CONTENTS.

History of Oratory and Orators

BY THE SAME AUTHOR

THE ART OF LIVING
LONG AND HAPPILY

12° $1.00

G. P. PUTNAM'S SONS

NEW YORK AND LONDON

History of Oratory

and Orators

A STUDY OF THE INFLUENCE OF ORATORY UPON POLITICS AND
LITERATURE, WITH SPECIAL REFERENCE TO CERTAIN
ORATORS SELECTED AS REPRESENTATIVE OF THEIR
SEVERAL EPOCHS, FROM THE EARLIEST
DAWN OF GRECIAN CIVILIZATION
DOWN TO THE PRESENT DAY

BY

HENRY HARDWICKE

Member of the New York Bar ; The New York Historical Society ; The New York
Genealogical and Biographical Society ; The Society of Medical
Jurisprudence, etc. Author of " The Art of Winning Cases,"
" The Art of Living Long and Happily," etc.

G. P. PUTNAM'S SONS

NEW YORK   LONDON
27 WEST TWENTY-THIRD STREET   24 BEDFORD STREET, STRAND

The Knickerbocker Press

1896

The Knickerbocker Press, New Rochelle, N. Y.

INTRODUCTION.

ORATORY is the parent of liberty. By the constitution of things it was ordained that eloquence should be the last stay and support of liberty, and that with her she is ever destined to live, flourish, and to die. It is to the interest of tyrants to cripple and debilitate every species of eloquence. They have no other safety. It is, then, the duty of free states to foster oratory.

The importance of oratory is attested by the belief, according to the fables of Greece and Egypt, that the art of eloquence was of celestial origin, ascribed to the invention of a god, who, from the possession of this art, was supposed to be the messenger and interpreter of Olympus. It is also witnessed by the care with which the art was cultivated at a period of the remotest antiquity.

With the first glimpse of historical truth which burst from the regions of mythology, in that dubious twilight which scarcely descries the distinction between the fictions of pagan superstition and the narrative of real events, a school of oratory, established in the Peloponnesus, dawns upon our view.

After the lapse of a thousand years from that time, Pausanius, a Grecian geographer and historian, says that he had read a treatise upon the art composed by the founder of this school, a contemporary and relative of Theseus in the age preceding that of the Trojan war.

As is stated elsewhere, the poems of Homer abound with still more decisive proofs of the estimation in which the powers of oratory were held, and of the attention with which it was honoured as an object of instruction in the education of youth.

From that time, through the long series of Greek and Roman history, down to the dark and forbidding period in which the glories of the Roman republic expired, the splendour and the triumphs of oratory are multiplied and conspicuous. Then it was that the practice of the art attained a perfection which has not since been rivalled.

Oratory was power, in the flourishing periods of Athens and Rome. Eloquence was the key to the highest dignities, the passport to the supreme dominion of the state. The voice of oratory was the thunder of Jupiter; the rod of Hermes was the sceptre of the empire. In proportion to the wonders she achieved, was the eagerness to acquire the art. Eloquence was taught as the occupation of a life. The course of instruction commenced with the infant in the cradle, and continued to manhood. It was one of the chief objects of education, and every other part of instruction for childhood was compelled to yield to it. Letters, the sciences, arts, were to be mastered, upon the theory that an orator must be a man of universal knowledge. Moral duties were taught, for the reason that none but a good man could be an orator.

Learning, wisdom, even virtue herself, were estimated by their subserviency to the purpose of eloquence, and the chief duty of man consisted in making himself a master of eloquence.

With the dissolution of Roman liberty, and the decline of Roman taste, oratory fell into decay.

In the United States, any one who knows the least of our system of government may perceive that every law that is passed must be submitted to the people in their representative or collective capacity, and there is no man, no matter how humble his station in life, who may not be called upon to serve as a legislator, or as a member of some body in which the art of speaking and the art of reasoning become absolutely necessary.

In political meetings which are held so often in our

country no man, thanks to the genius of our institutions, is precluded from delivering ·his sentiments with freedom upon any topic which it may be deemed expedient to consider, and the person who speaks well is sure never to miss applause, for by the aid of oratory useful truths are promulgated with effect. In order to succeed, however, natural abilities require the assistance of art. It is absurd to imagine that art imposes any fetters upon genius ; she aids and directs it.

Opinions differ as to the value of the ancient rhetorical writers. Lord Macaulay, in his essay, "*On the Athenian Orators,*" thought that the ancient writers upon the subject of oratory would afford us but little assistance. He says when they particularise they are generally trivial ; and when they would generalise they became indistinct. He says that while Aristotle was a great philosopher he was without imagination, and that in Quintilian he can look for nothing but rhetoric, and rhetoric not of the highest order. Quintilian, undoubtedly, speaks coldly of Æschylus, while he warmly praises the plays of Euripides, and makes other erroneous judgments of the great classical writers of antiquity. With the merits of Cicero, every school-boy is familiar.

Longinus gives us no general rules. He gives us, however, many eloquent sentences, and Macaulay suggests very pertinently that " The Sublimities of Longinus " would be a better title for his treatise than " Longinus on the Sublime."

It may be doubted, however, whether any compositions which have ever been produced since the dawn of civilisation are equally perfect in their kind with the best orations of antiquity. From these the author has drawn freely.

Bare allusion is made to the history of oratory in other countries than those in which we have given an account of it. The small opportunity afforded for a display of senatorial or forensic oratory by the different governments of Germany has almost entirely checked its growth in that country, and the same remark is applicable to Spain, Portugal, and Italy.

The difficulty which the author has experienced in selecting representative orators has been very great. He is aware of the fact that many eloquent men are not included whose lives would prove interesting and instructive.

The author ventures to indulge the hope that the noble lives he has put on record will act like an inspiration to others, for one of the great lessons of biography is to show what man can do by the development of his latent talents, and in this way the lives of great men are useful as guides, helps, and incentives to others. The splendour and variety of the lives of distinguished men make it somewhat difficult to distinguish the portion of time which ought to be admitted into history, from that which should be given to biography. These two parts are so distinct and unlike that they cannot be confounded without great injury to both; either when the writer of biography obscures the portrait of an individual by a crowded picture of events, or when the historian allows unconnected narratives of the lives of men to break the thread of history. The author belives that the biographer never ought to introduce public events except so far as they are necessary to the illustration of character, and that the historian should rarely digress in biographical particulars except as far as they contribute to the clearness of his narrative of occurrences.

The lives of the subjects of the following sketches cannot become too well known on account of the usefulness of their examples.

H. H.

NEW YORK, July, 1896.

HISTORY OF ORATORY AND ORATORS.

HISTORY OF ORATORY AND ORATORS.

CHAPTER I.

ORATORY IN GREECE.

TO trace the history of eloquence from its first rude origin through the various ramifications of human genius; to mark the powers, the characters of the many orators, in the different ages of society, who have employed with success this fascinating art, would be a pleasing task. It would be instructive even to pursue the science as long as the records of civilised man permit, and to trace the progress of oratory from Pericles to the present time. But unfortunately the materials for such a critical investigation are few. The best effusions of oratory are but winged words. The music, the cadence, the action, with which they were graced, are lost, and even the substance of very few of the orations of antiquity are transmitted to us.

Not many of the orations of Demosthenes have outlived the depredations of time. It is a well known fact that Cicero, for many years, spoke almost daily in public, and yet a very small proportion of his numerous orations were committed to writing.

Oratory was, undoubtedly, studied and practised with considerable effect from almost the earliest periods. This is conclusively proved by the specimens of eloquence which we find recorded in the oldest writings extant.

Like their poetry, the oratory of the Hebrews was short and sententious, but in the speeches of Moses, and Samuel, and in the Book of Job, we have many beautiful examples of the sublime and pathetic in oratory.

The speeches in Homer are worthy of study. It is said that these speeches were composed by Homer, and are not to be ascribed to the characters from whose mouths they are supposed to issue, nor to the period in which they existed. This may be true, but the Iliad is known to be a dramatic representation of the age in which the poet lived; hence two inferences will follow—that it was *then* customary to address public assemblies in the manner of the heroes of Homer—and that no inconsiderable progress must have been made in eloquence as an art.

Eloquence is only to be looked for in free states, and free states are only to be found where eloquence is assiduously cultivated. Longinus, in his treatise on the sublime, says that liberty is the nurse of true genius; it animates the spirit and invigorates the hopes of men ; excites honorable emulation, and a desire of excelling in every art.

In tracing the rise of oratory it is needless to go too far back in the early ages of the world, or delve for it among the monuments of Eastern or Egyptian antiquity. There was eloquence of a certain kind in those ages, but it was more like poetry than oratory. Philologists believe that the language of the first ages was passionate and metaphorical, owing to the small stock of words then known, and to the tincture which language naturally takes from the barbarous and uncultivated state of men, agitated by unrestrained passions, and struck by events, the causes of which, to them, were unknown. Rapture and enthusiasm, the parents of poetry, had an ample field in this state.

While the intercourse between different countries was unfrequent, when the words *stranger* and *enemy* were synonymous, and force and strength were the chief means employed in deciding controversies, the arts of oratory were compara-

tively unknown. The Assyrian and Egyptian empires, the
first that arose, were despotic in character, and the people
were led, or driven, not persuaded, and none of those refine-
ments of society which make public speaking an object of
importance were as yet introduced.

One of the earliest accounts of a trial is that which Homer
has given us in his description of the shield made by He-
phæstion, at the request of Thetis, for Achilles. The parties
are represented as pleading themselves before the judges.

> "The people thronged the forum, where arose
> The strife of tongues, and two contending stood :
> The one asserting that he had paid the mulct,
> The price of blood for having slain a man ;
> The other claiming still the fine as due.
> Both eager to the judges made appeal.
> The crowds, by heralds scarce kept back, with shouts
> And cheers applauded loudly each in turn.
> On smooth and polished stones, a sacred ring,
> The elders sat, and in their hands their staves
> Of office held, to hear and judge the cause ;
> While in the midst two golden talents lay,
> The prize of him who should most justly plead."

From the time of Homer to the age of Pericles, there are
no authentic orations on record.

The eloquence of Pericles must have been of a high order,
for by his eloquence and his policy his influence was supreme
in Athenian affairs for many years.

It is said that Pericles was the first Athenian who composed, and put into writing, an oration designed for the public. The golden age of Grecian eloquence extended from
the time of Solon (about 600 B.C.) to that of Alexander
(B.C. 336). Within this space the most renowned orators
flourished. This was the brightest period in the history of
Greece, at the close of which her sun went down in clouds,
and never rose again in its native, dazzling splendour. It is
said that Anaxagoras instructed Pericles in the sublimest
sciences, and that Pericles acquired from him not only an

elevation of sentiment, but a loftiness and purity of style
far superior to that of any of his cotemporaries. Pericles
was also noted for a remarkable gravity of countenance
which never relaxed into laughter, a firm and even tone of
voice, an easy deportment, and a decency of dress which no
vehemence of speaking ever put into disorder.

These things and others of a like nature excited the
admiration of his countrymen. In commenting upon the
character of this wonderful man, Plutarch says: " The beauty
of goodness has an attractive power; it kindles in us at
once an active principle; it forms our manners, and influences
our desires, not only when represented in a living example,
but even in an historical description."

When the name of Pericles is mentioned to a lover of
liberty, a crowd of glorious associations is called up. The
splendid funeral oration over those who fell in the Peloponnesian war, is one of the grandest productions of antiquity.
It exhibits a strong and ardent attachment to country,
which true patriots always feel, and an undaunted courage
in its defence, and willingness to pledge everything for the
maintenance of civil liberty. Many portions of this peerless oration are almost as applicable to America as to
Athens when delivered, but if the merits of the martyrs and
heroes of the American Revolution could be justly set forth
by an orator equal to the task, the renowned oration of
Pericles would be eclipsed.

The author cannot forbear quoting a few passages from
that celebrated address:

" I shall begin, first, with our ancestors, to whom it is at
once just and becoming, on such an occasion as the present,
that this honour of our commemoration should be paid; for
the country which was ever their own home, they have
handed down in the line of their successors to the present
day, free, through their valour. Both they indeed are
worthy of our praise, and still more our own fathers; for
having, in addition to what they inherited, acquired, not
without hardship, the dominion which we possess, they have
transmitted it to us.

"The greater portion of it indeed we ourselves, who are yet at the meridian of life, have still further augmented, till we have placed the city in all things in such a state of preparation that it is all-sufficient in itself for war and for peace.

"The warlike deeds by which all this has been effected, either by ourselves or by our fathers, in strenuously resisting the invasions, whether of barbarians or of Greeks, I omit, not wishing to enlarge upon them before the well informed; but by what conduct we have come to this condition, by what policy and by what manners these great results have been brought about, these I will set forth before the eulogy of the deceased, deeming these things not inappropriate to be spoken on this occasion; and that it will be beneficial to the whole assembly of strangers and citizens to listen to them.

" For we .enjoy a form of government not emulating the laws of neighbouring states, being ourselves rather a model to others than copying from them. It has been called by the name of Democracy, as being the government not of the few but of the majority. It secures to all, under the laws, equality in their private controversies,—in proportion as a citizen is in any respect in good repute, he is preferred above others, not more on account of the class to which he may belong than his own merit; while, on the other hand, as to poverty, no one qualified to serve the state is prevented from doing so by the obscurity of his condition. We perform our public duties on these liberal principles; and as to mutual supervision in reference to the daily course of life, we take no offence at our neighbour for following his own inclination, nor do we subject ourselves to the annoyance of austerities which are painful, if not injurious. In this panegyric of the state of things in Athens there is a constant, though tacit contrast with the Spartan institutions and character.

"While our private intercourse, therefore, is without offence in our public concerns, we mainly fear to act illegally, ever obeying the magistrates for the time being and

the laws, especially such of them as are passed for the protection of the oppressed, and such, though unwritten, as
cannot be broken without acknowledged shame.

.   .   .   .

" Having displayed our power in noble manifestations,
and most assuredly not without witnesses, we shall be the
admiration of the present age and of posterity, not needing
in addition the eulogy of Homer, or of any other poet,
whose descriptions will charm the ear at the time, but whose
conceptions of deeds is at variance with the truth; but having forced every sea and every land to be accessible to our
enterprise, and having everywhere planted, together with
our settlements, eternal monuments of injuries and of benefits. Combating therefore generously for such a city, and
thinking it unjust that it should be wrested from them,
these men laid down their lives; and, of those who survive,
it behooves every one to labour and suffer for it.

.   .   .   .

" Such, then, as became the city, were the departed. As for
those who remain, you may desire indeed a safer career, but
you must not deign to cherish a spirit in any degree less
resolute toward the enemy;—having regard not merely to
the words of persons not wiser than yourselves, who may
harangue you upon the honour of gallant resistance to the
foe, but rather daily contemplating indeed the power of the
state, till you become enamoured of it; and when you have
come to perceive its greatness, reflecting that brave men
knowing their duty, and in their deeds shrinking from dishonour, have achieved it,—men who, even though they might
fail in an enterprise, still felt that they ought not to deprive
the country of the benefit of their valour, but lavished upon
it the most precious offering. Thus giving their lives to the
public they received individually the praise that grows not
old, and a most distinguished sepulchre, not so much that in
which their bodies lie, as that in which their glory—on
every occasion of word or deed—shall be left in everlasting
remembrance.

" For of illustrious men the whole earth is the sepulchre, and not the inscription alone of columns in their native land indicates it, but in countries also not their own, the unwritten memory which abides with every man of the spirit more than the deed.

" Emulous of men like these, do you also, placing your happiness in liberty, and your liberty in courage, shun no warlike dangers in defence of your country."

Pericles was not only an orator, but a statesman, and a general; expert in business, and of consummate address. He had the surname of Olympias given him, and it was said, that, like Jupiter, he thundered when he spoke, but whether he could out-thunder Jupiter or not, is not certainly known. He was, however, humane, just, and patriotic, as well as generous, magnanimous, and public-spirited. The people had absolute confidence in his integrity, and never was that confidence betrayed. Although having ample opportunities to do so, he did not accumulate a fortune for himself, but spent vast sums of money in beautifying Athens, and in public works of great utility.

At his death he valued himself chiefly on having never obliged any citizen to wear mourning on his account.

After Pericles, those who were most noted for their eloquence, were Cleon, Alcibiades, Critias, and Theramenes.

The style of oratory which then prevailed was concise, vehement, and manly.

Eloquence was more assiduously cultivated after the death of Pericles than it was before. The precepts of oratory had not, until that time, been collected and reduced to anything like a system. There had been orators before the time of Pericles, of course, but in the nature of things, practice must precede theory. Oratory was undoubtedly prior in point of time to rhetoric. This must be the case with all arts. Many houses must have been built before a system of architecture could be formed; many poems composed before an art of poetry could be written.

All didactic treatises must, necessarily, consist of rules resulting from experience, and that experience must be founded on previous practice. So, at the period mentioned, a set of men called rhetoricians, and sometimes sophists, sprang up. They were especially plentiful during the Peloponnesian war. Among them were Protagoras, Prodicus, and Thrasymus. The most eminent of the sophists, however, was Gorgias of Leontium. The most of the sophists joined to the art of rhetoric as taught by them, a subtile logic —and they were a sort of metaphysical skeptics, according to some writers, but Gorgias was a professed master of eloquence only. He was highly venerated in Leontium of Sicily, his native city, and money is said to have been coined with his name upon it. His style was quaint and highly artificial, and the fragment of his, which has been preserved, abounds in antithetical expressions. In the hands of men like Gorgias, who professed to teach others how to speak for and against every cause whatever, oratory degenerated into a trifling and sophistical art. They were the first corrupters of true eloquence. The great and good Socrates exploded the doctrines of the sophists, and recalled the attention of the Athenians to natural language and useful thought.

Isocrates flourished in the same age, but a little later than Socrates. His writings are still extant. He was a teacher of eloquence, and an orator of ability, but his orations are greatly wanting in vigour. They have, however, been much admired on account of the sound morality which they inculcate, and for the smoothness and elegancy of the orator's style. Isocrates is said to have been the first rhetorician who introduced regular periods which had a studied music and harmonious cadence. He spent ten years in polishing one discourse, still extant, the *Panegyric*. Cicero was an admirer and, in some respects, an imitator of Isocrates, but it must be said to his credit, that he recognised and avoided his chief faults—his affectation, and the tiresomely uniform, regular cadence of his sentences.

Isæus and Lysias belong also to this period. Lysias was somewhat earlier than Isocrates, but, unlike the latter, his style was unaffected and simple. He was a lawyer by profession, and his eloquence is almost exclusively forensic.

Thirty-four of his orations have been transmitted to us, and for their acuteness, clearness, and the method shown in their composition would not be bad models for the forensic orators of our own day, if we could not hear better ones in our courts at almost any time.

Isæus is chiefly remarkable for being the teacher of Demosthenes, the greatest orator, in many respects, that ever lived. The circumstances of his life are well known, and it is needless to dwell upon them at length. His ambition to excel in the art of speaking; his frequent failures; his untiring perseverance in surmounting all the disadvantages of person and address which he laboured under; his resolution in shutting himself up in his subterranean retreat, that he might study without being disturbed; his declamations by the seashore that he might accustom himself to the noise of a tumultuous assembly, and his use of pebbles in his mouth while practising, in order to cure certain defects of speech; his speaking at home with a naked sword suspended over his shoulder, that he might check a habit which he had of raising and lowering it, to which he was subject,— all these circumstances show us how much can be accomplished by industry and application, and what great labour is necessary for the attainment of excellence in the art of oratory.

Demosthenes, despising the affected style of the orators of his day, chose Pericles as his model, hence the chief characteristics of his style were strength and vehemence.

Demosthenes had a wide field for the display of patriotic eloquence, when Philip of Macedon, by the aid of the most insidious arts, endeavoured to lay the Greeks asleep to their danger, and by force and fraud to overthrow Grecian liberty. He first crushed his enemies at home and then enlarged his kingdom abroad, then invited by the Thessalians to assist them against the Phocians, he sent an army into Thessaly, and made a determined and bold attempt to seize the key of Greece, the famous pass of Thermopylæ. This decisive movement alarmed the Athenians at last, and an assembly of the people was convened for the purpose of determining the

best course to be pursued for the purpose of arresting the
progress of the enterprising Macedonian tyrant. Rising,
like one inspired, Demosthenes, at this meeting, delivered,
in impassioned tones, his first Philippic, and urged his hearers to make vigorous war against Philip. He realised the
true state of affairs. He knew that many of the people had
become corrupt and degenerate and incapable of estimating
at its true value the great blessings of civil liberty ; that
traitors to their country, in the pay of Philip, were continually urging the people not to fight against him, and knowing
these facts he governed himself accordingly. The following
are some of the best passages from this famous speech :

"When, therefore, O my countrymen ! when will you
exert your vigour? Do you wait till roused by some dire
event? till forced by some necessity? What then are we to
think of our present condition? To freemen, the disgrace
attending on misconduct is, in my opinion, the most urgent
necessity. Or say, is it your sole ambition to wander through
the public places, each inquiring of the other, 'what new
advices?' Can anything be more new than that a man of
Macedon should conquer the Athenians and give law to
Greece? 'Is Philip dead?' 'No; but he is sick.' Pray
what is it to you whether Philip is sick or not. Supposing
he should die, you would raise up another Phillip, if you continue thus regardless of your interest !

"Then as to your own conduct, some wander about, crying, Philip hath joined with the Lacedemonians, and they
are concerting the destruction of Thebes. Others assure us
that he has sent an embassy to the king of Persia ; others,
that he is fortifying places in Illyria. Thus we all go about
framing our several tales. I do believe, indeed, Athenians !
he is intoxicated with his greatness, and does entertain his
imagination with many such visionary prospects, as he sees no
power rising to oppose him, and is elated with his success."

He continues in the same high strain in the third Philippic :

"All Greece, all the barbarian world, is too narrow for
this man's ambition. And though we Greeks see and

hear all this, we send no embassies to each other; we express no resentment; but into such wretchedness are we sunk, that even to this day we neglect what our interest and duty demand. Without engaging in associations, or forming confederacies, we look with unconcern upon Philip's growing power, each fondly imagining that the time in which another is destroyed is so much time gained on him; although no man can be ignorant that, like the regular periodic return of a fever, he is coming upon those who think themselves the most remote from danger.

"And what is the cause of our present passive disposition? For some cause sure there must be; why the Greeks, who have been so zealous heretofore in defence of liberty, are now so prone to slavery. The cause, Athenians, is that a principle which was formerly fixed in the minds of all, now exists no more; a principle which conquered the opulence of Persia, maintained the freedom of Greece, and triumphed over the powers of sea and land. That principle was an unanimous abhorrence of all those who accepted bribes from princes that were enemies to the liberties of Greece. To be convicted of bribery was then a crime altogether unpardonable. Neither orators nor generals would then sell for gold the favourable conjunctures which fortune put into their hands. No gold could impair our firm concord at home, our hatred of tyrants and barbarians. But now all things are exposed to sale as in a public market. Corruption has introduced such manners as have proved the bane and destruction of our country. Is a man known to have received foreign money? People envy him. Does he own it? They laugh. Is he convicted in form? They forgive him. So universally has this contagion diffused itself among us."

Sometimes Demosthenes found it difficult to arouse the Athenians to a just sense of their real danger. On one occasion when he was desirous of addressing a large meeting in the city, the people would not have heard him with attention, if he had not informed them that he only wished to tell them a story. Hearing this, he received their attention, and he commenced as follows: "Once upon a time there

was a man who hired an ass to go from this city to Megara.
About noon, when the sun was burning hot, both the driver
and the hirer sought the shade of the ass, and mutually hin-
dered each other. The owner said that the traveller had hired
his ass, and not its shadow. The traveller, in opposition to
him, maintained that the whole ass was under his jurisdiction."
Having thus commenced his story, he withdrew. The people
recalled him, and begged him to finish the story. He said
to them : " Ah! how eager you are to hear a story about
an ass's shadow, and you will not listen when I speak of your
most important affairs ! " Philip was not idle while the
Athenians were wasting their time in fruitless discussion.
Under pretence of attacking the Locrians, he marched his
army into Greece, captured Elatæa, a city of Phocis, not
very far distant from Athens. The capture of this place,
which was one of great importance, opened to Philip a
passage into Attica. The Athenians were struck with terror upon the announcement of this event. In his oration
on the crown Demosthenes graphically described the scene
of dismay and confusion which prevailed at Athens when
the news was received. He said :

"Thus successful in confirming the mutual separation of
our states, and elevated by these decrees and these replies,
Philip now leads his forces forward and seizes Elatæa. You
are no strangers to the confusion which this event raised
within these walls. Yet permit me to relate some few striking circumstances of our own consternation. It was evening.
A courier arrived, and repairing to the presidents of the
senate, informed them that Elatæa was taken. In a moment some started from supper, ran to the public place,
drove the traders from their stations, and set fire to their
sheds; some sent round to call the generals; others clamoured
for the trumpeter. Thus was the city one scene of tumult.
The next morning, by dawn of day, the presidents summoned the senate. The people were instantly collected, and
before any regular authority could convene their assembly,
the whole body of citizens had taken their places above.
Then the senate entered ; the presidents reported their

advices, and produced the courier. He repeated his intelligence. The herald then asked in form, 'Who chooses to
speak?' All was silence. The invitation was frequently
repeated. Still no man arose; though the ordinary speakers were all present; though the voice of Athens then called
on some man to speak and save her; for surely the regular
and legal proclamation of the herald may be fairly deemed
the voice of Athens. If an honest solicitude for the preservation of the state had on this occasion been sufficient to
call forth a speaker; then, my countrymen, ye must have all
risen and crowded to the gallery, for well I know this honest
solicitude had full possession of your hearts. If wealth had
obliged a man to speak, the three hundred must have risen.
If patriotic zeal and wealth united were the qualifications
necessary for the speaker, then should we have heard those
generous citizens, whose beneficence was afterward displayed
so nobly in the service of the state; for their beneficence
proceeded from this union of wealth and patriotic zeal.
But the occasion, the great day, it seems, called, not only
for a well-affected and an affluent citizen, but for the man
who had traced these affairs to their very source; who had
formed the exactest judgment of Philip's motives, of his
secret intentions in this his conduct. He who was not perfectly informed of these; he who had not watched the whole
progress of his actions with consummate vigilance, however
zealously affected to the state, however blessed with wealth,
was in no wise better qualified to conceive or to propose the
measures which your interests demanded on an occasion
so critical. On that day then, I was the man who stood
forth."

In commenting on this passage Mr. Goodrich eloquently
says: " Demosthenes gives us a picture of the scene by a few
distinct, characteristic touches—the presidents starting from
their seats in the midst of supper—rushing into the market-
place—tearing down the booths around it—burning up the
hurdles even, though the space would not be wanted till the
next day—sending for the generals—crying out for the
trumpeter—the council meeting on the morrow at break of

day—the people (usually so reluctant to attend) pouring
along to the assembly before the council had found a moment's opportunity to inquire or agree on measures—the
entering of the council into the assembly—their announcing
the news—their bringing forward the messenger to tell his
story ; and then the proclamation of the herald, '*Who will
speak?*'—the silence of all—the voice of their common
country, crying out again through the herald, 'Who will
speak for our deliverance?'—all remaining silent—when
Demosthenes arose, and suggested measures which caused
all these dangers to pass away like a cloud!"

An able writer, Mr. Harsha, says that "Demosthenes on
this occasion aroused his countrymen with a burst of eloquence which must have made even the iron will of Philip
to falter on the throne of Macedon. It was then that he delivered that exciting oration which made the whole assembly
cry out with one voice: 'To arms! to arms! Lead us
against Philip!'

"Two thousand years afterwards, the same enthusiasm
which then, amid their graceful columns, inspired the excitable Athenians, and filled their spacious amphitheatre with
a shout that rose to the warm, blue sky of Greece, awoke
among sterner men, in a colder climate, and made the plain
walls of a church in Virginia echo with a cry as bold and
more determined. That was in response to the words of
Patrick Henry, the forest-born Demosthenes, when he
uttered in tones of thunder those ever-memorable words:
'I know not what course others may take, but, as for me,
give me LIBERTY, or give me DEATH!'

" It is in the darkest crises of national struggles for independence, amid storms and tempests, that we see the greatest political orators arise, and hear the thunders of their
mighty eloquence, shaking thrones and kingdoms to their
centre. It is then that we hear them exclaim with Patrick
Henry, 'Whatever others do, I'll fight!' and with John
Adams, at the solemn crisis of the vote of the 4th of July,
1776, 'Independence *now*, and Independence forever!'"

The Athenians, on the proposal of Ctesiphon, decreed

Demosthenes a crown of gold, in consideration of the many valuable public services which he had rendered the state.

The reward was strongly opposed by his rival and personal enemy, Æschines—one of the greatest orators of that age,—who brought a suit against Ctesiphon which was intended to defeat Demosthenes. This famous prosecution was begun about the year 338 B.C.; the trial, however, was delayed eight years. When it came on an immense crowd of people from all parts of Greece went to Athens to witness the contest between the two great intellectual gladiators.

Æschines' speech was powerful and sarcastic. He was twelve years older than his rival, and it is said that his eloquence was distinguished by a happy flow of words, by an abundance and clearness of ideas, and by an air of great ease, which arose less from art than nature. The ancient writers appear to agree in this, that the manner of Æschines is softer, more insinuating, and more delicate than that of Demosthenes, but that the latter is more grave, forcible, and convincing. The one has more of address, and the other more of strength and energy. The one endeavours to steal, the other to force, the assent of his auditors. In the harmony and elegance, the strength and beauty of their language, both are deserving of high commendation, but the figures of the one are finer, of the other, bolder. In Demosthenes we see a more sustained effort; in Æschines, " vivid though momentary flashes of oratory."

The following brief extract from Æschines' oration will afford the reader a specimen of his style:

" When Demosthenes boasts to you, O Athenians, of his democratic zeal, examine not his harangues, but his life; not what he professes to be, but what he really is; redoubtable in words, impotent in deeds; plausible in speech, perfidious in action. As to his courage—has he not himself, before the assembled people, confessed his poltroonery? By the laws of Athens, the man who refuses to bear arms, the coward, the deserter of his post in battle, is excluded from all share in the public deliberations, denied admission to our religious rites, and rendered incapable of receiving the honour of a crown. Yet now it is proposed to crown a man whom your laws expressly disqualify!

"Which think you was the more worthy citizen, Themistocles, who commanded your fleet when you vanquished the Persians at Salamis, or Demosthenes, the deserter? Miltiades, who conquered the barbarians at Marathon, or this hireling traitor? Aristides, surnamed the Just, or Demosthenes, who merits a far different surname? By all the Gods of Olympus, it is a profanation to mention in the same breath this monster and those great men! Let him cite, if he can, one among them all to whom a crown was decreed. And was Athens ungrateful? No! She was magnanimous; and those uncrowned citizens were worthy of Athens. They placed their glory, not in the letter of a decree, but in the remembrance of a country, of which they had merited well, —in the living, imperishable remembrance!

"And now a popular orator— the mainspring of our calamities, a deserter from the field of battle, a deserter from the city—claims of us a crown, exacts the honour of a proclamation! Crown *him?* Proclaim *his* worth? My countrymen, this would not be to exalt Demosthenes, but to degrade yourselves,—to dishonor those brave men who perished for you in battle. Crown *him!* Shall *his* recreancy win what was denied to their devotion? This would indeed be to insult the memory of the dead, and to paralyse the emulation of the living!

"From those who fell at Marathon and at Platæa—from Themistocles—from the sepulchres of your ancestors—issues the protesting groan of condemnation and rebuke!"

Æschines did not receive a fifth part of the votes of the judges, and in consequence, by the laws of Athens, he thus became liable to fine and banishment, and accordingly went in exile to Rhodes. He established there a school in rhetoric, in which he read the two orations to his pupils. While his was received with approbation, that of Demosthenes was received with the greatest applause. "What then would you have thought, had you heard the lion himself," said Æschines.

"The greatest oration of the greatest orator," said Lord Brougham of this speech. The oration abounds in eloquent passages, and in magnificent expressions.

From this oration, which for sarcasm, invective, and declamation, as well as all that is glorious in eloquence, has no equal, in any language, the author selects the following passage, containing the celebrated oath by those who fell at Marathon, and setting forth the public spirit of the Athenians : "The Athenians never were known to live contented in a slavish though secure obedience to unjust and arbitrary power. No. Our whole history is a series of gallant contests for pre-eminence ; the whole period of our national existence hath been spent in braving dangers for the sake of glory and renown. And so highly do you esteem such conduct as characteristic of the Athenian spirit, that those of your ancestors who were most eminent for it are ever the most favourite objects of your praise. And with reason ; for who can reflect, without astonishment, on the magnanimity of those men who resigned their lands, gave up their city, and embarked in their ships rather than live at the bidding of a stranger? The Athenians of that day looked out for no speaker, no general, to procure them a state of easy slavery. They had the spirit to reject even life, unless they were allowed to enjoy that life in freedom. For it was a principle fixed deeply in every breast, that man was not born to his parents only, but to his country. And mark the distinction. He who regards himself as born only to his parents waits in passive submission for the hour of his natural dissolution. He who considers that he is the child of his country also, volunteers to meet death rather than behold that country reduced to vassalage ; and thinks those insults and disgraces which he must endure, in a state enslaved, much more terrible than death.

"Should I attempt to assert that it was I who inspired you with sentiments worthy of your ancestors, I should meet the just resentment of every hearer. No ; it is my point to show that such sentiments are properly your own ; that they were the sentiments of my country long before my

days. I claim but my share of merit in having acted on
such principles in every part of my administration. He,
then, who condemns every part of my administration ; he
who directs you to treat me with severity, as one who hath
involved the state in terrors and dangers, while he labours
to deprive me of present honour, robs you of all the applause of posterity. For, if you now pronounce that, as
my public conduct hath not been right, Ctesiphon must
stand condemned, it must be thought that you yourselves
have acted wrong, not that you owe your present state to the
caprice of fortune. But it cannot be ! No, my countrymen,
it cannot be that you have acted wrong in encountering danger bravely for the liberty and safety of all Greece. No ! I
swear it by the spirits of our sires, who rushed upon destruction at Marathon ! by those who stood arrayed at Platæa !
by those who fought the sea-fight at Salamis ! by the men
of Artemisium ! by the others so many and so brave, who
now rest in our public sepulchres ! all of whom their country
judged worthy of the same honour ; all, I say, Æschines ;
not those only who were victorious. And with reason.
What was the part of gallent men, they all performed.
Their success was such as the Supreme Ruler of the world
dispensed to each."

Panurge, in Rabelais, when in need, practised sixty-three
methods of procuring money, the most honest of which was
to steal. Æschines, the rival of Demosthenes, likewise left
no stone unturned when he got into a tight place. He was
guilty of dissimulation, inventions of various kinds, altera-
tions of dates, and texts—all arms, he thought, lawful, in
his contest with Demosthenes.

The style of Demosthenes is " strong and concise, though
sometimes, it must not be dissembled, harsh, and abrupt.
His words are very expressive ; his management is firm and
manly ; and though far from being unmusical, yet it seems
difficult to find in him that studied but concealed number
and rhythmus, which some of the ancient critics are fond
of attributing to him. Negligent of these lesser graces, one
would rather conceive him to have aimed at that sublime

which lies in sentiment. His action and pronunciation are recorded to have been uncommonly vehement and ardent ; which, from the manner of his composition, we are naturally led to believe. The character which one forms of him, from reading his works, is of the austere, rather than the gentle kind. He is on every occasion grave, serious, passionate ; takes everything on a high tone ; never lets himself down, nor attempts anything like pleasantry. If any fault can be found with his admirable eloquence, it is, that he sometimes borders on the high and dry. He may be thought to want smoothness and grace, which Dionysius of Halicarnassus attributes to his imitating too closely the manner of Thucydides, who was his great model for style, and whose history he is said to have written eight times over with his own hand. But these defects are far more than compensated, by that admirable and masterly force of masculine eloquence which, as it overpowered all who heard it, cannot at this day be read without emotion." Another critic says : " The style of Demosthenes is so strong, so close and nervous; it is everywhere so just, so exactly concise, that there is nothing too much or too little. What distinguishes his eloquence is the impetuosity of the expression, the choice of words, and the beauty of the disposition ; which, being supported throughout and accompanied with force and sweetness, keeps the attention of the judges perpetually fixed."

" What we admire in Demosthenes is the plan, the series, and the order and disposition of the oration ; it is the strength of the proofs, the solidity of the arguments, the grandeur and nobleness of the sentiments and of the style, the vivacity of the turns and figures ; in a word, the wonderful art of representing the subjects he treats in all their lustre, and displaying them in all their strength."

The author of the *Dialogues Concerning Eloquence* says : " Demosthenes moves, warms, and captivates the heart. Every oration of his is a close chain of reasoning that represents the generous notions of a soul who disdains any thought that is not great. His discourses gradually increase in force by greater light and new reasons, which are always illustrated by bold figures and lively images. One cannot but see that he has the good of the republic entirely at heart, and that nature itself speaks in all his transports, for his artful address is so masterly that it never appears. Nothing ever equalled the force and vehemence of his discourses."

To his admirable delivery, Demosthenes, in his orations, joined the equal force of great and noble expressions, of lively descriptions, of pathetic passages, and of rhetorical images proper to affect, and make strong impressions upon the mind. In short, nearly all his orations are full of expressive figures, of frequent apostrophes, and reiterated interrogations, which gave life and vigour to, and animated all he said.

Longinus, in his comparison between Demosthenes and Cicero, compares the eloquence of the former to lightning, and of the latter to a great fire. He says the eloquence of Demosthenes is a whirlwind and a clap of thunder that overturns all things, and that of Cicero like a great fire which devours all things. So that violence and impetuousness make up the character of Demosthenes' eloquence, and the progress of a great fire, which advances by degrees, together with the heat and insinuating virtue of fire, are the principal qualities of that of Cicero. The Grecian breaks out like thunder. The Roman warms and inflames like a great fire. Longinus therefore adds that Demosthenes never failed of success, when he was to strike terror into the minds of his audience, and to work upon them by strong representations and violent motions. But when it was necessary to go to the very heart, and to insinuate one's self into the mind, by all those graces and pleasing charms which eloquence is mistress of; then it was that Cicero's art was triumphant, and that his diffused, enlarged discourse succeeded far better than the more close and concise style of Demosthenes; and the one is no more prevalent by the *eclat*, the surprising strength of his reasons, than the other is by the warming and affecting emotions he raises.

It is said that before the time of Demosthenes, "there

existed three distinct styles of eloquence : that of Lysias, mild and persuasive, quietly engaged the attention, and won the assent of an audience ; that of Thucydides, bold and animated, awakened the feelings and powerfully forced conviction on the mind ; while that of Isocrates was, as it were, a combination of the two former. Demosthenes can scarcely be said to have proposed any individual as a model, although he bestowed so much untiring labor on the histo- ian of the Peloponnesian war. He rather culled all that was valuable from the various styles of his great predecessors, working them up, and blending them into one harmonious whole : not, however, that there is such a uniformity or mannerism in his works as prevents him from applying him- self with versatility to a variety of subjects ; on the contrary, he seems to have had the power of carrying each individual style to perfection, and of adapting himself with equal excel- lence to each successive topic. In the general structure of many of his sentences, he resembles Thucydides ; but he is more simple and perspicuous, and better calculated to be quickly comprehended by an audience. On the other hand his clearness in narration, his elegance and purity of diction, and (to borrow a metaphor from a sister art) his correct keeping, remind the reader of Lysias. But the argumenta- tive part of the speeches of Lysias are often deficient in vigour ; whereas earnestness, power, zeal, rapidity, and pas- sion, all exemplified in plain, unornamented language, and a strain of close, business-like reasoning, are the distinctive characteristics of Demosthenes. The general tone of his oratory was admirably adapted to an Athenian audience, constituted as it was of those whose habits of life were mechanical, and of those whom ambition or taste had led to the cultivation of literature. The former were captivated by sheer sense, urged with masculine force and inextinguish- able spirit, and by the forcible application of plain truths ; and yet there was enough of grace and variety to please more learned and fastidious auditors." Another writer says: " His style is rapid harmony, exactly adjusted to the sense ; it is vehement reasoning, without any appearance of art ; it is disdain, anger, boldness, freedom, involved in a continued stream of argument; and of all human productions, the orations of Demosthenes present to us the models which approach the nearest to perfection."

One of the most noticeable excellences of Demosthenes is the collocation of his words. The orators of ancient Greece studied assiduously the art of arranging sentences in such a manner that their cadences should be harmonious, and, to a certain degree, rhythmical, and the simplicity remarkable in the structure of the periods of Demosthenes is itself the result of art.

The question has often been asked, What is the secret of the success of Demosthenes? How did he attain pre-eminence among orators? Why is it, that in a faculty common to all mankind—that of communicating our thoughts and feelings, in language and by gestures—the palm is conceded to him by the consent of all ages and countries? His orations are not witty, humorous, nor, ordinarily, pathetic nor learned—all undeniable attributes of eloquence. Besides, he violates nearly every ancient rule of technical rhetoric. The secret of his success was this: He was an honest man; he was a patriot; his political principles were not assumed to serve an interested purpose, to be laid aside when he descended the Bema, and resumed when he sought to accomplish an object. No, his principles of patriotism were deeply seated in his heart, and emanated from its profoundest depths. The mystery of his wonderful influence, then, lay in his honesty. It is this, joined to his action, that gave warmth and tone to his feelings, an energy to his language, and an impression to his manner, before which every imputation of insincerity must have vanished. The chief characteristics of Demosthenes' oratory were strength, energy, and sublimity, aided by an emphatic and vehement elocution. Liberty and eloquence, which are twin born and which die together, expired in Greece, with their noble defender, Demosthenes, and eloquence relapsed again into the feeble manner introduced by the sophists.

Demetrius Phalereus, who lived in the next age to Demosthenes, attained some reputation as a speaker, but his chief attraction as an orator was his highly ornamented diction. He was not a convincing speaker, aiming as he did at grace rather than substance. Cicero says: " He amused the Athenians, rather than warmed them."

We hear no more of Grecian orators of note after his time.

CHAPTER II.

ORATORY IN ROME.

HAVING treated of the rise of eloquence, and of its state among the Greeks, the author will now proceed to notice its progress among the Romans. Here one model, at least, of eloquence, in its most dazzling and illustrious form, will be found.

The Romans derived their eloquence, poetry, and learning, chiefly from the Greeks. For a considerable period after the founding of Rome, the Romans were a rude, comparatively illiterate, and martial people, almost entirely unskilled in the polite arts, which were not much cultivated until after the conquest of Greece. In eloquence, it is thought, the Romans were inferior to the Greeks, in some respects. They were certainly more grave and magnificent, but less acute and spritely. Compared to the Greeks the Romans were a phlegmatic nation, their passions were not so easily moved, and their conceptions were not so lively. But after the introduction of Greek learning at Rome, eloquence, of all the arts next to war, was of most importance. For if war led to the conquests of foreign states, eloquence opened to each individual a path to dominion and empire over the minds and hearts of his countrymen. It was the opinion of Cicero that without this art wisdom itself could be of little avail for the advantage or glory of the commonwealth.

There was little room for the exercise of legal oratory during the existence of the monarchy, and in the early ages of the republic, because law proceedings were not numerous.

Civil suits were prevented to a great extent by the absolute dominion which a Roman father exercised over his family, and the severity of the decemviral laws, in which all the proceedings were extreme, frequently forced parties into an accommodation. At the same time, the purity of ancient manners, had not yet given rise to those criminal questions of bribery, extortion, and peculation at home or of oppression in the provinces, which disgraced the closing periods of the commonwealth, and furnished fruitful themes for the indignant oratory of Cicero and Hortensius. Consequently whatever eloquence may have been cultivated in the early ages of Rome was of a political character, and was exerted on affairs of state.

It must not be supposed, however, from what has been said, that there were no orators of eminence in Rome before the age of Hortensius and Cicero. From the earliest times of the republic the oratorical abilities of Junius Brutus, Publicola, and Appius Claudius were called into requisition for the purpose of allaying seditions, suppressing rebellions, and thwarting pernicious counsels. Romulus, by direction of his grandfather, made a speech to the people soon after the completion of the city, on the subject of the government to be established. This speech is given in Dionysius of Halicarnassus (Lib. II.).

Although many speeches are reported by Dionysius and Livy, no adequate opinion can be formed of their oratorical merits, for the reason that they were probably composed by these historians and adorned by them with all the arts of rhetoric. Judging, however, from the effect which the speeches of these orators in the early ages of Rome produced, they must have possessed a masculine vigour well calculated to protect the interests of the state, and to animate the courage of the Roman soldiery. But "a nation of outlaws, destined from their cradle to the profession of arms,—taught only to hurl the spear and the javelin, and inure their bodies to other martial exercises,—with souls breathing only conquest,—and regarded as the enemies of every state till they had become its masters, could have

possessed but few topics of illustration or embellishment,
and were not likely to cultivate any species of rhetorical
refinement. To convince by solid arguments when their
cause was good, and to fill their fellow-citizens with passions
corresponding to those with which they were themselves
animated, would be the great objects of an eloquence supplied by nature and unimproved by study. We are accordingly informed by some of the ancient writers "that though
there appeared in the ancient orations some traces of original
genius, and much force of argument, they bear in their
rugged and unpolished periods the signs of the times in
which they were delivered."

The speech of Appius Claudius in opposition to a peace
with Pyrrhus, is the only one mentioned by the Latin
writers as possessing the charms of oratory, prior to the
time of Cornelius Cethegus, who lived during the second
Punic war, and was consul about the year 550. Cethegus
was particularly distinguished for his "admirable sweetness
of elocution and powers of persuasion."

The speeches of Cato the Censor were chiefly noted for
their patriotism and their rude but masculine eloquence. It
is said that when Cato was in the decline of life "a more
rich and copious mode of speaking at length began to prevail. S. Galba, by the warmth and animation of his delivery,
eclipsed Cato and all his contemporaries. He was the first
among the Romans who displayed the distinguishing talents
of an orator, by embellishing his subject, by digressing, am-
plifying, entreating, and employing what are called topics,
or commonplaces of discourse. On one occasion, while
defending himself against a grave accusation, he melted his
judges to compassion by producing an orphan relative,
whose father had been a favourite of the people. When his
orations, however, were afterwards reduced to writing, their
fire appeared extinguished, and they preserved none of that
lustre with which his discourses are said to have shone
when given forth by the living orator. Cicero accounts for
this from his want of sufficient study and art in composition. While his mind was occupied and warmed with his

subject, his language was bold and rapid ; but when he took up the pen his emotion ceased, and the periods fell languid from its point, "which," continues he, "never happened to those who, having cultivated a more studied and polished style of oratory, wrote as they spoke. Hence the mind of Lælius yet breathes in his writings, though the force of Galba has failed."

Galba, however, was highly esteemed by the judges, the people, and Lælius himself, as appears from the following anecdote : " Lælius being entrusted with the defence of certain persons suspected of having committed a murder in the Sicilian forest, spoke for two days, correctly, eloquently, and with the approbation of all, after which the consuls deferred judgment. He then recommended the accused to carry their cause to Galba, as it would be defended by him with more heat and vehemence. Galba, in consequence, delivered a most forcible and pathetic harangue, and after it was finished, his clients were absolved as if by acclamation."

Cicero compares Lælius with his friend Scipio Africanus, in whose presence this question concerning the Sicilian murder was debated. They were almost equally distinguished for their eloquence ; and they were like each other in this respect, that they both always delivered themselves in a smooth manner, and never, like Galba, "exerted themselves with loudness of speech or violence of gesture." Their style of oratory, however was unlike,—Lælius adopting a much more ancient phraseology than that adopted by his friend. Cicero was most inclined to admire the oratory of Scipio, but his contemporaries awarded the palm of eloquence to Lælius.

The introduction of Greek learning about this time produced the same improvement in oratory that it had effected in every branch of literature.

M. Emilius Lepidus was younger than Galba or Scipio, and was consul in 617 A.U.C. His orations were extant in Cicero's time. It is said that he was the first Roman orator who, in imitation of the Greeks, gave sweetness and har-

mony to his periods, or "the graces of a style regularly
polished and improved by art."

Cicero mentions many other orators of the same age with
Lepidus, and gives a minute account of their different styles
of oratory. Among them are the most prominent men of
the period, as Scipio Nasica, Emilius Paulus, and Mucius
Scævola.

The political situation of Rome, consequent upon the
disputes which continually arose between the patricians
and the plebeians ; the frequent impeachment of corrupt
officials; the inquietude and unrest which succeeded its
foreign wars ; the debates concerning agrarian laws, afforded
ample room for the display of forensic and political oratory.

Oratory continued to open the most direct path to dignities during the whole period prior to the breaking out of the
civil wars, when her sweet voice was drowned by the horrid
din of war.

The Gracchi were factious demagogues who endeavoured
to inflame the passions of the poor against the rich. Instead
of pointing out to the rich the good qualities and the dire
necessities of the poor, and of calling the attention of the
poor to the many admirable qualities of the rich, they made
the vices of the rich the constant themes of their most impassioned declamations.   But, notwithstanding their dema-
gogical character, the influence which the celebrated brothers
exerted over the people is a sufficient proof of their
eloquence.

Tiberius Gracchus made oratory a serious study. He was
instructed in elocution, in his boyhood, by his mother Cor-
nelia. He was also constant in his attendance upon the
ablest masters from Greece. When he entered on the turbulent stage of Roman life, the land was owned by a few
people, and the middle classes which constituted the strength
of the ancient republic, were gradually rooted out. Tiberius
Gracchus while passing through Etruria on his way to
Numantia found the country almost depopulated of freemen, and at that time formed the project of agrarian law.
While much in his political conduct is worthy of condemna-

tion, he was undoubtedly eloquent, as the following specimen from Plutarch will show : " The wild beasts of Italy
have their dens to retire to—their places of refuge and repose ; while the brave men who shed their blood in the cause
of their country have nothing left but fresh air and sunshine. Without houses, without settled habitations, they
wander from place to place with their wives and children ;
and their commanders do but mock them when, at the head
of their armies, they exhort their soldiers to fight for their
sepulchres and altars. For, among such numbers, there is
not one Roman which belonged to his ancestors, or a tomb
in which their ashes repose. The private soldiers fight and
die to increase the wealth and luxury of the great ; and they
are styled sovereigns of the world, while they have not one
foot of ground they can call their own." The violent course
pursued by Tiberius Gracchus caused his death.

Caius Gracchus was endowed with greater ability than his
brother, but unfortunately he pursued the same course, that
of endeavouring to widen the breach between the senate and
the people. He was untiring in his exertions to lessen the
authority of the senate, and increase the authority of the
people. He advocated the colonisation of the public lands,
and their distribution among the poor ; the regulation of
the markets, so as to diminish the price of bread, and for
vesting the judicial power in the knights.

Though much alike in character, and in their political
conduct, there was a considerable difference between the
forensic demeanour and style of oratory of the two brothers.
" Tiberius, in his looks and gesture, was mild and composed,
Caius earnest and vehement ; so that when they spoke
in public Tiberius had the utmost moderation in his action
and moved not from his place ; whereas Caius was the first
of the Romans who, in addressing the people, walked to
and fro in the rostrum, threw his gown off his shoulder,
smote his thigh, and exposed his arm bare. The language
of Tiberius was laboured and accurate, that of Caius bold
and figurative. The oratory of the former was of a gentle
kind, and pity was the emotion it chiefly raised—that of

the latter was strongly impassioned, and calculated to excite
terror. In speaking, indeed, Caius was so often hurried
away by the violence of his passion that he exalted his
voice above the regular pitch, indulged in abusive expressions, and disordered the whole tenor of his oration. In
order to guard against such excesses, he stationed a slave
behind him with an ivory flute, which was modulated so as
to lead him to lower or heighten the tone of his voice, according as the subject required a higher or a softer key.
Says Cicero, " The flute you may as well leave at home, but
the meaning of the practice you must remember at the
bar."

Oratory became an object of assiduous study in the time
of the Gracchi. The custom was to introduce a young man
intended for the study of the law to one of the most distinguished orators of the city, whom he attended when he had
occasion to speak on a public or private cause, or in the
assemblies of the people. In doing this, he not only heard
him, but every other noted speaker. By pursuing this
course he became practically acquainted with business, and
the method of administering justice in the courts, and
learned the arts of oratorical conflict, as it were, in the field
of battle. " It animated the courage and quickened the
judgment of youth, thus to receive their instructions in the
eye of the world, and in the midst of affairs, where no one
could advance an absurd or weak argument without being
exposed by his adversary, and despised by the audience.
Hence, they also had an opportunity of acquainting themselves with the various sentiments of the people, and observing what pleased or disgusted them in the several orators
of the Forum. By these means they were furnished with
an instructor of the best and the most improving kind, exhibiting not the feigned resemblance of eloquence, but her
real and lively manifestation—not a pretended but genuine
adversary, armed in earnest for the combat—an audience
ever full and ever new, composed of foes as well as of friends,
and amongst whom not a single expression could fall but
was either censured or applauded."

The advantages derived from fictitious oratorical contests were also given to the youth of the city by the introduction of debating societies at Rome about the middle of its seventh century. In the year 661 A.U.C., Plotius Gallus, a Latin rhetorician, opened a declaiming school at Rome, but the declamations turned on questions of real business.

From these facts it is evident that in the middle of the seventh century oratory was sedulously studied, and universally practised, and that there must have been many proficients. It would be an endless task to enumerate all the public speakers mentioned by Cicero, the extensiveness of whose catalogue is only equalled by its dryness. The author will therefore proceed to Marcus Antonius and Lucius Crassus, whom Cicero celebrates as having first raised the glory of Roman eloquence to an equality with that of Greece.

Marcus Antonius was the grandfather of the famous triumvir. He was the most popular orator of his time, and was chiefly courted by clients because of his ability, and the fact that he was always ready to undertake any cause which was offered to him. It is said that he possessed a ready memory and remarkable talent of introducing everything where it could be placed with most effect. " He had a frankness of manner which precluded any suspicion of artifice, and gave to all his orations an appearance of being the unpremeditated effusions of an honest heart. But though there was no apparent preparation in his speeches, he always spoke so well, that the judges were never sufficiently prepared against the effects of his eloquence. His language was not perfectly pure, or of a constantly sustained elegance, but it was of a solid and judicious character, well adapted to his purpose ; his gesture, too, was appropriate and suited to his sentiments and language ; his voice was strong and durable, though naturally hoarse—but even this defect he turned to advantage, by frequently and easily adopting a mournful and querulous tone, which in criminal questions excited compassion, and more readily gained the belief of the judges."

According to Cicero he left very few orations behind him,

having determined never to publish any of his pleadings, lest he should be found to have maintained in one cause something which was inconsistent with what he had alleged in another. Cicero gives an account of Antony's defence of Aquilius which shows his power of moving the passions, and is also characteristic of the manner of Roman plead-ing. In the dialogue *De Oratore,* Antony, who is one of the characters, is introduced relating it himself. " Seeing his client, who had once been consul and a leader of armies reduced to a state of the utmost dejection and peril, he had no sooner begun to speak, with a view towards melting the compassion of others, than he was melted himself. Per-ceiving the emotion of the judges when he raised his client from the earth, on which he had thrown himself, he instantly took advantage of this favorable feeling. He tore open the garments of Aquilius, and showed the scars of those wounds which he had received in the service of his country. Even the stern Marius wept. Him the orator then apostrophized, imploring his protection, and invoking with many tears the gods, the citizens, and the allies of Rome. ' But whatever I could have said,' remarks he in the dialogue, ' had I delivered it without being myself moved, it would have ex-cited the derision, instead of the sympathy, of those who heard me.' "

Marius who was his enemy, in 666, had Antony's head cut off and affixed to the rostrum where he had defended the lives of so many of his fellow-citizens.

The greatest forensic rival of Antony, was Crassus, who had prepared himself diligently in his youth for public speak-ing by the study of oratory. He translated into Latin some of the best of the Greek orations, and he at the same time improved his voice, action, and memory by frequent exercises.

Crassus began his oratorical career at nineteen, when he acquired considerable reputation by his accusation of C. Carbo. Not long afterward he heightened his fame by his defence of Licinia.

The best speech which he delivered, however, and the

one that caused his death, which occurred in 662, he made in the senate against the Consul Philippus, who had declared, in one of the assemblies of the people, that some other advice must be resorted to, since he could no longer direct the affairs of the government with such a senate as then existed. Crassus arraigned the conduct of this consul in terms of the most glowing eloquence, alleging that, instead of acting as the guardian of the rights of the Senate, he sought to strip its members of their ancient inheritance of respect and dignity. It is said he was so greatly irritated by an attempt on the part of Philippus to compel him to comply with his demands, that he exerted, on this occasion, the utmost efforts of his genius and strength ; unfortunately, however, he returned home with a pleuritic fever, of which he died within seven days.

This oration of Crassus, followed as it was by his untimely death, made a deep and lasting impression on his countrymen, who long afterwards were accustomed to repair to the Senate-house, for the purpose of looking at the spot where he last stood and had fallen, virtually in defence of the privileges of his order.

Crassus left very few orations behind him. Cicero was in his boyhood when he died, and having collected the opinions of those who had heard him, speaks with a minute and perfect intelligence of his style of oratory.

His diction was perhaps more highly ornamented than that of any speaker that had appeared before his time in the Forum.

He was grave, dignified, and forcible, but these qualities were happily blended with the utmost politeness, urbanity, ease, and gaiety. His language was pure and accurate, and he expressed himself with the greatest elegance.

Clearness and copiousness of argument and illustration were the chief excellences for which his orations were distinguished.

He was diffident in manner while speaking, and was so much embarrassed on one occasion, when a young man, that Q. Maximus, seeing that he was disabled by confu-

3

sion and in danger of making an utter failure, adjourned the
court. Crassus always remembered his kindness with the
highest sense of gratitude. Cicero says that this diffidence
never entirely forsook him, and after the practice of a long
life at the bar he was frequently so much agitated in the
exordium of his discourse that he was observed to grow pale,
and tremble in every part of his frame. It is said that
" some persons considered Crassus as only equal to Antony ;
others preferred him as the most perfect and accomplished
orator. Antony chiefly trusted to his intimate acquaintance
with affairs and ordinary life. He was not, however, so
destitute of knowledge as he seemed ; but he thought the
best way to recommend his eloquence to the people was to
appear as if he had never learned anything. Crassus, on the
other hand, was well instructed in literature, and showed off
his information to the best advantage. Antony possessed
the greater power of promoting conjecture, and of allaying
or exciting suspicion, by apposite and well-timed insinuations ; but no one could have more copiousness or facility
than Crassus in defining, interpreting, and discussing the
principles of equity. The language of Crassus was indis-
putably preferable to that of Antony ; but the action and
gesture of Antony were as incontestably superior to those
of Crassus.

Sulpicius and Cotta were born about 630 A.U.C. They
were for some time contemporaries of Antony and Crassus,
but were younger orators. They had, however, achieved
considerable reputation before the death of the latter and
assassination of the former. For some years Sulpicius was
respected and admired, but about the year 665, being then
a tribune, he espoused the cause of Marius, at the first
breaking out of the dissensions between Sylla and Marius.
At this time, it may be safely said that he became one of
the greatest villains in Rome, although that city could boast
of a large assortment of villains at this conjuncture. Cruel
and avaricious, he committed, without hesitation or reluctance, the most criminal actions. It is said that he sold by
public auction the freedom of Rome to foreigners, telling

out the purchase money on counters erected in the Forum for that purpose. He kept three thousand swordsmen about him in constant pay, ready on any occasion to do his bidding, and these he called his anti-senatorian band. While Marius was in power, Sulpicius, as tribune, transacted all public affairs by violence and force of arms. He decreed to Marius the command in the Mithridatic war. With his band he attacked the consuls while they were holding an assembly of the people in the temple of Castor and Pollux, and deposed one of them. Sylla, however, having at length gained the ascendency, Marius was expelled and Sulpicius was seized and put to death in the bloom of his youth and beauty, justly punished for the many crimes which he had committed. Notwithstanding his villainy he was endowed with great oratoric powers. It is said that he was the most lofty, and what Cicero called the most tragic, orator of Rome; that "his attitudes, deportment, and figure were of supreme dignity; his voice was powerful and sonorous; his elocution rapid; his action variable and animated.

Cotta, being constitutionally weak, was not vehement in manner, but soft and relaxed. Everything he said, however, was in good taste, and he often led the judges to the same conclusion to which Sulpicius impelled them. Says Cicero: "No two things were ever more unlike than they are to each other. The one, in a polite, delicate manner, sets forth his subject in well-chosen expressions. He still keeps to the point; and as he sees with the greatest penetration what he has to prove to the court, he directs to that the whole strength of his reasoning and eloquence, without regarding other arguments. But Sulpicius, endowed with irresistible energy, with a full, strong voice, with the greatest vehemence and dignity of action, accompanied with so much weight and variety of expression, seemed, of all mankind, the best fitted by nature for eloquence."

The renown, however, of all preceding orators at Rome was eclipsed by Hortensius, who "burst forth in eloquence at once calculated to delight and astonish his fellow-citizens." This famous orator was born in the year 640, and was ten years younger than Cotta and Sulpicius. At the early age of nineteen he made his first appearance in the Forum, and Cicero, his rival, but his just and impartial critic, says: "His excellence was immediately acknowledged, like that of a statue by Phidias, which only requires to be seen in order to be admired."

The case in which he first appeared was one of considerable importance, being an accusation at the instance of the Roman province of Africa against its governors for rapacity. It was heard before Scævola and Crassus, as judges—the former being the ablest lawyer, and the latter the most accomplished speaker, of his age. The young orator had the good fortune to win not only their approbation but that of every one present at the trial. For many years he was the greatest forensic orator at Rome, and was the acknowledged head of the Roman bar. Cicero says: "Nature had given him so happy a memory that he never had need of committing to writing any discourse which he had meditated, while, after his opponent had finished speaking, he could recall, word by word, not only what the other had said, but also the authorities which had been cited against himself." As a proof of his excellent memory, Seneca says that, for a trial of it, he remained a whole day at a public auction, and when it was concluded, he repeated in order *what had been sold, to whom, and at what price.* His statement was compared with the clerk's account, and his memory was found to have served him faithfully in every particular. Cicero also says of him : "His industry was indefatigable. He never let a day pass without speaking in the forum, or preparing himself to appear on the morrow ; oftentimes he did both. He excelled particularly in the art of dividing his subject, and in then reuniting it in a luminous manner, calling in, at the same time, even some of the arguments which had been used against him. His diction was elegant, noble, and rich ; his voice was strong and pleasing ; his gestures carefully studied."

The elegance and aptitude for public business of Hortensius procured for him not only a fortune, but the highest official honours of the state. Want of competition, and the formation of luxurious habits, however, caused him gradually to relax that assiduity which had contributed so largely to his success. The growing fame of Cicero, however, stimulated him to renew his exertions. He never, however, recovered his former reputation. Cicero partly accounts for this decline from the peculiar nature and genius of his oratory. His oratory was Asiatic in character, being full of brilliant thought and sparkling expressions, and was much more florid and ornamental than that of Cicero himself.

This glowing style of oratory, though lacking in deficiency and weight, was not unsuitable in a young man, and being further recommended by a beautiful cadence, met with the greatest applause. Hortensius, as he advanced in years, retained the florid style of oratory which he had acquired in his youth. The grave fathers of the senatorial order thought his glittering phraseology totally inconsistent with his advanced age and consular dignity, consequently his reputation diminished with increase of years.

The orations of Hortensius, it has been said, suffered much when transferred to paper, as his chief excellence consisted in delivery.

As the speeches of Hortensius have not been preserved, his oratorical character rests almost entirely upon the opinion of his great, but unprejudiced rival, Cicero. The friendship and friendly rivalry of Hortensius and Cicero presents an agreeable contrast to the bitter enmity of Æschines and Demosthenes. Hortensius also was free from any feeling of that envy which is such an infallible mark of an ignoble mind. Cicero has certainly done the oratorical talents of Hortensius ample justice, representing him as endowed with nearly all the qualities necessary to form a great orator, as has been said. Macrobius, however, says that, on account of his affected gestures, he was much ridiculed by some of his contemporaries. His adversaries accused him of being too theatrical in his gestures. It seems that in pleading it was his custom to keep his hands almost constantly in motion. Roscius, the celebrated Roman actor, often attended his

pleadings to catch his gestures and imitate them on the
stage. According to Valerius Maximus, his exertion in action was so great that it was commonly said that it could not
be determined whether people went to hear or to see him.
Like Demosthenes, he chose and put on his dress with the
most studied care and neatness. He also is said to have
bathed himself in odoriferous waters, and to have daily per-
fumed himself with the most precious essences. The only
blemishes in his oratorical character appear to have been
this minute attention to his person and his gesticulation.
His moral conduct was not free from blame, because of his
practice of sometimes corrupting the judges of the causes in
which he appeared, when he could do so with impunity—unfortunately, in his time, there were many defects in the judicial system of Rome, and corruption of the courts was one
of the greatest evils of the age.

It would be unfair to omit all mention of Hortensia, the
daughter of Hortensius, for she inherited something of the
spirit and eloquence of her father, and Valerius Maximus
tells us that when the triumvirs Octavius, Lepidus, and
Antony had imposed a tax upon the Roman matrons, and
the advocates of the day were too cowardly to accept the
perilous task of speaking on their behalf against the obnoxious law, Hortensia came forward as the champion of
her sex, and made such an eloquent and effective speech
that the greatest part of the tax was remitted. Quintillian
says of Hortensia that her speech was well worthy of perusal
without taking into account the sex of the speaker.

Mention ought also to be made of another Roman lady,
Amæsia Sentia, who appeared in her own behalf in an action
which had been brought against her. Attracted by the novelty of the spectacle, an immense crowd had gathered in
court to hear her. She pleaded her cause with such eloquence
that she received at once an almost unanimous judgment in
her favour.

Afrania, the wife of Licinius Buccio, a Senator, sometimes
pleaded her own causes in person out of sheer impudence.
She was a quarrelsome and litigious dame, and was perpetu-

ally getting into legal scrapes. Her voice was so harsh and unmusical that it was compared to the yelp of a dog. After a while at Rome to be called an Afrania was a reproach amongst the women of the city.

Licinius Calvus was considered as the rival of Hortensius in eloquence, but his style of speaking was the reverse of that of Hortensius. The orations of Lysias were his models. " Hence that correct and slender delicacy at which he so studiously aimed, and which he conducted with great skill and elegance; but, from being too much afraid of the faults of redundance and unsuitable ornament, he refined and attenuated his discourse till it lost its raciness and spirit. He compensated, however, for his sterility of language and diminutive figure, by his force of elocution and vivacity of action." Says Quintillian: " I have met with persons who preferred Calvus to all our orators; and others who were of opinion that the too great rigor which he exercised on himself, in point of precision, had debilitated his oratorical talents. Nevertheless, his speeches, though chaste, grave, and correct, are frequently also vehement. His taste of writing was Attic; and his untimely death was an injury to his reputation, if he designed to add to his compositions, and not to retrench them. He delivered his most noted oration against Votinius when he was twenty years of age. Votinius, overpowered and alarmed, interrupted him by exclaiming to the judges: " Must I be condemned because he is eloquent ? "

Calvus died at the early age of thirty. He left behind him twenty-one books of orations. Pliny, the younger, made these orations his models.

Calidius merits a short notice. He is said to have been different from all other orators—chiefly on account of " the soft and polished language in which he arrayed his exquisitely delicate sentiments."

" Nothing could be more easy, pliable, and ductile than the turn of his periods; his words flowed like a pure and limpid stream, without anything hard or muddy to impede or pollute their course; his action was genteel, his mode of

address sober and calm, his arrangement the perfection of
art. Cicero says, while discussing the merits of Calidius:
' The three great objects of an orator are to instruct, delight, and move.' Two of these he admirably accomplished.
He rendered the most abstruse subject clear by illustration,
and enchained the minds of his hearers with delight. But
the third praise of moving and exciting the soul must be
denied him ; he had no force, pathos, or animation."

These were the greatest orators who preceded Cicero, or
who were contemporaries with him. It is said that at
Rome, in the time of Cicero, "the organisation of the judicial tribunals was wretched, and their practice scandalous.
The Senate, Prætors, and Comitia, all partook of the legislative and judicial power, and had a sort of reciprocal right
of opposition and reversal, which they exercised to gratify
their avarice or prejudices, and not with any view to the
ends of justice. But however injurious this system might
be to those who had claims to urge, or rights to defend, it
afforded the most ample fields for the excursions of eloquence. The Prætors, though the supreme judges, were
not men bred to the law, advanced in years, familiarised
with precedents, secure of independence, and fixed in their
stations for life. They were young men of little experience,
who held the office for a season, and proceeded, through it,
to what were considered as the most important situations
of the republic. Though their procedure was strict in some
trivial points of preliminary form, devised by the ancient
jurisconsults, they enjoyed in more essential matters a
perilous latitude. On the dangerous pretext of equity, they
eluded the law by various subtilties or fictions ; and thus,
without being endued with legislative authority, they abro-
gated ancient enactments according to caprice. It was worse,
when, in civil cases, the powers of the Prætors were intrusted
to the judges ; or when, in criminal trials, the jurisdiction was
assumed by the whole people. The inexperience, ignorance,
and popular prejudices of those who were to decide them,
rendered litigations extremely uncertain, and dependent, not
on any fixed law or principle, but on the opinions or pas-

sions of tumultuary judges, which were to be influenced and moved by the arts of oratory. This furnished ample scope for displaying all that interesting and various eloquence with which the pleadings of the ancient orators abounded. The means to be employed for success were conciliating favour, rousing attention, removing or fomenting prejudice, but, above all, exciting compassion. Hence we find that, in the defence of a criminal, while a law or precedent was seldom mentioned, everything was introduced which could serve to gain the favour of the judges or move their pity. The accused, as soon as the day of trial was fixed, assumed an apparently neglected garb; and although allowed, whatever was the crime, to go at large till sentence was pronounced, he usually attended in court surrounded by his friends, and sometimes accompanied by his children, in order to give a more piteous effect to the lamentations and exclamations of his counsel, when he came to that part of the oration in which the fallen and helpless state of his client was to be suitably bewailed. Piso, justly accused of oppression toward the allies, having prostrated himself on the earth in order to kiss the feet of his judges, and having risen with his face defiled with mud, obtained an immediate acquittal. Even where the cause was good, it was necessary to address the passions, and to rely on the judge's feelings of compassion, rather than on his perceptions of right. Rutilius prohibited all exclamations and entreaties to be used in his defence. He even forbade the accustomed and expected excitement of invocations, and stamping with the feet; and "he was condemned," says Cicero, "though the most virtuous of the Romans, because his counsel was compelled to plead for him as he would have done in the Republic of Plato." It thus appears that it was dangerous to trust to innocence alone, and that the judges were the capricious arbiters of the fate of their fellow-citizens, and not (as their situation so urgently required) the inflexible interpreters of the laws of their exalted country.

"But if the manner of treating causes was favourable to the exertions of eloquence, much also must be allowed for the nature of the questions themselves, especially those of a criminal description, tried before the Prætor or people. One can scarcely figure more glorious opportunities for the display of oratory than were afforded by those complaints of the oppressed and plundered provinces against their rapacious governors.   From the extensive ramifications of the Roman power, there continually arose numerous cases of a description that can rarely occur in other countries, and which are unexampled in the history of Britain, except in a memorable impeachment, which not merely displayed, but created such eloquence as can be called forth only by splendid topics, without which rhetorical indignation would seem extravagant, and attempted pathos ridiculous."

" The spot, too, on which the courts of justice assembled, was calculated to heighten and inspire eloquence.   The Roman Forum presented one of the most splendid spectacles that eye could behold, or fancy conceive.   This space formed an oblong square between the Palatine and Capitoline hills, composed of a vast assemblage of sumptuous though irregular edifices.   On the side next the Palatine Hill stood the ancient Senate-house, and Comitium, and Temple of Romulus the Founder.   On the opposite quarter it was bounded by the Capitol, with its ascending range of porticos, and the temple of the tutelar deity on the summit.   The other sides of the square were adorned with basilicæ, and piazzas terminated by triumphal arches ; and were bordered with statues, erected to the memory of the ancient heroes or preservers of their country.   Having been long the theatre of the factions, the politics, the intrigues, the crimes, and the revolutions of the capital, every spot of its surface was consecrated to the recollection of some great incident in the domestic history of the Romans ; while their triumphs over foreign enemies were vividly called to remembrance by the Rostrum itself, which stood in the centre of the vacant area, and by other trophies gained from vanquished nations.

" A vast variety of shops, stored with a profusion of the most costly merchandise, likewise surrounded this heart and centre of the world, so that it was the mart for all important commercial transactions. Being thus the emporium of law, politics, and trade, it became the resort of men of business, as well as of those loiterers whom Horace calls *Forenses*. Each Roman citizen regarding himself as a member of the same vast and illustrious family, scrutinised with jealous watchfulness the conduct of his rulers, and looked with anxious solicitude to the issue of every important cause. In all trials of oppression or extortion, the Roman multitude took a particular interest,—repairing in such numbers to the Forum that even its spacious square was hardly sufficient to contain those who were attracted to it by curiosity; and who in the course of the trial, were in the habit of expressing their feelings by shouts and acclamations, so that the orator was ever surrounded by a crowded and tumultuary audience. This numerous assembly, too, while it inspired the orator with confidence and animation, after he had commenced his harangue, created in prospect that anxiety which led to the most careful preparation previous to his appearance in public. The apprehension and even trepidation felt by the greatest speakers at Rome on the approach of the day fixed for the hearing of momentous causes, is evident from the many passages of the rhetorical works of Cicero. The Roman orator thus addressed his judges with all the advantages derived both from the earnest study of the closet, and the exhilaration imparted to him by unrestrained and promiscuous applause.

" Next to the courts of justice, the great theatre for the display of eloquence was the Comitia, or assemblies of the people, met to deliberate on the proposal of passing a new law, or abrogating an old one. A law was seldom offered for consideration but some orator was found to dissuade its adoption; and as in the courts of justice the passions of the judges were addressed, so the favourers or opposers of a law did not confine themselves to the expediency of the measure, but availed themselves of the prejudices of the people, alternately confirming their errors, indulging their caprices, gratifying their predilections, exciting their jealousies, and fomenting their dislikes. Here, more than anywhere, the

many were to be courted by the few—here more than anywhere, was created that excitement which is most favourable
to the influence of eloquence, and forms indeed the element
in which alone it breathes with freedom.

" Finally the deliberations of the Senate, which was the
great council of the state, afforded, at least to its members,
the noblest opportunities for the exertions of eloquence.
This august and numerous body consisted of individuals who
had reached a certain age, who were possessed of a certain
extent of property, who were supposed to be of un-
blemished reputation, and most of whom had passed through
the annual magistracies of the state. They were consulted
upon almost everything that regarded the administration or
safety of the commonwealth. The power of making war
and peace, though it ultimately lay with the people assembled in the Comitia Centuriata, was generally left by them
entirely to the Senate, who passed a decree of peace or war
previous to the suffrages of the Comitia. The Senate, too,
had always reserved to itself the supreme direction and
superintendence of the religion of the country, and distribution of the public revenue—the levying or disbanding troops,
and fixing the service on which they should be employed—
the nomination of governors for the provinces—the rewards
assigned to successful generals for their victories—and the
guardianship of the state in times of civil dissension. These
were the great subjects of debate in the Senate, and they
were discussed on certain fixed days of the year, when its
members assembled of course, or when they were summoned
together for any emergency. They invariably met in a temple, or other consecrated place, in order to give solemnity to
their proceedings, as being conducted under the immediate
eye of Heaven. The Consul, who presided, opened the
business of the day by a brief exposition of the question
which was to be considered by the assembly. He then
asked the opinions of the members in the order of rank and
seniority. Freedom of debate was allowed in its greatest
latitude ; for though no Senator was permitted to deliver
his sentiments till it came to his turn, he had then a right

to speak as long as he thought proper, without being in the smallest degree confined to the point in question. Sometimes indeed the Conscript Fathers consulted on the state of the commonwealth in general; but even when summoned to deliberate on a particular subject, they seem to have enjoyed the privilege of talking about anything else which happened to be uppermost in their minds. Thus we find that Cicero took the opportunity of delivering his seventh Philippic when the Senate was consulted concerning the Appian Way, the coinage, and Luperci—subjects which had no relation to Antony, against whom he inveighed from one end of his oration to the other, without taking the least notice of the only points which were referred to the consideration of the senators. The resolution of the majority was expressed in the shape of a decree, which, though not properly a law, was entitled to the same reverence on the point to which it related; and, except in matters where the interests of the state required concealment, all pains were taken to give the utmost publicity to the whole proceedings of the Senate.

The number of the Senate varied, but in the time of Cicero it was nearly the same as the British House of Commons; but it required a larger number to make a quorum. Sometimes there were between four hundred and five hundred members present; but two hundred, at least during certain seasons of the year, formed what was accounted a full house. This gave to senatorial eloquence something of the spirit and animation created by the presence of a popular assembly, while at the same time the deliberative majesty of the proceedings required a weight of argument and dignity of demeanour unlooked for in the Comitia or Forum. Accordingly, the levity, ingenuity, and wit, which were there so often crowned with success and applause, were considered as misplaced in the Senate, where the consular, or prætorian orator, had to prevail by depth of reasoning, purity of expression, and an apparent zeal for the public good.

It was the authority of the Senate, with the calm and im-

posing aspect of its deliberations, that gave to Latin oratory
a somewhat different character from the eloquence of Greece,
to which, in consequence of the Roman spirit of imitation,
it bore, in many respects, so close a resemblance. The
power of the Areopagus, which was originally the most dignified assembly at Athens, had been retrenched amid the
democratic innovations of Pericles. From that period,
everything, even the most important affairs of state, depended entirely, in the pure democracy of Athens, on the
opinion, or rather the momentary caprice, of an inconstant
people, who were fond of pleasure and repose, who were
easily swayed by novelty, and were confident in their power.
As their precipitate decisions thus often hung on an instant
of enthusiasm, the orator required to dart into their bosoms
those electric sparks of eloquence which inflamed their passions, and left no corner of the mind fitted for cool consideration. It was the business of the speaker to allow them
no time to recover from the shock, for its force could have
been spent had they been permitted to occupy themselves
with the beauties and style of diction. "Applaud not the
orator," says Demosthenes, at the end of one of his Philippics, "but do what I have recommended. I cannot save
you by my words, you must save yourselves by your
actions." When the people were persuaded, everything was
accomplished, and their decision was embodied in a sort of
decree by the orator. The people of Rome, on the other
hand, were more reflective and moderate, and less vain than
the Athenians; nor was the whole authority of the state
vested in them. There was, on the contrary, an accumulation of powers, and a complication of different interests to
be managed. Theoretically, indeed, the sovereignty was in
the people, but the practical government was entrusted to
the Senate. As we see from Cicero's third oration, *De Lege
Agraria*, the same affairs were often treated at the same
time in the Senate and on the Rostrum. Hence, in the
judicial and legislative proceedings, in which, as we have
seen, the feelings of the judges and prejudices of the vulgar
were so frequently appealed to, some portion of the sena-

torial spirit pervaded and controlled the popular assemblies, restrained the impetuosity of decision, and gave to those orators of the Forum, or Comitia, who had just spoken, or were to speak next day in the Senate, a more grave and temperate tone, than if their tongues had never been employed but for the purpose of impelling a headlong multitude.

But if the Greeks were a more impetuous and inconstant, they were also a more intellectual people than the Romans. Literature and refinement were more advanced in the age of Pericles than of Pompey. Now, in oratory, a popular audience must be moved by what corresponds to the feelings and taste of the age. With such an intelligent race as the Greeks, the orator was obliged to employ the most accurate reasoning, and most methodical arrangement of his arguments. The flowers of rhetoric, unless they grew from the stem of his discourse, were little admired. The Romans, on the other hand, required the excitation of fancy, of comparison, and metaphors, and rhetorical decoration. Hence, the Roman orator was more anxious to seduce the imagination than convince the understanding; his discourse was adorned with frequent digressions into the fields of morals and philanthropy, and he was less studious of precision than of ornament.

On the whole, the circumstances of the Roman constitution and judicial procedure appear to have wonderfully conspired to render Cicero an accomplished orator. He was born and educated at a period when he must have formed the most exalted idea of his country. She had reached the height of power, and had not yet sunk into submission or servility. " The subjects to be discussed, and characters to be canvassed, were thus of the most imposing magnitude, and could still be treated with freedom and independence. The education, too, which Cicero had received, was highly favourable to his improvement."

If the character of this work required that the author should treat of Cicero as a statesman, a philosopher, a philanthropist, and as a writer, he would shrink from the

attempt, and would feel inclined to imitate the example of
the Greek artist, who, having chosen as the subject of his
picture the sacrifice of Iphigenia, employed the resources of
his art on the other figures of the group, but concealed the
countenance of Agamemnon in the folds of his robe, and
left to the imagination to conceive what he dared not venture to portray. But the scope of the present sketch is not
so ambitious. It is not "Cicero as a statesman, saluted by
the title of *Pater Patriæ* for his successful efforts against the
enemies of the republic; or as a philosopher, discussing
amidst the shades of Tusculum the immortality of the soul,
and inquiring into the principles and grounds of moral
duty"; but Cicero as an orator, whom he has to consider.

Marcus Tullius Cicero was born on the 3d day of January,
107 B. C., at Arpinum, in ancient times a small town of Lati-
um, now part of Naples.

As a child Cicero discovered a great ardour for study, and
made great progress under his teachers. His thirst for
knowledge was remarkably great, and his mind was well
fitted by nature, not only for acquiring, but for retaining information upon all subjects. In early life he was very fond
of the study of poetry, and one of his first teachers was the
poet Archias, who taught him the art of poetry. From his
earliest years he is said to have distinguished himself in such
a remarkable manner among those of his own age, that,
hearing of his extraordinary genius, the parents of his school-
fellows came on purpose to the school to be eye-witnesses of
it, and were delighted with what they saw and heard.

The Roman youth were allowed to wear the *toga virilis*,
or manly gown, at sixteen. As has been said, it was a custom
at Rome at this time for the relations or friends of a youth,
when he arrived at the age of sixteen, and was designed
for the bar, to put him under the protection of one of the
most celebrated orators. After this he devoted himself to
his patron in a particular manner; went to hear him plead,
consulted him about his studies, and did nothing without
his advice. He was thus early accustomed, as it were, to
breathe the air of the bar, which is the best school for a

young lawyer, and as he was the disciple of the greatest lawyers, and formed on the most finished models, he was soon able to imitate them.

From Scævola, the famous Roman lawyer, he acquired a profound knowledge of the civil law, and the political institutions of the Romans. He likewise studied philosophy in all its branches, with the greatest assiduity, and it was his opinion that it contributed more to making him an orator than rhetoric.

Milo was the most celebrated teacher of eloquence in Rome, and under his direction Cicero applied himself with the greatest diligence to the study of oratory. He practised declamation daily, repeating the finest passages of the best poets and orators. He also translated the passages of the most eminent Greek orators into Latin—thus enriching his own style with choice expressions. Cicero knew that, notwithstanding his great natural endowments, he could not reach an exalted position in the oratorical world, unless he submitted to the severest intellectual discipline and study, consequently he was unremitting in his efforts to master the art of oratory.

By giving careful attention to the following passage from the writings of Cicero, the reader will understand why Cicero distanced all his competitors:

" No person at that time made polite literature his particular study, without which there is no perfect eloquence; no one studied philosophy thoroughly, which alone teaches us at one and the same time, to live and speak well; no one learned the civil law, which is absolutely necessary for an orator, to enable him to plead well in private causes, and form a true judgment of public affairs; there was no person well skilled in the Roman history, or able to make proper use of it in pleading; no one could raise a cheerfulness in the judges, and unruffle them, as it were, by seasonable railleries, after having vigorously pushed his adversary, by the strength and solidity of his arguments; no one had the art of transferring or converting the circumstance of a private affair into a common or general one; no person could some-

4

times depart from his subject by prudent digressions, to
throw in the agreeable into his discourse; in fine, no person
could incline the judges sometimes to anger, sometimes to
compassion, and inspire them with whatever sentiments he
pleased, wherein, however, the principal merit of an orator
consists."

Cicero began to plead when he was about twenty-six
years of age. He was prevented by the troubles of the
state from attempting it sooner. At the age of twenty-
seven he undertook his first important case, the defence of
S. Roscius in a criminal prosecution. His speech, especially
that portion of it relating to the punishment of parricides,
which consisted in throwing the criminal, tied up in a sack,
into a river, gained him great applause, but was condemned
by the severer taste of his more advanced years. The passage mentioned is as follows: "Its intention was to strike
the parricide at once out of the system of nature, by de-
priving him of air, light, water, and earth, so that he who
had destroyed the author of his existence, might be excluded
from those elements whence all things derived their being.
He was not thrown to wild beasts, lest their ferocity should
be augmented by the contagion of such guilt—he was not
committed naked to the stream, lest he should contaminate
that sea which washed away all other pollutions. Everything in nature, however common, was accounted too good
for him to share in; for what is so common as air to the
living, earth to the dead, the sea to those who float, the
shore to those who are cast up. But the parricide lives so
as not to breathe the air of heaven, dies so that the earth
cannot receive his bones, is tossed by the waves so as not
to be washed by them, so cast on the shore as to find no
rest on its rocks."

Not only was his eloquence worthy of the commendation
of his countrymen, but the courage which he exhibited as
well. He was the only advocate who dared to brave the
anger of Chrysogonus, the favorite of Sylla, the dictator,
whose power in the commonwealth was at that time practically unlimited. Cicero was triumphant, and procured the

acquittal of his client. In the management of the case, he is said to have displayed the loftiest eloquence, which was received with shouts of applause by the audience. The successful defence of Roscius firmly established the reputation of Cicero as an orator, and placed him in the first class of advocates.

Shortly after the trial of Roscius, Cicero set out upon a tour to Greece and Asia Minor. He spent two years in these two countries in the study of philosophy and oratory, under the best philosophers and rhetoricians. He returned to Rome at the age of thirty, with his mind enriched with the treasures of Grecian literature, and with his style of eloquence polished and perfected.

The following remarks of a judicious critic upon the style of Cicero's oratory will be found interesting and instructive to the student of eloquence: " The object in this period most worthy to draw our attention, is Cicero himself; whose name alone suggests everything that is splendid in oratory. With the history of his life and with his character, as a man and a politician, we have not at present any direct concern. We consider him only as an eloquent speaker; and, in this view, it is our business to remark both his virtues, and his defects, if he has any. His virtues are, beyond controversy, eminently great. In all his orations there is high art. He begins, generally, with a regular exordium ; and with much preparation and insinuation prepossesses the hearers and studies to gain their affections. His method is clear, and his arguments are arranged with great propriety. His method is indeed more clear than that of Demosthenes; and this is one advantage which he has over him. We find every thing in its proper place; he never attempts to move till he has endeavoured to convince: and in moving, especially the softer passions, he is very successful. No man, that ever wrote, knew the power and force of words better than Cicero. He rolls them along with the greatest beauty and pomp ; and in the structure of his sentences, is curious and exact to the highest degree. He is always full and flowing, never abrupt. He is a great amplifier of every subject;

magnificent, and in his sentiments highly moral. His manner is on the whole diffuse, yet it is often happily varied,
and suited to the subject. In his four orations, for instance,
against Catiline, the tone and style of each of them, particularly the first and last, is very different, and accommodated
with a great deal of judgment to the occasion and the situation in which they were spoken. When a great public object roused his mind, and demanded indignation and force,
he departs considerably from that loose and declamatory
manner to which he inclines at other times, and becomes
exceedingly cogent and vehement. This is the case in his
orations against Antony, and in those too against Verres
and Catiline."

That he had defects there can be no question. It is said
that : "Together with those high qualities which Cicero possesses, he is not exempt from certain defects, of which it is
necessary to take notice. For the Ciceronian eloquence is
a pattern so dazzling by its beauties, that, if not examined
with accuracy and judgment, it is apt to betray the unwary
into a faulty imitation ; and I am of opinion that it has
sometimes produced this effect. In most of his orations,
especially those composed in the early part of his life, there
is too much art ; even carried the length of ostentation.
There is too visible a parade of eloquence. He seems often
to aim at obtaining admiration, rather than at operating
conviction, by what he says. Hence, on some occasions, he
is showy, rather than solid ; and diffuse, where he ought to
have been pressing. His sentences are at all times round
and sonorous ; they cannot be accused of monotony, for
they possess variety of cadence ; but from too great a study
of magnificence, he is sometimes deficient in strength. On
all occasions, where there is the least room for it, he is full
of himself. His great actions, and the real services which
he had performed to his country, apologise for this in
part ; ancient manners, too, imposed fewer restraints from
the side of decorum ; but, even after these allowances are
made, Cicero's ostentation of himself cannot be wholly pal-
liated ; and his orations, indeed all his works, leave on our

minds the impression of a good man, but, withal of a vain man."

The following comparison of Cicero and Demosthenes is worthy of insertion here:

" On the subject of comparing Cicero and Demosthenes, much has been said by critical writers. The different manners of these two princes of eloquence, and the distinguishing characters of each, are so strongly marked in their writings, that the comparison is, in many respects, obvious and easy. The character of Demosthenes is vigour and austerity; that of Cicero is gentleness and insinuation. In the one, you find more manliness; in the other, more ornament. The one is more harsh, but more spirited and cogent; the other more agreeable, but, withal, looser and weaker.

" To account for this difference, without any prejudice to Cicero, it has been said, that we must look to the nature of their different auditories: that the refined Athenians followed with ease the concise and convincing eloquence of Demosthenes; but that a manner more popular, more flowery, and declamatory was requisite in speaking to the Romans, a people less acute, and less acquainted with the arts of speech. But this is not satisfactory. For we must observe, that the Greek orator spoke much oftener before a mixed multitude than the Roman. Almost all the public business of Athens was transacted in popular assemblies. The common people were his hearers and his judges; whereas Cicero generally addressed himself to the ' Patres Conscripti,' or, in criminal trials, to the Prætor and the Select Judges; and it cannot be imagined that the persons of highest rank and best education in Rome required a more diffuse manner of pleading than the common citizens of Athens, in order to make them understand the cause, or relish the speaker. Perhaps we shall come nearer the truth by observing, that to unite together all the qualities, without the least exception, that form a perfect orator, and to excel equally in each of those qualities, is not to be expected from the limited powers of human genius. The highest degree of strength is, I suspect, never found united with the highest degree of smoothness and ornament; equal attentions to both are incompatible; and the genius that carries ornament to its utmost length is not of such a kind as can excel as much in vigour. For there plainly lies the characteristical difference between these two celebrated orators.

" It is a disadvantage to Demosthenes that, besides his conciseness, which sometimes produces obscurity, the language in which he writes is less familiar to most of us than the Latin, and that we are less acquainted with the Greek antiquities than we are with the Roman. We read Cicero with more ease, and of course with more pleasure. Independent of this circumstance too, he is no doubt, in himself, a more agreeable writer than the other. But notwithstanding this advantage, I am of opinion that, were the state in danger, or some great public interest at stake, which drew the serious attention of men, an oration in the spirit and strain of Demosthenes would have more weight, and produce greater effects, than one in the Ciceronian manner. Were Demosthenes' Philippics spoken in a British assembly, in a similar conjuncture of affairs, they would convince and persuade at this day. The rapid style, the vehement reasoning, the disdain, anger, boldness, freedom, which perpetually animate them, would render their success infallible over any modern assembly. I question whether the same can be said of Cicero's orations; whose eloquence, however beautiful, and however well suited to the Roman taste, yet borders oftener on declamation, and is more remote from the manner in which we now expect to hear real business and causes of importance treated."

Cicero's orations against Verres have been regarded by many writers as among the most splendid monuments of his genius. Of the six orations against Verres which have come down to us, Cicero delivered but one. Soon after the trial was begun, Verres, overwhelmed by the evidence of guilt which was produced against him, without awaiting the decision of the court, went into voluntary exile. If he had made a defence, the other five speeches would doubtless have been delivered. These orations contain many beautiful

passages. Perhaps the most eloquent was that in which
he described the crucifixion of Publius Gavius Cosanus, an
innocent Roman citizen. "Its conception is grand; its
arrangement, beautiful; its pathos, deep and thrilling. It
is not surpassed by anything of the kind in the history of
ancient eloquence."

Before introducing this passage, the author will give a
judicious reflection of an able critic: "The punishments of
death and torture usually reserved for slaves, but inflicted
by Verres on freemen of Rome, formed the climax of his
atrocities, which are detailed in oratorical progression. After
the vivid description of his former crimes, one scarcely expects that new terms of indignation will be found; but the
expressions of the orator become more glowing, in proportion as Verres grows more daring in his guilt. The sacred
character borne over all the world by a Roman citizen, must
be fully remembered, in order to read with due feeling the
description of the punishment of Gavius, who was scourged,
and then nailed to a cross, which, by a refinement in cruelty,
was erected on the shore, and facing Italy, that he might
suffer death with his view directed towards home and a
land of liberty. The whole is poured forth in a torrent of
the most rapid and fervid composition; and had it actually
flowed from the lips of the speaker, we can not doubt the
prodigious effect it would have had on a Roman audience
and on Roman judges."

Here we have the orator's touching description of the
punishment and execution of Gavius: "For why should I
speak," said Cicero, "of Publius Gavius, a citizen of the
municipality of Cosa, O judges! or with what vigour of
language, with what gravity of expression, with what grief
of mind shall I mention him? But, indeed, that indignation
fails me. I must take more care than usual that what I am
going to say be worthy of my subject—worthy of the indignation which I feel. For the charge is of such a nature,
that when I was first informed of it I thought I should not
avail myself of it. For although I knew that it was entirely
true, still I thought that it would not appear credible.

Being compelled by the tears of all the Roman citizens who are living as traders in Sicily, being influenced by the testimonies of the men of Valentia, most honourable men, and by those of all the Rhegians, and of many Roman knights who happened at that time to be at Messana, I produced at the previous pleading only just that amount of evidence which might prevent the matter from appearing doubtful to any one. What shall I do now? When I have been speaking for so many hours of one class of offences, and of that man's nefarious cruelty,—when I have now expended nearly all my treasures of words of such a sort as are worthy of that man's wickedness on other matters, and have omitted to take precautions to keep your attention on the stretch by diversifying my accusations, how am I to deal with an affair of the importance that this is? There is, I think, but one method, but one line open to me. I will place the matter plainly before you, which is of itself of such importance that there is no need of my eloquence—and eloquence, indeed, I have none, but there is no need of any one's eloquence to excite your feelings. This Gavius whom I am speaking of, a citizen of Cosa, when he (among that vast number of Roman citizens who had been treated in the same way) had been thrown by Verres into prison, and somehow or other had escaped secretly out of the stone quarries, and had come to Messana, being now almost within sight of Italy and of the walls of Rhegium, and being revived, after that fear of death and that darkness, by the light, as it were, of liberty and of the fragrance of the laws, began to talk at Messana, and to complain that he, a Roman citizen, had been thrown into prison. He said that he was now going straight to Rome, and that he would meet Verres on his arrival there.

" The miserable man was not aware that it made no difference whether he said this at Messana, or before the man's face in his own prætorian palace. For, as I have shown you before, that man had selected this city as the assistant in his crimes, the receiver of his thefts, the partner in all his wickedness. Accordingly, Gavius is at once brought before the Mamertine magistrates; and, as it happened, Verres

came on that very day to Messana. The matter is brought
before him. He is told that the man was a Roman citizen,
who was complaining that at Syracuse he had been confined
in the stone-quarries, and who, when he was actually em-
barking on board ship, and uttering violent threats against
Verres, had been brought back by them, and reserved in
order that he himself might decide what should be done
with him. He thanks the men and praises their good-will
and diligence in his behalf. He himself, inflamed with wickedness and frenzy, comes into the forum. His eyes glared ;
cruelty was visible in his whole appearance. All men waited
to see what steps he was going to take—what he was going
to do ; when all of a sudden he orders the man to be
seized, and to be stripped and bound in the middle of
the forum, and the rods to be got ready. The miserable
man cried out that he was a Roman citizen, a citizen also, of
the municipal town of Cosa,—that he had served with Lucius
Pretius, a most illustrious Roman knight, who was living
as a trader at Panormus, and from whom Verres might know
that he was speaking the truth. Then Verres says that he
has ascertained that he had been sent into Sicily by the
leaders of the runaway slaves, in order to act as a spy ; a
matter as to which there was no witness, no trace, nor even
the slightest suspicion in the mind of any one. Then he
orders the man to be most violently scourged on all sides.
In the middle of the forum of Messana a Roman citizen, O
judges, was beaten with rods ; while in the meantime no
groan was heard, no other expression was heard from that
wretched man, amid all his pain, and between the sound of
the blows, except these words, 'I am a citizen of Rome.'
He fancied that by this one statement of his citizenship he
could ward off all blows, and remove all torture from his
person. He not only did not succeed in averting by his
entreaties the violence of the rods, but as he kept on
repeating his entreaties and the assertion of his citizenship,
a cross—a cross, I say—was got ready for that miserable
man, who had never witnessed such a stretch of power.

" O the sweet name of liberty ! O the admirable privileges

of our citizenship! O Porcian law! O Sempronian laws!
O power of the tribunes, bitterly regretted by, and at last
restored to, the Roman people! Have all our rights fallen
so far, that in a province of the Roman people,—in a town
of our confederate allies,—a Roman citizen should be bound
in the forum, and beaten with rods by a man who only had
the fasces and the axes through the kindness of the Roman
people? What shall I say? When fire, and red-hot plates
and other instruments of torture were employed? If the
bitter entreaties and the miserable cries of that man had no
power to restrain you, were you not moved even by the weeping and loud groans of the Roman citizens who were present
at that time? Did you dare to drag anyone to the cross
who said that he was a Roman citizen?

"If you, O Verres! being taken among the Persians or in
the remotest parts of India, were being led to execution,
what else would you cry out but that you were a Roman
citizen? And if that name of your city, honoured and renowned as it is among all men, would have availed you, a
stranger among strangers, among barbarians, among men
placed in the most remote and distant corners of the earth,
ought not he, whoever he was, whom you were hurrying to
the cross, who was a stranger to you, to have been able,
when he said that he was a Roman citizen, to obtain from
you, the prætor, if not an escape, at least a respite from
death by his mention of and claims to citizenship?

"Men of no importance, born in an obscure rank, go to
sea; they go to places which they have never seen before;
where they can neither be known to the men among whom
they have arrived, nor always find people to vouch for them.
But still, owing to this confidence in the mere fact of their
citizenship, they think that they shall be safe, not only
among our own magistrates, who are restrained by fear of
the laws and of public opinion, nor among our fellow-citizens
only, who are united with them by community of language,
of rights, and of many other things; but wherever they come
they think that this will be a protection to them. Take away
this protection from Roman citizens, establish the fact that

there is no assistance to be found in the words 'I am a
Roman citizen'; that a prætor, or any other officer, may
with impunity order any punishment he pleases to be inflicted on a man who says that he is a Roman citizen, though
no one knows that it is not true ; and at one blow, by admitting that defence, you cut off from the Roman citizens all
the provinces, and the kingdoms, all free cities, and indeed
the whole world, which has hitherto been open most especially to our countrymen.

"But why need I say more about Gavius? as if you were
hostile to Gavius, and not rather an enemy to the name and
class of citizens, and to all their rights. You were not, I say,
an enemy to the individual, but to the common cause of
liberty. For what was our object in ordering the Mamer-
tines, when, according to their regular custom and usage,
they had erected the cross behind the city in the Pompeian
road, to place it where it looked towards the strait ; and in
adding, what you can by no means deny, what you said
openly in the hearing of everyone, that you chose that place
in order that the man who said that he was a Roman citizen,
might be able from his cross to behold Italy and to look
towards his own home ? And accordingly, O judges, that
cross, for the first time since the foundation of Messana, was
erected in that place. A spot commanding a view of Italy
was picked out by that man, for the express purpose that the
wretched man who was dying in agony and torture might see
that the rights of liberty and of slavery were only separated
by a very narrow strait, and that Italy might behold her son
murdered by the most miserable and most painful punishment appropriate to slaves alone.

"It is a crime to bind a Roman citizen; to scourge him is
a wickedness; to put him to death is almost parricide. What
shall I say of crucifying him ? So guilty an action cannot
by any possibility be adequately expressed by any name bad
enough for it. Yet with all this that man was not content.
'Let him behold his country,' said he ; 'let him die within
sight of laws and liberty.' It was not Gavius, it was not one
individual, I know not whom,—it was not one Roman citi-

zen,—it was the common cause of freedom and citizenship that you exposed to that torture and nailed on that cross. But now consider the audacity of the man. Do not you think that he was indignant that he could not erect that cross for Roman citizens in the forum, in the comitium, in the very rostra? For the place in his province which was the most like those places in celebrity, and the nearest to them in point of distance, he did select. He chose that monument of his wickedness and audacity to be in the sight of Italy, in the very vestibule of Sicily, within sight of all passers-by as they sailed to and fro."

Cicero, however, acquired his greatest renown as a statesman and an orator by detecting and crushing the famous conspiracy of Catiline. His orations against Catiline are the greatest which he delivered. They are among the best models of style that adorn Roman literature.

Sallust and other historians have given a history of the Catilinarian conspiracy, which was crushed B.C. 63, and it is doubtless familiar to the reader. It is therefore unnecessary to give a full account of this plot, which had for objects the burning of Rome and the ruin of the republic.

" It was to have been carried into effect in this manner : Catiline was to leave Rome and join his forces, assembled in different parts of Italy, while his accomplices in the city were to burn the Capitol, and massacre the senators and citizens. Cicero, by his vigilance, having discovered their infernal design, summoned the senate to meet in the temple of Jupiter (this temple was only used for this purpose on occasions of great danger), in the Capitol, that he might lay before it the whole circumstance of the deep-laid plot. The presence of Catiline, who had the boldness to appear in the midst of the assembly, so inflamed the orator that he immediately rose and broke out in that severe, overwhelming invective which produced such an electric effect when delivered, and which cannot, at this day, be read without emotion. It was in a thundering tone of exasperated eloquence that Cicero exclaimed, as he fixed his eye upon the conspirator:

" ' When, O Catiline, do you mean to cease abusing our patience? How long is that madness of yours still to mock us? When is there to be an end of that unbridled audacity of yours, swaggering about as it does now? Do not the mighty guards placed on the Palatine Hill—do not the watches posted throughout the city—does not the alarm of the people, and the union of all good men—does not the precaution taken of assembling the senate in this most defensible place—do not the looks and countenances of this venerable body here present, have any effect upon you? Do you not feel that your plans are detected? Do you not see that your conspiracy is already arrested and rendered powerless by the knowledge which everyone here possesses of it? What is there that you did last night, what the night before—where is it that you were—who was there that you summoned to meet you—what design was there which was adopted by you with which you think that any one of us is unacquainted?

" ' Shame on the age and on its principles! The senate is aware of these things; the consul sees them; and yet this man lives. Lives! aye, he comes even into the senate. He takes part in the public deliberations; he is watching and marking down and checking off for slaughter every individual among us. And we, gallant men that we are, think that we are doing our duty to the republic if we keep out of the way of his frenzied attacks.

" ' You ought, O Catiline, long ago to have been led to execution by command of the consul. That destruction which you have been long plotting against us ought to have already fallen on your own head.

" ' I wish, O conscript fathers, to be merciful; I wish not to appear negligent amid such danger to the state; but I do now accuse myself of remissness and culpable inactivity. A camp is pitched in Italy, at the entrance of Etruria, in hostility to the republic; the number of the enemy increases every day; and yet the general of that camp, the leader of those enemies we see within the walls—aye, and even in the senate—planning every day some internal injury to the re-

public. If, O Catiline, I should now order you to be
arrested, to be put to death, I should, I suppose, have to
fear lest all good men should say that I had acted tardily,
rather than that any one should affirm that I acted cruelly.
But yet this, which ought to have been done long since, I
have good reason for not doing as yet; I will put you to
death, then, when there shall be not one person possible to
be found so wicked, so abandoned, so like yourself, as not
to allow that it has been rightly done. As long as one person exists who can dare to defend you, you shall live; but
you shall live as you do now, surrounded by my many and
trusty guards so that you shall not be able to stir one finger
against the republic : many eyes and ears shall still observe
and watch you, as they have hitherto done, though you shall
not perceive them.

"'As, then, this is the case, O Catiline, continue as you
have begun. Leave the city at least : the gates are open;
depart. That Manlian camp of yours has been waiting too
long for you as its general. And lead forth with you all
your friends, or at least as many as you can ; purge the city
of your presence ; you will deliver me from a great fear,
when there is a wall between me and you. Among us you
can dwell no longer. I will not bear it, I will not permit it,
I will not tolerate it.

"'For what is there, O Catiline, that can now afford you
any pleasure in this city? for there is no one in it, except
that band of profligate conspirators of yours, who does not
fear you—no one who does not hate you. What brand of
domestic baseness is not stamped upon your life? What
disgraceful circumstance is wanting to your infamy in
your private affairs? From what licentiousness have your
eyes, from what atrocity have your hands, from what iniquity
has your whole body ever abstained? Is there one youth
when you have once entangled him in the temptations of
your corruption, to whom you have not held out a sword
for audacious crime, or a torch for licentious wickedness?

"'Begone from the city, O Catiline, deliver the republic
from fear; depart into banishment, if that is the word you

are waiting for. What now, O Catiline? Do you not perceive, do you not•see the silence of these men; they permit it, they say nothing; why wait you for the authority of
their words when you see their wishes in their silence?

" ' Wherefore, O conscript fathers, let the worthless begone,
—let them separate themselves from the good,—let them
collect in one place,—let them, as I have often said before,
be separated from us by a wall; let them cease to plot
against the consul in his own house,—to surround the tribunal of the city prætor,—to besiege the senate house with
swords,—to prepare brands and torches to burn the city;
let it, in short, be written on the brow of every citizen, what
are his sentiments about the republic. I promise you this,
O conscript fathers, that there shall be so much diligence in
us the consuls, so much authority in you, so much virtue
in the Roman knights, so much unanimity in all good men,
that you shall see everything made plain and manifest by the
departure of Catiline,—everything checked and punished.'

" Catiline did not venture to make any reply to this
speech, but he begged the senate not to be too hasty in believing everything which was said to his prejudice by one
who had always been his enemy, as Cicero had; and alleged
his high birth, and the stake which he had in the prosperity
of the commonwealth, as arguments to make it appear im-
probable that he should seek to injure it; and called Cicero
a stranger, and a new inhabitant of Rome. But the senate
interrupted him with a general outcry, calling him traitor
and parricide. Upon which, being rendered furious and
desperate, he declared aloud what he had before said to
Cato, that since he was circumvented and driven headlong
by his enemies, he would quench the flame which his enemies
were kindling around him in the common ruin. And so he
rushed out of the temple.

" In point of effect, this oration must have been perfectly
electric. The disclosure to the criminal himself of his most
secret purposes—their flagitious nature, threatening the life
of every one present—the whole course of his villainies and
treasons, blazoned forth with the fire of increased eloquence

—and the adjuration to him, by flying from Rome, to free his country from such a pestilence, were all wonderfully calculated to excite astonishment, admiration, and horror."

This speech produced a powerful effect. It was the means of driving Catiline from Rome, and of saving the commonwealth from utter ruin. After the conspirator had fled from the city, Cicero called the people together into the forum, and delivered his second Catilinarian oration, which commences as follows:

" At length, O Romans, we have dismissed from the city, or driven out, or, when he was departing of his own accord, we have pursued with words, Lucius Catiline, mad with audacity, breathing wickedness, impiously planning mischief to his country, threatening fire and sword to you and to this city. He is gone, he has departed, he has disappeared, he has rushed out. No injury will now be prepared against these walls within the walls themselves by that monster and prodigy of wickedness. And we have, without controversy, defeated him, the sole general of this domestic war. For now that dagger will no longer hover about our sides ; we shall not be afraid in the campus, in the forum, in the senate-house,—ay, and within our own private walls. He was moved from his place when he was driven from the city. Now we shall openly carry on a regular war with an enemy without hindrance. Beyond all question we ruin the man ; we have defeated him splendidly when we have driven him from secret treachery into open warfare. But that he has not taken with him his sword red with blood as he intended, —that he has left us alive,—that we wrested the weapon from his hands,—that he has left the citizens safe and the city standing, what great and overwhelming grief must you think that this is to him ! Now he lies prostrate, O Romans, and feels himself stricken down and abject, and often casts back his eyes towards this city, which he mourns over as snatched from his jaws, but which seems to me to rejoice at having vomited forth such a pest, and cast it out of doors."

The conspiracy was suppressed finally by the execution of five of the principal conspirators, and by the fall of Catiline himself in battle. Cicero for his services on this occasion received the thanks of the senate, and was universally hailed as the deliverer and father of his country.

All of the orations of Cicero deserve careful reading and study ; especially is this true of the speech for Archias and that for Milo.

The orations against Marc Antony were the last which Cicero delivered. Cicero looked upon Antony as the greatest enemy to the liberties of the Roman people. From their resemblance to speeches of Demosthenes against Philip, these orations received the name of *Philippics*.

The peroration of the second Philippic contains a bold exclamation against Antony : "Consider, I beg you, Marcus Antoninus, do some time or other consider the republic; think of the family of which you are born, not of the men with whom you are living. Be reconciled to the republic. However, do you decide on your conduct. As to mine, I myself will declare what that shall be. *I defended the republic as a young man, I will not abandon it now that I am old. I scorned the sword of Catiline, I will not quail before yours. No, I will rather cheerfully expose my own person if the liberty of the city can be restored by my death.*

"May the indignation of the Roman people at last bring forth what it has been so long labouring with. In truth, if twenty years ago in this very temple I asserted that death would not come prematurely upon a man of consular rank, with how much more truth must I now say the same of an old man? To me, indeed, O conscript fathers, death is even now desirable, after all the honours which I have gained, and the deeds which I have done. I only pray for these two things : one, that dying I may leave the Roman people free. No greater boon than this can be granted me by the immortal gods. The other, that every one may meet with a fate suitable to his deserts and conduct toward the republic."

The last extract which the author will give, is the peroration of the sixth Philippic, addressed to the people, in which the orator endeavours to show that Roman citizens cannot be reduced to slavery:

5

" It is impossible for the Roman people to be slaves; that people whom the immortal gods have ordained should rule over all nations. Matters are now come to a crisis. We are fighting for our freedom. Either you must conquer, O Romans, which indeed you will do if you continue to act with such piety and such unanimity, or you must do anything rather than become slaves. Other nations can endure slavery. Liberty is the inalienable possession of the Roman people."

But the fetters of the Roman people had been forged, and their liberty was at an end. They did not heed the notes of warning which he sounded. He was included in the proscription of Antony, and was assassinated in the sixty-fourth year of his age, B.C. 43.

Quintilian has said of Cicero that his name " is only another for eloquence itself, and that he united in his manner the vehemence of Demosthenes, the copiousness of Plato, and the sweetness of Isocrates."

No adequate conception can now be formed of Cicero's impassioned eloquence. The most glowing description can but imperfectly paint the charms of his oratory. Its greatest force lay in the living voice—the graceful gesture—the expressive countenance—the beaming eye—the pathos and power of tone which thrill the hearer;—these were some of the characteristics of that oratory which so often thrilled the heart of a Roman audience.

Forensic oratory may be said to have passed away, at Rome, with the republic. Eloquence cannot exist under a despotic form of government. It can only be found in countries where free institutions flourish. Crematius Cardus, in the reign of Tiberius, thought otherwise, and on one occasion, he alluded in terms of praise to the patriots of the republic. He eulogised Brutus, and designated Cassius as the last of the Romans, but his temerity cost him his life.

In the dialogue on the " Causes of the Corruption of Eloquence," written, it is thought, by Tacitus a little more than a century after the death of Cicero, the author feelingly laments that oratory was extinct. He says: " Often have you

asked me, Justus Fabius, why, when former ages were so distinguished by the genius and renown of orators, our own age,
destitute and bereft of glory, scarce retains the very name.
For we style none such now except the ancients; but the
speakers of the present day are called pleaders, and advocates, and barristers, and anything rather than orators."

Judging from what Juvenal says of it, the bar in his time,
at Rome, was by no means in a prosperous and satisfactory
state:

" Say now what honours advocates attend,
　Whose shelves beneath a load of volumes bend ;
　The voice stentorian in the courts we hear,
　But chiefly when some creditor is near :
　A show of business eager to display,
　Their lungs like panting bellows work away.
　Alas ! a hundred lawyers scarce can gain,
　What one successful jockey will obtain.—
　The court has met : with pale and careworn face
　You rise to plead some helpless client's case,
　And crack your voice; for what ? when all is o'er,
　To see a bunch of laurel on your door.
　This is the meed of eloquence ; to dine
　On dried-up hams, and cabbage, and sour wine :
　If by good luck four briefs you chance to hold,
　And your eye glistens at the sight of gold ;
　Think not to pocket all the hard-won fee,
　For the attorney claims his share with thee.
　Large sums Æmilius can command, 't is true,
　Although a far worse advocate than you ;
　But then his steed of bronze and brazen car
　The rich Æmilius to the world declare ;
　While lance in hand he rides a sculptur'd knight,
　And seems a warrior charging in the fight."

Pliny the younger also speaks of the changed condition of
the forum in his day, and of the unprofessional and unworthy
arts which were resorted to to gain a reputation and attract
clients.　In one of his epistles to a friend he says: "You are
right in your conjecture.　I am tired to death of causes in

the centumviral courts, which give me practice rather than
pleasure, for they are for the most part trifling and trumpery.
A case seldom occurs distinguished either by the rank of the
parties, or the importance of the matter in dispute.   Besides,
there are very few counsel with whom it is at all agreeable to
be engaged.   The rest are generally obscure young men
with plenty of effrontery, who go there to make declamatory
speeches with such rashness and want of modesty, that my
friend Attilius seems to have said, with great truth, that boys
at the bar begin with causes in those courts, just as they did
with Homer at school."

Pliny also mentions, with disapproval, the practice of
certain advocates who hired *claqueurs* to attend upon them
and applaud their speeches in court.   He says: "If you
chance to pass through the hall, and wish to know how each
counsel acquits himself, you have no occasion to listen to
what he says.   You may rest assured that he is the worst
speaker who has the loudest applause."   Pliny says that
Sergius Licinius first introduced this practice: "Once, when
Domitius Afer was pleading a cause before the centumvirs,
he suddenly heard, in the adjoining court, a loud and unusual shouting, and for a few moments he stopped.   When
the noise ceased he went on, but soon there was another
shout of applause and he again paused.   After he had resumed his argument, he was again interrupted, and he then
asked who was speaking in the other court.   He was told
that it was Licinius ; upon which he said, addressing the
judges, 'This is a death-blow to the profession.'"

Ulpian in his treatise *Ad Edictum* tells us that an express
law was enacted to prevent the fair sex from pleading in the
courts of law, "that they might not intermeddle in such
matters, contrary to the modesty befitting their sex, nor engage in employments proper to men."   The cause of this
edict being passed, is said to have been the conduct of a
virago named Carfania, a most troublesome and ill-condi-
tioned lady, who gave the magistrates a great deal of trouble
by her importunity in court.   An exception was made, however, in favour of the daughters of advocates who could not

attend in person on account of sickness or infirmity, and who could not get anyone else to plead for them."

In one of the books written during the middle ages the following advice is given to the forensic orator. He was told that, in order that his discourse " might have dignity and beauty, there are three things necessary : first, it must please; secondly, it must convince; thirdly, it must persuade. For the first effect the pleader must speak gracefully; for the second plainly; for the third with great ardour and fervency."

CHAPTER III.

MODERN ORATORY.

ORATORY is immortal. In some form or other oratory will live, and have its influence upon mankind, as in past ages, and in different countries, as long as the human heart is inhabited by the passions which are inherent to our nature and which have taken up their residence there, and as long as it is necessary to discuss important questions in the pulpit, the senate, and the bar.

"*Not until human nature is other than it is, will the function of the living voice—the greatest force on earth among men—cease,*" said Henry Ward Beecher. The same magnificent orator said, also: "*I advocate, therefore, in its full extent, and for every reason of humanity, of patriotism, and of religion, a more thorough culture of oratory; and I define oratory to be the art of influencing conduct with the truth set home by all the resources of the living man.*"

The study of oratory has of late years been too much neglected by public speakers—especially by lawyers. They do not give enough attention to general literature. By giving a portion of their time to the study of polite literature, aside from the benefits derived from an accumulation of valuable facts and felicitous phrases, they would return to their more rugged pursuits with greater alacrity and with renewed strength.

The mind is invigorated, strengthened, and improved by turning it into other channels occasionally.

"A mere lawyer is a mere jackass, and has never the power to unload himself ; whereas I consider the advocate—the thoroughly accomplished advocate—the highest style of man. He is always ready to learn, and always ready to ¡teach. Hortensius was a lawyer, Cicero an orator. The one is forgotten, the other is immortal," said one of the greatest of American lawyers—David Paul Brown.

Good speaking, in a republican form of government like our own, is usually a direct road to riches and honour, and it should be cultivated assiduously by those who are endowed by nature with the requisite natural ability.

The oratory of the American bar is not as good as it should be. Too many of our speakers imagine they are heaven-born geniuses, and that it is useless for them to study the art of oratory. The success of many of our forensic orators is owing in a great measure to the exertions of strong parts and masculine understandings, breaking through and surmounting the incumbrances of a bad style and an ungraceful elocution. We are often content to fatigue our attention in listening to these men, because we know that their matter and their acuteness in the application of it will, in the end, make us compensation. The pleasure of hearing them, however, is greatly diminished by the incorrectness of their language, the want of conclusiveness of their arguments, and the dryness of their diction.

There are, however, bright stars in our legal hemisphere to whom this criticism does not apply. But their eloquence derives that dazzling lustre with which it is irradiated, from the acquirements of logical and rhetorical support and ornament.

Neither Greece nor Rome, in their palmiest days, presented a fairer field than that which now invites the culture of the enlightened citizens of America. We enjoy as much liberty as is consistent with the nature of man. We possess as a nation all the advantages which climate, soil, and situation can bestow, and nothing but *merit* is here required as a qualification for the highest offices of state. Eloquence never had more ample scope.

We must not rest satisfied with admiring the celebrated
orators of Greece and Rome. Oratory, that most sublime
of all arts, must not be neglected, while every other useful
and ornamental art speeds swiftly toward perfection.

American eloquence should be raised above all Greek,
above all Roman fame. To our young readers, especially,
we would repeat the words of Adams:

" Is it your intention to devote the labours of your maturity to the cause of justice ; to defend the persons, the
property, and the fame of your fellow-citizens from the open
assaults of violence, and the secret encroachments of fraud?
Fill the fountains of your eloquence from inexhaustible
sources, that their streams, when they shall begin to flow,
may themselves prove inexhaustible.

" Is there among you a youth whose bosom burns with
the fires of honourable ambition ; who aspires to immortalise
his name by the extent and importance of his services to his
country ; whose visions of futurity glow with the hope of
presiding in her councils, of directing her affairs, of appearing to future ages, on the rolls of fame, as her ornament and
pride? Let him catch from the relics of ancient oratory
those unresisted powers which mould the mind of a man to
the will of the speaker, and yield the guidance of a nation
to the dominion of the voice.

" Under governments purely republican, where every
citizen has a deep interest in the affairs of the nation, and, in
some form of public assembly or other, has the means and
opportunity of delivering his opinions, and of communicating
his sentiments by speech,—where government itself has no
arms but those of persuasion,—where prejudice has not acquired an uncontrolled ascendancy, and faction is yet confined
within the barriers of peace, the voice of eloquence will not
be heard in vain.

" March then with firm, with steady, with undeviating
step to the prize of your high calling. Gather fragrance
from the whole paradise of science, and learn to distil from
your lips all the honeys of persuasion. Consecrate, above
all, the faculties of your life to the cause of truth, of freedom,

and of humanity. So shall your country ever gladden at
the sound of your voice, and every talent, added to your
accomplishments, become another blessing to mankind."

The advance of civilisation is great, and the engines of
force are mighty, but man is greater than that which he produces. Unspeakably great and useful is the Press, and the
voice is its most important auxiliary. There is work for
both. It has been said that our greatest orators have not
been trained. This is not true. On the contrary, the most
successful forensic and political orators of ancient and modern times have been diligent students of oratory from the
time of Demosthenes to the present, and including that
great forensic orator, Hon. Joseph H. Choate, the most
successful advocate of the present day.

Henry Clay, by his own exertions, chiefly, became an
accomplished and cultured orator, and it is said that Daniel
Webster was studious of everything he did, even to the
selection of the buttons for his coat.

He who does not believe that industry is necessary to the
attainment of eloquence, should read the following extract
from the works of an able writer upon the subject:

" The history of the world is full of testimony to prove
how much depends upon industry. Not an eminent orator
has lived but is an example of it. Yet, in contradiction to
all this, the almost universal feeling appears to be, that
industry can effect nothing, that eminence is the result of
accident, and that every one must be content to remain just
what he may happen to be. Thus, multitudes, who come
forward as teachers and guides, suffer themselves to be
satisfied with the most indifferent attainments, and a
miserable mediocrity, without so much as inquiring how
they may rise higher, much less, making any attempt to
rise. For any other art they would have served an appren-
ticeship and would be ashamed to practise it in public
before they had learned it. If any one would sing, he
attends a master, and is drilled in the very elementary principles ; and it is only after the most laborious process that
he dares to exercise his voice in public. This he does,

though he has scarcely anything to learn but the mechanical execution of what lies in sensible forms before the eye.
But the extempore speaker, who is to invent, as well as to
utter, to carry on an operation of the mind, as well as to
produce sound, enters upon the work without preparatory
discipline, and then wonders that he fails! If he were
learning to play on the flute for public exhibition, how
many hours and days would he spend in giving facility to
his fingers, and in attaining the power of the sweetest and
most expressive execution!"

The author cannot commend too highly the following
comparison between ancient and modern oratory by John
Quincy Adams:

"At the revival of letters in modern Europe, Eloquence,
together with her sister muses, awoke, and shook the pop-
pies from her brow. But their torpors still tingled in her
veins. In the interval her voice was gone; her favourite
languages were extinct; her organs were no longer attuned
to harmony, and her hearers could no longer understand her
speech. The discordant jargon of feudal anarchy had banished the musical dialects, in which she had always
delighted. The theatres of her former triumphs were
either deserted, or they were filled with the babblers of
sophistry and chicane. She shrunk intuitively from the
forum, for the last object she remembered to have seen
there was the head of her darling Cicero, planted upon the
rostrum. She ascended the tribunals of justice; there she
found her child, Persuasion, manacled and pinioned by the
letter of the law; there she beheld an image of herself, stam-
mering in barbarous Latin, and staggering under the lum-
ber of a thousand volumes. Her heart fainted within her.
She lost all confidence in herself. Together with her irresistible powers, she lost proportionally the consideration of
the world, until, instead of comprising the whole system of
public education, she found herself excluded from the circle
of sciences, and declared an outlaw from the realms of
learning. She was not, however, doomed to eternal silence.
With the progress of freedom and of liberal science, in vari-

ous parts of modern Europe, she obtained access to mingle
in the deliberations of their parliaments. With labour and
difficulty she learned their languages, and lent her aid in
giving them form and polish. But she has never recovered
the graces of her former beauty, nor the energies of her
ancient vigour.

"The immeasurable superiority of ancient over modern
oratory is one of the most remarkable circumstances which
offer themselves to the scrutiny of reflecting minds, and it is
in the languages, the institutions, and the manners of modern
Europe, that the solution of a phenomenon so extraordinary must be sought. The assemblies of the people, of the
select councils, or of the senate in Athens and Rome, were
held for the purpose of real deliberation. The fate of measures was not decided before they were proposed. Eloquence
produced a powerful effect, not only upon the minds of the
hearers, but upon the issue of the deliberation. In the only
countries of modern Europe, where the semblance of deliberative assemblies has been preserved, corruption, here in
the form of executive influence, there in the guise of party
spirit, by introducing a more compendious mode of securing
decisions, has crippled the sublimest efforts of oratory, and
the votes upon questions of magnitude to the interest of
nations are all told, long before the questions themselves
are submitted to discussion. Hence those nations, which
for ages have gloried in the devotion to literature, science,
and the arts, have never been able to exhibit a specimen of
deliberative oratory that can bear a comparison with those
transmitted down to us from antiquity.

"Religion indeed has opened one new avenue to the
career of eloquence. Amidst the sacrifices of paganism to
her three hundred thousand gods, amidst her sagacious and
solemn consultations in the entrails of slaughtered brutes,
in the flight of birds, and the feeding of fowls, it had never
entered her imagination to call upon the pontiff, the haru-
spex, or the augur, for discourses to the people, on the
nature of their duties to their Maker, their fellow-mortals,
and themselves. This was an idea, too august to be mingled

with the absurd and ridiculous, or profligate and barbarous
rites of her deplorable superstition. It is an institution, for
which mankind are indebted to Christianity; introduced by
the Founder himself of this divine religion, and in every
point of view worthy of its high original. Its effects have
been to soften the tempers and purify the morals of mankind; not in so high a degree as benevolence could wish,
but enough to call forth our strains of warmest gratitude to
that good Being, who provides us with the means of promoting our own felicity, and gives us power to stand,
though leaving us free to fall. Here then is an unbounded
and inexhaustible field for eloquence, never explored by the
ancient orators; and here alone have the modern Europeans
cultivated the art with much success. In vain should we
enter the halls of justice, in vain should we listen to debates
of senates for strains of oratory worthy of remembrance
beyond the duration of the occasion which called them
forth. The art of embalming thought by oratory, like that
of embalming bodies by aromatics, would have perished,
but for the exercises of religion. These alone have in the
latter ages furnished discourses which remind us that eloquence is yet a faculty of the human mind.

" Among the causes which have contributed thus to depress
the oratory of modern times, must be numbered the indifference with which it has been treated as an article of education. The ancients had fostered an opinion, that this talent
was in a more than usual degree the creature of discipline;
and it is one of the maxims handed down to us as a result
of their experience, that men must be born to poetry, and
bred to eloquence; that the bard is always the child of
nature, and the orator always the issue of instruction. The
doctrine seems to be not entirely without foundation, but
was by them carried in both its parts to an extravagant
excess.

" The foundations for the oratorical talent, as well as those
of the poetical faculty, must be laid in the bounties of
nature; and as the muse in Homer, impartial in her distribution of good and evil, struck the bard with blindness,

when she gave him the powers of song, her sister not unfrequently, by a like mixture of tenderness and rigour, bestows
the blessing of wisdom, while she refuses the readiness of
utterance. Without entering however into a disquisition
which would lead me far beyond the limits of this occasion,
I may remark that the modern Europeans have run into
the adverse extreme, and appear, during a considerable
period, in their system of public education, to have passed
upon eloquence a sentence of proscription. Even when
they studied RHETORIC as a theory, they neglected
ORATORY as an art; and while assiduously unfolding to
their pupils the bright displays of Greek and Roman eloquence, they never attempted to make them eloquent
themselves."

The golden age of modern parliamentary and forensic
oratory was the latter part of the eighteenth century. This
period was illuminated by the brilliant genius of Vergniaud
and Mirabeau in France; of Chatham, Burke, Pitt, Fox,
Sheridan, Grattan, Curran, and Erskine in England; of
Henry, Otis, Warren, the Adamses, and many others in
America. It was not only an age of oratorical glory; but of
literary and scientific greatness.

It was an illustrious period, too, in political history for
some of the most important events that have ever occurred.

Mr. Alison has so beautifully described this era, which
may be designated as that of George III., that the author
cannot forbear repeating a passage of his graphic description, affording a grand view of the world when the "flame
of eloquence shone so steadily and burned so brightly in
Europe and America." The eloquent historian mentioned
says:

"The reign of George III. embraces, beyond all question,
the most eventful and important period in the annals of
mankind. In its eventful days were combined the growth
of Grecian democracy with the passions of Roman ambition; the fervour of plebeian zeal with the pride of aristocratic power; the blood of Marius with the genius of Cæsar;
the opening of a nobler hemisphere to the enterprise of Co-

lumbus, with the rise of a social agent as mighty as the press
or the powers of steam.

"But if new elements were called into action in the social
world, of surpassing strength and energy, in the course of
this memorable reign, still more remarkable were the characters which rose to eminence during its continuance. The
military genius, unconquerable courage, and enduring constancy of Frederick; the ardent mind, burning eloquence,
and lofty patriotism of Chatham; the incorruptible integrity,
sagacious intellect, and philosophic spirit of Franklin; the
disinterested virtue, prophetic wisdom, and imperturbable
fortitude of Washington; the masculine understanding, fem-
inine passions, and blood-stained ambition of Catharine,
would alone have been sufficient to cast a radiance over any
other age of the world. But bright as were the stars of its
morning light, more brilliant still was the constellation
which shone forth in its meridian splendour, or cast a glow
over the twilight of its evening shades. Then were to be
seen the rival genius of Pitt and Fox, which, emblematic of
the antagonist powers which then convulsed mankind, shook
the British senate by their vehemence, and roused the spirit
destined, ere long, for the dearest interests of humanity, to
array the world in arms; then the great soul of Burke cast
off the unworldly fetters of ambition or party, and, fraught
with a giant's force and a prophet's wisdom, regained its
destiny in the cause of mankind; then the arm of Nelson
cast its thunderbolts on every shore, and preserved un-
scathed in the deep the ark of European freedom; and, ere
his reign expired, the wisdom of Wellington had erected an
impassable barrier to Gallic ambition, and said, even to the
deluge of imperial power, 'Hitherto shalt thou come and
no farther, and here shall thy proud waves be stayed.' Nor
were splendid genius, heroic virtue, gigantic wickedness
wanting on the opposite side of this heart-stirring conflict.
Mirabeau had thrown over the morning of the French
Revolution the brilliant but deceitful light of democratic
genius; Danton had coloured its noontide glow with the
passions and the energy of tribunitian power; Carnot had

exhibited the combination, rare in a corrupted age, of republican energy with private virtue ; Robespierre had darkened its evening days by the blood and agony of selfish ambition ; Napoleon had risen like a meteor over its midnight darkness, dazzled the world by the brightness of his genius and the lustre of his deeds, and lured its votaries, by the deceitful blaze of glory, to perdition.

" In calmer pursuits in the tranquil walks of science and literature, the same age was, beyond all others, fruitful in illustrious men. Doctor Johnson, the strongest intellect and the most profound observer of the eighteenth century ; Gibbon, the architect of a bridge over the dark gulf which separates ancient from modern times, whose vivid genius has tinged with brilliant colours the greatest historical work in existence ; Hume, whose simple but profound history will be coeval with the long and eventful thread of English story ; Robertson, who first threw over the maze of human events the light of philosophic genius and the spirit of enlightened reflection ; Gray, whose burning thoughts had been condensed in words of more than classic beauty ; Burns, whose lofty soul spread its own pathos and dignity over the ' short and simple annals of the poor ' ; Smith, who called into existence a new science, fraught with the dearest interests of humanity, and nearly brought it to perfection in a single lifetime ; Reid, who carried into the recesses of the human mind the torch of cool and sagacious inquiry ; Stewart, who cast a luminous glance over the philosophy of mind, and warmed the inmost recesses of metaphysical inquiry by the delicacy of taste and the glow of eloquence ; Watt, who added an unknown power to the resources of art, and in the regulated force of steam discovered the means of approximating the most distant parts of the earth and spreading in the wilderness of nature the wonders of European enterprise and the blessings of Christian civilisation ; these formed some of the ornaments of the period, during its earlier and more pacific times, forever memorable in the annals of scientific acquisition and literary greatness."

The author feels that he would not do his subject justice

if he did not here quote the valuable, and in the main just, observations of Dr. Blair upon modern eloquence. He differs, however, from that author when he says, agreeing with Mr. Hume, that the English bar does not afford a fine theatre for oratory. In forming this conclusion these distinguished writers laboured under some disadvantage, for they had only before their view the Scottish bar, where the trial by jury is allowed only in criminal cases, or was at least at the time he wrote. But in England and America, where in the superior as well as inferior judicatures, almost every cause is tried by a jury of twelve men, fairly selected by ballot, the very finest opportunity for the display of eloquence is afforded the advocate. The author will grant what Dr. Blair says, that he is in some degree confined by the precision of our laws, still he speaks to the jury largely on matters of fact, and the less of technical language he uses the greater will be the effect of what he says. Of course, the sober character of the people in the countries mentioned, and the feeling of jurymen that they are bound by their oaths, prevent them from being unduly swayed by the eloquence of advocates. As Dr. Blair's work has been largely used as a text-book, the author is inclined to believe that his *dictum* has influenced many lawyers to pay less attention to the study of forensic oratory than they should have given it. Eloquence is, or should be, spoken wisdom, and it is so described by Cicero. It is certain that nearly every successful aspirant for political or forensic honours, even in America, has been an untiring student of oratory. With these remarks of a prefatory character, the author inserts at this place Dr. Blair's observations upon modern eloquence:

"In the decline of the Roman empire, the introduction of Christianity gave rise to a new species of eloquence, in the apologies, sermons, and pastoral writings of the Fathers of the Church. Among the Latin Fathers, Lactantius and Minutius Felix are the most remarkable for purity of style; and, in a later age, the famous St. Augustine possesses a considerable share of sprightliness and strength. But none of the Fathers afford any just models of eloquence. Their language, as soon as we descend to the third or fourth century, becomes harsh; and they are, in general, infected with the taste of that age, a love of swollen and strained thoughts, and of the play of words. Among the Greek Fathers, the most distinguished by far, for his oratorical merit, is St. Chrysostom. His language is pure, his style highly figured. He is copious, smooth, and sometimes pathetic. But he retains, at the same time, much of that character which has been always attributed to the Asiatic eloquence, diffuse and redundant to a great degree, and often overwrought and tumid. He may be read, however, with advantage, for the eloquence of the pulpit, as being freer from false ornaments than the Latin Fathers.

"As there is nothing more that occurs to me, deserving particular attention in the middle age, I pass now to the state of eloquence in modern times. Here, it must be confessed, that in no European nation public speaking has been considered as so great an object, or been cultivated with so much care, as in Greece or Rome. Its reputation has never been so high; its effects have never been so considerable: nor has that high and sublime kind of it, which prevailed in those ancient states, been so much as aimed at: notwithstanding, too, that a new profession has been established, which gives peculiar advantages to oratory, and affords it the noblest field; I mean that of the Church. The genius of the world seems, in this respect, to have undergone some alteration. The two countries where we might expect to find most of the spirit of eloquence are France and Great Britain: France, on account of the distinguished turn of the nation towards all the liberal arts, and of the encouragement which, for this century past, these arts have received from the public; Great Britain, on account both of the public capacity and genius, and of the free government which it enjoys. Yet so it is, that, in neither of those countries, has the talent of public speaking risen near to the degree of its ancient splendour; while in other productions of genius, both in prose and in poetry, they have contended for the prize with Greece and Rome; nay, in some compositions,

6

may be thought to have surpassed them : the names of Demosthenes and Cicero stand, at this day, unrivalled in fame ;
and it would be held presumptuous and absurd to pretend
to place any modern whatever in the same, or even in a
nearly equal rank.

" It seems particularly surprising that Great Britain should
not have made a more conspicuous figure in eloquence than
it has hitherto attained ; when we consider the enlightened,
and, at the same time, the free and bold genius of the country, which seems not a little to favour oratory ; and when
we consider that, of all the polite nations, it alone possesses
a popular government, or admits into the legislature such
numerous assemblies as can be supposed to lie under the
dominion of eloquence. Notwithstanding this advantage,
it must be confessed that, in most parts of eloquence, we
are undoubtedly inferior, not only to the Greeks and Romans by many degrees, but also to the French. We have
philosophers, eminent and conspicuous, perhaps, beyond
any nation, in all the parts of science. We have both taste
and erudition in a high degree. We have historians, we
have poets of the greatest name ; but of orators, of public
speakers, how little have we to boast ! And where are the
monuments of their genius to be found ! In every period
we have had some who made a figure, by managing the
debates in parliament ; but that figure was commonly owing
to their wisdom, or their experience in business, more than
to their talent for oratory ; and unless in some few instances,
wherein the power of oratory has appeared, indeed, with
much lustre, the art of parliamentary speaking rather obtained to several a temporary applause, than conferred upon
any a lasting renown. At the bar, though questionless, we
have many able pleaders, yet few or none of their pleadings
have been thought worthy to be transmitted to posterity,
or have commanded attention any longer than the cause
which was the subject of them interested the public ; while
in France, the pleadings of Patru, in the former age, and
those of Couching and D'Aguesseau, in later times, are read
with pleasure, and are often quoted as examples of eloquence

by the French critics. In the same manner, in the pulpit, the British divines have distinguished themselves by the most accurate and rational compositions which, perhaps, any nation can boast of. Many printed sermons we have, full of good sense, and of sound divinity and morality; but the eloquence to be found in them, the power of persuasion, of interesting and engaging the heart, which is, or ought to be, the great object of the pulpit, is far from bearing a suitable proportion to the excellence of the matter. There are few arts, in my opinion, farther from perfection than that of preaching is among us; the reasons of which I shall afterwards have occasion to discuss. In proof of the fact, it is sufficient to observe, that an English sermon, instead of being a persuasive, animated oration, seldom rises beyond the strain of correct and dry reasoning; whereas, in the sermons of Bossuet, Massilon, Bourdaloue, and Flechier, among the French, we see a much higher species of eloquence aimed at, and in a great measure attained, than the British preachers have in view.

"In general, the characteristical difference between the state of eloquence in France and in Great Britain is, that the French have adopted higher ideas both of pleasing and persuading by means of oratory, though, sometimes, in the execution, they fail. In Great Britain we have taken up eloquence in a lower key; but in our execution, as was naturally to be expected, have been more correct. In France, the style of their orators is ornamented with bolder figure, and their discourse carried on with more amplification, more warmth and elevation. The composition is often very beautiful; but sometimes, also, too diffuse and deficient in that strength and cogency which renders eloquence powerful; a defect owing, perhaps, in part, to the genius of the people, which leads them to attend fully as much to ornament as to substance, and, in part, to the nature of their government, which by excluding public speaking from having much influence on the conduct of public affairs, deprives eloquence of its best opportunity for acquiring nerves and strength. Hence the pulpit is the principal field which is left for their eloquence. The members, too, of the French Academy give harangues at their admission, in which genius often appears; but, labouring under the misfortune of having no subject to discourse upon, they run commonly into flattery and panegyric, the most barren and insipid of all topics.

" I observed before, that the Greeks and Romans aspired to a more sublime species of eloquence than is aimed at by the moderns. Theirs was of the vehement and passionate kind, by which they endeavoured to inflame the minds of their hearers, and hurry their imaginations away; and, suitable to this vehemence of thought, was their vehemence of gesture and action; the 'supplosio pedis,' the 'percussio frontis et femoris,' were, as we learn from Cicero's writings, usual gestures among them at the bar; though now they would be reckoned extravagant anywhere, except upon the stage. Modern eloquence is much more cool and temperate; and in Great Britain especially, has confined itself almost wholly to the argumentative and rational. It is much of that species which the ancient critics called the 'Tenuis,' or 'Subtilis'; which aims at convincing and instructing, rather than affecting the passions, and assumes a tone not much higher than common argument and discourse.

" Several reasons may be given why modern eloquence has been so limited, and humble in its efforts. In the first place, I am of opinion that this change must, in part, be ascribed to that correct turn of thinking which has been so much studied in modern times. It can hardly be doubted that, in many efforts of mere genius, the ancient Greeks and Romans excelled us, but, on the other hand, that, in accuracy and closeness of reasoning on many subjects, we have some advantage over them, ought, I think, to be admitted also. In proportion as the world has advanced, philosophy has made greater progress. A certain strictness of good sense has, in this island particularly, been cultivated and introduced into every subject. Hence we are more on our guard against the flowers of elocution; we are now on the watch; we are jealous of being deceived by oratory. Our public speakers are obliged to be more reserved than the ancients, in their attempts to elevate the imagination, and warm the passions; and by the influence of prevailing taste, their own genius is sobered and chastened, perhaps, in too great a degree. It is likely too, I confess, that what we fondly ascribe to our correctness and good sense, is owing in a great measure to our phlegm and natural coldness. For the vivacity and sensibility of the Greeks and Romans, more especially of the former, seem to have been much greater than ours, and to have given them a higher relish of all the beauties of oratory.

" Besides these national considerations, we must, in the next place, attend to peculiar circumstances in the three great scenes of public speaking, which have proved disadvantageous to the growth of eloquence among us. Though the parliament of Great Britain be the noblest field which Europe, at this day, affords to a public speaker, yet eloquence has never been so powerful an instrument there as it was in the popular assemblies of Greece and Rome. Under some former reigns, the right hand of arbitrary power bore a violent sway ; and in latter times, ministerial influence has generally prevailed. The power of speaking, though always considerable, yet has been often found too feeble to counterbalance either of these ; and, of course, has not been studied with so much zeal and favour as where its effect on business was irresistible and certain.

" At the bar, our disadvantage, in comparison of the ancients, is great. Among them, the judges were generally numerous ; the laws were few and simple ; the decision of causes was left, in a great measure, to equity and the sense of mankind. Here was an ample field for what they termed judicial eloquence. But among the moderns the case is quite altered. The system of law is become much more complicated. The knowledge of it is thereby rendered so laborious an attainment, as to be the chief object of a lawyer's education, and in a manner the study of his life. The art of speaking is but a secondary accomplishment to

which he can afford to devote much less of his time and
labour. The bounds of eloquence, besides, are now much
circumscribed at the bar; and, except in a few cases, reduced
to arguing from strict law, statute, or precedent, by which
means knowledge, much more than oratory, is become the
principal requisite.

" With regard to the pulpit, it has certainly been a great
disadvantage that the practice of reading sermons, instead
of repeating them from memory, has prevailed so universally in England. They may, indeed, have introduced accuracy, but it has done great prejudice to eloquence, for a
discourse read is far inferior to an oration spoken. It leads
to a different sort of composition, as well as of delivery, and
can never have an equal effect upon any audience. Another circumstance, too, has been unfortunate. The secta-
ries and fanatics, before the Restoration, adopted a warm,
zealous, and popular manner of preaching; and those who
adhered to them, in after times, continued to distinguish
themselves by somewhat of the same manner. The odium
of these sects drove the established church from that warmth
which they were judged to have carried too far, into the
opposite extreme of a studied coolness and composure of
manner. Hence, from the art of persuasion, which preaching ought always to be, it has passed, in England, into mere
reasoning and instruction, which not only has brought down
the eloquence of the pulpit to a lower tone than it might
justly assume, but has produced this farther effect that, by
accustoming the public ear to such cool and dispassionate
discourses, it has tended to fashion other kinds of public
speaking upon the same model.

" Thus I have given some view of the state of eloquence
in modern times, and endeavoured to account for it. It has,
as we have seen, fallen below that splendour which it maintained in ancient ages, and from being sublime and vehement,
has come down to be temperate and cool. Yet, still, in that
region which it occupies, it admits great scope; and to the
defect of zeal and application, more than to the want of
capacity and genius, we may ascribe its not having hitherto

risen higher. It is a field where there is much honour yet to be reaped ; it is an instrument which may be employed for purposes of the highest importance. The ancient models may still, with much advantage, be set before us for imitation, though in that imitation we must, doubtless, have some regard to what modern taste and modern manners will bear, of which I shall afterwards have occasion to say more.

Lawyers, eloquent, fearless, and honest, have always been among the first to resist the encroachments of tyranny, and promote the welfare of the human race.

History proves the truth of this assertion.

Demosthenes, who roused the Athenians to arms against the tyrannical Philip, was a lawyer; Cicero, who did such valiant service for the cause of freedom, and whose eloquent orations still nerve the patriot's arm and fire his heart, was a lawyer. When Charles I. endeavoured to establish an absolute monarchy in England, he was first opposed by lawyers. France has been regenerated by lawyers, and at the present moment her greatest statesmen are lawyers.

When Great Britain endeavoured to deprive the Colonies of their rights, they were aroused to conquest by the voices of Otis, Henry, Adams, and other lawyers, and the beacon lights of patriotism and law are kept burning by lawyers at the present moment in England and America, and it is to be hoped that they will be perpetually kindled by them until time is merged into eternity.

CHAPTER IV.

ORATORY IN ENGLAND.

THE conduct of advocates in England has been subjected to very little legislative interference. A statute, however, which is still in force, was passed in 1275, in the reign of Edward I., whereby it was provided, "That if any sergeant, countor, or others, do any manner of deceit or collusion in the king's court, or consent unto it, in deceit of the court, or to beguile the court, or the party, and thereof be attainted, he shall be imprisoned for a year and a day, and from thenceforth shall not be heard to plead in that court for any man; and if he be no countor, he shall be imprisoned in like manner by the space of a year and a day at least; and if the trespass shall require greater punishment it shall be at the king's pleasure."

In the *Mirroir des Justices*, one of the most ancient English law books extant, it is laid down that every pleader (or countor as he is called) on behalf of others ought to have regard to four things: First, that he be a person receivable in judgment; that he be no heretic, excommunicate person, nor criminal, nor a man of religion, nor a woman, nor a beneficed clerk with cure of souls, nor under the age of twenty-one years, nor judge in the same cause, nor attainted of falsity against the right of his office. Secondly, every pleader is to be charged by oath that he will not maintain nor defend what is wrong or false to his knowledge, but will fight (*guerra*) for his client to the utmost of his ability. Thirdly, he is to put in before the court no false delays (dilatory pleas), nor false evidence, nor move nor offer any corruptions, deceits, or tricks, or false lies, nor consent to any such, but truly maintain the right of his client, so that it fail not through any folly, negligence, or default in him. Fourthly, in respect to his salary four things are to be con- sidered—the value of the cause ; the pains of the sergeant ; the worth of the pleader in point of knowledge, eloquence, and gifts ; the usage of the court. And a pleader is to be suspended if he be attainted of having received fees from both sides in the same cause, and if he say or do anything in contempt of the court."

In England, forensic eloquence was almost unknown until the latter part of the eighteenth century. Finch, afterwards Lord Nottingham, was called in his day the " English Cicero," and the English Roscius, but the speeches of his which have come down to us do not justify these epithets. The *State Trials*, that voluminous and interesting repository of cases, may be searched in vain for the higher efforts of forensic oratory. Immense learning, and research, a remarkable familiarity with precedents, and sound and logical argu- ments are found, however.

Eloquence has always been comparatively rare among the advocates of England, but there are causes to account for this. One reason is the technicality which formerly per- vaded every branch of English law. Special pleading seems to have the effect of cramping and confining the intellect.

Owing to its enormous and unwieldy mass, the English law is unfavourable to the cultivation of oratory. " This tends to suffocate the fire of genius, and deadens the imagi- nation which shrinks back in affright from the aspect of the thousand volumes in which are enshrined the mysteries of our jurisprudence." It is said that in six hundred volumes of law reports there are not less than two hundred and forty thousand points. The immense number of law books, it must be remembered, continues yearly to increase both in England and in this country. Each session of parliament, there, or of the legislature here, gives birth to a bulky volume of statutes to swell the numerous progeny of legislation. The increase of law reports is also alarming.

The effect of this system of laws, then, upon eloquence must be very great.

In ancient times, during the flourishing periods of Greek and Roman eloquence, the laws were few in number and simple in phraseology, and the judges were vested with a large discretion, and were governed to a large extent by equity and common sense. The study of the laws was not such a laborious occupation, requiring the drudgery of years to finish it. The statesmen and generals of Rome were nearly all lawyers, and Cicero, amongst the multiplicity of his engagements, declared that he would undertake in a few days to make himself a complete civilian. And of course when an advocate addresses himself to the equity of the judges he has greater room for the display of eloquence, than where he must draw his arguments from strict laws. In the former case many personal considerations may be regarded, and even favour and inclination, which it belongs to the advocate to conciliate by his eloquence, may be disguised under the appearance of equity.

The chief reason, however, of the absence of eloquence is a neglect of the means necessary to acquire the habit of graceful and fluent elocution. It is strange that so little pains should be taken by advocates to qualify themselves for success in speaking. They seem to believe that eloquence must spring into being like Minerva from the head of Jove, instantaneously, in full and perfect panoply, and that it requires no discipline and study in advance. Or else they dread the infinite labor which they must undergo, in order to perfect themselves in the art of speaking.

If the poet, the musician, the sculptor, and the artist all devote themselves with untiring assiduity to a study of the principles of their art, why should the advocate imagine that he is exempt from the necessity of toil?

In studying the history of modern parliamentary eloquence there is little to interest us until we come to the time of Lord Chatham, if we except the traditionary accounts of the wonderful oratorical ability of Lord Bolingbroke. Of course we find some sudden bursts of genuine eloquence

in the speeches of Pym, Eliot, Vane, and other statesmen of
the English Commonwealth under Cromwell, yet we hear not
the highest notes until Chatham arises and sways the British
senate by the spell of his magnificent oratory. The author
will now proceed to contemplate some of the most celebrated
orators and statesmen, beginning with Lord Bolingbroke.

Bolingbroke.—Henry St. John, Lord Viscount Bolingbroke, was born in October, 1678, at Battersea in Surrey, at
a seat that had been in the possession of his ancestors for
ages before. He was educated at Eton and Oxford, and
there laid the foundation of his classical education which he
afterward completed. He was more extensively acquainted
with Latin than Greek literature.

St. John's handsome person, and a face in which dignity
was happily blended with sweetness, his commanding
presence, his fascinating address, his vivacity, his wit, his extraordinary memory, his subtlety in thinking and reasoning,
and oratorical powers of the very highest order, contributed
to his phenomenal success as a parliamentary orator.

Very few fragments of his speeches have come down to
us, but from criticisms of those who heard him speak, and
from his published writings, they must have been brilliant,
sarcastic, and extremely effective, and Lord Chatham said
that the loss of his speeches was to be more greatly deplored
than the lost books of Livy.

His application to business was prodigious, and he would
sometimes plod for whole days and nights in succession, like
the lowest clerk in an office.

Bolingbroke died on the 12th day of December, 1751.

The following testimony of Lord Brougham to his oratorical powers is convincing:

"Few men, whose public life was so short, have filled a
greater space in the eyes of the world during his own times
than Lord Bolingbroke, or left behind them a more brilliant
reputation. Not more than fifteen years elapsed between
his first coming into parliament and his attainder; during not
more than ten of these years was he brought before the
public in the course of its proceedings; and yet, as a states-

man and an orator, his name ranks among the most famous
in our history, independent of the brilliant literary reputation which places him among the best classics of our
Augustan age.   Much of his rhetorical fame may certainly
be ascribed to the merit of his written works; but had he
never composed a page, he would still have come down to
our times as one of the most able and eloquent men of
whom this country could boast.

"They who look down upon even the purely ethical and
purely metaphysical writings of Bolingbroke, would do well
to show us any statesman or any orator, except perhaps
Cicero, who in any age has brought to the senate the same
resources of moral science, which even the failures of Bolingbroke, as a professed author on these subjects, prove him to
have possessed; and it is hardly necessary to remark how
vast an accession of force to his eloquence, whether in its
argumentative, its pathetic, or its declamatory department,
would have been gained by even far less skill, capacity, or
practice, than he had as a moral philosopher, a student of
the nature of the mind, or an expert logician.

"Accordingly, when all these accomplishments, joined to
his strong natural sagacity, his penetrating acuteness, his extraordinary quickness of apprehension, a clearness of
understanding, against which sophistry set itself up in
vain, as the difficulties of the most complicated subjects in
vain opposed his industry and his courage, with a fancy rich,
lively, various beyond that of most men, a wit exuberant
and sparkling, a vehemence of passion belonging to his
whole temperament, even to his physical powers, came to be
displayed before the assembly which he was to address, and
when the mighty '*armentaria cæli*' were found under the
command of one whose rich endowments of mind and
whose ample stores of acquired virtue resided in a person
of singularly animated countenance, at once beautiful and
expressive, and made themselves heard in the strains of an
unrivalled voice, it is easy to comprehend how vast, how
irresistible must have been their impression.

"But all agree in describing the external qualities of his

oratory as perfect. A symmetrical, beautiful, and animated
countenance, a noble and dignified person, a sonorous and
flexible voice, action graceful and correct, though unstudied,
gave an inexpressible charm to those who witnessed his
extraordinary displays as spectators or critics, and armed
his eloquence with resistless effect over those whom it was
intended to sway, or persuade, or control. If the concurring
accounts of witnesses, and the testimony to his merits borne
by his writings, may be trusted, he must be pronounced to
stand, upon the whole, *at the head of modern orators.*
There may have been more measure and matured power
in Pitt, more fire in the occasional bursts of Chatham, more
unbridled vehemence, more intent reasoning in Fox, more
deep-toned declamation in passages of Sheridan, more
learned imagery in Burke, more wit and humour in Canning,
but, as a whole, and taking in all rhetorical gifts, and all the
orator's accomplishments, no one, perhaps hardly the union
of several of them, can match what we are taught by
tradition to admire in Bolingbroke's spoken eloquence, and
what the study of his works makes us easily believe to be
true."

St. John devoted much time to the study of metaphysics
—a study which he thought absolutely essential to the man
who seeks to make the minds of others acknowledge his own
mind's dominion.

He recognised the fact that the law is a science, worthy
of the most assiduous study, and the standard of excellence
which he set for the legal profession was high, as will be
seen from the following passage from his dissertation on the
Study of History: "There have been lawyers that were
orators, philosophers, historians: there have been Bacons
and Clarendons, my lord. There will be none such any
more, till, in some better age, true ambition, or the love of
fame, prevails over avarice, and till men find leisure and encouragement to prepare themselves for the exercise of this
profession, by climbing up to the *vantage ground,* so my
Lord Bacon calls it, of science; instead of grovelling all
their lives below, in a mean, but gainful application to all

the little arts of chicane. Till this happen, the profession of the law will scarce deserve to be ranked among the learned professions; and whenever it happens, one of the vantage grounds to which men must climb, is metaphysical, and the other historical, knowledge. They must pry into the secret recesses of the human heart, and become well acquainted with the whole moral world, that they may discover the abstract reason of all laws; and they must trace the laws of particular states, especially of their own, from the first rough sketches to the more perfect draughts, from the first causes or occasions that produced them, through all the effects, good and bad, that they produced."

St. John was well read in both ancient and modern history. He says upon the study of history:

" Man is the subject of every history; and to know him well we must see him and consider him, as history alone can present him to us, in every age, in every country, in every state, in life, and in death. History, therefore, of all kinds, of civilised and uncivilised, of ancient and modern nations, in short, all history that descends to a sufficient detail of human actions and characters, is useful to bring us acquainted with our species, nay, with ourselves. To teach and to inculcate the general principles of virtue, and the general rules of wisdom and good policy, which result from such details of actions and characters, comes for the most part, and always should come, expressly and directly into the design of those who are capable of giving such details ;. and therefore whilst they narrate as historians they hint often as philosophers, they put into our hands as it were, on every proper occasion, the end of a clue that serves to remind us of searching, and to guide in the search of that truth which the example before us either establishes or illustrates. If a writer neglects this part, we are able, however, to supply his neglect by our attention and industry, and when he gives us a good history of Peruvians or Mexicans, of Chinese or Tartars, of Muscovites or Negroes, we may blame him, but we must blame ourselves much more if we do not make it a good lesson of philosophy. This being the general use of history, it is not to be neglected. Every one may make it who is able to read and to reflect on what he reads, and every one who makes it will find in his degree the benefit that arises from an early acquaintance contracted in this manner with mankind. We are not only passengers and sojourners in this world, but we are absolute strangers at the first steps we make in it. Our guides are often ignorant, often unfaithful. By this map of the country which history spreads before us, we may learn, if we please, to guide ourselves. In our journey through it we are beset on every side. We are besieged sometimes even in our strongest holds. Terrors and temptations, conducted by the passions of other men, assault us, and our own passions, which correspond with these, betray us. History is a collection of the journals of those who have travelled through the same country and been exposed to the same accidents, and their good and their ill success are equally instructive. In this pursuit of knowledge an immense field is spread to us: general histories, sacred and profane; the histories of particular countries, particular events, particular orders, particular men; memorials, anecdotes, travels. But we must not ramble in this field without discernment or choice, nor even with these must we ramble too long. . . .

" As soon as we have taken this general view of mankind, and of the course of human affairs in different ages and different parts of the world, we ought to apply, and, the shortness of human life considered, to confine ourselves almost entirely in our study of history to such histories as have an immediate relation to our professions, or to our rank and situation in the society to which we belong. Let me instance the profession of divinity as the noblest and the most important."

The foregoing extract is worthy of the closest study.

Sir Edward Creasy, a recent English writer, says of St. John: " I unhesitatingly place him at the head of all the prose writers in our language."

The beauty and propriety of his images and illustrations are never introduced for mere purposes of adornment, but to support the arguments they adorn. In a letter to Wind-

ham he says : " The ocean which environs us is an emblem
of our government, and the pilot and the minister are in
similar circumstances. It seldom happens that either of
them can steer a direct course, and they both arrive at their
part by means which frequently seem to carry them from
it." In "The Spirit of the Times" he truthfully and beautifully says : " Eloquence must flow like a stream that is fed
by an abundant stream, and not spout forth a little frothy
water on some gaudy day, and remain dry all the rest of the
year."

The literary works of Bolingbroke undoubtedly resemble
spoken eloquence far more than those of any man that ever
wrote.

He disliked, exceedingly, the mechanical drudgery of
writing, and dictated many of his literary productions to an
amanuensis.

Chatham.—Few great English parliamentary orators who
preceded Lord Chatham will be remembered by posterity.
In his external appearance no person was ever more beautifully gifted by nature for an orator than this extraordinary
man.

Grace and dignity were wonderfully combined in his look
and gesture, but dignity presided ; "the terrors of his beak,
the lightning of his eye," were insufferable. His voice was
marvellously clear and full, and his lowest whisper was
audible in every part of the house. His middle tones were
sweet, rich, and beautifully varied. When he elevated his
voice the house was completely filled with the sound, and
the effect is said to have been awful, except when he wished
to cheer or animate; and then he had "spirit-stirring" notes,
which could not be resisted. He often suddenly rose from
a very low to a very high key, but the effort was not
apparent. His vocabulary was full and varied, but his
diction was simple.

He is said to have read Bailey's *Dictionary* through twice,
in order to increase his stock of words.

Unfortunately very few of Lord Chatham's speeches have
come down to us, as he delivered them. This was owing to

the imperfect state of parliamentary reporting in his day. From the time he entered the House of Commons until he left it, the privileges of parliament almost wholly precluded the possibility of full and regular accounts of debates being communicated to the public. They were given at one time under feigned names, as if held in the senate of Rome by the ancient orators and statesmen; at another they were conveyed by the initials only of the names of the real speakers. Later, when these disguises were no longer used, speeches were composed by reporters who had not been present at the debates, but were only familiar with a few heads of each speaker's topics from some one who had heard him. The fullest accounts given of the speeches delivered at this period are mere meagre outlines of the subjects touched upon, and do not even present an approximation to the execution of the orators. Many of Lord Chatham's earlier speeches in the House of Commons, as transmitted to us, were avowedly composed by Dr. Johnson, and it is said that his "measured style, formal periods, balanced antitheses, and total want of pure, racy English, betray their author at every line, while each debate is made to speak exactly in the same manner." The only speech which there is reason to believe was revised by Lord Chatham himself, and the one most celebrated of all, was the one upon the employment of the Indians in the American war.

Of Chatham's patriotism there can be no question. He was far superior to the paltry objects of a grovelling ambition. When party ties or interests interfered with his duty to his country, they were set aside. He believed that the highest duty of man was to further the interest of the human species.

Lord Chatham, when a young member, having expressed himself in the house with great energy, in opposition to one of the measures then in agitation, his speech produced an answer from Mr. Walpole, who in the course of it charged him, among other things, with youthful inexperience and theatrical enunciation. Mr. Walpole said:

7

"*Sir :* I was unwilling to interrupt the course of this debate, while it was carried on with calmness and decency, by
men who do not suffer the ardour of opposition to cloud
their reason, or transport them to such expressions as the
dignity of this assembly does not admit.   I have hitherto
deferred to answer the gentleman who declaimed against
the bill with such fluency of rhetoric, and such vehemence of
gesture ; who charged the advocates of the expedients now
proposed with having no regard to any interests but their
own, and with making laws only to consume paper, and
threatened them with the defection of their adherents, and
the loss of their influence, upon this new discovery of their
folly and their ignorance.   Nor, sir, do I now answer him
for any other purpose than to remind him how little the
clamours of rage, and petulancy of invectives, contribute to
the purposes for which this assembly is called together ;
how little the discovery of truth is promoted, and the security of the nation established, by pompous diction and
theatrical emotions.   Formidable sounds and furious declamations, confident assertions, and lofty periods, may affect
the young and inexperienced ; and perhaps the gentleman
may have contracted his habits of oratory by conversing
more with those of his own age, than with such as have had
more opportunities of acquiring knowledge, and more successful methods of communicating their sentiments.   If the
heat of his temper, sir, would suffer him to attend to those
whose age and long acquaintance with business give them
an indisputable right to deference and superiority, he would
learn, in time, to reason rather than declaim ; to prefer justness of argument, and an accurate knowledge of facts, to
sounding epithets, and splendid superlatives, which may disturb the imagination for a moment, but leave no lasting impression on the mind.   He will learn, sir, that to accuse and
prove are very different, and that reproaches, unsupported
by evidence, affect only the character of him that utters
them.   Excursions of fancy and flights of oratory are indeed pardonable in young men, but in no other ; and it
would surely contribute more, even to the purpose for which

some gentlemen appear to speak (that of depreciating the conduct of the administration), to prove the inconvenience and injustice of this bill, than barely to assert them, with whatever magnificence of language, or appearance of zeal, honesty, or compassion."

As soon as Mr. Walpole sat down, Mr. Pitt got up and replied to his ill-timed reflections as follows:

"*Sir:* The atrocious crime of being a young man, which the honourable gentleman has, with such spirit and decency, charged upon me, I shall neither attempt to palliate nor deny; but content myself with wishing—that I may be one of those whose follies cease with their youth; and not of that number who are ignorant in spite of experience.

"Whether youth can be imputed to any man as a re- proach, I will not, sir, assume the province of determining— but surely age may become justly contemptible—if the op- portunities which it brings have passed away without im- provement, and vice appears to prevail when the passions have subsided. The wretch who, after having seen the conse- quences of a thousand errors, continues still to blunder, and whose age has only added obstinacy to stupidity, is surely the object of either abhorrence or contempt; and deserves not that his grey hairs should secure him from insult. Much more, sir, is he to be abhorred—who, as he has advanced in age, has receded from virtue, and becomes more wicked with less temptation: who prostitutes himself for money which he cannot enjoy, and spends the remains of his life in the ruin of his country.

"But youth, sir, is not my only crime. I have been ac- cused of acting a theatrical part.

"A theatrical part may either imply—some peculiarities of gesture,—or a dissimulation of my real sentiments, and the adoption of the opinions and language of another man.

"In the first sense, the charge is too trifling to be con- futed; and deserves only to be mentioned that it may be despised. I am at liberty, like every other man, to use my own language; and though I may, perhaps, have some am- bition,—yet to please this gentleman, I shall not lay myself

under any restraint, nor very solicitously copy his dictum
or his mien, however matured by age or modelled by experience. If any man shall, by charging me with theatrical
behaviour, imply that I utter any sentiments but my own, I
shall treat him as a calumniator and a villain ; nor shall any
protection shelter him from the treatment he deserves.   I
shall, on such an occasion, without scruple trample upon all
those forms with which wealth and dignity intrench themselves ; nor shall anything but age restrain my resentment ;
age, which always brings one privilege, that of being inso-
lent and supercilious without punishment. But with regard,
sir, to those whom I have offended, I am of opinion, that if
I had acted a borrowed part I should have avoided their
censure; the heat that offended them is the ardour of conviction, and that zeal for the service of my country which
neither hope nor fear shall influence me to suppress.   I will
not sit unconcerned while my liberty is invaded, nor look
in silence upon public robbery. I will exert my endeavours,
at whatever hazard, to repel the aggressor, and drag the
thief to justice,—whoever may protect them in their villainy, and whoever may partake of their plunder."

Brougham said of the administration of Lord Chatham :

"As soon as Mr. Pitt took the helm, the steadiness of
the hand that held it was instantly felt in every motion of
the vessel.   There was no more of wavering counsels,
of torpid inaction, of listless expectancy, of abject despondency. His firmness gave confidence, his spirit roused courage, his vigilance secured exertion, in every department
under his sway. Each man, from the first Lord of the Admiralty down to the most humble clerk in the Victualling
Office—each soldier, from the Commander-in-chief to the
most obscure contractor or commissary—now felt assured
that he was acting or was indolent under the eye of one
who knew his duties and his means as well as his own, and
who would very certainly make all defaulters, whether
through misfeasance or through nonfeasance, accountable
for whatever detriment the commonwealth might sustain at
their hands.

"Over his immediate coadjutors his influence swiftly obtained an ascendant which it ever after retained uninterrupted. Upon his first proposition for changing the conduct of the war he stood single among his colleagues, and tendered his resignation should they persist in their dissent; they at once succumbed, and from that hour ceased to have an opinion of their own upon any branch of the public affairs. Nay, so absolutely was he determined to have the control of those measures, of which he knew the responsibility rested upon him alone, that he insisted upon the first Lord of the Admiralty not having the correspondence of his own department; and no less eminent a naval character than Lord Anson, as well as his junior Lords, was obliged to sign the naval orders issued by Mr. Pitt while the writing was covered over from their eyes!"

From the speech of Lord Chatham on the American war, which has been already mentioned, the following extract richly deserves a perusal:

"I cannot, my lords, I will not, join in congratulation on misfortune and disgrace. This, my lords, is a perilous and tremendous moment. It is not a time for adulation. The smoothness of flattery cannot save us in this rugged and awful crisis. It is now necessary to instruct the throne in the language of truth. We must, if possible, dispel the illusion and darkness which envelop it, and display, in its full danger and genuine colours, the ruin which is brought to our doors,

"Can ministers still presume to expect support in their infatuation? Can parliament be so dead to its dignity and duty, as to give their support to measures thus obtruded and forced upon them? Measures, my lords, which have reduced this late flourishing empire to ruin and contempt! But yesterday, and England might have stood against the world; now, none so poor as to do her reverence.

"The people whom we at first despised as rebels, but whom we now acknowledge as enemies, are abetted against us; supplied with every military store, their interest consulted, and their ambassadors entertained by our inveterate enemy !—and ministers do not, and dare not, interpose with dignity or effect. The desperate state of our army abroad is in part known. No man more highly esteems and honours the English troops than I do ; I know their virtues and their valour; I know they can achieve anything but impossibilities ; and I know that the conquest of English America *is an impossibility.*

"You cannot, my lords, *you cannot conquer America.* What is your present situation there? We do not know the *worst;* but we know that in three campaigns we have done nothing, and suffered much. You may swell every expense, accumulate every assistance, and extend your traffic to the shambles of every German despot: your attempts will be forever vain and impotent—doubly so, indeed, from this mercenary aid on which you rely ; for it irritates, to an incurable resentment, the minds of your adversaries, to overrun them with the mercenary sons of rapine and plunder, devoting them and their possessions to the rapacity of hireling cruelty. If I were an American, as I am an Englishman, while a foreign troop was landed in my country, I never would lay down my arms—*never, never, never !*

"But, my lords, who is the man that, in addition to the disgrace and mischiefs of the war, has dared to authorise and associate to our arms the *tomahawk* and *scalping-knife* of the savage?—to call into civilised alliance the wild and inhuman inhabitants of the woods?—to delegate to the merciless Indian the defence of disputed rights, and to wage the horrors of his barbarous war against our brethren? My lords, these enormities cry aloud for redress and punishment.

"But, my lords, this barbarous measure has been defended, not only on the principles of policy and necessity, but also on those of morality ; 'for it is perfectly allowable,' says Lord Suffolk, 'to use all the means which God and Nature have put into our hands.' I am astonished, I am shocked, to hear such principles confessed ; to hear them avowed in this house, or in this country !

"My lords, I did not intend to encroach so much upon

your attention, but I cannot repress my indignation. I feel myself impelled to speak. My lords, we are called upon as members of this house, as men, as Christian men, to protest against such horrible barbarity. 'That God and Nature have put into our hands!' What ideas of God and Nature that noble lord may entertain, I know not ; but I know that such detestable principles are equally abhorrent to religion and humanity.

"What! to attribute the sacred sanction of God and Nature to the massacres of the Indian scalping-knife!—to the cannibal savage, torturing, murdering, devouring, drinking the blood of his mangled victims! Such notions shock every precept of morality, every feeling of humanity, every sentiment of honour. These abominable principles, and this more abominable avowal of them, demand the most decisive indignation.

"I call upon that right reverend, and this most learned bench, to vindicate the religion of their God, to support the justice of their country. I call upon the bishops to interpose the unsullied sanctity of their lawn ; upon the judges to interpose the purity of their ermine, to save us from this pollution. I call upon the honour of your lordships to reverence the dignity of your ancestors, and maintain your own. I call upon the spirit and humanity of my country to vindicate the national character."

One of the finest passages from the speeches of Lord Chatham is his allusion to the legal maxim, that every man's house is his castle :

"The poorest man may in his cottage bid defiance to all the forces of the crown. It may be frail—its roof may shake —the wind may blow through it—the storm may enter— the rain may enter—but the king of England cannot enter ! —all his force dares not cross the threshold of the ruined tenement ! "

Another extract from his " Speech on the Address to the Throne," in 1770, shows his love for the ancient political institutions of his country. Speaking of the Charter of Runnymede, he said :

"My lords, I have better hopes of the constitution, and a firmer confidence in the wisdom and constitutional authority of this house. It is to *your* ancestors, my lords, it is to the English barons, that we are indebted for the laws and constitution we possess. Their virtues were rude and uncultivated, but they were great and sincere. Their understandings were as little polished as their manners, but they had hearts to distinguish right from wrong; they had heads to distinguish truth from falsehood; they understood the rights of humanity, and they had spirit to maintain them.

"My lords, I think that history has not done justice to their conduct. When they obtained from their sovereign that great acknowledgment of national rights contained in Magna Charta, they did not confine it to themselves alone, but delivered it as a common blessing to the whole people. They did not say, these are the rights of the great barons, or these are the rights of the great prelates:—No, my lords; they said, in the simple Latin of the times, *nullus liber homo,* and provided as carefully for the meanest subject as for the greatest. These are uncouth words, and sound but poorly in the ears of scholars; neither are they addressed to the criticism of scholars, but to the hearts of free men. These three words, *nullus liber homo,* have a meaning which interests us all: they deserve to be remembered—they deserve to be inculcated in our minds—they are worth all the classics. Let us not, then, degenerate from the glorious example of our ancestors. Those iron barons (for so I may call them when compared with the silken barons of modern days) were the guardians of the people; yet *their* virtues, my lords, were never engaged in a question of such importance as the present. A breach has been made in the constitution —the battlements are dismantled—the citadel is open to the first invader—the walls totter—the constitution is not tenable. What remains, then, but for us to stand foremost in the breach, to repair it, or perish in it?"

Lord Chatham's remark on confidence, when it was asked by the ministry of 1766, for whom he had "some forebearance rather than any great respect," is worthy of repetition.

He said their characters were fair enough, and he was always glad to see such persons engaged in the public service; but, turning to them with a smile, very courteous, but not very respectful, he said: "Confide in you? Oh, no—you must pardon me, gentlemen—*youth* is the season of credulity—*confidence* is a plant of slow growth in an aged bosom!"

Many splendid tributes have been paid to the oratorical talents of Lord Chatham, and from among them the author selects the following from Lord Brougham and others. Lord Brougham said of his eloquence: "All accounts, however, concur in representing those effects to have been prodigious. The spirit and vehemence which animated its greater passages—their perfect application to the subject-matter of debate—the appositeness of his invective to the individual assailed—the boldness of the feats which he ventured upon—the grandeur of the ideas which he unfolded—the heart-stirring nature of his appeals,—are all confessed by the united testimony of his contemporaries; and the fragments which remain bear out to a considerable extent such representations; nor are we likely to be misled by those fragments, for the more striking portions were certainly the ones least likely to be either forgotten or fabricated. To these mighty attractions was added the imposing, the animating, the commanding power of a countenance singularly expressive; an eye so piercing that hardly any one could stand its glare; and a manner altogether singularly striking, original, and characteristic; notwithstanding a peculiarly defective and even awkward action. Latterly, indeed, his infirmities precluded all action; and he is described as standing in the House of Lords leaning upon his crutch, and speaking for ten minutes together in an undertone of voice scarcely audible, but raising his notes to their full pitch when he broke out into one of his grand bursts of invective or exclamation. But in his earlier time, his whole manner is represented as having been, beyond conception, animated and imposing. Indeed the things which he effected principally by means of it, or at least which noth-

ing but a most striking and commanding tone could have
made it possible to attempt, almost exceed belief."

A splendid tribute to the talents of Lord Chatham was
also paid by the celebrated Wirt :

"Talents, whenever they have had a suitable theatre,
have never failed to emerge from obscurity, and assume
their proper rank in the estimation of the world. The
jealous pride of power may attempt to repress and crush
them ; the base and malignant rancour of impotent spleen
and envy may strive to embarrass and retard their flight :
but these efforts, so far from achieving their ignoble purpose, so far from producing a discernible obliquity in the
ascent of genuine and vigorous talents, will serve only to
increase their momentum, and mark their transit with an
additional gleam of glory.

"When the great Earl of Chatham first made his appearance in the House of Commons, and began to astonish and
transport the British parliament and the British nation, by
the boldness, the force, and range of his thoughts, and the
celestial fire, and pathos of his eloquence, it is well known
that the minister, Walpole, and his brother Horace, from
motives very easily understood, exerted all their wit, all
their oratory, all their acquirements of every description,
sustained and enforced by the unfeeling 'insolence of
office,' to heave a mountain on his gigantic genius, and
hide it from the world.—Poor and powerless attempt !—The
tables were turned. He rose upon them in the might and
irresistible energy of his genius, and in spite of all their convulsions, frantic agonies, and spasms, he strangled them and
their whole faction, with as much ease as Hercules did the
serpent Python.

"Who can turn over the debates of the day, and read
the account of this conflict between youthful ardour and
hoary-headed cunning and power, without kindling in the
cause of the tyro, and shouting at his victory? That they
should have attempted to pass off the grand, yet solid and
judicious operations of a mind like his, as being mere theatrical start and emotion ; the giddy, hair-brained eccentrici-

ties of a romantic boy! That they should have had the presumption to suppose themselves capable of chaining down to the floor of the parliament a genius so ethereal, towering, and sublime, seems unaccountable! Why did they not, in the next breath, by way of crowning the climax of vanity, bid the magnificent fire-ball to descend from its exalted and appropriate region, and perform its splendid tour along the surface of the earth?

"Talents which are before the public have nothing to dread, either from the jealous pride of power, or from the transient misrepresentations of party, spleen, or envy. In spite of opposition from any cause, their buoyant spirit will lift them to their proper grade.

"The man who comes fairly before the world, and who possesses the great and vigorous stamina which entitle him to a niche in the temple of glory, has no reason to dread the ultimate result; however slow his progress may be, he will, in the end, most indubitably receive that distinction. While the rest, 'the swallows of science,' the butterflies of genius, may flutter for their spring; but they will soon pass away, and be remembered no more. No enterprising man, therefore, and least of all the truly great man, has reason to droop or repine at any efforts which he may suppose to be made with the view to depress him. Let, then, the tempest of envy or of malice howl around him. His genius will consecrate him; and any attempt to extinguish that, will be as unavailing, as would a human effort 'to quench the stars.'

The following observations concerning the eloquence of Lord Chatham were made soon after his death:

"Those who have been witnesses to the wonders of his eloquence—who have listened to the music of his voice, or trembled at its majesty—who have seen the graceful persuasiveness of his action, or have felt its force;—those who have caught the flame of eloquence from his eye—who have rejoiced in the glories of his countenance—or shrunk from his frowns, —will remember the resistless power with which he impressed conviction. But to those who never heard nor saw this accomplished orator, the utmost effort of imagination will be necessary to form a just idea of that combination of excellence which gave perfection to his eloquence :—his elevated aspect, commanding the awe and mute attention of all who beheld him ; whilst a certain grace in his manner, conscious of all the dignities of his situation, of the solemn scene he acted in, as well as his own exalted character, seemed to acknowledge and repay the respect he received ;— his memorable form, bowed with infirmity and age, but animated by a mind which nothing could subdue ;—his spirit shining through him, arming his eye with lightning, and clothing his lips with thunder ;—or if milder topics offered, harmonising his countenance in smiles, and his voice in softness ;—for the compass of his powers was infinite. As no idea was too vast, no imagination too sublime, for the grandeur and majesty of his manner; so no fancy was too playful, nor any allusion too comic, for the ease and gaiety with which he could accommodate to the occasion. But the character of his oratory was dignity : this presided throughout; giving force, because securing respect, even to his sallies of pleasantry. This elevated the most familiar language, and gave novelty and grace to the most familiar allusions ; so that, in his hand, even the crutch became a weapon of oratory."

William Pitt.—William Pitt, the second son of William Pitt, Earl of Chatham, and of Lady Hester Granville, daughter of Hester, Countess Temple, was born on the 28th of May, 1759.

Pitt's genius and ambition when a child displayed themselves with a rare and almost unnatural precocity. He amazed his parents and teachers when only seven years of age by the interest he took in grave subjects, the ardour with which he pursued his studies, and the sound judgment with which he criticised books and events. When his father was made Earl of Chatham, he exclaimed : "I am glad that I am not the eldest son. I want to speak in the House of Commons like papa." Pitt, when a young man, paid but little attention to English literature. He was unacquainted with any livîng language except French, and that he knew imperfectly. He was intimate, however, with a few of the best English writers, particularly with Shakespeare and Milton.

The debate in Pandemonium was one of his favourite passages, and his early friends used to speak of the just emphasis and melodious cadence with which they had heard him recite the incomparable speech of Belial.

Pitt had been trained by his father from infancy in the art of managing his voice, which was naturally clear and deep-toned. The wits of Brooke's, at a later period, irritated by observing, night after night, how powerfully Pitt's fascinating elocution affected the rows of country gentlemen, reproached him with having been "taught by his dad on a stool."

Pitt's education was well adapted to form a great parliamentary orator. His classical studies, from the way he carried them on, had the effect of greatly enriching his English vocabulary, and of making him wonderfully expert in the difficulty of constructing strikingly beautiful and correct English sentences.

It was his practice "to look over a page or two of a Greek or Latin author, to make himself master of the meaning, and then to read the passage straightforward into his own language. It is not strange that a young man of great abilities, should soon become an accomplished speaker by following this course."

"Of all the remains of antiquity, the orations were those on which he bestowed the most minute examination. His favourite employment was to compare harangues on opposite sides of the same question, to analyse them, and to observe which of the arguments of the first speaker were refuted by the second, which were evaded, and which were left untouched. Nor was it only in books that he at this time studied the art of parliamentary fencing. When he was at home, he had frequent opportunities of hearing important debates at Westminister; and he heard them not only with interest and enjoyment, but with a close scientific attention resembling that with which a diligent pupil at Guy's Hospital watches every turn of the hand of a great surgeon through a difficult operation." (*Enc. Brit.*, Art. "Pitt.")

" If from the statesman we turn to the orator, Pitt is to be placed, without any doubt, in the highest class. With a sparing use of ornament, hardly indulging more in figures, or even in figurative expression, than the most severe examples of ancient chasteness allowed—with little variety of style, hardly any graces of manner—he no sooner rose than he carried away every hearer, and kept the attention fixed and unflagging till it pleased him to let it go ; and then

> " ' So charming left his voice, that we, awhile,
>   Still thought him speaking ; still stood fixed to hear.'

This magical effect was produced by his unbroken flow, which never for a moment left the hearer in pain or doubt, and yet was not the mean fluency of mere relaxation, requiring no effort of the speaker, but imposing on the listener a heavy task ; by his lucid arrangement, which made all parts of the most complicated subject quit their entanglement, and fall each into its place ; by the clearness of his statements, which presented at once a picture to the mind ; by the forcible appeals to strict reason and strong feeling, which formed the great staple of the discourse ; by the majesty of the diction ; by the depth and fulness of the most sonorous voice, and the unbending dignity of the manner, which ever reminded us that we were in the presence of more than an advocate or debater—that there stood before us a ruler of the people. Such were invariably the effects of this singular eloquence, and they were as certainly on ordinary occasions, as in those grander displays when he rose to the height of some great argument, or indulged in vehement invective against some individual, and variegated his speech with that sarcasm of which he was so great a master, and indeed so little sparing an employer,—although even here all was uniform and consistent, nor did anything, in any mood of mind, ever drop from him that was unsuited to the majestic frame of the whole, or could disturb the serenity of the full and copious flood rolled along."

The subjoined remarks were made by Mr. Pitt in reference to a resolution declaring that immediate measures ought to be adopted for concluding peace with the American colonies:

"Gentlemen have passed the highest eulogiums on the American war. Its justice has been denied in the most fervent manner. A noble lord, in the heat of his zeal, has called it a holy war. For my part, although the honourable gentleman who made this motion, and some other gentlemen, have been, more than once, in the course of the debate, severely reprehended for calling it a wicked and accursed war, I am persuaded, and would affirm, that it was a most accursed, wicked, barbarous, cruel, unnatural, unjust, and diabolical war! It was conceived in injustice; it was nurtured and brought forth in folly; its footsteps were marked with blood, slaughter, persecution, and devastation;—in truth, everything which went to constitute moral depravity and human turpitude were to be found in it. It was pregnant with misery of every kind.

"The mischief, however, recoiled on the unhappy people of this country, who were made the instruments by which the wicked purposes of the authors of the war were effected. The nation was drained of its best blood, and of its vital resources of men and money. The expense of the war was enormous,—much beyond any former experience. And yet, what has the British nation received in return? Nothing but a series of ineffective victories, or severe defeats;—victories celebrated only by a temporary triumph over our brethren, whom we would trample down and destroy; victories, which filled the land with mourning for the loss of dear and valued relatives, slain in the impious cause of enforcing unconditional submission, or with narratives of the glorious exertions of men struggling in the holy cause of liberty, though struggling in the absence of all the facilities and advantages which are in general deemed the necessary concomitants of victory and success. Where was the Eng-

lishman, who, on reading the narratives of those bloody and
well-fought contests, could refrain from lamenting the loss
of so much British blood spilt in such a cause ; or from
weeping, on whatever side victory might be declared ? "

Certain resolutions were passed by the house in 1784 for
the removal of his Majesty's ministers, at the head of whom
was Mr. Pitt. These resolutions, however, his Majesty had
not thought proper to comply with. A reference having
been made to them, Mr. Pitt spoke as follows, replying to
Mr. Fox:

" Can anything that I have said, Mr. Speaker, subject me
to be branded with the imputation of preferring my personal
situation to the public happiness? Sir, I have declared,
again and again, only prove to me that there is any reasonable hope—show me but the most distant prospect—that
my resignation will at all contribute to restore peace and
happiness to the country, and I will instantly resign. But,
sir, I declare, at the same time, I will not be induced to resign as a preliminary to negotiation. I will not abandon
this situation, in order to throw myself upon the mercy of
that right honourable gentleman. He calls me now a mere
nominal minister, the mere puppet of secret influence. Sir,
it is because I will not become a mere nominal minister of
his creation,—it is because I disdain to become the puppet
of that right honourable gentleman,—that I will not resign ;
neither shall his contemptuous expressions provoke me to
resignation : my own honour and reputation I never will
resign.

" Let this house beware of suffering any individual to in-
volve his own cause, and to interweave his own interests, in
the resolutions of the House of Commons. The dignity of
the house is forever appealed to. Let us beware that it is
not the dignity of any set of men. Let us beware that
personal prejudices have no share in deciding these great
constitutional questions. The right honourable gentleman
is possessed of those enchanting arts whereby he can give
grace to deformity. He holds before your eyes a beautiful
and delusive image ; he pushes it forward to your observa-

tion ; but, as sure as you embrace it, the pleasing vision will vanish, and this fair phantom of liberty will be succeeded by anarchy, confusion, and ruin to the constitution. For, in truth, sir, if the constitutional independence of the crown is thus reduced to the very verge of annihilation, where is the boasted equipoise of the Constitution? Dreadful, therefore, as the conflict is, my conscience, my duty, my fixed regard for the Constitution of our ancestors, maintain me still in this arduous situation. It is not any proud contempt, or defiance of the constitutional resolutions of this house,—it is no personal point of honour,—much less is it any lust of power, that makes me still cling to office. The situation of the times requires of me—and, I will add, the country calls aloud to me—that I should defend this castle ; and I am determined, therefore, I WILL defend it ! "

Pitt's speech on the war in 1803 is supposed to have excelled all his other speeches in " vehement and spirit-stirring declamation." Mr. Fox, in his reply, said : " The orators of antiquity would have admired, probably would have envied, it."

Probably his finest speech is that upon the peace of 1783 and the coalition, " when he so happily closed his magnificent peroration by that noble yet simple figure ": " And if this inauspicious union be not already consummated, in the name of my country I forbid the banns."

" But," says an able critic, " all authorities agree in placing his speech on the slave trade, in 1791, before any other effort of his genius ; because it combined, with the most impassioned declamation, the deepest pathos, the most lively imagination, and the closest reasoning." Fox is said to have listened to this speech with the greatest interest. Sheridan praised it highly, and Mr. Windham said that he " walked home lost in amazement at the compass, till then unknown to him, of human eloquence."

As a parliamentary orator Mr. Pitt's powers were various. In statement he was perspicuous, in declamation animated. If he had to explain a financial account he was clear and accurate. If he wanted to rouse a just indignation for the

8

wrongs of the country he was rapid, vehement, glowing, and
impassioned. And whether his discourse was argumentative
or declamatory, it always displayed a happy choice of expression and a fluency of diction, which could not fail to delight
his hearers. So singularly select, felicitous, and appropriate
was his language that, it has often been remarked, a word of
his speech could scarcely be changed without prejudice to its
harmony, vigour, or effect. He seldom was satisfied with
standing on the defensive in debate ; but was proud to contrast his own actions with the avowed intentions of his
opponents. These intentions, too, he often exposed with
the most pointed sarcasm ; a weapon which, perhaps, no
speaker wielded with more dexterity and force than himself.

"Of his eloquence, it may be observed generally, that it
combined the eloquence of Tully with the energy of
Demosthenes. It was spontaneous; always great, it shone
with peculiar, with unequalled splendour, in a reply, which
precluded the possibility of previous study ; while it fascinated the imagination by the brilliancy of language, it convinced the judgment by the force of argument,—like an
impetuous torrent, it bore down all resistance, extorting the
admiration even of those who most severely felt its strength,
and who most earnestly deprecated its effect. It is unnecessary, and might be presumptuous to enter more minutely
into the character of Mr. Pitt's eloquence ;—there are many
living witnesses of its power—it will be admired as long as
it shall be remembered."

The sketch of Mr. Pitt by his political associate and
ardent admirer, Mr. Canning, is interesting:

"The character of this illustrious statesman early passed
its ordeal. Scarcely had he attained the age at which reflection commences, when Europe with astonishment beheld
him filling the first place in the councils of his country, and
managing the vast mass of its concerns with all the vigour
and steadiness of the most matured wisdom. Dignity—
strength—discretion,—these were among the masterly qualities of his mind at its first dawn. He had been nurtured a
statesman, and his knowledge was of that kind which always

lay ready for application. Not dealing in the subtleties of abstract politics, but moving in the slow, steady procession of reason, his conceptions were reflective, and his views correct. Habitually attentive to the concerns of government, he spared no pains to acquaint himself with whatever was connected, however minutely, with its prosperity. He was devoted to the state. Its interests engrossed all his study and engaged all his care. It was the element alone in which he seemed to live and move. He allowed himself but little recreation from his labours. His mind was always on its station, and its activity was unremitted.

"He did not hastily adopt a measure nor hastily abandon it. The plan struck out by him for the preservation of Europe was the result of prophetic wisdom and profound policy. But, though defeated in many respects by the selfish ambition and short-sighted imbecility of foreign powers—whose rulers were too venal or too weak to follow the flight of that mind which would have taught them to outwing the storm—the policy involved in it has still a secret operation on the conduct of surrounding states. His plans were full of energy, and the principles which inspired them looked beyond the consequences of the hour.

"He knew nothing of that timid and wavering cast of mind which dares not abide by its own decision. He never suffered popular prejudice or party clamour to turn him aside from any measure which his deliberate judgment had adopted. He had a proud reliance on himself, and it was justified. Like the sturdy warrior leaning on his own battle-axe, conscious where his strength lay, he did not readily look beyond it.

"As a debater in the House of Commons, his speeches were logical and argumentative. If they did not often abound in the graces of metaphor, or sparkle with the brilliancy of wit, they were always animated, elegant, and classical. The strength of his oratory was intrinsic; it presented the rich and abundant resource of a clear discernment and a correct taste. His speeches are stamped with inimitable marks of originality. When replying to his opponents, his readiness was not more conspicuous than his energy. He was always prompt and always dignified. He could sometimes have recourse to the sportiveness of irony, but he did not often seek any other aid than was to be derived from an arranged and extensive knowledge of his subject. This qualified him fully to discuss the arguments of others, and forcibly to defend his own. Thus armed, it was rarely in the power of his adversaries, mighty as they were, to beat him from the field. His eloquence occasionally rapid, electric, and vehement, was always chaste, winning, and persuasive—not awing into acquiescence, but arguing into conviction. His understanding was bold and comprehensive. Nothing seemed too remote for its reach or too large for its grasp.

" Unallured by dissipation and unswayed by pleasure, he never sacrificed the national duty to the one or the national interest to the other. To his unswerving integrity the most authentic of all testimony is to be found in that unbounded public confidence which followed him throughout the whole of his political career.

" Absorbed as he was in the pursuits of public life, he did not neglect to prepare himself in silence for that higher destination, which is at once the incentive and the reward of human virtue. His talents, superior and splendid as they were, never made him forgetful of that Eternal Wisdom from which they emanated. The faith and fortitude of his last moments were affecting and exemplary."

The following observations on the style of Fox and Pitt are interesting and instructive :

" Mr. Burke may be said to have belonged to a Triumvirate of eloquence—the greatest, unquestionably, that ever divided among them the empire of mind. Mr. Fox though a much younger man, entered on his parliamentary career, nearly at the same time with Burke. For a while he was willing to rank as his disciple and follower; but in a few years his growing abilities—his great skill in debate—the charm of his disposition and manners—and his superior political connections, gave him the ascendancy, and made him the acknowledged leader of the opposition ranks. When some twelve years later the youthful Pitt appeared upon the scene, he found those great men in full possession of the stage. The ease and suddenness with which he vaulted to the first place of honour and power is well known. That he should succeed against *such* competition, was the strongest proof of talent he could give. At the age of twenty-three years, he had vanquished an opposing majority in the House of Commons, led by Fox, Sheridan, and Burke—had won the nation to his side—and was wielding the destinies of the British Empire.

"The oratory of Fox and Pitt was very unlike that of the great Triumvir already described. *Their* scene of glory was the arena of debate. Theirs was the skill and power acquired by the breaking of lances, by the parrying and giving of blows, in many a 'passage of arms'. More dexterous or powerful combatants never engaged in political warfare: a warfare maintained by them with scarce an intermission, for more than twenty years. The question of their comparative greatness it would be difficult to settle, but we can easily perceive that they were very unlike. Fox was persuasive, impetuous, powerful. To strong argument, and vehement appeal, he could add the lighter but often more effective weapons of ridicule and wit. Before his rushing charge, nothing for the moment could stand. But he was often incautious, and generally lacked that higher power, which is necessary to turn even victory to account. His antagonist had far more dignity, vigilance, and prudence. He could never be thrown from his guard. He was lofty and fluent, but not impassioned ; sarcastic, but not witty. The conflict of these rival statesmen was often that of Roderick Dhu and Snowdon's Knight. The giant strength and fiery valor of the highland chief are wasted on the air. But 'Fitz James's blade is sword and shield.' Even the personal qualities of the two men influenced, probably in some degree, the judgments which were formed of their eloquence. Who can doubt that Mr. Fox would have been even more admired, and trusted, and beloved, if to his winning manners and brilliant powers he had added the virtuous circumspection of his illustrious rival?"

In private life Pitt's integrity was without a stain. He was exceedingly amiable; "his spirits were naturally buoyant and even playful," his affections were warm, his veracity never questioned.

Fox.—Charles James Fox, if not the greatest orator, was the most accomplished debater that ever appeared upon the theatre of public affairs in any age or country.

He was unacquainted with even the rudiments of metaphysical philosophy, natural science, or political economy. His acquaintance, however, with the Greek and Latin classics was intimate. His knowledge of general history was not very extensive, but his knowledge of the history of England and of other modern states was accurate and profound, and it is said that no politician in any age ever knew so perfectly the various interests and the exact position of all the countries with which England had dealings to conduct or relations to maintain. His knowledge of modern languages was minute.

Fox was largely indebted to his charming social qualities, his amiable disposition, sweetness of temper, sunny humour, and generous, open, manly nature for his popularity.

He abhorred duplicity or dissimulation, and was the uncompromising enemy of corruption in all its forms.

He determined at an early age to excel as a parliamentary speaker, and he was untiring in his efforts to accomplish his purpose. He said on one occasion: "During five whole sessions I spoke every night but one; and I reget that I did not speak on that night too."

Fox was very careless in his dress.

Directly after he heard him in the House of Commons, Horace Walpole said of him: "Fox's abilities are amazing at so very early a period, especially under the circumstances of such a dissolute life. He was just arrived from Newmarket and had sat up drinking all night, and had not been in bed. How such talents make one laugh at Tully's rules for an orator, and his indefatigable application! His laboured orations are puerile in comparison to this boy's manly reason."

From the speech of Mr. Fox in 1797 on "Parliamentary Reform," the following passage upon the progress of liberty will be found interesting:

" Liberty is order. Liberty is strength. Look round the world, and admire, as you must, the instructive spectacle. You will see that liberty not only is power and order, but that it is power and order predominant and invincible,— that it derides all other sources of strength. And shall the preposterous imagination be fostered, that men bred in liberty,—the first of human kind who asserted the glorious distinction of forming for themselves their social compact,— can be condemned to silence upon their rights? Is it to be conceived that men who have enjoyed, for such a length of days, the light and happiness of freedom, can be restrained, and shut up again in the gloom of ignorance and degradation? As well might you try, by a miserable dam, to shut up the flowing of a rapid river! The rolling and impetuous tide would burst through every impediment that man might throw in its way; and the only consequence of the impotent attempt would be that, having collected new force by its temporary suspension, enforcing itself through new channels, it would spread devastation and ruin on every side. The progress of liberty is like the progress of the stream. Kept within its bounds, it is sure to fertilise the country through which it runs; but no power can arrest it in its passage; and short-sighted, as well as wicked, must be the heart of the projector that would strive to divert its course."

Mr. Fox was always a warm friend of America. In 1778, he said in parliament among other things in regard to the American motive to war:

" Every blow you strike in America is against yourselves; it is against all idea of reconciliation, and against your own interest, though you should be able, as you never will be, to force them to submit. Every stroke against France is of advantage to you: America must be conquered in France; France never can be conquered in America.

"The war of the Americans is a war of passion : it is of
such a nature as to be supported by the most powerful virtues, love of liberty and of their country ; and, at the same
time, by those passions in the human heart which give
courage, strength, and perseverance to man ; the spirit of
revenge for the injuries you have done them ; of retaliation
for the hardships you have inflicted on them ; and of opposition to the unjust powers you have exercised over them.
Everything combines to animate them to this war, and such
a war is without end ; for whatever obstinacy enthusiasm
ever inspired man with, you will now find in America. No
matter what gives birth to that enthusiasm ; whether the
name of religion or of liberty, the effects are the same ; it
inspires a spirit which is unconquerable, and solicitous to
undergo difficulty, danger, and hardship: and as long as
there is a man in America, a being formed such as we are,
you will have him present himself against you in the field."

In 1780, speaking of the results of the American war, Mr.
Fox said :

"We are charged with expressing joy at the triumphs of
America. True it is that, in a former session, I proclaimed
it as my sincere opinion, that if the Ministry had succeeded
in their first scheme on the liberties of America, the liberties
of this country would have been at an end. Thinking this,
as I did, in the sincerity of an honest heart, I rejoiced at the
resistance which the ministry had met to their attempt.
That great and glorious statesman, the late Earl of Chatham,
feeling for the liberties of his native country, thanked God
that America had resisted. But, it seems, ' all the calamities
of the country are to be ascribed to the wishes, and the joy,
and the speeches, of opposition.' O miserable and unfortunate ministry ! O blind and incapable men! whose
measures are framed with so little foresight, and executed
with so little firmness, that they not only crumble to pieces,
but bring on the ruin of their country, merely because one
rash, weak, or wicked man, in the House of Commons, makes
a speech against them !

"But who is he who arraigns gentlemen on this side of

the house with causing, by their inflammatory speeches, the misfortunes of their country ? The accusation comes from one whose inflammatory harangues have led the nation, step by step, from violence to violence, in that inhuman, unfeeling system of blood and massacre, which every honest man must detest, which every good man must abhor, and every wise man condemn ! And this man imputes the guilt of such measures to those who had all along foretold the consequences ; who had prayed, entreated, and supplicated, not only for America, but for the credit of the nation and its eventual welfare, to arrest the hand of power, meditating slaughter, and directed by injustice !

"What was the consequence of the sanguinary measures recommended in those bloody, inflammatory speeches? Though Boston was to be starved, though Hancock and Adams were proscribed, yet at the feet of these very men the Parliament of Great Britain was obliged to kneel, flatter, and cringe ; and, as it had the cruelty at one time to denounce vengeance against these men, so it had the meanness afterwards to implore their forgiveness. Shall he who called the Americans 'Hancock and his crew,'—shall he presume to reprehend any set of men for inflammatory speeches ? It is this accursed American war that has led us, step by step, into all our present misfortunes and national disgraces. What was the cause of our wasting forty millions of money, and sixty thousand lives? The American war ! What was it that produced the French rescript and a French war? The American war ! What was it that produced the Spanish manifesto and Spanish war ? The American war ! What was it that armed forty-two thousand men in Ireland with the arguments carried on the points of forty thousand bayonets ? The American war ! For what are we about to incur an additional debt of twelve or fourteen millions? This accursed, cruel, diabolical American war !"

In 1797, speaking of the vigour of democratic governments, Mr. Fox said :

"When we look at the democracies of the ancient world, we are compelled to acknowledge their oppressions to their

dependencies; their horrible acts of injustice and of ingrati-
tude to their own citizens; but they compel us, also, to
admiration, by their vigour, their constancy, their spirit, and
their exertions, in every great emergency in which they were
called upon to act. We are compelled to own that the
democratic form of government gives a power of which no
other form is capable. Why? Because it incorporates
every man with the state. Because it arouses everything
that belongs to the soul, as well as to the body, of man.
Because it makes every individual feel that he is fighting for
himself; that it is his own cause, his own safety, his own
dignity, on the face of the earth, that he is asserting. Who,
that reads the history of the Persian War—what boy, whose
heart is warmed by the grand and sublime actions which the
democratic spirit produced,—does not find, in this principle,
the key to all the wonders which were achieved at Thermopylæ and elsewhere, and of which the recent and marvellous
acts of the French people are pregnant examples? Without
disguising the vices of France,—without overlooking the horrors that have been committed, and that have tarnished the
glory of the Revolution,—it cannot be denied that they have
exemplified the doctrine, that, *if you wish for power, you
must look to liberty.* If ever there was a moment when this
maxim ought to be dear to us, it is the present. We have
tried all other means. We have addressed ourselves to all
the base passions of the people. We have tried to terrify
them into exertion; and all has been unequal to our emergency. Let us try them by the only means which experience
demonstrates to be invincible. Let us address ourselves to
their love! Let us identify them with ourselves!—let us
make it their own cause, as well as ours!"

A great deal has been said and written of Mr. Fox's
oratory. From all accounts of it, in order to comprehend
and appreciate it, the orator himself must have been heard.

When Mr. Fox became deeply engaged in his subject he
was earnest, pathetic, and impetuous, as the occasion demanded. At times his tones were so thrilling and so sweet
that every heart was subdued. Simplicity and vehemence

were two of the most prominent traits in his character as an orator. Mr. Goodwin says: " I have seen his countenance lighten up with more than mortal ardour and goodness; I have been present when his voice was suffocated with tears."

Coleridge says: " His feeling was all intellect, and his intellect all feeling."

Says Sir James Mackintosh : " To speak of him justly as an orator would require a long essay. Everywhere natural, he carried into public something of that simple and negligent exterior which belonged to him in private. When he began to speak, a common observer might have thought him awkward ; and even a consummate judge could only have been struck with the exquisite justness of his ideas, and the transparent simplicity of his manners. But no sooner had he spoken for some time, than he was changed into another being. He forgot himself and everything around him. He thought only of his subject. His genius warmed and kindled as he went on. He darted fire into his audience. Torrents of impetuous and irresistible eloquence swept along their feelings and conviction. He certainly possessed above all moderns, that union of reason, simplicity, and vehemence which formed the prince of orators. He was the most Demosthenean speaker since Demosthenes."

Lord Brougham in contradiction to this last sentence remarks :

" There never was a greater mistake, than the fancying a close resemblance between his eloquence and that of Demosthenes; although an excellent judge (Sir James Mackintosh) fell into it when he pronounced him the most Demosthenean speaker since Demosthenes. That he resembled his immortal predecessor in despising all useless ornament, and all declamation for declamation's sake, is true enough ; but it applies to every good speaker as well as to those two signal ornaments of ancient and modern rhetoric. That he resembled him in keeping more close to the subject in hand than many good and even great speakers have often done, may also be affirmed ; yet this is far too vague and remote a likeness to justify the proposition in question ; and it is only a difference in degree, and not a specific distinction between him and others. That his eloquence was fervid, rapid, copious, carrying along with it the minds of the audience, not suffering them to dwell upon the speaker or the speech, but engrossing their whole attention, and keeping it fixed on the question, is equally certain, and is the only real resemblance which the comparison affords. But then the points of difference are as numerous as they are important, and they strike indeed upon the most cursory glance. The one was full of repetitions, recurring again and again to the same topic, nay to the same view of it, till he had made his impression complete; the other never came back upon a ground which he had utterly wasted and withered up by the tide of fire he had rolled over it. The one dwelt at length, and with many words, on his topics; the other performed the whole at a blow, sometimes with a word, always with the smallest number of words possible. The one frequently was digressive, even narrative and copious in illustration ; in the other no deviation from his course was ever to be perceived ; no disporting on the borders of his way, more than any lingering upon it ; but carried rapidly forward, and without swerving to the right or to the left, like the engines flying along a railway, and like them driving everything out of sight that obstructed his resistless course."

Professor Goodrich, after quoting the conflicting remarks of Brougham and Mackintosh, adds:

"When two such men differ on a point like this, we may safely say that both are in the right and in the wrong. As to certain qualities, Fox was the very reverse of the great Athenian; as to others they had much in common. In whatever relates to the forms of oratory—symmetry, dignity, grace, the working up of thought and language to their most perfect expression,—Mr. Fox was not only inferior to Demosthenes, but wholly unlike him, having no rhetoric and no ideality ; while, at the same time, in the structure of his understanding, the modes of its operation, the soul and spirit which breathe throughout his eloquence, there was a striking resemblance. This will appear as we dwell for a moment on his leading peculiarities.

"(1) He had a luminous simplicity, which gave his speeches the most absolute unity of impression, however irregular might be their arrangement. No man ever kept the great points of his case more steadily and vividly before the minds of his audience.

"(2) He took everything in the concrete. If he discussed principles, it was always in direct connection with the subject before him. Usually, however, he did not even discuss a subject—he grappled with an antagonist. Nothing gives such life and interest to a speech, or so delights an audience, as a direct contest of man with man.

"(3) He struck instantly at the heart of his subject. He was eager to meet his opponent at once on the real points at issue; and the moment of his greatest power was when he stated the argument against himself, with more force than his adversary or any other man could give it, and then seized it with the hand of a giant, tore it to pieces, and trampled it under foot.

"(4) His mode of enforcing a subject on the minds of his audience was to come back again and again to the strong points of his case. Mr. Pitt *amplified* when he wished to impress; Mr. Fox *repeated*. Demosthenes also repeated, but he had more adroitness in varying the mode of doing it.

"(5) He had rarely any preconceived method or arrangement of his thoughts. This was one of his greatest faults, in which he differed most from the Athenian artist. If it had not been for the unity of impression and feeling mentioned above, his strength would have been wasted in disconnected efforts.

"(6) Reasoning was his forte and his passion. But he was not a regular reasoner. In his eagerness to press forward, he threw away everything he could part with, and compacted the rest into a single mass. Facts, principles, analogies, were all wrought together like the strands of a cable, and intermingled with wit, ridicule, or impassioned feeling. His arguments were usually personal in their nature, *ad hominem*, etc., and were brought home to his antagonist with stinging severity and force.

"(7) He abounded in *hits*—those abrupt and startling turns of thought which rouse an audience and give them more delight than the loftiest strains of eloquence.

"(8) He was equally distinguished for his *side blows*, for keen and pungent remarks flashed out upon his antagonist in passing as he pressed on with his argument.

"(9) He was often dramatic, personating the character of his opponents or others, and carrying on a dialogue between them, which added greatly to the liveliness and force of his oratory.

"(10) He had astonishing dexterity in evading difficulties, and turning to his own advantage everything that occurred in debate.

" In nearly all these qualities he had a close resemblance to Demosthenes.

" In his language Mr. Fox studied simplicity, strength, and boldness. 'Give me an elegant Latin and a homely Saxon word,' said he, ' and I will always choose the latter.' Another of his sayings was this. 'Did the speech read well when reported? If so it was a bad one.' These two remarks give us the secret of his style as an orator.

" The life of Mr. Fox has this lesson for young men, that early habits of recklessness and vice can hardly fail to destroy the influence of the most splendid abilities and the most humane and generous dispositions."

Burke.—Although men may differ as to the soundness of Mr. Burke's doctrines, or the purity of his public conduct, there can be no doubt that he was one of the most remarkable persons that has ever lived. He possessed a fund of knowledge that was extensive, and of the most various description. He was well acquainted with human nature. His vast store of information was always available for the purpose of illustrating his subject or enriching his diction. Consequently his speeches and writings show that he was a great reasoner and a great teacher, to whom all branches of knowledge were familiar.

One of Burke's critics, after saying that he was a writer of the first class, and excelled in almost every kind of prose composition, continued as follows: " The kinds of composition are various and he excels in them all, with the exception of two, the very highest, given but to few, and when given, almost always possessed alone—fierce, nervous, overwhelming declamation, and close, rapid argument. Every other he uses easily, abundantly, and successfully. . . .

" As in the various kinds of writing, so in the different styles, he had an almost universal excellence, one only being deficient—the plain and unadorned."

Mr. Burke fully entered on his political career in 1765, when he obtained a seat in parliament as member for Wendover. He entered parliament at an eventful period in English history—when American taxation was the most important topic under discussion.

In January, 1766, Mr. Burke made his maiden speech on the Stamp Act. It was one of great power and eloquence, and was completely successful, and it placed him at once among the greatest orators of the age. Dr. Johnson said that probably no man at his first appearance ever obtained so much reputation before. Lord Chatham, who followed in a speech on the same subject, commenced by saying, that the young member had proved a very able advocate. He had himself intended to enter at length into the details, but he had been anticipated with such ingenuity and eloquence, that there was but little left for him to say. He congratulated him on his success, and his friends on the value of the acquisition they had made. Such an encomium from Lord Chatham gave Burke at once a high reputation in the House of Commons.

The three great subjects to which Mr. Burke gave greatest attention in the house were those relating to America, India, and France.

Notwithstanding the fact that his delivery was so poor—being ungraceful and inelegant in the highest degree—Mr. Burke is ranked among the greatest English orators. One writer says : " The variety and extent of his powers in debate was greater than that of any other orator in ancient or modern times. No one ever poured forth such a flood of thought; so many original combinations of inventive genius; so much knowledge of man and the working of political systems; so many just remarks on the relation of government to the manners, the spirit, and even the prejudices of a people; so many wise maxims as to a change in constitution and laws; so many beautiful effusions of lofty and generous sentiments; such exuberant stores of illustration, ornament, and apt allusion; all intermingled with the liveliest sallies of wit or the boldest flights of a sublime imagination."

Mr. Goodrich says: " As an orator Burke derived little or no advantage from his personal qualifications. He was tall, but not robust; his gait and gesture were awkward; his countenance, though intellectual, was destitute of softness, and rarely relaxed into a smile; and as he always wore spectacles, his eye gave him no command over an audience."

Undoubtedly, the extent of Mr. Burke's knowledge, the beauty of his imagery, the richness, variety, and brilliancy of his oratory, were wonderful.

Sir N. W. Wraxall, a parliamentary contemporary, thus writes of him:

"Nature had bestowed on him a boundless imagination, aided by a memory of equal strength and tenacity. His fancy was so vivid, that it seemed to light up by its own powers, and to burn without consuming the element on which it fed; sometimes bearing him away into ideal scenes created by his own exuberant mind, but from which he, sooner or later, returned to the subject of debate; descending from his most aërial flights by a gentle and imperceptible gradation, till he again touched the ground. Learning waited on him like a handmaid, presenting to his choice all that antiquity has culled or invented, most elucidatory of the topic under discussion. He always seemed to be oppressed under the load and variety of his intellectual treasures. Every power of oratory was wielded by him in turn; for he could be during the same evening, often within the space of a few minutes, pathetic and humorous; acrimonious and conciliating; now giving loose to his indignation or severity; and then, almost in the same breath, calling to his assistance wit and ridicule. It would be endless to cite instances of this versatility of disposition, and of the rapidity of his transitions

' From grave to gay, from lively to severe,'

that I have myself witnessed."

Edward Burke, in his person, was about five feet ten inches high, erect and well-formed. His countenance was frank and open, and, except by an occasional bend of his brow, caused by his being near-sighted, indicated none of those great traits of mind, which he was otherwise well known to possess.

The richness of his mind illustrated every subject he spoke or wrote upon. In conversing with him he attracted by his novelty, variety, and research; in parting from him, strangers and friends alike involuntarily exclaimed: " What an extraordinary man." As an orator, though not so grand and commanding in his manner as Lord Chatham, yet he had excellencies that gave him great influence in the senate. His prolixity and irritability, however, lessened his usefulness.

He was often interrupted while he spoke, and some members made a point of laughing, beating the ground with their feet, and even hooting. The dignity of conscious superiority ought to have rendered Burke indifferent to such disturbances. Instead of indifference, however, he fell into the most outrageous fits of passion, and once told them, that he could discipline a pack of hounds to yelp with much more melody and equal comprehension.

Unaccustomed to dissipation, he devoted to reading and conversation those hours which were not employed in parliamentary duty, in exercise, or in the discharge of the duties incident to private life. He generally read with a pen in his hand to make notes, though his memory was wonderfully retentive.

As a writer he deserves a high rank, and judging him from
9

his earliest to his latest productions, he must be considered as one of those prodigies which are sometimes given to the world to be admired, but cannot be imitated. He believed firmly in the Christian religion, and exercised its principles in its duties, wisely considering, "that whatever disunites man from God, disunites man from man."

He looked within himself for the regulation of his conduct, which was exemplary in all the relations of life; he was warm in his affections, simple in his manners, and free from the follies and dissipations of the times in which he lived.

Speaking on American affairs, but with special reference to magnanimity in politics, in 1775, Burke said:

"A revenue for America, transmitted hither? Do not delude yourselves! You never can receive it—no, not a shilling! Let the Colonies always keep the idea of their civil rights associated with your government, and they will cling and grapple to you. These are ties which, though light as air, are strong as links of iron. But let it once be understood that your government may be one thing and their privileges another,—the cement is gone, the cohesion is loosened! Do not entertain so weak an imagination as that your registers and your bonds, your affidavits and your sufferances, your cockets and your clearances, are what form the great securities of your commerce. These things do not make your government. Dead instruments, passive tools, as they are, it is the spirit of the English communion that gives all their life and efficacy to them. It is the spirit of the English Constitution which, infused through the mighty mass, pervades, feeds, unites, invigorates, vivifies, every part of the Empire, even down to the minutest member.

"Do you imagine that it is the land tax which raises your revenue? that it is the annual vote in the committee of supply which gives you your army? or that it is the mutiny bill which inspires it with bravery and discipline? No! Surely no! It is the love of the people; it is their attachment to their government from the sense of the deep stake they have in such a glorious institution, which gives you your army and your navy, and infuses into both that liberal obedience, without which your army would be a base rabble, and your navy nothing but rotten timber.

"All this, I know well enough, will sound wild and chimerical to the profane herd of those vulgar and mechanical politicians, who have no place among us; a sort of people who think that nothing exists but what is gross and material; and who, therefore, far from being qualified to be directors of the great movement of empire, are not fit to turn a wheel in the machine. But, to men truly initiated and rightly taught, these ruling and master principles, which, in the opinion of such men as I have mentioned, have no substantial existence, are, in truth, everything, and all in all. Magnanimity in politics is not seldom the truest wisdom; and a great empire and little minds go ill together. Let us get an American revenue, as we have got an American empire. English privileges have made it all that it is; English privileges alone will make it all it can be!"

Referring to American taxation, Mr. Burke said:

"Could anything be a subject of more just alarm to America, than to see you go out of the plain highroad of finance, and give up your most certain revenues and your clearest interests, merely for the sake of insulting your colonies? No man ever doubted that the commodity of tea could bear an imposition of three-pence. But no commodity will bear three-pence, or will bear a penny, when the general feelings of men are irritated, and two millions of men are resolved not to pay. The feelings of the colonies were formerly the feelings of Great Britain. Theirs were formerly the feelings of Mr. Hampden, when called upon for the payment of twenty shillings. Would twenty shillings have ruined Mr. Hampden's fortune? No! but the payment of half twenty shillings, on the principle it was demanded, would have made him a slave! It is the weight of that preamble, of which you are so fond, and not the weight of the duty, that the Americans are unable and unwilling to bear. You are, therefore, at this moment, in the awkward

situation of fighting for a phantom; a quiddity; a thing
that wants, not only a substance, but even a name; for a
thing which is neither abstract right, nor profitable enjoyment.

"They tell you, sir, that your dignity is tied to it. I
know not how it happens, but this dignity of yours is a
terrible incumbrance to you; for it has of late been ever at
war with your interest, your equity, and every idea of your
policy. Show the thing you contend for to be reason, show
it to be common sense, show it to be the means of obtaining some useful end, and then I am content to allow it what
dignity you please. But what dignity is derived from the
perseverance in absurdity, is more than I ever could discern!
Let us, sir, embrace some system or other before we end
this session. Do you mean to tax America, and to draw a
protective revenue from thence? If you do, speak out:
name, fix, ascertain this revenue; settle its quantity; define
its objects; provide for its collection; and then fight, when
you have something to fight for. If you murder, rob; if
you kill, take possession: and do not appear in the character of madmen, as well as assassins,—violent, vindictive,
bloody, and tyrannical, without an object. But may better
counsels guide you!"

· Speaking of the incompatibility of despotism with right
in the trial of Mr. Hastings, in 1788, Mr. Burke said:

"My lords, you have now heard the principles on which
Mr. Hastings governs the part of Asia subjected to the
British Empire. Here he has declared his opinion, that he
is a despotic prince; that he is to use arbitrary power; and,
of course, all his acts are covered with that shield. 'I know,
says he, 'the Constitution of Asia only from its practice.'
Will your lordships submit to hear the corrupt practices of
mankind made the principles of government? *He* have
arbitrary power!—My lords, the East-India Company have
not arbitrary power to give him; the king has no arbitrary
power to give him; your lordships have not; nor the
Commons; nor the whole legislature. We have no arbitrary power to give, because arbitrary power is a thing

which neither any man can hold nor any man can give. No man can lawfully govern himself according to his own will,—much less can one person be governed by the will of another. We are all born in subjection,—all born equally, high and low, governors and governed, in subjection to one great, immutable, pre-existent law, prior to all our devices, and prior to all our contrivances, paramount to all our ideas and to all our sensations, antecedent to our very existence, by which we are knit and connected in the eternal frame of the universe, out of which we cannot stir.

"This great law does not arise from our conventions or compacts; on the contrary, it gives to our conventions and compacts all the force and sanction they can have ;—it does not arise from our vain institutions. Every good gift is of God; all power is of God ;—and he who has given the power, and from whom alone it originates, will never suffer the exercise of it to be practised upon any less solid foundation than the power itself. If, then, all dominion of man over man is the effect of the divine disposition, it is bound by the eternal laws of him that gave it, with which no human authority can dispense; neither he that exercises it, nor even those who are subject to it; and, if they were mad enough to make an express compact, that should release their magistrate from his duty, and should declare their lives, liberties, properties, dependent upon, not rules and laws, but his mere capricious will, that covenant would be void.

"This arbitrary power is not to be had by conquest. Nor can any sovereign have it by succession; for no man can succeed to fraud, rapine, and violence. Those who give and those who receive arbitrary power are alike criminal; and there is no man but is bound to resist it to the best of his power, wherever it shall show its face to the world.

"Law and arbitrary power are in eternal enmity. Name me a magistrate, and I will name property; name me power, and I will name protection. It is a contradiction in terms, it is blasphemy in religion, it is wickedness in politics, to say that any man can have arbitrary power. In every patent of office the duty is included. For what else does a magistrate exist? To suppose for power, is an absurdity in idea. Judges are guided and governed by the eternal laws of justice, to which we are all subject. We may bite our chains, if we will; but we shall be made to know ourselves, and be taught that man is born to be governed by *law;* and he that will substitute *will* in the place of it is an enemy to God."

Mr. Burke said on the impeachment of Mr. Hastings, in part.:

" My lords, I do not mean now to go further than just to remind your lordships of this,—that Mr. Hastings's government was one whole system of oppression, of robbery of individuals, of spoliation of the public, and of supersession of the whole system of the English government, in order to vest in the worst of the natives all the power that could possibly exist in any government; in order to defeat the ends which all governments ought, in common, to have in view. In the name of the Commons of England, I charge all this villainy upon Warren Hastings, in this last moment of my application to you.

" My lords, what is it that we want here, to a great act of national justice? Do we want a cause, my lords? You have the cause of oppressed princes, of undone women of the first rank, of desolated provinces, and of wasted kingdoms.

"Do you want a criminal, my lords? When was there so much iniquity ever laid to the charge of any one?—No, my Lords, you must not look to punish any other such delinquent from India. Warren Hastings has not left substance enough in India to nourish such another delinquent.

" My lords, is it a prosecutor you want? You have before you the Commons of Great Britain as prosecutors; and I believe, my lords, that the sun, in his beneficent progress round the world, does not behold a more glorious sight than that of men, separated from a remote people by the material bonds and barriers of nature, united by the bonds of a social and moral community;—all the Commons of England resenting, as their own, the indignities and cruelties that are offered to the people of India.

" Do we want a tribunal? My lords, no example of antiquity, nothing in the modern world, nothing in the range
of human imagination, can supply us with a tribunal like
this. We commit safely the interests of India and humanity
into your hands. Therefore, it is with confidence that,
ordered by the Commons,

" I impeach Warren Hastings, Esquire, of high crimes and
misdemeanours.

" I impeach him in the name of the Commons of Great
Britain in parliament assembled, whose parliamentary trust
he has betrayed.

" I impeach him in the name of all the Commons of Great
Britain, whose national character he has dishonoured.

" I impeach him in the name of the people of India, whose
laws, rights, and liberties he has subverted ; whose properties he has destroyed ; whose country he has laid waste
and desolate.

" I impeach him in the name and by virtue of those eternal
laws of justice which he has violated.

" I impeach him in the name of human nature itself, which
he has cruelly outraged, injured, and oppressed, in both
sexes, in every age, rank, situation, and condition of life."

The peroration of Mr. Burke's speech against Hastings
was as follows :

" My lords, at this awful close, in the name of the Commons, and surrounded by them, I attest the retiring, I attest
the advancing generations, between which, as a link in the
great chain of eternal order, we stand. We call this nation,
we call the world to witness, that the Commons have shrunk
from no labour; that we have been guilty of no prevarica-
tion; that we have made no compromise with crime; that
we have not feared any odium whatsoever, in the long warfare which we have carried on with the crimes, with the
vices, with the exorbitant wealth, with the enormous and
overpowering influence of Eastern corruption.

" My lords, it has pleased Providence to place us in such
a state that we appear every moment to be upon the verge
of some great mutations. There is one thing, and one thing

only, which defies all mutation: that which existed before
the world, and will survive the fabric of the world itself,—
I mean justice; that justice which, emanating from the
Divinity, has a place in the breast of every one of us, given
us for our guide with regard to ourselves and with regard to
others, and which will stand, after this globe is burned to
ashes, our advocate or our accuser, before the great Judge,
when He comes to call upon us for the tenor of a well-spent
life.

"My lords, the Commons will share in every fate with
your lordships; there is nothing sinister which can happen
to you, in which we shall not all be involved; and, if it
should so happen that we shall be subjected to some of
those frightful changes which we have seen,—if it should
happen that your lordships, stripped of all the decorous distinctions of human society, should, by hands at once base
and cruel, be led to those scaffolds and machines of murder
upon which great kings and glorious queens have shed their
blood, amidst the prelates, amidst the nobles, amidst the
magistrates, who supported their thrones,—may you in those
moments feel that consolation which I am persuaded they
felt in the critical moments of their dreadful agony!

"My lords, if you must fall, may you so fall! but, if you
stand,—and stand I trust you will,—together with the fortune of this ancient monarchy, together with the ancient
laws and liberties of this great and illustrious kingdom, may
you stand as unimpeached in honour as in power; may you
stand, not as a substitute for virtue, but as an ornament of
virtue, as a security of virtue; may you stand long, and long
stand the terror of tyrants; may you stand the refuge of the
afflicted nations; may you stand a sacred temple, for the
perpetual residence of an inviolable justice!"

Henry Grattan.—Henry Grattan was born at Dublin on
the 3d of July, 1746. He entered Trinity College, Dublin,
where he soon became noted for his diligence as a student,
for the impetuosity of his feelings, and for the energy of his
character. He graduated in 1767, with a high literary reputation, and soon after went to London and commenced the

study of the law. He had not been there long before politics began to engage his attention. He frequently attended the debates in parliament, and became an ardent admirer of Lord Chatham—then in the zenith of his fame.

The powerful oratory of this great statesman made a deep impression on the glowing mind of young Grattan, who listened with indescribable pleasure to those magnificent bursts of declamation which rolled from the lips of the orator.

The eloquence of Chatham, bold, nervous, and fiery, was exactly suited to the nature of Grattan, upon whom it acted with such fascination as seemed completely to form his destiny. It is said that he now determined to become an orator and chose Lord Chatham as his model. " Everything was forgotten in the one great object of cultivating his powers as a public speaker. To emulate and express, through the peculiar forms of his own genius, the lofty conceptions of the great English orator, was from this time the object of his continual study and most fervent aspirations."

" Even in those early days Grattan was preparing sedulously for his future destination. He had taken a residence near Windsor Forest, and there it was his custom to rove about moonlight nights, addressing the trees as if they were an audience. His landlady took such manifestations much to heart. ' What a sad thing it was,' she would say, ' to see the poor young gentleman all day talking to somebody he calls Mr. Speaker, when there is no speaker in the house except himself!' Her mind was completely made up upon the subject.'

Mr. Grattan returned to Ireland in 1772, and became a member of the Irish parliament, in 1775.

The complete independence of his country was the one great object which he had in view, during his brilliant political career.

Ireland had been long treated by the English like a conquered nation. During the reign of George I., an act was passed, asserting, " that Ireland was a subordinate and dependent kingdom ;—that the Kings, Lords, and Commons of England had power to make laws to bind Ireland ; that the Irish House of Lords had no jurisdiction, and that all proceedings before that court were void."

Mr. Grattan determined that the parliament of his country should be free if it was in his power to break the chains thrown around her. He resolved to effect the repeal of this act. Accordingly on the 19th of April, 1780, he made his memorable motion for a Declaration of Irish Right, which denied the authority of the British parliament to make laws for Ireland. Mr. Grattan was cheered on in taking this bold step by the whole body of the Irish nation. It is said that the speech which he delivered on that occasion in support of his motion "was the most splendid piece of eloquence that had ever been heard in Ireland." The orator himself always thought it his finest oratorical effort. Says Professor Goodrich : "As a specimen of condensed and fervid argumentation, it indicates a high order of talent ; while in brilliancy of style, pungency of application, and impassioned vehemence of spirit, it has rarely, if ever, been surpassed. The conclusion, especially, is one of the most magnificent passages in our eloquence." Mr. Grattan thus finished his speech in the boldest tone:

"I might, as a constituent, come to your bar and demand my liberty. I do call upon you by the laws of the land, and their violation ; by the instructions of eighteen centuries; by the arms, inspiration, and providence of the present movement—tell us the rule by which we shall go ; assert the law of Ireland ; declare the liberty of the land ! I will not be answered by a public lie, in the shape of an amendment ; nor, speaking for the subject's freedom, am I to hear of faction. I wish for nothing but to breathe in this our island, in common with my fellow-subjects, the air of liberty. I have no ambition, unless it be to break your chain and contemplate your glory. I never will be satisfied so long as the meanest cottager in Ireland has a link of the British chain clanking to his rags. He may be naked, he shall not be in irons. And I do see the time at hand ; the spirit has gone forth; the Declaration of Right is planted and though great men should fall off, the cause will live; and though he who utters this should die, yet the immortal fire shall outlast the organ that conveys it, and the breath of liberty, like the word of the holy man, will not die with the prophet, but survive him."

Professor Goodrich says: " The reader will be interested to observe the *rhythmus* of the last three paragraphs, so slow and dignified in its movement; so weighty as it falls on the ear; so perfectly adapted to the sentiments expressed in this magnificent passage. The effect will be heightened by comparing it with the rapid and iambic movement of the passage containing Mr. Erskine's description of the Indian chief."

Mr. Grattan's motion did not pass at that time; but notwithstanding his temporary defeat, he never faltered for a moment: he ever kept his eye fixed on parliamentary emancipation. Mr. Grattan availed himself of the general enthusiasm for liberty which prevailed in Ireland, and mainly by his efforts the Irish Revolution of 1782 was carried, thus achieving, to use the language of Lord Brougham, a victory " which stands at the head of all the triumphs ever won by a patriot for his country in modern times; he had effected an important revolution in the government without violence of any kind, and had broken chains of the most degrading kind by which the injustice and usurpation of three centuries had bowed her down."

While his countrymen were armed, ready for open rebellion, on the 16th of April, 1782, Mr. Grattan repeated his motion in the Irish House of Commons for a Declaration of Irish Right. His speech on that occasion, it is said, was universally admired for its boldness, sublimity, and compass of thought. The untiring efforts of the orator were at last crowned with complete success. The grievances of Ireland were redressed, a bill repealing the act of George I. was soon after passed.

Mr. Grattan's services were remunerated by a grant of £100,000 from the parliament of Ireland. He at first de-

clined the reception of this high expression of gratitude ; but
by the interposition of his friends he was subsequently induced to accept one-half of the amount granted.

Shortly after this victory Mr. Grattan was led into a personal quarrel with Mr. Flood, a rival member of parliament.
A bitter animosity had arisen between them ; and Grattan
having unfortunately led the way in personality, by speaking of his opponent's " affectation of infirmity," Flood
replied with great asperity, denouncing Grattan as " a men-
dicant patriot," who, " bought by his country for a sum of
money, then sold his country for prompt payment." He
also sneered at Grattan's " aping the style of Lord Chatham." To these taunts Grattan replied in a speech, an
abridgment of which will be given. An arrangement for a
hostile meeting between the parties was the consequence of
this speech ; but Flood was arrested, and the crime of a duel
was not added to the offence of vindictive personality of
which both had been guilty. It is said that Grattan lived to
regret his harshness, and spoke in generous terms of his rival.
Mr. Grattan said :

" It is not the slander of an evil tongue that can defame
me. I maintain my reputation in public and in private life.
No man, who has not a bad character, can ever say that I
deceived. No country can call me a cheat. But I will suppose such a public character. I will suppose such a man to
have existence. I will begin with his character in his political cradle, and I will follow him to the last stage of political
dissolution. I will suppose him, in the first stage of his life,
to have been intemperate ; in the second, to have been corrupt ; and in the last, seditious ;—that, after an envenomed
attack on the persons and measures of a succession of viceroys, and after much declamation against their illegalities
and their profusion, he took office, and became a supporter
of government, when the profusion of ministers had greatly
increased, and their crimes multiplied beyond example.

" With regard to the liberties of America, which were inseparable from ours, I will suppose this gentleman to have
been an enemy decided and unreserved ; that he voted

against her liberty, and voted, moreover, for an address to send four thousand Irish troops to cut the throats of the Americans; that he called these butchers ' armed negotiators', and stood with a metaphor in his mouth and a bribe in his pocket, a champion against the rights of America,—of America, the only hope of Ireland, and the only refuge of the liberties of mankind. Thus defective in every relationship, whether to constitution, commerce, and toleration, I will suppose this man to have added much private improbity to public crimes; that his probity was like his patriotism, and his honour on a level with his oath. He loves to deliver panegyrics on himself. I will interrupt him and say :

" Sir, you are much mistaken if you think that your talents have been as great as your life has been reprehensible. You began your parliamentary career with an acrimony and personality which could have been justified only by a supposition of virtue ; after a rank and clamorous opposition, you became, on a sudden, *silent ;* you were silent for seven years ; you were silent on the greatest questions, and you were silent for money ! You supported the unparalleled profusion and jobbing of Lord Harcourt's scandalous ministry. You, sir, who manufacture stage thunder against Mr. Eden for his anti-American principles,—you, sir, whom it pleases to chant a hymn to the immortal Hampden ;—you, sir, approved of the tyranny exercised against America,—and you, sir, voted four thousand Irish troops to cut the throats of the Americans fighting for their freedom, fighting for your freedom, fighting for the great principle, *liberty !* But you found, at last, that the court had bought, but would not trust you. Mortified at the discovery, you try the sorry game of a trimmer in your progress to the acts of an incendiary ; and observing, with regard to prince and people, the most impartial treachery and desertion, you justify the suspicion of your sovereign by betraying the government, as you had sold the people. Such has been your conduct, and at such conduct every order of your fellow-subjects have a right to exclaim ! The merchant may say to you, the constitutionalist may say to you, the American may say to you,

—and I, I now say, and say to your beard, sir,—you are not an honest man!"

The invectives of Mr. Grattan were terrible, and one of the most scathing pieces of this kind which he ever pronounced was that against Mr. Corry, Chancellor of the Exchequer, delivered during the debate on the union of Ireland with England, February 14, 1800. A duel, in which Mr. Corry was wounded in the arm, was the sequel to this speech. The immediate provocation of the speech was a remark from Corry that Grattan, instead of having a voice in the councils of his country, should have been standing as a culprit at her bar.

Mr. Grattan said :

"Has the gentleman done? Has he completely done? He was unparliamentary from the beginning to the end of his speech. There was scarce a word that he uttered that was not a violation of the privileges of the house. But I did not call him to order. Why? Because the limited talents of some men render it impossible for them to be severe without being unparliamentary. But before I sit down I shall show him how to be severe and parliamentary at the same time. On any other occasion, I should think myself justifiable in treating with silent contempt anything which might fall from that honourable member; but there are times when the insignificance of the accuser is lost in the magnitude of the accusation. I know the difficulty the honourable gentleman laboured under when he attacked me, conscious that, on a comparative view of our characters, public and private, there is nothing he could say which would injure me. The public would not believe the charge. I despise the falsehood. If such a charge were made by an honest man, I would answer it in the manner I shall do before I sit down. But I shall first reply to it when not made by an honest man.

"The right honourable gentleman has called me 'an un-impeached traitor.' I ask, why not 'traitor,' unqualified by any epithet? I will tell him; it was because he dare not ! It was the act of a coward, who raises his arm to strike, but has not courage to give the blow! I will not call him villain, because it would be unparliamentary, and he is a privy councillor. I will not call him fool, because he happens to be Chancellor of the Exchequer. But I say he is one who has abused the privilege of parliament and freedom of debate, to the uttering language which, if spoken out of the house, I should answer only with a blow! I care not how high his situation, how low his character, how contemptible his speech; whether a privy councillor or a parasite, my answer would be a blow! He has charged me with being connected with the rebels. The charge is utterly, totally, and meanly false. Does the honourable gentleman rely on the report of the House of Lords for the foundation of his assertion? If he does, I can prove to the committee there was a physical impossibility of that report being true. But I scorn to answer any man for my conduct, whether he be a political coxcomb, or whether he brought himself into power by a false glare of courage or not.

"I have returned, not as the right honourable member has said, to raise another storm,—I have returned to discharge an honourable debt of gratitude to my country, that conferred a great reward for past services, which, I am proud to say, was not greater than my desert. I have returned to protect that constitution, of which I was the parent and the founder, from the assassination of such men as the honourable gentleman and his unworthy associates. They are corrupt—they are seditious—and they, at this very moment, are in a conspiracy against their country! I have returned to refute a libel, as false as it is malicious, given to the public under the appellation of a report of the committee of the lords. Here I stand for impeachment or trial! I dare accusation! I defy the honourable gentleman! I defy the government! I defy the whole phalanx; let them come forth! I tell the ministers I shall neither give them quarter nor take it! I am here to lay the shattered remains of my constitution on the floor of this house, in defence of the liberties of my country.

"The right honourable gentleman has said that this was

not my place—that instead of having a voice in the councils
of my country, I shall now stand a culprit at her bar—at the
bar of a court of criminal judicature, to answer for my
treasons. The Irish people have not so read my history;
but let that pass ; if I am what he said I am, the people are
not therefore to forfeit their constitution. In point of argument, therefore, the attack is bad—in point of taste or feeling,
if he had either, it is worse—in point of fact it is false,
utterly and absolutely false—as rancorous a falsehood as the
most malignant motives could suggest to the prompt sympathy of a shameless and a venal defence. The right honourable gentleman has suggested examples which I should
have shunned, and examples which I should have followed.
I shall never follow his, and I have ever avoided it. I shall
never be ambitious to purchase public scorn by private
infamy—the lighter characters of the model have as little
chance of weaning me from the habits of a life spent, if not
exhausted, in the cause of my native land. Am I to re-
nounce those habits now forever and at the beck of whom,
I should rather say of what—half a minister, half a monkey
—a 'prentice politician, and a master coxcomb? He has
told you that what he said of me here, he would say anywhere. I believe he would say thus of me in any place
where he thought himself safe in saying it. Nothing can
limit his calumnies but his fears—in parliament he has ca-
lumniated me to-night, in the king's courts he would calum-
niate me to-morrow; but had he said or dared to insinuate
one half as much elsewhere, the indignant spirit of an
honest man would have answered the vile and venal slan-
derer with—a blow."

Mr. Grattan was always opposed to the union of Ireland
with England. To prevent it in 1800, when the question
was discussed, he delivered a speech of great ability, from
which the following eloquent passage is taken:

"The ministers of the crown will, or may, perhaps, at
length find that it is not so easy, by abilities however great,
and by power and corruption however irresistible, to put
down forever an ancient and respectable nation. Liberty

may repair her golden beams, and with redoubled heat animate the country. The cry of loyalty will not long continue against the principles of liberty. Loyalty is a noble, a judicious, and a capacious principle; but in these countries, loyalty, distinct from liberty, is corruption, not loyalty.

" The cry of disaffection will not, in the end, avail against the principles of liberty. Yet I do not give up the country. I see her in a swoon, but she is not dead. Though in her tomb she lies helpless and motionless, still there is on her lips a spirit of life, and on her cheek a glow of beauty:

> ' Thou art not conquered ; beauty's ensign yet
> Is crimson in thy lips and in thy cheeks,
> And death's pale flag is not advancéd there.'

." While a plank of the vessel sticks together, I will not leave her. Let the courtier present his flimsy sail, and carry the light bark of his faith with every new breath of wind; I will remain anchored here, with fidelity to the fortunes of my country, faithful to her freedom, faithful to her fall."

His countrymen, however, were so much divided that his efforts were unavailing. He exerted his oratorical powers in vain on this subject.

Mr. Grattan became a member of the British parliament in 1805, where he stood eminent among the leading orators and statesmen of the age. Charles Phillips says: "His debut in the imperial parliament was a bold and hazardous experiment. He had told Flood, and somewhat prophetically, ' that an oak of the forest was too old to be transplanted at fifty '; and yet here he was himself; whether he would take root was the question, and for some moments very questionable it was. When he rose, every voice in that crowded house was hushed—the great rivals, Pitt and Fox, rivetted their eyes on him—he strode forth and gesticulated —the hush became ominous, not a cheer was heard, men looked in one another's faces, and then at the phenomenon before them, as if doubting his identity ; at last and on a sudden the indication of the master-spirit came. Pitt was the first generously to recognise it ; he smote his thigh

10

hastily with his hand—it was an impulse when he was pleased—his followers saw it, and knew it, and with a universal burst they hailed the advent and the triumph of the stranger."

Grattan died in London on the 14th of May, 1820. Mr. Grattan's personal appearance is thus described by Charles Phillips: " He was short in stature and unprepossessing in appearance. His arms were disproportionately long. His walk was a stride. With a person swaying like a pendulum, and an abstracted air, he seemed always in thought, and each thought provoked an attendant gesticulation. Such was the outward and visible form of one whom the passenger would stop to stare at as a droll, and the philosopher contemplate as a study. How strange it seems that a mind so replete with grace and symmetry, and power and splendour, should have been allotted such a dwelling for its residence. Yet so it was; and so also was it one of his highest attributes that his genius, by its ' excessive light,' blinded the hearer to his physical imperfections. It was the victory of mind over matter. The man was forgotten in the orator."

The outlines of Mr. Grattan's character as an orator will next be given.

His son says: " The style of his speaking was strikingly remarkable,—bold, figurative, and impassioned,—always adapted to the time and circumstance, and peculiarly well suited to the taste and temper of the audience that he had to address. In the latter part of his career, his arguments were more closely arranged; there was less ornament, but more fact and reasoning; less to dazzle the sight, and more to convince the understanding."

Grattan endeavoured, as has been said, to form his manner of speaking after the style of Lord Chatham. His eloquence resembled that of the great Englishman in many respects. " Like him, he excelled in the highest characteristics of oratory—in vehemence of action, condensation of style, rapidity of thought, closeness of argumentation, striking figures, grand metaphors, beautiful rhythmus, luminous statements, vivid descriptions, touching pathos, lofty declama-

tion, bitter sarcasm, and fierce invective. His language, like
that of Chatham, is remarkable for its terseness, expressiveness, and energy. His periods are made up of short clauses
which flash upon the mind with uncommon vividness. Passing over the minutiæ of his discourse, he seized the principal
points in debate and presented them in the strongest light.
The intensity of feeling by which his mental operations were
governed, gave rise to this characteristic of eloquence which
distinguishes the most powerful orators. Aiming directly at
his object, he generally struck the decisive blow in a few
words.

" Deep emotion strikes directly at its object. It struggles
to get free from all secondary ideas—all mere accessories.
Hence the simplicity and even barrenness of thought, which
we usually find in the great passages of Chatham and Demosthenes. The whole turns often on a single phrase, a
word, an allusion. They put forward a few great objects,
sharply defined, and standing boldly out in the glowing atmosphere of emotion. They pour their burning thoughts
instantaneously upon the mind, as a person might catch the
rays of the sun in a concave mirror, and turn them on their
object with a sudden and consuming power."

Lord Brougham, an excellent critic, says of Mr. Grattan:
"Among the orators, as among the statesmen of his age,
Mr. Grattan occupies a place in the foremost rank; and it
was the age of the Pitts, the Foxes, and the Sheridans. His
eloquence was of a very high order, all but of the very highest, and it was eminently original. In the constant stream
of a diction replete with epigram and point, a stream on
which floated gracefully, because naturally, flowers of various
hues,—was poured forth the closest reasoning, the most
luminous statement, the most persuasive display of all the
motives that could influence, and of all the details that could
enlighten, his audience. Often a different strain was heard,
and it was declamatory and vehement—or pity was to be
moved, and its pathos was as touching as it was simple—or,
above all, an adversary sunk in baseness, or covered with
crimes, was to be punished or to be destroyed, and a storm

of the most terrible invective raged, with all the blights of
sarcasm and the thunders of abuse."

Professor Goodrich, in a splendid critique on the genius
of Grattan, says : " The speeches of Mr. Grattan offered un-
equivocal proof, not only of a powerful intellect, but of a
high and original genius.   There was nothing commonplace
in his thoughts, his images, or his sentiments.   Everything
came fresh from his mind with the vividness of a new creation.   His most striking characteristic was condensation and
rapidity of thought.   '*Semper instans sibi*,' pressing continually upon himself, he never dwelt upon an idea, however
important ; he rarely presented it under more than one
aspect ; he hardly ever stopped to fill out the immediate
steps of his argument.   His forte was reasoning, but it was
'logic or fire'; and he seemed ever to delight in flashing
his ideas on the mind with a sudden, startling abruptness.
Hence a distinguished writer has spoken of his eloquence as
a ' combination of *cloud, whirlwind*, and *flame*'—a striking
representation of the occasional obscurity and the rapid
force and brilliancy of his style.   But his incessant effort
to be strong sometimes made him unnatural.   He seems to
be continually straining after effect.   He wanted that calmness and self-possession which mark the highest order of
minds, and show their consciousness of great strength.
When he had mastered, his subject mastered him.   His
great efforts have too much the air of harangues.   They
sound more like the battle speeches of Tacitus than the
orations of Demosthenes.

" His style was elaborated with great care.   It abounds in
metaphors which were always striking and often grand.   It
is full of antitheses and epigrammatic turns, which give it
uncommon point and brilliancy, but have too often an
appearance of labour and affectation.   His language is select.
His periods are easy and fluent—made up of short clauses,
with but few or brief qualifications, all uniting in the expression of some one leading thought.   His rhythmus is often
uncommonly fine.   In the peroration of his great speech of
April 19, 1780, we have one of the best specimens in our

language of that admirable adaptation of the sound to the sense which distinguished the ancient orators.

"Though Mr. Grattan is not a safe model in every respect, there are certain purposes for which his speeches may be studied with great advantage. Nothing can be better suited to break up a dull monotony of style—to give raciness and point—to teach a young speaker the value of that terse and expressive language which is to the orator, especially, the finest instrument of thought."

The delivery of Mr. Grattan is vividly described by Charles Phillips: "The chief difficulty in this speaker's way was the first five minutes. During his exordium laughter was imminent. He bent his body almost to the ground, swung his arms over his head, up and down and around him, and added to the grotesqueness of his manner a hesitating tone and drawling emphasis. Still, there was an earnestness about him that at first besought, and as he warmed, enforced, nay commanded, attention. The elevation of his mind, the grandeur of his diction, the majesty of his declamation, the splendour of his imagery, and the soundness of his logic, displayed in turn the ascendancy of a genius. He was fine and judicious in his panegyric; but his forte—that which seemed to conjure up and concentrate all his faculties—was the overwhelming, withering severity of his invective. It was like the torrent-lava; brilliant, inevitable, fatal. It required such qualifications to overcome the peculiarity of his appearance and the disadvantages of his manner. Truly indeed might it be said of him, as he said of Chatham, he was 'very great and *very odd*.' For a time the eye dissented from the verdict of the mind; but at last his genius carried all before it, and, as in the oracle of old, the contortions vanished as the inspiration became manifest."

It is said that the character of Mr. Grattan was irreproachable. It was remarked by Sir James Mackintosh, that he was as eminent in his observance of all the duties of private life as he was heroic in the discharge of his public ones. He may be said to have lived only for his country, and died in advocating her cause. Wilberforce declared that he never knew a man whose patriotism and love for his country seemed so completely to extinguish all private interests, and to induce him to look invariably and exclusively to the public good.

Curran.—John Philpot Curran was born at Newmarket, a small village in the County of Cork, Ireland, on the 24th of July, 1750.

He entered Trinity College, Dublin, at the age of nineteen. After the completion of his college course he went to London, and commenced the study of the law in the Middle Temple. He pursued his studies here with great ardour.

His mornings were spent reading law, even to exhaustion, and the rest of the day in the more congenial pursuits of literature.

He usually read law seven hours every day before his admission to the bar, and devoted about three hours each day to the study of history and the general principles of politics.

In order to master the art of oratory, Mr. Curran commenced a system of discipline almost as severe as that adopted by the great Athenian. He knew that the art of speaking well cannot be acquired without the closest application, extensive practice, repeated trials, deep sagacity, and a ready invention.

When Curran commenced speaking, his voice was so bad, and his articulation so hasty and confused, that he was called " stuttering Jack Curran."

His manner was extremely awkward, his gestures were extravagant and meaningless as many of those we daily see in ordinary practice, and his whole appearance was only calculated to produce laughter. All these faults he overcame by patient labour.

Mr. Curran regularly attended the London debating societies; but he was at first ridiculed by his opponents, and mortified by frequent failures.

Mr. Curran gives a graphic account of one of his earliest

efforts at a debating club. After he became a distinguished orator, some one speaking to him of his eloquence said, "It must have been born with you." Curran replied: "Indeed, my dear sir, it was not. It was born three and twenty years and some months after me. When I was at the Temple, a few of us formed a little debating club, where all the great questions in ethics and politics were discussed, and irrevocably settled. Upon the first night of our assembling, I attended, my foolish heart throbbing with the anticipated honour of being styled, 'the honoured member that opened the debate,' or 'the very eloquent gentleman who had just sat down.' All day the scene had been flitting before my fancy and cajoling it; my ear already caught the glorious melody of 'hear him! hear him!' I stood up. I have forgotten what the question was. My mind was stored with about a folio volume of matter. I stood up trembling through every fibre, but remembering that in this I was imitating Cicero, I took courage, and had actually proceeded as far as 'Mr. Chairman,' when to my astonishment and terror I perceived that every eye was rivetted upon me. There were but six or seven present, and the little room could not hold as many more, yet was it to my panic-struck imagination as if I were the central object in nature, and assembled millions were gazing on me with breathless expectation. I became dismayed and dumb. My friends cried 'hear him!' but there was nothing to hear. So you see it was not born in me. My friends despaired of my ever making a speaker, but I would not give it up. I attended the debates punctually, I said yes and no, till at length one in his speech referred to me, calling me 'orator mum,' who he doubted not possessed wonderful talents for eloquence although he would recommend him to show it in future by some more popular method than his silence. I followed his advice."

One of his friends says: "He turned his shrill and stumbling brogue into a flexible, sustained, and finely modulated voice; his action became free and forcible; he acquired perfect readiness in thinking on his legs; he put down every opponent by the mingled force of his argument

and wit, and was at last crowned with the universal applause
of the society, and invited by the president to an entertainment in their behalf."

Mr. Curran was a member of the Irish House of Commons from 1783 to 1797, but he never became a distinguished parliamentary orator.

. His education fitted him for the forum rather than the
senate. His greatest speeches were made at the state trials
arising out of the United Irish conspiracy.

Probably, the most eloquent speech he made was the one
in defence of Mr. Rowan, who was indicted for the publication of a seditious libel. This speech was delivered on the
29th of January, 1794. This speech contains those strikingly
beautiful and highly finished passages on universal emancipation and the liberty of the press. In reading them it
must be borne in mind that it was not so much his *matter*,
although that was excellent, but the *manner* in which his
speech was made which invested it with such irresistible
power, and caused it to produce such wonderful effects.

In order, then, to form an adequate idea of that wonderful
eloquence which subdued every heart, " we must call up in
our minds the living speaker, with his glowing eye and
expressive countenance ; his bold and impassioned gestures ;
his finely modulated voice and musical tones ; his wit and
mimicry ; his tenderness and pathos ; his cutting sarcasm
and overwhelming invective."

The first extract which the author will give from his speech
in defence of Mr. Rowan, is on the Liberty of the Press :

" What then remains? The liberty of the Press *only*—
that sacred palladium which no influence, no power, no
minister, no government, which nothing but the depravity,
or folly, or corruption of a jury can ever destroy.

" In that awful moment of a nation's travail, of the last
gasp of tyranny, and the first breath of freedom, how pregnant is the example ! The press extinguished, the people
enslaved, and the prince undone. As the advocate of society, therefore—of peace—of domestic liberty—and the
lasting union of the two countries—I conjure you to guard

the liberty of the press, that great sentinel of the state, that great detecter of public imposture ; guard it, because, when it sinks, there sinks with it, in one common grave, the liberty of the subject and the security of the crown.

"There is a sort of aspiring and adventurous credulity which disdains assenting to obvious truths, and delights in catching at the improbability of circumstance, as its best ground of faith. To what other cause, gentlemen, can you ascribe that, in the wise, the reflecting, and the philosophical nation of Great Britain, a printer has been found guilty of a libel for publishing those resolutions, to which the present minister of that kingdom had actually subscribed his name? To what other cause can you ascribe, what in my mind is still more astonishing, in such a country as Scotland, a nation cast in the happy medium between the spiritless acquiescence of submissive poverty and the sturdy credulity of pampered wealth ; cool and ardent, adventurous and per-severing ; winging her eagle flight against the blaze of every science, with an eye that never winks, and a wing that never tires ; crowned as she is with the spoils of every art, and decked with the wreath of every muse ; from the deep and scrutinising researches of her Hume, to the sweet and sim-ple, but not less sublime and pathetic morality of her Burns —how, from the bosom of a country like that, genius and character and talents should be banished to a distant, bar-barous soil, condemned to pine under the horrid communion of vulgar vice and base-born profligacy, for twice the period that ordinary calculation gives to the continuance of human life? But I will not further press any idea that is painful to me, and I am sure must be painful to you. I will only say, you have now an example of which neither England nor Scotland had the advantage. You have the example of the panic, the infatuation, and the contrition of both. It is now for you to decide whether you will profit by their experience of idle panic and idle regret, or whether you merely prefer to palliate a servile imitation of their frailty by a paltry affectation of their repentance. It is now for you to show that you are not carried away by the same hectic delusions,

to acts of which no tears can wash away the consequences
or the indelible reproach."

The eloquent passage on Universal Emancipation reads as
follows: "I speak in the spirit of the British law, which
makes liberty commensurate with, and inseparable from, the
British soil—which proclaims even to the stranger and the
sojourner the moment he sets foot upon British earth, that
the ground on which he treads is holy and consecrated by
the genius of Universal Emancipation. No matter in what
language his doom may be pronounced; no matter what
complexion incompatible with freedom an Indian or an
African sun may have burned upon him; no matter in what
disastrous battle his liberty may have been cloven down; no
matter with what solemnities he may have been devoted
upon the altar of slavery,—the first moment he touches the
sacred soil of Britain, the altar and the god sink together in
the dust; his soul walks abroad in her own majesty; his
body swells beyond the measure of his chains, that burst
from around him, and he stands redeemed, regenerated,
and disenthralled by the irresistible genius of Universal
Emancipation."

Beautifully conceived is the peroration of this great
speech: "Upon this subject credit me when I say that I
am still more anxious for you than I can be for him. I
cannot but feel the peculiarity of your situation. Not the
jury of his own choice, which the law of England allows,
but which ours refuses, collected in that box by a person
certainly no friend to Mr. Rowan, certainly not very deeply
interested in giving him a very impartial jury. Feeling
this, as I am persuaded you do, you cannot be surprised,
however you may be distressed, at the mournful presage
with which an anxious public is led to fear the worst from
your possible determination. But I will not, for the justice
and honour of our common country, suffer my mind to be
borne away by such melancholy anticipations. I will not
relinquish the confidence that this day will be the period of
his sufferings; and however merciless he has been hitherto
pursued, that your verdict will send him home to the arms

of his family and the wishes of his country. But if, which Heaven forbid, it hath still been unfortunately determined that, because he has not bent to power and authority, because he would not bow down before the golden calf and worship it, he is to be bound and cast into the furnace, I do trust in God that there is a redeeming spirit in the Constitution which will be seen to walk with the sufferer through the flames, and to preserve him unhurt by the conflagration."

Mr. Curran's personal appearance is vividly described by his friend and biographer, the celebrated Charles Phillips: "Mr. Curran was short of stature, with a swarthy complexion, and ' an eye that glowed like a live coal.' His countenance was singularly expressive; and as he stood before a jury he not only read their hearts with a searching glance, but he gave them back his own in all the fluctuations of his feelings, from laughter to tears. His gesture was bold and impassioned; his articulation was uncommonly distinct and deliberate; the modulations of his voice were varied in a high degree, and perfectly suited to the widest range of his eloquence."

Mr. Curran's oratory was of the most copious, fervid, and expressive kind. It sparkled with wit, humour, fun, and ridicule. Bitter sarcasm and terrible invective sometimes predominated, however. At other times his deep pathos caused tears to flow from every eye. The strength and variety of his emotions were wonderful. " He delighted a jury by his wit; he turned the court-room into a scene of the broadest farce by his humour, mimicry, and fun; he made it ' a place of tears,' by a tenderness and pathos which subdued every heart; he poured out his invective like a stream of lava, and inflamed the minds of his countrymen almost to madness by the recital of their wrongs. His rich and powerful imagination furnished the materials for these appeals, and his instinctive knowledge of the heart taught him how to use them with unfailing success."

Mr. Curran's ascendancy over the feelings of his countrymen was complete. He was one of the most popular orators of his day. " He spoke—and the nation listened. He put forth his thoughts in language that stirred the hearts of all. His imagination was fertile ; his language was striking and appropriate ; his pathos was refined and thrilling ; his whole appearance indicated earnestness and sincerity. In many respects, his eloquence was similar to that of his intimate associate and illustrious rival, Thomas Addis Emmet."

Judge Story's remarks on the character of Mr. Emmet apply with equal truth to Mr. Curran. " His mind was quick, vigorous, searching, and buoyant. He kindled as he spoke. There was a spontaneous combustion, as it were, not sparkling, but clear and glowing. His object seemed to be, not to excite wonder or surprise, to captivate by bright pictures, and varied images, and graceful groups, and start-ling apparitions ; but by earnest and close reasoning to con-vince the judgment, or to overwhelm the heart by awakening its most profound emotions. His own feelings were warm and easily touched. His sensibility was keen, and refined itself almost into a melting tenderness. His knowledge of the human heart was various and exact. He was easily captivated by a belief that his own cause was first. Hence his eloquence was most striking for its persuasiveness. He said what he felt, and he felt what he said. His command over the passions of others was an instantaneous and sympa-thetic action. The tones of his voice, when he touched on topics calling for deep feeling, were instinct with meaning. They were utterances of the soul as well as of the lips."

O'Connell.—Daniel O'Connell, one of the greatest forensic and political orators which Ireland has produced, was born August 6, 1775, in Kerry. He was of a long-lived family : his uncle Maurice, was ninety-seven at the time of his death, and another uncle, General O'Connell, died in the French service at the age of ninety-one. O'Connell was called to the Irish bar in Easter Term, 1798, and his industry and ability soon obtained him business.

The following sketch of O'Connell was written during his lifetime, by Sheil, for many years his warm personal friend, and political associate :

" His frame is tall, expanded, and muscular ; precisely

such as befits a man of the people—for the physical classes ever look with double confidence and affection upon a leader who represents in his own person the qualities upon which they rely. In his face he has been equally fortunate : it is extremely comely. The features are at once soft and manly ; the florid glow of health and a sanguine temperament are diffused over the whole countenance, which is national in the outline, and beaming with national emotion. The expression is open and confiding, and inviting confidence ; there is not a trace of malignity or wile— if there were, the bright and sweet blue eyes, the most kindly and honest-looking that can be conceived, would repel the imputation. These popular gifts of nature O'Connell has not neglected to set off by his external carriage and deportment, or, perhaps, I should rather say, that the same hand which has moulded the exterior has supersaturated the inner man with a fund of restless propensity, which it is quite beyond his power, as it is certainly beyond his inclination, to control. A large portion of this is necessarily expended upon his legal avocations ; but the labours of the most laborious of professions cannot tame him into repose : after deducting the daily drains of the study and the courts, there remains an ample residuum of animal spirits and ardour for occupation, which go to form a distinct, and, I might say, a predominant character—the political chieftain. The existence of this overweening vivacity is conspicuous in O'Connell's manners and movements, and being a popular, and more particularly a national quality, greatly recommends him to the Irish people. . . .

"As a professional man O'Connell is, perhaps, for general business, the most competent advocate at the Irish bar. Every requisite for a barrister of all-work is combined in him ; some in perfection—all in sufficiency. He is not understood to be a deep scientific lawyer. He is, what is far better for himself and his clients, an admirably practical one. He is a thorough adept in all the complicated and fantastic forms with which justice, like a Chinese monarch, insists that her votaries shall approach her. A suitor ad-

vancing toward her throne, cannot go through the evolutions
of the indispensable *Ko-tou* under a more skilful master of
the ceremonies.   In this department of his profession, the
knowledge of the practice of the courts, and in a perfect
familiarity with the general principles of law that are applicable to questions discussed in open court, O'Connell is on a
level with the most experienced of his competitors ; and with
few exceptions, perhaps with the single one of Mr. Plunket,
he surpasses them all in the vehement and pertinacious
talent with which he contends to the last for victory, or,
where victory is impossible, for an honourable retreat.   If
his mind had been duly disciplined, he would have been a
first-rate reasoner and a most formidable sophist.   He has all
the requisites from nature—singular clearness, promptitude,
and acuteness.   When occasion requires, he evinces a metaphysical subtlety of perception which nothing can elude.
The most slippery distinction that glides across him, he can
grasp and hold '*pressis manibus*,' until he pleases to set it
free.   But his argumentative powers lose much of their
effect from want of arrangement.   His thoughts have too
much of the impatience of conscious strength to submit to
an orderly disposition.   Instead of moving to the conflict in
compact array, they rush forward like a tumultuary insur-
gent mass, jostling and overturning one another in the confusion of the charge ; and, though finally beating down all
opposition by sheer strength and numbers, still reminding
us of the far greater things they might have achieved had
they been better drilled.

   " But, O'Connell has, by temperament, a disdain of everything that is methodical and sedate.   You can see this
running through his whole deportment in court.   I never
knew a learned personage who resorted so little to the ordinary tricks of his vocation.   As he sits waiting till his turn
comes to 'blaze away,' he appears totally exempt from the
usual throes and heavings of animo-gestation.   There is no
hermetically-sealing of the lips, as if nothing else could
restrain the fermentation within ; there are no traces of abstraction, as if the thoughts had left their home on a distant

voyage of discovery; no haughty swellings of the mind into
alto-relievos on the learned brow;—there is nothing of this
about O'Connell. On the contrary, his countenance and
manner impress you with the notion, that he looks forward
to the coming effort as a pastime in which he takes delight.
Instead of assuming the 'Sir Oracle,' he is all gayety and
good-humour, and seldom fails to disturb the gravity of the
proceedings by a series of disorderly jokes, for which he is
duly rebuked by his antagonists with a solemnity of indignation that provokes a repetition of the offence; but his
insubordinate levity is, for the most part, so redeemed by
his *imperturbable* good-temper, that even the judges, when
compelled to interfere and pronounce him out of order, are
generally shaking their sides as heartily as the most enraptured of his admirers in the galleries. In the midst, however, of this seeming carelessness, his mind is, in reality,
attending with the keenest vigilance to the subject-matter
of discussion; and the contrast is often quite amusing. . . .

"Mr. O'Connell is in particular request in jury cases. There
he is in his element. Next to the 'harp of his country,' an
Irish jury is the instrument on which he delights to play;
and no one better understands its qualities and compass. I
have already glanced at his versatility. It is here that it is
displayed. His powers as a *Nisi-Prius* advocate, consist
not so much in the perfection of any of the qualities necessary to the art of persuasion, as in the number of them he
has at command, and the skill with which he selects and
adapts them to the exigency of each particular case. He
has a thorough knowledge of human nature, as it prevails
in the class of men whom he has to mould to his purposes.
I know of no one that exhibits a more quick and accurate
perception of the essential peculiarities of the Irish character. It is not merely with reference to their passions that
he understands them, though here he is pre-eminently adroit.
He can cajole a dozen of miserable corporation-hacks into
the persuasion that the honour of their country is concen-
trated in their persons. His mere acting on such occasions
is admirable; no matter how base and stupid, and how

poisoned by political antipathy to himself, he may believe
them to be, he affects the most complimentary ignorance of
their real characters. He hides his scorn and contempt
under a look of unbounded reliance. He addresses them
with all the deference due to upright and high-minded
jurors. He talks to them of 'the eyes of all Europe,' and
the present gratitude of Ireland, and the residuary blessings
of posterity, with the most perfidious command of countenance. In short, by dint of unmerited commendations, he
belabours them into the belief that, after all, they have some
reputation to sustain, and sets them chuckling, with anticipated exultation, at the honours with which a verdict according to the evidence is to consecrate their names.

" But, in addition to the art of heating the passions of his
hearers to the malleable point, O'Connell manifests powers
of observation of another, and, for general purposes, a more
valuable kind. He knows that strange modification of humanity—the Irish mind,—not only in its moral, but in its
metaphysical peculiarities. Throw him upon any particular
class of men, and you would imagine that he must have
lived among them all his life, so intuitively does he accommodate his style of argument to their particular modes of
thinking and reasoning. He knows the exact quantity of
strict logic which they will bear or can comprehend. Hence
(where it serves his purpose), instead of trying to drag them
along with him, whether they will or no, by a chain of unbroken demonstration, he has the address to make them
imagine that their movements are directed solely by themselves. He pays their compliments the compliment of not
making things too clear. Familiar with the habitual tendencies of their minds, he contents himself with throwing off
rather materials for reasoning than elaborate reasonings—
mere fragments or seeds of thought, which, from his knowledge of the soil in which they drop, he confidently predicts
will shoot up and expand into precisely the conclusions that
he wants. This method has the disadvantage, as far as personally regards the speaker, of giving the character of more
than his usual looseness and irregularity to O'Connell's jury

speeches; but his client, for whom alone he labours, is a gainer by it—directly in the way I have been stating, and indirectly for this reason, that it keeps the jury in the dark as to the points of the case in which he feels he is weak. By abstaining from a show of rigorous demonstration, where all the argument is evidently upon his side, he excites no suspicion by keeping at an equal distance from topics which he could not venture to approach. This, of course, is not to be taken as O'Connell's invariable manner, for he has no invariable manner, but as a specimen of that dexterous accommodation of particular means to a particular end, from which his general powers as a *Nisi-Prius* advocate may be inferred. And so, too, of the tone in which he labours to extort a verdict; for though, when compelled by circumstances, he can be soft and soothing, as I have above described him, yet on other occasions, where it can be done with safety, he does not hesitate to apprise a jury, whose purity he suspects, of his real opinion of their merits, and indeed, not infrequently, in the roundest terms defies them to balance for an instant between their malignant prejudices and the clear and resistless justice of the case. .

"There is one, the most difficult, it is said, and certainly the most anxious and responsible part of an advocate's duties, in which O'Connell is without a rival at the Irish bar —I allude to his skill in conducting defences in the crown court. His ability in this branch of his profession illustrates one of those inconsistencies in his character to which I have already adverted. Though habitually so bold and sanguine, he is here a model of forethought and undeviating caution. In his most rapid cross-examinations he never puts a dangerous question. He presses a witness upon collateral facts, and beats him down by arguments and jokes and vociferations; but wisely presuming his client to be guilty until he has the good luck to escape conviction, he never affords the witness an opportunity of repeating his original narrative, and perhaps, by supplying an omitted item, of sealing the doom of the accused.

"O'Connell's ordinary style is vigorous and copious, but

incorrect. The want of compactness in his periods, however, I attribute chiefly to inattention. He has phrase in
abundance at command, is sensible of melody. Every now
and then he throws off sentences not only free from all
defect, but extremely felicitous specimens of diction. As
to his general powers of eloquence, he rarely fails in a case
admitting of emotion to make a deep impression upon a
jury; and in a popular assembly he is supreme. Still there
is much more of eloquence in his manner and topics than in
his conceptions. He unquestionably proves, by occasional
bursts, that the elements of oratory, and perhaps of the
highest order, are about him; but he has had too many
pressing demands of another kind to distract him from the
cultivation of this the rarest of all attainments, and accordingly I am not aware that any of his efforts, however able
and successful, have deserved, as examples of public speaking, to survive the occasion. His manner, though far from
graceful, is earnest and impressive. It has a steady and
natural warmth, without any of that snappish animation in
which gentlemen of the long robe are prone to indulge. His
voice is powerful, and the intonations full and graduated.
I understand that when he first appeared at the bar, his
accent at once betrayed his foreign education. To this day
there is a remaining dash of Foigardism in his pronunciation
of particular words; but on the whole he has brought himself, as far as delivery is concerned, to talk pretty much like
a British subject.'

Curran gives the following sketch of O'Connell: "The
inmate of the carriage was about five feet eleven and a half
inches high, and wore a portly, stout, hale, and agreeable
appearance. His shoulders were broad, and his legs stoutly
built, and, as he at that moment stood, one arm in his side-
pocket, the other thrust into a waistcoat, which was almost
completely unbuttoned from the heat of the day, he would
have made a good figure for the rapid but fine-finishing
pencil of Harlowe. His head was covered with a light fur
cap, which, partly thrown back, displayed the breadth of
forehead which I have never yet seen absent from real

talent. His eyes appeared to me at that instant to be between a light-blue and a grey colour. His face was pale and sallow, as if the turmoil of business, the shade of care, or the study of midnight had chased away the glow of health and youth. Around his mouth played a cast of sarcasm, which, to a quick eye, at once betrayed satire ; and it appeared as if the lips could be easily resolved into the *risus sardonicus.* His head was somewhat larger than that which a modern doctrine denominates the " medium size "; and it was well supported by a stout and well-foundationed pedestal, which was based on a breast, full, round, prominent, and capacious. The eye was shaded by a brow which I thought would be more congenial to sunshine than storm ; and the nose was neither Grecian nor Roman, but was large enough to admit him into the chosen band of that " immortal rebel " (as Lord Byron called Cromwell), who chose his body-guard with capacious lungs and noses, as affording greater capability of undergoing toil and hardship. Altogether he appeared to possess strong physical powers. . . .

" Were O'Connell addressing a mixed assembly where the lower orders predominated, I scarcely know any one who would have such a power of wielding the passions. He has a knack of speaking to a mob which I have never heard exceeded. His manner has at times the rhodomontade of Hunt; but he is infinitely superior, of course, to this well-known democrat in choice of language and power of expression. The same remark may apply, were I to draw any comparison between him and another well-known mob-speaker, Cobbett. Were he opposed to these two persons in any assembly of the people, he would infallibly prove himself the victor. A balcony outside a high window, and a large mob beneath him, is the very spot for O'Connell. There he would be best seen, and his powers and person best observed; but were he in the House of Commons, I do not think I am incorrect when I say that he would make little impression on the house, supposing he was heard with every prepossession in his favour. [It is needless to say that O'Connell afterward became one of the best speakers in the

House of Commons.]   His action wants grace and suavity—
qualities so eminently fascinating in an elegant and classical
speaker, but which perhaps are overlooked in an 'orator of
the people.'   The motions of his body are often sharp and
angular.   His arms swing about ungracefully ; and at times
the right hand plays slovenly with his watch-chain.

   " Though I shall not, perhaps, find many to agree with
me, yet I am free to confess that he does not appear to me
to possess that very rare gift—*genuine* satire.   He wants the
cultivated grace of language which his compeer, Sheil, possesses, and the brilliancy of metaphor.   .   .   .   His language
is often coarse, and seldom elegant.   Strong, fierce, and perhaps bold, it often is ; but vituperation and personality make
up too much of the *matériel.*   His voice is sometimes harsh
and dissonant ; and I could wish more of that round, full
mellow tone, which is essential to a good delivery, and which
captivates the ear.   'The voice is the key which unlocks the
heart,' says Madame Roland.   I believe it.   Let the reader
listen to the fine round voice of Lord Chief-Justice Bushe,
and then let him hear the sometimes grating tones of O'Connell, and he will soon perceive the difference.   The voice of
the latter much reminds me of the harsh thinness of Mr. J.
D. Latouche's (whose conversational tone by-the-by, is far
beyond his oratorical one); and yet the coolness and the
astuteness which the latter gentleman possesses in an argument, would be no bad substitute for the headlong impetuosity and violent sarcasm in which O'Connell sometimes
indulges.

   " As he cannot clothe his language in the same elegance as
Sheil, he consequently cannot give the same insinuation to
his discourses.   In this respect his contemporary has greatly
the advantage.   Sheil gives us the poetry of eloquence—
O'Connell gives us the prose.   The attempts of the latter at
wit are clumsy, while the former can bring both that and
metaphor to his aid, and he often uses them with much effect.

   " O'Connell, however, can attempt humour with effect,
and he has a peculiar tact in suiting this humour to the
Irish people.   I have not often seen a good exordium from

O'Connell an integral part of a discourse which it is extremely difficult to make ; and I think his perorations want grace, point, and force, and that which the Italians would denominate ' espressivo.' "

O'Connell was able at the bar. He was studious, industrious, and ambitious. His knowledge of human nature was profound. He had an athletic understanding, much sensibility, imagination, and great force of passion. His caution, coolness, and powers of labour were extraordinary.

While accounted one of the best advocates of his time, he was also in great repute in civil cases.

His knowledge of character, as has been said, was wonderful. He dissected the motives of parties and witnesses with inimitable skill. His combination of knowledge of the world and legal information, his aptness and ingenuity, his inexhaustible supply of humour, his torrents of ridicule, his zeal for his client, and untiring physical energies, rendered him a formidable antagonist at the bar.

On one occasion O'Connell defended a man named Hogan, charged with murder. A hat, which the prosecution insisted belonged to the prisoner, was found close to the body of the murdered man, and this was the principal ground for supposing that Hogan was the perpetrator of the horrible deed. The state of the body showed that the deceased had come to his death by violence, and O'Connell felt that the case for the prisoner required the utmost of his powers. The crown counsel made a strong point on the hat, which was produced in court. O'Connell cross-examined the neighbour of the prisoner who identified it.

" It is not different from other hats," said O'Connell.

" Well, seemingly, but I know the hat."

" Are you perfectly sure that this was the hat found near the body ? "

" Sartin sure."

O'Connell proceeded to inspect the *caubeen*, and turned up the lining as he looked inside.

" Was the prisoner's name, PAT HOGAN [he spelled each letter slowly], in it at the time you found it ? "

" 'T was, of course."

" You could not be mistaken ? "

" No, sir."

" And all you sware is as true as that ? "

" Quite."

" Then go off the table this minute ! " cried O'Connell, triumphantly. Addressing the Judge, he said : " My lord, there can be no conviction here. *There is no name in the hat !* "

The prisoner was at once acquitted.

O'Connell was retained in a Kerry case in which the venue or place of trial (it being in law a transitory action) was laid in Dublin. O'Connell was instructed to try and change the bench, so that the case might be tried in Tralee. This motion was opposed, and Mr. Scriven, the counsel opposed to O'Connell, happened to be a gentleman of a very plain, even forbidding countenance, and of high tory politics. He stated that he had no knowledge of Kerry, and had never been in that part of Ireland.

" Oh ! " replied O'Connell, " we 'll be very glad to welcome my learned friend, and show him the lovely lakes of Killarney."

" Yes," growled Mr. Scriven, " I suppose the bottom of them."

" No, no," retorted O'Connell ; " *I would not frighten the fish !* "

The criminal law in the days of O'Connell was much more favourable to criminals than now, when indictments may be amended. Many of O'Connell's triumphs in defending prisoners were owing to his skill in detecting flaws in the indictments. Thus a man was charged with stealing a cow ; the prosecutor swore that the prisoner was caught in the field where he left the cow to graze, but that the carcass was found in the next field. O'Connell submitted the indictment was bad, for when the cow was killed it was no longer a cow ; and if the prisoner was to be tried for stealing a dead animal, it should be so stated. He relied on the dictum of Judge Holroyd that an indictment for stealing a dead animal should state it was dead; for upon a general statement that a party stole the animal, it is to be intended that he stole it alive.[1]

The court, of course, held the indictment bad, and directed the jury to acquit the prisoner. It was said the cow in question was the fattest of a number of cows, and the night on which it was killed was dark as pitch. The grateful cattle-stealer came in the evening to O'Connell's lodgings, to thank him for having saved his life, for in those days cattle-stealing was punished by hanging.

" How did you contrive to select the fattest cow when the night was quite dark?" inquired O'Connell, wishing to increase his stock of useful knowledge.

" Well, your honour, you saved my life," replied the culprit, " so I will put you up to the dodge. When you go to steal a cow, and wish, av coorse, to take the best—for ' in for a penny in for a pound '—be sure to take her that 's on the outside. The wakest craturs always make for the ditch fer shelter, but the fat bastes are outside."

O'Connell died at Genoa, on the 15th of May, 1847. One of O'Connell's biographers says of him : " For several years he went the Munster Circuit, and gained the reputation of being the best criminal lawyer in Europe. He was called to the bar in the troubled year of 1798, and having relations in almost every county in Munster, he naturally selected the Munster Circuit. He had great personal and physical advantages—a fine, well-developed figure, clear blue eye, features expressive of keen intelligence, and a voice of great power, now rolling like tones of a grand organ, bursting forth in thunder, then dying away into deep pathos, rushing into rapid declamation, or, if engaged in denunciation, pouring forth epithets, strong, fierce, and stinging. He was well versed in the technicalities of his profession, and soon his large practice, and the necessary reading it involved, made him a first-rate advocate. Then he possessed a wonderful knowledge of his countrymen ; and who can compete with a Kerry man? He was irresistibly comic when a joke was

[1] Edwards's Case, Russell and Ryan, 497.

needed, and no man was more sarcastic when vituperation
was required. He was extremely vigilant, and never lost a
case through inattention. It was, I believe, at Tralee he
completely silenced an attorney who defied all gentle rebuke. This individual possessed a love for fighting not inferior to the Scotch terrier that lost his appetite when he
had ' naething to worrit.' His person, we are told, was indicative of his disposition. His face was bold, menacing,
and scornful in its expression. He had stamped upon him
the defiance and resolution of a pugilist. Upon either temple there stood erect a lock of hair which no brush could
smooth down. The locks looked like horns, and added to
the combative expression of his countenance. He was fiery
in his nature, excessively spirited, and ejaculated rather than
spoke to an audience ; his speeches consisting of a series of
short, hissing, spluttering sentences, by no means devoid of
talent of a certain kind.   .   .   .

"Upon the occasion referred to, this irrepressible attorney
gave O'Connell great annoyance. He interrupted O'Connell
several times ; he improperly addressed the witnesses as they
mounted to the witness-chair, and altogether was quite unruly. The counsel engaged with O'Connell tried to keep
him quiet ; more than once the judge severely rebuked his
improper interference—it was all in vain ; up he would shoot
like a Jack-in-a-box—hiss out some remark which was sure
to provoke O'Connell. At last, when O'Connell was pressing a hostile witness with a vital question, which the witness
was seeking to evade answering, and this individual again
interfered, as if for the purpose of annoyance, O'Connell,
losing all patience, scowling at this man with a stern countenance, shouted, in a voice of thunder, ' Sit down, you
audacious, snarling, pugnacious ramcat ! ' We are told the
words were no sooner uttered than every one in court saw
their truth. Judge, jury, counsel, attorneys, were convulsed
with laughter. The judge extremely enjoyed the happy
epithets, which completely suited the combative attorney,
who gasped with suppressed rage. He bore the *sobriquet* of
Ramcat for the rest of his natural life."

Canning.—George Canning, the brilliant English orator, was born in London, on the 11th day of April, 1770. After his graduation from Oxford, in the twenty-second year of his age, he was brought into parliament by William Pitt, who had heard of his oratorical ability and talents, and who was anxious to obtain the aid of such men as Canning to resist the tide of opposition.

Mr. Canning's subsequent conduct justified Pitt's choice. In Mr. Canning he found a warm friend, a faithful follower, and an ardent champion of his political measures, and after Mr. Pitt's death he paid many eloquent tributes to his memory, and before he himself died he requested that in death they should not be separated, and when he died he was buried in Westminster Abbey, at the foot of Mr. Pitt's tomb.

In January, 1794, Mr. Canning made his first speech in the House of Commons. His oratorical powers commanded respect, but did not cause that enthusiastic admiration which he afterward called forth when he reached the summit of his fame.

In his speech on Bank-Notes and Coin, in 1811, Mr. Canning said:

"Are bank-notes equivalent to the legal standard coin of the realm? This is the question which divides and agitates the public opinion. Says the right honourable gentleman, 'I will devise a mode of settling this question to the satisfaction of the public.' By advising a proclamation? No. By bringing a bill into parliament? No. By proposing to declare the joint opinion of both houses, or the separate opinion of one? No. By what process then? Why, simply by telling the disputants that they are, and have been all along, however unconsciously, agreed upon the subject of their variance; and gravely resolving for them, respectively, an unanimous opinion! This is the very judgment, I should imagine, which Milton ascribes to the venerable Anarch, whom he represents as adjusting the disputes of the conflicting element:

> 'Chaos umpire sits,
> And by decision more embroils the fray.'

" ' In public estimation,' says the right honourable gentleman's resolution, ' bank-notes and coin are equivalent.' Indeed! What, then, is become of all those persons who, for
the last six months, have been, by every outward and visible
indication, evincing, maintaining, and inculcating an opinion
diametrically opposite? Who wrote that multitude of
pamphlets, with the recollection of which one's head is still
dizzy? Does the honourable gentleman apprehend that his
arguments must have wrought their conversion?

"When Bonaparte, not long ago, was desirous of reconciling the nations under his dominion to the privations resulting from the exclusion of all colonial produce, he
published an edict, which commenced in something like the
following manner: ' Whereas, sugar made from beet-root,
or the maple-tree,' is infinitely preferable to that of the
sugar-cane,'—and he then proceeded to denounce penalties
against those who should persist in the use of the inferior
commodity. The denunciation might be more effectual than
the right honourable gentleman's resolution, but the preamble did not go near so far; for, though it asserted the
superiority of the maple and beet-root sugar, it rested that
assertion merely on the authority of the state, and did not
pretend to sanction it by ' public estimation.'

"When Galileo first promulgated the doctrine that the
earth turned round the sun, and that the sun remained
stationary in the centre of the universe, the holy fathers of
the Inquisition took alarm at so daring an innovation, and
forthwith declared the first of these propositions to be false
and heretical, and the other to be erroneous in point of faith.
The Holy Office ' pledged itself to believe ' that the earth
was stationary, and the sun movable. This pledge had
little effect in changing the natural course of things; the sun
and the earth continued, in spite of it, to preserve their
accustomed relations to each other, just as the coin and the
bank-note will, in spite of the right honourable gentleman's
resolution.

" Let us leave the evil, if it must be so, to the chance of
a gradual and noiseless correction. But let us not resolve,

as law, what is an incorrect and imperfect exposition of the
law. Let us not resolve, as fact, what is contradictory to
universal experience. Let us not expose ourselves to ridicule by resolving, as the opinions of the people, opinions
which the people do not, and which it is impossible they
should, entertain."

On Mr. Tierney's motion December 11, 1798, Mr. Canning said :

"The friendship of Holland! The independence of Spain!
Is there a man so besotted as to suppose that there is one
hour of peace with France preserved by either of these unhappy countries, that there is one syllable of friendship
uttered by them towards France, but what is extorted by
the immediate pressure, or by the dread and terror, of
French arms?—

> ' Mouth-honour, breath,
> Which the poor heart would fain refuse, but dare not ! '

Have the regenerated republic of Holland, the degraded
monarchy of Spain, such reason to rejoice in the protection
of the French republic, that they would voluntarily throw
themselves between her and any blow which might menace
her existence?

"But does the honourable gentleman intend his motion
as a motion for peace? If he really thinks this a moment for
opening a negotiation, why has he not the candour and manliness to say so? Mark, I entreat you, how delicately he
manages it ! He will not speak *to* France, but he would speak
at her. He will not propose—not he—that we should say to the
Directory, ' Will you make peace?' No, sir; we are merely
to say to ourselves, loud enough for the Directory to overhear us, 'I wish these French gentlemen would make an
overture to us.' Now, sir, does this save the dignity of the
country? or is it only a sneaking, shabby way of doing what,
if fit to be done at all, must, to have any serious effect, be
done openly, unequivocally, and directly? But I beg the
honourable gentleman's pardon ;—I misrepresent him ; I
certainly do. His motion does not amount even to so much

as I have stated. He begins further off. The soliloquy which he prompts us, by his motion, is no more than this: 'We must continue to make war against France, to be sure, —and we are sorry for it; but we will not do it as if we bore malice. We will not make an ill-natured, hostile kind of war any longer,—that we wont. And who knows but, if they should happen to overhear this resolution, as the Directory are good-natured at bottom, their hearts may soften and grow kind towards us—and then they will offer to make a peace!' And thus, sir, and thus only, is the motion a motion for peace.

" Since then, sir, this motion appears to me to be founded on no principle of policy or necessity; since, if it be intended for a censure on ministers, it is unjust,—if for a control, it is nugatory; as its tendency is to impair the power of prosecuting war with vigour, and to diminish the chance of negotiating peace with dignity, or concluding it with safety; as it contradicts, without reason, and without advantage, the established policy of our ancestors; as it must degrade in the eyes of the world the character of this country; as it must carry dismay and terror throughout Europe: and, above all, as it must administer consolation, and hope, and power, and confidence, to France,—I shall give it my most hearty and decided negative."

On Men and Measures, Mr. Canning expressed the following sentiments:

"If I am pushed to the wall, and forced to speak my opinion, I have no disguise nor reservation:—I do think that this is a time when the administration of the government ought to be in the ablest and fittest hands; I do not think the hands in which it is now placed answer to that description. I do not pretend to conceal in what quarter I think that fitness most eminently resides; I do not subscribe to the doctrines which have been advanced, that, in times like the present, the fitness of individuals for their political situation is no part of the consideration to which a member of parliament may fairly turn his attention. I know not a more solemn or important duty that a member of parliament can have to discharge, than by giving, at fit seasons, a free opinion upon the character and qualities of public men. Away with the cant of 'measures, not men!' the idle supposition that it is the harness, and not the horses, that draw the chariot along! No, sir; if the comparison must be made, if the distinction must be taken, men are everything, measures comparatively nothing. I speak, sir, of times of difficulty and danger; of times when systems are shaken, when precedents and general rules of conduct fail. Then it is that, not to this or that measure, however prudently devised, however blameless in execution,—but to the energy and character of individuals, a state must be indebted for its salvation. Then it is that kingdoms rise or fall in proportion as they are upheld, not by well-meant endeavours (laudable though they may be), but by commanding, overawing talents,—by able men.

"And what is the nature of the times in which we live? Look at France, and see what we have to cope with, and consider what has made her what she is. A man! You will tell me that she was great, and powerful, and formidable, before the days of Bonaparte's government; that he found in her great physical and moral resources; that he had but to turn them to account. True, and he did so. Compare the situation in which he found France with that to which he has raised her. I am no panegyrist of Bonaparte; but I cannot shut my eyes to the superiority of his talents, to the amazing ascendancy of his genius. Tell me not of his measures and his policy. It is his genius, his character, that keeps the world in awe. Sir, to meet, to check, to curb, to stand up against him, we want arms of the same kind. I am far from objecting to the large military establishments which are proposed to you. I vote for them with all my heart. But, for the purpose of coping with Bonaparte, one great, commanding spirit is worth them all."

On the Philosophy of Hatred, Mr. Canning made the following remarks:

"My honourable friend has expended abundant research and subtility upon this inquiry, and having resolved the phrase into its elements, in the crucible of his philosophical mind, has produced it to us purified and refined, to a degree that must command the admiration of all who take delight in metaphysical alchemy. My honourable and learned friend began by telling us, that, after all, hatred is no bad thing in itself. 'I hate a tory,' says my honourable friend— 'and another man hates a cat; but it does not follow that he would hunt down the cat, or I the tory.' Nay, so far from it—hatred, if it be properly managed, is, according to my honourable friend's theory, no bad preface to a rational esteem and affection. It prepares its votaries for a reconciliation of differences—for lying down with their most inveterate enemies, like the leopard and the kid, in the vision of the prophet. This dogma is a little startling, but it is not altogether without precedent. It is borrowed from a character in a play which is, I dare say, as great a favourite with my learned friend as it is with me: I mean, the comedy of *The Rivals;* in which Mrs. Malaprop, giving a lecture on the subject of marriage to her niece, (who is unreasonable enough to talk of liking, as a necessary preliminary to such an union,) says: 'What have you to do with your likings and your preferences, child? Depend upon it, it is safest to begin with a little aversion. I am sure I hated your poor dear uncle like a blackamoor, before we were married; and yet you know, my dear, what a good wife I made him.' Such is my learned friend's argument to a hair. But finding that this doctrine did not appear to go down with the house so glibly as he had expected, my honourable and learned friend presently changed his tack, and put forward a theory which, whether for novelty or for beauty, I pronounce to be incomparable, and, in short, as wanting nothing to recommend it but a slight foundation in truth. 'True philosophy,' says my honourable friend, 'will always continue to lead men to virtue by the instrumentality of their conflicting vices. The virtues, where more than one exist, may live harmoniously together; but the vices bear moral antipathy to one another, and therefore furnish, to the moral engineer, the power by which he can make each keep the other under control.'

Admirable! but, upon this doctrine, the poor man who has but one single vice must be in a very bad way. No fulcrum, no moral power for effecting his cure. Whereas his more fortunate neighbour, who has two or more vices in his composition, is in a fair way of becoming a very virtuous member of society. I wonder how my learned friend would like to have this doctrine introduced into his domestic establishment. For instance, suppose that I discharge a servant because he is addicted to liquor, I could not venture to recommend him to my honourable and learned friend. It might be the poor man's only fault, and therefore clearly incorrigible. · But if I had the good fortune to find out that he was also addicted to stealing, might I not, with a safe conscience, send him to my learned 'friend with a strong recommendation, saying, I send you a man whom I know to be a drunkard, but I am happy to assure you he is also a thief; you cannot do better than employ him; you will make his drunkenness counteract his thievery, and no doubt you will bring him out of the conflict a very moral personage?"

Mr. Canning dressed plainly, but in excellent taste. He seemed to partake, in most things, of the character of his eloquence: open and manly, with that consciousness of power which is consistent with modesty, and consequently simple and unpretentious.

In the prime of life, he was a handsome man, tall, well-formed, strong, and active.

He had a mild and expressive countenance indicative of intellect and firmness. His head was bald, his forehead lofty and broad, "his eyes reflective and at times lively."

Lord Brougham has given us the following estimate of his oratory:

"His declamation, though often powerful, always beautifully ornate, never deficient in admirable diction, was certainly not of the highest class. It wanted depth; it came from the mouth, not from the heart; and it tickled or even filled the ear rather than penetrated the bosom of the listener. The orator never seemed to forget himself and be absorbed in his theme; he was not carried away by his passions, and he carried not his audience along with him. An actor stood before us, a first-rate one, no doubt, but still an actor; and we never forgot that it was a representation we were witnessing, not a real scene. The Grecian artist was of the second class only, at whose fruit the *birds* pecked; while, on seeing Parrhasius's picture, *men* cried out to have the curtain drawn aside. Mr. Canning's declamation entertained his hearers, so artistically was it executed; but only an inexperienced critic could mistake it for the highest reach of rhetorical art. The truly great orator is he who carries away his hearer, or fixes his whole attention on the subject—with the subject fills his whole soul—than the subject, will suffer him to think of no other thing—of the subject's existence alone will let him be conscious, while the vehement inspiration lasts on his own mind which he communicates to his hearer—and will only suffer him to reflect on the admirable execution of what he has heard after the burst is over, the whirlwind has passed away, and the excited feelings have in the succeeding lull sunk into repose."

Brougham.—Henry Brougham was born in Edinburgh on the 19th day of September, 1779. He obtained the rudiments of his education at the High School in that city.

He entered the University of Edinburgh at the age of sixteen, and soon became noted for his attainments in mathematical studies. His knowledge of science was, indeed, extraordinary for one so young. Before he was seventeen years of age, his essay on the "Flection and Reflection of Light was inserted in the Edinburgh *Philosophical Transactions.*

After completing his college course, Mr. Brougham studied law, as a profession. He was soon called to the bar, and began his practice with great success in Edinburgh. He gave a large share of his time to history, politics, and literature, besides attending to his legal business.

Brougham was one of the most remarkable men of modern times. He was a lawyer, a statesman, an author, and a scientist.

Lord Campbell, who does not do him justice, in his *Lives of the Chancellors*, after reciting the fact that in parliament he spoke on every occasion and on every subject, says that in his opinion, "of all the sons of men, since the flood at least, Brougham had uttered the most words by far." It has been the fashion, of late, to speak slightingly of Brougham's ability as a lawyer, but his critics indulge in general observations, and fail to give particular instances which prove their statements to be true. He had, at the time of his elevation to the bench, a lucrative practice, and as he was employed in many of the most important causes which were tried while he was at the bar, and was opposed to the greatest advocates of his day, his inefficiency or shallowness would have soon been shown if he had not been a well read lawyer and an accomplished advocate. His stock of knowledge was simply prodigious. Campbell says: "If shut up in a tower without books, at the end of a year he would have produced (barring a few ludicrous blunders) a very tolerable *Encyclopædia.*"

If Brougham had known less of other subjects, his critics would have doubtless thought him a more profound lawyer. The world will not tolerate an assumption of universal knowledge, even if it is well founded.

In trivial causes Brougham could not rouse himself to take the interest he always manifested in important matters. In cases involving any great principle of civil or religious liberty, Brougham was perhaps the equal of any of his contemporaries. It is said that he usually rose, "in a calm and collected manner, enunciated a few sentences in a subdued tone, expressive of the sense he entertained of the importance of the task he had undertaken, and solicited the indulgence of the jury while he trespassed on their attention for a short time. He then proceeded, in slow accents and in measured sentences, to develop the generalities of the case, gradually rising in animation of manner and increasing in the loudness of his voice and the rapidity of his utterance, until he arrived at the most important parts of his subject. The first indication he usually gave of

12

having reached those points in his speech to which he meant
to apply all the energies of his mind, was that of pulling his
gown further up on his shoulders, and putting his tall, gaunt
figure into as erect and commanding a posture as he could
assume without endangering his equilibrium.   Then came
his vehement gesticulation—the rapid movement of his right
arm, with an occasional wafture of the left hand, and the
turning and twisting of his body into every variety of form.
His eye, which before was destitute of fire, and his features,
which were composed and placid as those of a marble statue,
were now pressed as auxiliaries into the service of his client.
His eye flashed with the fire of one whose bosom heaved
with tumultuous emotions, and the whole expression of his
face was that of a man whose mind was worked up to the
utmost intensity of feeling.   And this was really the case
with Brougham wherever the interests of his client were
identified with some great principle.

"To have seen him in some of these moods was truly a
spectacle worthy of name.   It was only on such occasions
that any accurate estimate could be formed of the vast resources of his mind.   He then poured from his lips strains
of the loftiest order of eloquence.   Idea followed idea,
principle succeeded principle, illustration accompanied illustration with a rapidity which was astonishing.   One moment
he was strictly argumentative—the next declamatory.   Now
he stated, in a winning language and in an engaging manner,
whatever was in favour of his client—then he inveighed in
the fiercest strains and in tones which resounded through
the place in which he spoke, against that client's opponent.
In such moments there would have been something absolutely withering to him against whom his denunciations were
directed in the very countenance of the orator, even had he
not uttered a word.   His dark, bristly hair stood on end, or
at least appeared to do so.   His brow was knit.   There was
a piercing stare and wildness in his eye; and his sallow complexion and haggard features altogether presented an aspect
which it was frightful to behold.   The jury on such occasions
often forgot the purpose for which they had been called into

court; they forgot the case in the advocate. He diverted
their minds from the subject-matter before them to himself.
They lost sight, for the moment, of the merits of the case
they were impanelled to decide, in their boundless admiration of the gigantic talents and brilliant eloquence of the
speaker.

"The jury often, in some of Brougham's happier efforts, forgot, for the time, that they were jurymen. In
the court not a breath was to be heard; all was still, save
his own powerful though somewhat harsh voice. In his
denunciations of witnesses whose testimony had made
against his client, he was terrible. And yet, notwithstanding all the vehemence of his manner, and the intensity of
passion into which he worked himself, his speeches, though
he sometimes purposely wandered from the principal point
before the court, were as well arranged, and every sentence
was as correctly constructed—that is to say, according to
the massy and involved style which he always preferred—
as they could have been had he been speaking in the calmest and most collected manner. He seldom displayed much
legal knowledge; and though he could on occasion argue
closely, he very rarely in his greatest efforts exhibited much
of argumentative acuteness. He disdained, indeed, when
he threw his whole soul into his speeches, to be fettered by
what he considered in such a case the trammels of law or
logic. Hence he could not so well be said to have gained
the great triumphs he so often achieved at the bar by convincing, as by confounding, the jury,—just as we often see a
person silenced rather than convinced by the dexterity of a
skilful disputant. Mr. Brougham may be said to have taken
the jury on such occasions by storm. He *compelled* them to
surrender themselves to him. His appeals to their feelings
and passions were so powerful, and his eloquence so dazzling,
that he deprived them for a time of the capacity of dis-
passionately examining and comparing the conflicting evidence on either side. It is true that the cool and careful
summing up of the judge followed his address; but the
impressions made on their minds by that address were not

yet effaced. Apparently they were all attention to the statements and observations of the judge, but in reality they scarcely knew what he was saying. The penetrating and expressive looks of Brougham still haunted their mental vision ; his vehement and impressive, though often uncouth, gesticulation was still before them ; the deep and varied in-tonations of his voice still rang in their ears ; and the matchless and overwhelming brilliance of his eloquence continued to exert its way in their minds to the exclusion of everything else. It is in this way alone that the fact can be accounted for, that he often extorted a verdict from the jury in favour of his client when it was equally notorious to the bench and every professional gentleman in court, that all the law and the argument were on the opposite side."

Lord Brougham sometimes prepared speeches which he delivered to juries, but ordinarily he is said to have spoken without having made the least previous preparation, farther than making himself acquainted with the facts in the case. No one had the ability to master the details of a case more perfectly than Brougham in the short time he usually de-voted to this task. He was resourceful, and he depended upon the inspiration of the moment for the language he used. But when he was to speak on an extraordinary occa-sion he prepared his speeches, or at least portions of them, with great care. He prepared the peroration of his speech before the House of Lords in Queen Caroline's case with such care that he re-wrote it no less than seventeen times before it suited him.

Sergeant Talfourd's estimate of Lord Brougham as an advocate is both interesting and instructive. He said of him : " Mr. Brougham may, at first, appear to form an ex-ception to the doctrines we have endeavoured to establish ; but, on attentive consideration, will be found their most striking example. True it is that this extraordinary man, who, without high birth, splendid fortune, or aristocratic connection, has, by mere intellectual power, become the parliamentary leader of the whigs of England, is at last be-ginning to succeed in the profession he has condescended to follow. But, stupendous as his abilities, and various as his acquisitions are, he has that one presiding faculty, imagination, which, as it concentrates all others, chiefly renders them unavailing for inferior uses. Mr. Brougham's powers are not thus united and rendered unwieldy and prodigious, but remain apart, and neither assist nor impede each other. The same speech, indeed, may give scope to several talents—to lucid narration, to brilliant wit, to irresistible reasoning, and even to heart-touching pathos ; but these will be found in parcels, not blended and interfused in one superhuman burst of passionate eloquence. The single power in which he excels all others is sarcasm, and his deepest inspiration—scorn. Hence he can awaken terror and shame far better than he can melt, agitate, and raise. Animated by this blasting spirit, he can ' bare the mean hearts' which 'lurk beneath ' a hundred 'stars,' and smite a majority of lordly persecutors into the dust ! His power is all directed to the practical and earthy. It is rather that of a giant than a magician ; of Briareus than of Prospero. He can do a hundred things well, and almost at once; but he cannot do the one highest thing : he cannot by a single touch reveal the hidden treasures of the soul, and astonish the world with truth and beauty unknown till disclosed at his bidding. Over his vast domain he ranges with amazing activity, and is a different man in each province which he occupies. He is not one but legion. At three in the morning he will make a reply in parliament, which shall blanch the cheeks and appal the hearts of his enemies; and at half past nine he will be found at his place in court, working out a case, in which a bill of five pounds is disputed, with all the plodding care of the most laborious junior. This multiplicity of avocation, and division of talent, suit the temper of his constitution and mind. Not only does he accomplish a greater variety of purposes than any other man—not only does he give anxious attention to every petty cause, while he is fighting a great political battle, and weighing the relative interests of nations—not only does he write an article for the *Edinburgh Review,* while contesting a county, and prepare complicated arguments on Scotch appeals by way of rest from his generous endeavours to educate a people ; but he does all this as if it were perfectly natural to him, in a manner so unpretending and quiet, that a stranger would think him a merry gentleman, who had nothing to do but to enjoy himself and fascinate others. The fire which burns in the tough fibres of his intellect does not quicken his pulse, or kindle his blood to more than a genial warmth. He, therefore, is one man in the senate, another in the study, another in a committee room, and another in a petty cause ; and consequently is never above the work which he has to perform. His powers are all as distinct and as ready for use as those of the most accomplished of Old Bailey practitioners. His most remarkable faculty, taken singly, the power of sarcasm, can be understood even by a Lancaster jury. And yet, though worthy to rank with statesmen before whom Erskine sank into insignificance, and though following his profession with zeal and perseverance almost unequalled, he has hardly been able to conquer the impediment of that splendid reputation, which to any other man must have been fatal."

Brougham was greatly interested in the question of Law Reform, and the following extract from his speech on that subject affords a good specimen of his manner:

"You saw the greatest warrior of the age,—conqueror of Italy, humbler of Germany, terror of the North,—saw him account all his matchless victories poor compared with the triumph you are now in a condition to win,—saw him contemn the fickleness of fortune, while in despite of her he could pronounce his memorable boast : 'I shall go down to posterity with the Code in my hand.' You have vanquished him in the field ; strive now to rival him in the sacred arts of peace ! Outstrip him as lawyer whom in arms you overcame ! The lustre of the Regency will be eclipsed by the more solid and enduring splendour of the Reign. It was the boast of Augustus,—it formed part of the glare in which the perfidies of his earlier years were lost,—that he found Rome of brick and left it of marble. But how much nobler will be the Sovereign's boast when he shall have it to say, that he found law dear and left it cheap; found it a sealed book, left it a living letter; found it the patrimony of the rich, left it the inheritance of the poor; found it the two-edged sword of craft and oppression, left it the staff of honesty and the shield of innocence!"

That he could be severe when tried, the following quota- tion from his speech in the House of Lords on the Emancipation of Negro Apprentices, will afford ample evidence:

"I have read with astonishment and I repel with scorn the insinuation that I had acted the part of an advocate, and that some of my statements were collected to serve a cause. How dares any man so to accuse me? How dares anyone, skulking under a fictitious name, to launch his slanderous imputations from his covert? I come forward in my own person. I make the charge in the face of day. I drag the criminal to trial. I openly call down justice on his head. I defy his attacks. I defy his defenders. I challenge investigation. How dares any concealed adversary to charge me as an advocate speaking from a brief, and misrepresenting the facts to serve a purpose? But the absurdity of this charge even outstrips its malice."

Lord Brougham had a just appreciation of the character of Washington, and paid him the following tribute:

"How grateful the relief which the friend of mankind, the lover of virtue, experiences, when, turning from the contemplation of such a character as Napoleon, his eye rests upon the greatest man of our own or any age,—the only man upon whom an epithet, so thoughtlessly lavished by men, to foster the crimes of their worst enemies, may be innocently and justly bestowed!

"This eminent person is presented to our observation, clothed in attributes as modest, as unpretending, as little calculated to strike or to astonish, as if he had passed unknown through some secluded region of private life. But he had a judgment sure and sound; a steadiness of mind which never suffered any passion, or even any feeling, to ruffle its calm; a strength of understanding which worked rather than forced its way through all obstacles,—removing or avoiding rather than overleaping them.

"If these things, joined to the most absolute self-denial, the most habitual and exclusive devotion to principle, can constitute a great character, without either quickness of apprehension, remarkable resources of information, or inventive powers, or any brilliant quality that might dazzle the vulgar,—then surely Washington was the greatest man that ever lived in this world, uninspired by divine wisdom, and unsustained by supernatural virtue.

"His courage, whether in battle or in council, was as perfect as might be expected from this pure and steady temper of soul. A perfect just man, with a thoroughly firm resolution never to be misled by others, any more than to be by others overawed; never to be seduced or betrayed, or hurried away by his own weaknesses or self-delusions, any more than by other men's arts; nor ever to be disheartened by the most complicated difficulties, any more than to be spoilt on the giddy heights of fortune;—such was this great man.

"Great he was, pre-eminently great, whether we regard him sustaining alone the whole weight of campaigns all but desperate, or gloriously terminating a just warfare by his resources and his courage; presiding over the jarring elements of his political council, alike deaf to the storms of all extremes, or directing the formation of a new government for a great people, the first time that so vast an experiment had ever been tried by man; or, finally, retiring from the supreme power to which his virtue had raised him over the nation he had created, and whose destinies he had guided as long as his aid was required,—retiring with the veneration of all parties, of all nations, of all mankind, in order that the rights of men might be conserved, and that his example never might be appealed to by vulgar tyrants.

"This is the consummate glory of Washington: a triumphant warrior where the most sanguine had a right to despair; a successful ruler in all the difficulties of a course wholly untried; but a warrior, whose sword only left its sheath when the first law of our nature commanded it to be drawn ; and a ruler who, having tasted of supreme power, gently and unostentatiously desired that the cup might pass from him, nor would suffer more to wet his lips than the most solemn and sacred duty to his country and his God required !

" To his latest breath did this great patriot maintain the noble character of a captain the patron of peace, and a statesman the friend of justice. Dying, he bequeathed to his heirs the sword which he had worn in the war for liberty, and charged them ' never to take it from the scabbard but in self-defence, or in defence of their country and her freedom ' ; and commanded them that, 'when it should thus be drawn, they should never sheathe it, nor ever give it up, but prefer falling with it in their hands to the relinquishment thereof,'—words, the majesty and simple eloquence of which are not surpassed in the oratory of Athens and Rome.

" It will be the duty of the historian and the sage, in all ages, to let no occasion pass of commemorating this illustrious man ; and, until time shall be no more, will a test of the progress which our race has made in wisdom and in virtue be derived from the veneration paid to the immortal name of Washington ! "

In 1830, speaking of the fate of the Reformer, Lord Brougham said :

"I have heard it said that, when one lifts up his voice against things that are, and wishes for a change, he is raising a clamour against existing institutions, a clamour against our venerable establishments, a clamour against the law of the land ; but this is no clamour against the one or the other, —it is a clamour against the abuse of them all. It is a clamour raised against the grievances that are felt. Mr. Burke, who was no friend to popular excitement,—who was no ready tool of agitation, no hot-headed enemy of existing establishments, no under-valuer of the wisdom of our ancestors, no scoffer against institutions as they are,—has said, and it deserves to be fixed, in letters of gold, over the hall

of every assembly which calls itself a legislative body :
'WHERE THERE IS ABUSE, THERE OUGHT TO BE CLAMOUR;
BECAUSE IT IS BETTER TO HAVE OUR SLUMBER BROKEN BY
THE FIRE-BELL, THAN TO PERISH, AMIDST THE FLAMES, IN
OUR BED.' I have been told, by some who have little objection to the clamour, that I am a timid and a mock reformer ; and by others, if I go on firmly and steadily, and
do not allow myself to be driven aside by either one outcry
or another, and care for neither, that it is a rash and dangerous innovation which I propound ; and that I am taking, for
the subject of my reckless experiments, things which are the
objects of all men's veneration. I disregard the one as much
as I disregard the other of these charges.

> ' False honour charms, and lying slander scares,
>   . Whom, but the false and faulty ? '

"It has been the lot of all men, in all ages, who have aspired
at the honour of guiding, instructing, or mending mankind, to
have their paths beset by every persecution from adversaries,
by every misconstruction from friends ; no quarter from the
one,—no charitable construction from the other! To be
misconstrued, misrepresented, borne down, till it was in
vain to bear down any longer, has been their fate. But
truth will survive, and calumny has its day. I say that, if
this be the fate of the reformer,—if he be the object of misrepresentation,—may not an inference be drawn favourable
to myself ? Taunted by the enemies of reform as being too
rash, by the over-zealous friends of reform as being too slow
or too cold, there is every reason for presuming that I have
chosen the right course. A reformer must proceed steadily
in his career; not misled, on the one hand, by panegyric,
nor discouraged by slander, on the other. He wants no
praise. I would rather say, ' Woe to him when all men
speak well of him ! ' I shall go on in the course which I
have laid down for myself; pursuing the footsteps of those
who have gone before us, who have left us their instructions
and success,—their instructions to guide our walk, and their
success to cheer our spirits."

Lord Brougham made the following comparison between the conqueror and the schoolmaster:

"But there is nothing which the adversaries of improvement are more wont to make themselves merry with than what is termed the '*march of intellect*'; and here I will confess, that I think, as far as the phrase goes, they are in the right. It is a very absurd, because a very incorrect expression. It is little calculated to describe the operation in question. It does not picture an image at all resembling the proceedings of the true friends of mankind. It much more resembles the progress of the enemy to all improvement. The conqueror moves in a march. He stalks onward with the 'pride, pomp, and circumstance of war'— banners flying—shouts rending the air—guns thundering —and martial music pealing, to drown the shrieks of the wounded and the lamentations for the slain.

"Not thus the schoolmaster, in his peaceful vocation. He meditates and prepares in secret the plans which are to bless mankind; he slowly gathers round him those who are to further their execution; he quietly, though firmly, advances in his humble path, labouring steadily, but calmly, till he has opened to the light all the recesses of ignorance, and torn up by the roots the weeds of vice. His is a progress not to be compared with anything like a march; but it leads to a far more brilliant triumph, and to laurels more imperishable than the destroyer of his species, the scourge of the world, ever won.

"Such men—men deserving the glorious title of Teachers of Mankind—I have found, labouring conscientiously, though, perhaps, obscurely, in their blessed vocation, wherever I have gone. I have found them, and shared their fellowship, among the daring, the ambitious, the ardent, the indomitably active French; I have found them among the persevering, resolute, industrious Swiss; I have found them among the laborious, the warm-hearted, the enthusiastic Germans; I have found them among the high-minded, but enslaved Italians; and in our own country, God be thanked! their numbers everywhere abound, and are every day increasing.'

" Their calling is high and holy ; their fame is the property of nations; their renown will fill the earth in after ages, in proportion as it sounds not far off in their own times.   Each one of those great teachers of the world, possessing his soul in peace, performs his appointed course ; awaits in patience the fulfilment of the promises ; and, resting from his labours, bequeaths his memory to the generation whom his works have blessed, and sleeps under the humble but not inglorious epitaph, commemorating ' one in whom mankind lost a friend, and no man got rid of an enemy.' "

Lord Brougham died at Cannes, upon the 7th day of May, 1868, in the ninetieth year of his age.

Nothwithstanding his faults, and they were many, Lord Brougham had, at bottom, genuine warmth of heart and good nature.   He was an affectionate son, and a devoted parent and brother, and keenly sensible to the sufferings and sympathies of the poor.

Erskine.—Lord Erskine was, undoubtedly, one of the most remarkable advocates of any age or country, and the history of his life cannot be too carefully studied by the student of forensic oratory.   His successes at the bar were not accidental.   They were due to his own indefatigable energy and industry.   His competitors for fame had been, almost without a notable exception, educated at the public schools and English universities, and while they were being instructed by the ablest teachers which could be found, he was laying in the stores of knowledge which were, after-wards, so useful to him, on board a man-of-war, or in the barracks of a marching regiment.   To an ordinary aspirant for intellectual distinction, the difficulties which confronted Erskine would have proved insurmountable, but instead of being discouraged by them, Erskine was only stimulated to greater exertion.

In a small and poorly furnished room in an upper "flat " of a very high house in Edinburgh, Thomas Erskine was born, on the 10th day of January, 1750.   He was the youngest son of Henry David, tenth Earl of Buchan, and counted in his line many distinguished ancestors.   One of

these distinguished ancestors, whose name it is not necessary to mention, having wasted the ample patrimony which
once belonged to the family, Henry David was left with a
very large family and a very small income, amounting to
about £200 a year. His wife was a most extraordinary
woman, equally eminent for piety, and good common-sense.
She was the daughter of Sir James Stewart of Goodtrees in
the county of Mid-Lothian. Erskine's parents were compelled to abandon an old castle standing on their small
estate, for the wretched habitation in Edinburgh which has
been mentioned, where their poverty would not be so conspicuous and their children better educated. Erskine's
mother taught her children to read, and instilled at an early
age, into their minds, the doctrines of the Presbyterian faith.

That buoyancy of spirit and sprightliness of fancy which
he was noted for in after life was discovered in his youth.
He attended for some years the High School of Edinburgh,
eating, with considerable fortitude, his oatmeal porridge for
breakfast, and *soup maigre*, called " kail," for dinner. Notwithstanding the economy practised, Edinburgh was found
too expensive for the slender finances of the family, and in
1762 they removed to St. Andrew's in Fife, where house
rent was lower, and educational advantages not inferior.

At this time Erskine is said to have been " of quick parts
and retentive memory, rather idly inclined, but capable of
great application,—full of fun and frolic,—and ever the
favourite of his master and his playmates."

One of his letters, written at this period to his eldest
brother, Lord Cardross, who was then at Edinburgh, is of
interest :

" My Dear Brother :

" I received your letter, and it gave me great joy to hear
that you were in health, which I hope will always continue.
I am in my second month at the dancing-school. I have
learned *shantrews* and the single *hornpipe*, and am just now
learning the *double-hornpipe*. There is a pretty large Norway
ship in the harbour ; the captain took Harry and me into the

cabin, and entertained us with French claret, Danish biscuit, and smoked salmon; and the captain was up in the town seeing Papa to-day. He is to sail on Friday, because the stream is great. Yesterday I saw Captain Sutherland exercise his party of Highlanders, which I liked very well to see. In the time of the vacation Harry and me writes themes, reads Livy and French, with Mr. Douglas, between ten and eleven. Papa made me a present of a ring-dial, which I am very fond of, for it tells me what o'clock it is very exactly. You bid me, in your last letter, write to you when I had nothing better to do: but, I assure you, I think I cannot employ myself better than to write to you, which I shall take care to do very often. Adieu, my dear brother, and believe me, with great affection.

"Yours,   T. E."

This note is said to have been very neatly written with lines. His grammatical errors in speaking of himself and brother Harry cannot fairly be complained of, for in fraternal affection they were one.

At the grammar school of St. Andrew's, under Mr. Hackett, whose scholarly attainments were not equal to his zeal as a teacher, Erskine attained only a moderate proficiency in Latin, and learned little of Greek beyond the alphabet. But happily for him he was taught to compose in English, as if it had been a foreign tongue, and being extremely fond of books, he read many volumes of English poems, plays, voyages, and travels. It is said that he was never matriculated in the university of St. Andrew's, but in the session of 1762–3 he attended the mathematical and natural philosophy classes, taught by professors of considerable eminence, and from them he imbibed the small portion of science of which he could ever boast.

Early in life he began to consider, with a seriousness which could not have been expected from one of his years and gay disposition, how he was to make his way in the world. His parents were so poor that they could do nothing better than send him to sea as a midshipman, but being desirous of improving his mind, and of being bred to one of the learned professions, and having a particular aversion to the sea service, he asked that·a commission in the army might be procured for him. After a correspondence between his father and some of his friends, this point seems to have been conceded to him. Believing this, he wrote the following letter to Lady Stewart, his aunt, which does him great credit for the noble aspirations which it discloses:

" Nov. 4, 1763.

" MY DEAR AUNT :

" I received your letter about a week ago with great pleasure, and thank you for the good advice contained in it, which I hope by God's assistance I shall be able to follow.

" I am extremely glad that you approve of my not going to sea. I shall tell my reasons for it.

" In the first place, Papa got a letter from Commodore Dennis, laying before him the disadvantages at present of the sea service, on account of the many half-pay officers on the list, which all behoved to be promoted before me ; he also acquainted Papa that he was sorry that if I did go he could be of no service to me, as he had at present no command, and had no prospects of getting any : he at the same time did not forget the advantages of it ; but when I weighed the two in scales, the disadvantages prevailed, and still more when added to my own objections, which are as follows ;— In the first place, I could have no opportunity of improving my learning, whereas in the army the regiment is often quartered in places where I might have all advantages. I assure you I could by no means put up without improving myself in my studies, for I can be as happy as the day is long with them, and would ten times rather be at St. Andrew's, attending the classes there, and even those which I was at last year, viz. natural philosophy and mathematics (both of which I am extremely fond of), than at the most beautiful place in the world, with all manner of diversions and amusements. My second objection is, that I would be obliged to keep company with a most abandoned set of people that would corrupt my morals; whereas in the army, though they be bad enough, yet I should have the advantage of choosing my company when I pleased, without being constrained to any particular set;—and thirdly, I think my constitution would not agree with it, as I am very subject to rheumatic pains. [Then follow some little family matters and messages.]

"I shall now conclude with assuring you that I am, my dear aunt,

"Your most affectionate nephew,

THOMAS ERSKINE."

The arrangements, however, were not consummated, because a commission could not be obtained without purchase, and the original intention of sending him to sea was resumed. In the following year he was put under Sir David Lindsay, a nephew of Lord Mansfield, and an experienced sea captain in command of a man-of-war. Young Erskine being supplied with a blue jacket, cocked hat, and sword, embarked at Leith, after taking an affecting leave of his family whom he tenderly loved. He never saw his father again alive, but his talented mother survived to encourage and animate him for many years, and to witness the commencement of his brilliant career.

Erskine left his native land discouraged and dispirited, but when he next revisited it, he had achieved the reputation of the greatest forensic orator that England ever produced, and he was besides an ex-Chancellor, a Peer, and a Knight of the Thistle.

Erskine remained in the *Tartar*, the name of the ship in which he sailed, four years, cruising about in the West Indies and on the coast of America. One of his biographers says: "The life of a midshipman has been much improved of late years by superior comforts, and by anxious attention to professional and general education while he is afloat; but in Erskine's time the interior of a man-of-war presented nearly the same spectacle which we find described in so lively a manner in *Roderic Random*,—and the young officers were taught little else than to smoke tobacco, to drink flip, and to eat salmagundy. Erskine, however,—never neglecting his professional duties,—contrived often to escape from the dark and noisy abode of the midshipmen to a quiet corner of the vessel, where he amused and improved himself in reading books which he had brought on board with him—picking up some new volume at every port he visited. He was soon reconciled to his situation—and his elastic spirits and gay temperament made him not only take a deep interest in the new scenes which presented themselves to him, but to be pleased with all he saw. . . . He was so warm an admirer of the open, straightforward, light-hearted, brave though thoughtless and indiscreet character of English seamen, that he would not hear of any plan for rendering them more sober and orderly on shore, saying, 'You may scour an old coin to make it legible ; but if you go on scouring, it will be no coin at all.' "

Erskine did not remain long enough in the service to obtain the commission of lieutenant, thought he acted for some time in that capacity, through the friendship of his commander. In this capacity Erskine made the voyage home to England, believing that his promotion would be confirmed, but on arriving at Portsmouth the ship was paid off, and he was told at the Admiralty that, on account of the great number of midshipmen who had served longer than himself, he could not yet have a lieutenant's commission, and there was no telling when he might be advanced.

At eighteen Erskine entered the army, as an ensign in the Royals, or 1st regiment of foot. On the 1st day of September, 1768, he obtained his commission. Most of the officers of the corps were his countrymen. In this regiment he remained seven years, and was not raised to a lieutenancy until the 21st of April 1773. On the 29th day of March, 1770, he was married to a lady of good family, but as poor as himself. His wife was a daughter of Daniel Moore, Esq., M.P. for Marlow. His marriage was a most happy one. She became the fond parent of numerous children, and lived till within a few months of the time when Erskine was made

13

Lord Chancellor, having richly deserved the tribute which he had inscribed on her monument, that she was the most faithful and the most affectionate of women.

While at Minorca where his regiment had been ordered, Erskine read many of the old English authors, and it is said that " he was more familiar with Shakespeare than almost any man of his age, and Milton he had nearly by heart. The noble speeches in *Paradise Lost* may be deemed as good a substitute as could have been discovered by the future orator for the immortal originals in the Greek models. The works of Dryden and Pope were next read, and committed to memory, with the avidity of a refined and well formed taste."

Even the hours of garrison life, when not devoted to his favorite authors, were not wholly wasted, for Erskine acquired among his brother officers a knowledge of the world, a frank and gallant bearing, and that self-respect for which he was afterwards noted, and which greatly contributed to his success at the bar. When he returned to England with his regiment in 1772, he mixed much with the men of letters of the metropolis, and even tried authorship himself. Said Jeremy Bentham: " I saw a letter written by Erskine when he was an officer in the army—it complained of insufficient pay. That letter was characterized by something different from common writing, though it had many defects of which he afterwards got rid. When the Fragment was published Erskine sought me out. I met him sometimes [said the gossiping octogenarian] at Dr. Burton's. He was so shabbily dressed as to be quite remarkable. He was astonished when I told him I did not mean to practice. I remember his calling on me, and not finding me at home, he wrote his name with chalk on my door."

Erskine also attended the assemblies of Mrs. Montagu, frequented by Dr. Johnson, Sir Joshua Reynolds, the Bishop of St. Asaph, Dr. Burney and many other celebrated men of that day.

Boswell in his *Life of Johnson*, says:

" On Monday, April 6, I dined with him at Sir Alexander Macdonald's where was a young officer in the Regimentals of the Scots Royals, who talked with vivacity, fluency, and precision, so uncommon that he attracted particular attention. He proved to be the Honourable Thomas Erskine, youngest brother to the Earl of Buchan, who has since risen into such brilliant reputation at the Bar in Westminster Hall." It appears that, after the example of David and Goliath, the ensign ventured to combat the literary giant. A controversy arising about the respective merits of the authors of *Tom Jones* and *Clarissa*, and Johnson pronouncing Fielding to be " a blockhead " and " a barren rascal," and saying " there is more knowledge of the heart in one letter of Richardson's than in all Tom Jones,"—Erskine objected : " Surely, sir, Richardson is very tedious." He received only this answer, which, I think, is not very satisfactory : " Why, sir, if you were to read Richardson for the story, your impatience would be so much fretted that you would hang yourself ! But you must read him for the sentiment, and consider the story as only giving occasion to the sentiment."

Various conjectures have been made by Erskine's biographers as to the motives which led him to adopt the legal profession. While little is certainly known it is highly probable that he was encouraged to study law by his mother, a woman of uncommon acquirements and great penetration, and by Lord Mansfield, but that the idea of becoming a lawyer first suggested itself to his own mind there can hardly be room for doubt after reading the following extract from his biography by Lord Campbell :

" Having been some time the senior ensign in his regiment, on the 21st of April, 1773, he was raised to be a lieutenant. The pleasure of promotion speedily passed away, and he became more and more dissatisfied with his situation and his prospects. He was again moving about with his regiment from one country town to another. This mode of life had lost the charm of novelty which once made it endurable, and was now become doubly irksome from his having to keep a wife and family in a barrack-room, or in lodgings, the expense of which he could ill afford. He had

no money to purchase higher commissions, and he might
wait many years before he gained another step by seniority.
Notwithstanding some disputes with the American colonies,
there seemed a probability of long and profound peace. He
thought himself fit for better things than the wretched
existence that seemed lengthening before him—to be spent
in listlessness and penury.   •

"It so happened that in the midst of these lucubrations,
the assizes were held in the town in which he was quartered.
The lounging lieutenant entering the court in his regimentals, Lord Mansfield, the presiding judge, inquired who he
was, and, finding that this was the youngest son of the late
Earl of Buchan, who had sailed with his nephew, invited
him to sit on the bench by his side, explained to him the
nature of the proceedings that were going forward, and
showed him the utmost civility. Erskine heard a cause of
considerable interest tried, in which the counsel were supposed to display great eloquence. Never undervaluing his
own powers, he thought within himself, that he could have
made a better speech than any of them, on whichever side
he had been retained. Yet these gentlemen were the leaders
of the circuit, each making a larger income than the pay of
all the officers of the Royals put together,—with the chance
of being raised by their own abilities to the Woolsack. The
thought then suddenly struck him that it might not even
now be too late for him to study the law and be called to
the bar. He saw the difficulties in his way, but there was
no effort which he was not willing to make, no privation to
which he would not cheerfully submit, that he might rescue
himself from his present forlorn condition,—that he might
have a chance of gaining intellectual distinction,—above all,
that he might make a decent provision for his family. Lord
Mansfield invited him to dinner, and being greatly struck
with his conversation and pleased with his manners, detained
him till late in the evening. When the rest of the company
had withdrawn, the Lieutenant, who ever showed great
moral courage, in consideration of the connection between
the Murrays and the Erskines, and the venerable Earl's

great condescension and kindness, disclosed to him his plan of a change of profession, with a modest statement of his reasons. Lord Mansfield by no means discouraged him; but advised him before he took a step so serious to consult his near relations."

He accordingly wrote to his mother, and she, justly appreciating the energy and perseverance as well as the enthusiasm belonging to his nature, strongly advised him to quit the army for the law. His brothers did not oppose,—although Henry warned him of the thorny and uphill path on which he was entering. His resolution was now firmly taken, and he came up to London to carry it into effect. It was not till the spring of the following year that financial difficulties were so far removed as to render it possible for him to make the experiment. Craddock says: "At the house of Admiral Walsingham I first met with Erskine and Sheridan, and it was there the scheme was laid that the former should exchange the army for the law"; but he had not been made acquainted with the previous consultations, or he would have said that the plan was there *matured*, and the arrangements made for his legal studies and his call to the bar. "The period of five years was then required by all the inns of court for a student to be on the books of the society before he could be called—with this proviso, that it was reduced to three years for those who had the degree of M. A. from either of the universities of Oxford or Cambridge. It was resolved that Erskine should immediately be at an inn of court; that he should likewise be matriculated at Cambridge, and take a degree there; that he should keep his academical and law terms concurrently, and that as soon as it could be managed, he should become a pupil to some eminent pleader, so as to be well grounded in the technicalities of his craft." On the 26th day of April, 1775, Erskine was admitted a student of Lincoln's Inn, and on the 13th of January, 1776, he was matriculated at Cambridge, and entered on the books of Trinity College, as a Gentleman Commoner. He took the honorary degree of A. M. in June, 1778. It is said that while still a student at Cambridge he kept his

terms at Lincoln's Inn. He had not yet actually quitted
the army, but had succeeded in getting six months' leave of
absence.   During Easter he created a sensation in the dining hall by appearing with a student's black gown over the
scarlet regimentals of the Royals, probably not having a
decent suit of plain clothes to put on.   By the sale of his
lieutenancy he obtained a small supply of cash on the 19th
day of September, 1775.

Erskine became a pupil in the chambers of Mr. Justice
Buller, the great *Nisi Prius* judge, who said his idea of
heaven was a place where he could hear causes all day and
play whist all night, and when Buller was made a judge, he
entered himself with another famous lawyer, George Wood,
afterwards made Baron of the Exchequer, with whom he
continued for nearly a year after his admission to the bar.

Erskine never became a profound lawyer, but he had a
logical understanding, and it is said that by severe application he made considerable progress, and that he was able
thoroughly to understand and appreciate, in all its bearings,
any question of law which he had occasion to consider—and
to collect and arrange the authorities upon it, and to argue
it lucidly and scientifically.   For three years after his retirement from the army Erskine was often in need of money.
Although practising the strictest economy, and the most
rigid self-denial, he often found it difficult to provide the
necessaries of life for his family.   But like most men of
ability and determination, he had carefully calculated the
chances of success and failure, and had made up his mind to
do his best, and leave the consequences to Infinite wisdom.

Poverty too often presents such a discouraging front to
struggling genius as to paralyse every effort, but, fortunately,
Erskine was endowed by nature with a sanguine temperament and an indomitable will which enabled him to overcome all obstacles.

It is, unhappily, but too true, that men of genius are often
doomed to languish in obscurity at the bar for many years
after their admission ; but by a fortunate accident Erskine
was soon given an opportunity to demonstrate his capacity

to the bench and bar of London. Be it said to the credit
of the legal profession both in this country and in England,
that the leaders of the bar are rarely guilty of the unutterable meanness of attempting to prevent the rise of a talented
lawyer, but, on the contrary, are only too glad to assist him,
in every possible way, to tread the thorny and difficult path
which he finds before him.

Captain Baillie, the lieutenant-governor of Greenwich Hospital, and a veteran seaman of excellent character, having
discovered gross abuses in the administration of that charity,
presented various petitions to the directors, governors, and
at last, to the lords of the admiralty, asking for enquiry and
redress. No attention being paid to his petitions and remonstrances, he published a statement of the case and distributed
copies amongst the general-governors of the hospital. In
this paper he animadverted with great severity upon the introduction of landsmen into the hospital, charging that they
had been placed there, at the instance, and to serve the election purposes, of Lord Sandwich, the First Lord of the
Admiralty. The circulation of the pamphlet caused the
suspension of Captain Baillie soon after its publication, and
certain officers who had been censured applied to the Court
of King's Bench for a criminal information. Erskine's successful connection with the case has been graphically told
by himself, as follows :

"I had scarcely a shilling in my pocket when I got my
first retainer. It was sent me by Captain Baillie of the navy,
who held an office at the Board of Greenwich Hospital, and
I was to show cause at the Michaelmas term against a rule
that had been obtained in the preceding term, calling on him
to show cause why a criminal information reflecting on Lord
Sandwich's conduct as governor of that charity should not
be filed against him. I had met, during the long vacation,
this Captain Baillie at a friend's table, and after dinner I expressed myself with some warmth, probably with some eloquence, on the corruption of Lord Sandwich as First Lord
of the Admiralty, and then adverted to the scandalous practices imputed to him with regard to Greenwich Hospital.

Baillie nudged the person who sat next to him, and asked who I was. Being told that I had just been called to the bar, and had formerly been in the navy, Baillie exclaimed with an oath: 'Then I 'll have him for my counsel!' I trudged down to Westminster Hall when I got the brief, and being the junior of five, who would be heard before me, never dreamt that the court would hear me at all. The argument came on. Dunning, Bearcroft, Wallace, Bower, Hargave, were all heard at considerable length, and I was to follow. Hargrave was long-winded and tired the court. It was a bad omen; but, as my good fortune would have it, he was afflicted with the· strangury, and was obliged to retire once or twice in the course of his argument. This protracted the cause so long, that Lord Mansfield, when he had finished, said that the remaining counsel should be heard the next morning. This was exactly what I wished. I had the whole night to arrange in my chambers what I had to say in court the next morning, and I took the court with their faculties awake and freshened, succeeded quite to my own satisfaction (sometimes the surest proof that you have satisfied others), and, as I marched along the Hall after the rising of the judges, the attorneys flocked around me with their retainers. I have since flourished, but I have always blessed God for the providential strangury of poor Hargrave."

In his defence of Baillie, Erskine displayed great courage in attacking those who came forward as prosecutors. He paid his respects to one of them as follows: " In this enumeration of delinquents, the Reverend Mr. —— looks round, as if he thought I had forgotten him. He is mistaken; I well remember him: but his infamy is worn threadbare. Mr. Murphy has already treated him with that ridicule which his folly, and Mr. Peckham with that invective which his wickedness, deserve. I shall therefore forbear to taint the ear of the court further with his name,—a name which would bring dishonour upon his country and its religion, if human nature were not happily compelled to bear the greater part of the disgrace, and to share it amongst mankind."

Erskine's attack upon the prosecutors of Baillie was occasionally varied by pathetic references to the saddest features of the case : " This simple and honest tribute was the signal for all that followed. The leader of these unfortunate people was turned out of office ; and the affidavit of Charles Smith is filed in court, which, I thank my God, I have not been able to read without tears ; how, indeed, could any man, when he swears that for this cause alone his place was taken from him : that he received his dismission when languishing with sickness in the infirmary, the consequence of which was, that his unfortunate wife and several of his helpless innocent children died in want and misery, *the woman actually expiring at the gates of the hospital.* That such wretches should escape chains and a dungeon is a reproach to humanity and to all order and government ; but that they should become *prosecutors* is a degree of effrontery that would not be believed by any man who did not accustom himself to observe the shameless scenes which the monstrous age we live in is every day producing."

Erskine then commenced his famous attack upon Lord Sandwich, when Lord Mansfield observed that Lord Sandwich was not before the court. The dauntless advocate said : " I know that he is not before the court, but for that very reason *I will bring him before the court.* He has placed these men in the front of the battle, in hopes to escape under their shelter ; but I will not join in battle with *them* : *their* vices, though screwed up to the highest pitch of human depravity, are not of dignity enough to vindicate the combat with *me.* I assert that the Earl of Sandwich has but one road to escape out of this business without pollution and disgrace ; and that is by publicly disavowing the acts of the prosecutors, and restoring Captain Baillie to his command. If he does this then his offence will be no more than the too common one of having suffered his own personal interests to prevail over his public duty, in placing his voters in the hospital. But if, on the contrary, he continues to protect the prosecutors, in spite of the evidence of their guilt, which has excited the abhorrence of the numerous audience that crowd this court ; if he keeps this injured man suspended, or dares

to turn that suspension into a removal, I shall then not scruple to declare him an accomplice in their guilt, a shameless
oppressor, a disgrace to his rank, and a traitor to his trust."

The panegyric, delivered in an impassioned manner, upon
his client's conduct, was fine. He said : " *Fine and imprisonment !* The man deserves a palace instead of a prison, who
prevents the palace built by the bounty of his country from
being converted into a dungeon, and who sacrifices his own
security to the interests of humanity and virtue."

After his successful defence of Baillie, Erskine found
himself at once in full business, strange to say, for, notwithstanding the brilliancy of his first forensic effort, the
attorneys, who are proverbially cold and cautious, and dis-
trustful of displays of eloquence, flocked around him with
briefs and fees, large and small. His sudden success has
always been justly regarded as phenomenal by the wisest
members of the legal profession both in England and in this
country, and the younger members of the legal profession
are constantly warned, by their judicious friends, that no
matter how great their attainments they cannot hope to
succeed as Erskine did. Erskine himself could not perform
such an oratorical feat at this day, because of the change
which the style of oratory has undergone, because our
courts are more prosaic, and more business-like in their
methods than they were in his time.

In the year 1779, Erskine was employed, at the instance
of Dunning, himself one of the brightest ornaments of the
English bar, to assist in the defence of Admiral Keppel.
The charges brought against Keppel were of incapacity and
misconduct in the battle of Ushant, with the French fleet
under the command of Count d'Orvilliers. Erskine was not
permitted to address the court-martial in defence of Keppel,
but he wrote the speech which the Admiral read himself.
The whole speech is worthy of a careful perusal, on account
of the tact displayed in its composition. Erskine always
had a happy knack of placing the accusers of his clients on
the defensive, and in this case he made the Admiral say :
" I could almost wish, in pity to my accuser, that appear-

ances were not so strong against him. The trial has left my accuser without excuse, and he now cuts that sort of figure which I trust in God all accusers of innocence will ever exhibit! As to this Court, I entreat you, gentlemen, who compose it, to recollect that you sit here as a Court of honour, as well as a Court of justice ; and I now stand before you not merely to save my life, but for a purpose of infinitely greater moment—to clear my fame. My conscience is perfectly clear—I have no secret machination, no dark contrivance, to answer for. My heart does not reproach me. As to my enemies, I would not wish the greatest enemy I have in the world to be afflicted with so heavy a punishment as my accuser's conscience."

When Keppel's speech was finished the Hall resounded with shouts of acclamation, and he was fully and honorably acquitted by an unanimous verdict.

Keppel gratefully presented to Erskine one thousand pounds. Lord Campbell relates a curious incident, in Erskine's career, which, if true, is illustrative of the old saying that, "Coming events cast their shadows before." He says: "This spring, he (Erskine) joined the Home Circuit, where his fame had preceded him, and he was immediately in full employment. Riding over a blasted heath between Lewes and Guildford with his friend William Adam, afterwards Lord Chief Commissioner of the Jury Court in Scotland, (whether from some supernatural communication, or the workings of his own fancy, I know not,) he exclaimed after a long silence : ' Willie, the time will come when I will be invested with the robes of Lord Chancellor, and the Star of the Thistle shall blaze on my bosom ! ' "

Truly, there are more things in heaven and earth than are dreamed of in our philosophies!

Of Erskine's defence of Lord George Gordon for high treason, Lord Campbell says : " Regularly trained to the profession of the law—having practised thirty years at the bar—having been Attorney-General above seven years—having been present at many trials for high treason, and having conducted several myself,—I again peruse, with

increased astonishment and delight, the speech delivered
on this occasion by him who had recently thrown aside
the scarlet uniform of a subaltern in the army—which he
had substituted for the blue jacket of a midshipman, thrust
upon him while he was a school-boy. Here I find not only
wonderful acuteness, powerful reasoning, enthusiastic zeal,
and burning eloquence, but the most masterly view ever
given of the English law of high treason,—the foundation
of all our liberties."

The reader will remember that Lord George Gordon was
"President of the Protestant Association," and that at
the head of forty thousand persons he had proceeded to
the House of Commons to present a petition against the
repeal of certain penal laws against the Catholics. While
the petitioners were assembled, certain riots took place
which Lord George Gordon was accused, erroneously, as
the jury found, of having incited.

Erskine's speech in this case—in the humble opinion of
the writer—was one of the best that he ever delivered, and
the student of forensic eloquence cannot read it too often.

It is difficult to give a just notion of this speech by
quotations from it. After an eloquent and judicious
exordium, Erskine proceeded to lay down the law of high
treason. Then, with great tact, he referred to the destruction of the house of the presiding judge, Lord Mansfield,
during these riots—drawing from it an argument in favor
of Gordon :

"Can any man living believe that Lord George Gordon
could possibly have excited the mob to destroy the house of
that great and venerable magistrate, who has presided so long
in this great and high tribunal, that the oldest of us do not
remember him with any other impression than the awful form
and figure of justice,—a magistrate who had always been the
friend of the Protestant dissenters against the ill-timed jealousies of the establishment ;—his countryman, too, and, without adverting to the partiality not unjustly imputed to men
of that country, a man of whom any country might be proud ?
No, gentlemen, it is not credible that a man of noble birth

and liberal education (unless agitated by the most implac-
able personal resentment, which is not imputed to the prisoner) could possibly consent to this burning of the house of
Lord Mansfield."

Lord Campbell says again : " He then reviewed the whole
of the evidence, varying his tone from mild explanation to
furious invective,—always equally skilful and impressive,
and ever carrying the sympathies of his hearers along with
him in the most daring flights of his eloquence. Now was
witnessed the single instance recorded in our judicial annals,
of an advocate in a court of justice introducing an oath by
the sacred name of the Divinity,—and it was introduced not
only without any violation of taste, or offence to pious ears,
but with the thrilling sensations of religious rapture, caught
from the lips of the man who, as if by inspiration, uttered
the awful sound. Arguing upon the construction of certain
words attributed to Lord George Gordon, he exclaimed :
' But this I will say, that he must be a *ruffian*, and not a lawyer, who would dare to tell an English jury that ambiguous
words, hemmed closely between others not only innocent,
but meritorious, are to be adopted to constitute guilt by rejecting both introduction and sequel.' "

Lord Erskine's defence of the Dean of St. Asaph against
the charge of publishing a seditious libel added greatly to
his fame as a forensic orator, and to his reputation as a man
of courage. By defying the threat of committal, made by
Justice Buller, he did his profession an excellent service.
For it must never be forgotten that the members of the Bar
have rights which the Bench has no right to violate. His
manner to the court was not lacking in courtesy, and neither
in manner nor matter did he commit a contempt. The Justice himself saw that he had committed an error, and did not
dare carry his threat of committal into execution, because he
knew that, if he did so, public opinion, which then was, and
is now, omnipotent, would not have sustained him.

Lack of space alone prevents the insertion of extracts from
Erskine's able speech in this case. It seemed for a while that
the abominable doctrine, that *libel or no libel* was a pure

question of law, would be forever established, but, thank
Heaven! it led instead to the entire subversion of that fatal
doctrine, and the establishment of the liberty of the press
under the guardianship of English juries. The consequences
of this decision so alarmed the public mind that Mr. Fox's
Libel Bill was called for, which declared the rights of jurors
in cases of libel, and while in the opinion of eminent lawyers
that great constitutional triumph is largely due to the exertions of the illustrious Lord Camden, who fought half a century in the cause, had it not been for Erskine's magnificent
speech in defence of the Dean of St. Asaph, the Star Chamber
might have been re-established in England.

Charles James Fox had such great admiration for this
speech that he repeatedly declared that he thought it the
finest argument in the English language.

The writer, however, is inclined to believe that Erskine's
speech in Stockdale's case is even superior to the speech in
defence of Gordon, and that it is in many respects the most
eloquent speech ever delivered at the English bar.

While the impeachment of Warren Hastings was pending,
after the articles drawn up against him by Mr. Burke, in
greatly exaggerated language, had appeared in nearly every
prominent newspaper in England, together with the abusive
speeches of the eloquent managers at the bar of the House
of Lords, Mr. Logan, a minister of the Church of Scotland,
wrote a pamphlet in his defence which contained many severe
accusations against the prosecution.   Mr. Logan said, among
other things, that the charges against Mr. Hastings, " originated from misrepresentation and falsehood "; the House .
of Commons, for making one of these charges, was compared
to "a tribunal of inquisition rather than a Court of Parliament." These and many other charges were made, one of
the severest of which was, that the impeachment was " carried
on from motives of personal animosity, not from regard to
public justice."   But Mr. Logan entered into the merits of
the case, and the arguments he used were very strong, and
he seemed sincerely desirous of establishing the innocence
of Mr. Hastings.

Mr. Stockdale, a bookseller of good character, in Piccadilly, published this pamphlet in the way of his trade. At the instance of some of the managers of the impeachment, a criminal information for libel was filed by the Attorney-General against Mr. Stockdale, and the case came on to be tried before Lord Kenyon and a special jury in the Court of King's Bench, at Westminster. No lawyer should try a case of libel without first reading, over and over again, Erskine's speech in this case. The principles which the eloquent advocate laid down were clearly and forcibly stated, illustrated, and established, and a well connected chain of reasoning will be found to run through it.

In order to win the compassion of the jury for Mr. Hastings, Erskine gives the following picturesque description of Westminster Hall:

"There the most august and striking spectacle was daily exhibited which the world ever witnessed. A vast stage of justice was erected, awful from its high authority, splendid from its illustrious dignity, venerable from the learning and wisdom of its judges, captivating and affecting from the mighty concourse of all ranks and conditions which daily flocked into it as into a theatre of pleasure. Here, when the whole public mind was at once awed and softened to the impression of every human affection, there appeared day after day, one after another, men of the most powerful and exalted talents, eclipsing by their accusing eloquence the most boasted harangues of antiquity, rousing the pride of national resentment by the boldest invectives against broken faith and violated treaties, and shaking the bosom with alternate pity and horror by the most glowing pictures of insulted nature and humanity;—ever animated and energetic, from the love of fame, which is the inherent passion of genius; firm and indefatigable, from a strong prepossession of the justice of their cause. Gentlemen, when the author sat down to write the book now before you, all this terrible, unceasing, exhaustless artillery of warm zeal, matchless vigour of understanding, consuming and devouring eloquence, united with the highest dignity, was daily, and with-

out prospect of conclusion, pouring forth upon one private
unprotected man who was bound to hear it in the face of
the whole people of England with reverential submission and
silence.   I do not complain of this as I did of the publication
of the charges, because it is what the law allowed and
sanctioned in the course of a public trial; but when it is
remembered that we are not angels, but weak, fallible men;
and that even the noble judges of that high tribunal are
clothed beneath their ermines with the common infirmities
of man's nature, it will bring us all to a proper temper for
considering the book itself which will in a few moments be laid
before you.   But, first, let me once more remind you, that it
was under all these circumstances, and amidst the blaze of
passion and prejudice which the scene I have been endeavouring faintly to describe to you might be supposed likely
to produce, that the author sat down to compose the book
which is prosecuted to-day as a libel."

After paying that gentleman some compliments, Erskine
thus states the motive by which he had been actuated, and
the issue which the jury had to try: " He felt for the situation of a fellow-citizen, exposed to a trial which, whether
right or wrong, is undoubtedly a severe one ;—a trial certainly not confined to a few criminal acts, like those we are
accustomed to, but comprehending the transactions of a
whole life, and the complicated policies of numerous and
distant nations ;—a trial which had neither visible limits to
its duration, bounds to its expense, nor circumscribed compass for the grasp of memory or understanding ;—a trial
which had, therefore, broke loose from the common form of
decision, and had become the universal topic of discussion
in the world, superseding not only every grave pursuit, but
every fashionable dissipation.   Gentlemen, the question you
have, therefore, to try upon all this matter, is extremely
simple.   It is neither more nor less than this.   At a time
when the charges against Mr. Hastings were, by the implied
consent of the Commons, in every hand and on every table,—
when by their harangues the lightning of eloquence was
incessantly consuming him, and flashing in the eyes of the

public,—when every man was, with perfect impunity, saying, and writing, and publishing just what he pleased of the supposed plunderer and devastator of nations,—would it have been criminal *in Mr. Hastings himself* to have reminded the public that he was a native of this free land, entitled to the common protection of her justice, and that he had a defence in his turn to offer them, the outlines of which he implored them, in the meantime, to receive as an antidote to the unlimited and unpunished poison in circulation against him? THIS is without colour or exaggeration, the true question you are to decide. Gentlemen, I tremble with indignation to be driven to put such a question in England. Shall it be endured that a subject of this country—instead of being arraigned and tried for some single act in her ordinary courts, where the accusation, as soon at least as it is made public, is followed in a few hours by the decision—may be impeached by the House of Commons for the transactions of twenty years—that the accusation shall spread as wide as the region of letters—that the accused shall stand, day after day and year after year, as a spectacle before the public, which shall be kept in a perpetual state of inflammation against him,—yet that he shall not, without the severest penalties, be permitted to say anything to the judgment of mankind in his defence? If this be law (which it is for you to-day to decide), such a man has no trial;—that great hall, built by our fathers for English justice, is no longer a court, but an altar,—and an Englishman, instead of being judged in it *by God and his country, is a victim and a sacrifice.*

"If you think, gentlemen, that the common duty of self-preservation in the accused himself, which nature writes as a law in the hearts of even savages and brutes, is nevertheless too high a privilege to be enjoyed by an impeached and suffering Englishman; or if you think it beyond the offices of humanity and justice, when brought home to the hand of a brother, or a friend, you will say so by your verdict of *guilty.* The decision will then be *yours,* and the consolation *mine,*—that I laboured to avert it. A very small part of the

14

misery which will follow from it is likely to light upon *me ;*
the rest will be divided amongst *yourselves and your children.*" ·

" Having," says Campbell, in commenting upon this
speech, " at great length and with unflagging spirit, examined
the contents of the pamphlet, and commented on the passage
charged in the information to be libellous,—with the view
of ingratiating Mr. Hastings defender with the jury, he proceeds to take a favourable view of the conduct of Mr. Hastings
himself,—not venturing to defend all his acts, but palliating
them so as to make them be forgiven, or even applauded,
from the circumstances in which he was placed, and the
instructions which he had received." Then follows the finest
passage to be found in ancient or modern oratory—for
imagery, for passion, for pathos, for variety and beauty of
cadence, for the concealment of art, for effect in gaining the
object of the orator: ' If your dependencies have been
secured, and their interests promoted, I am driven in the
defence of my client to remark, that it is mad and preposterous to bring to the standard of justice and humanity the
exercise of a dominion founded upon violence and terror. It
may and must be true that Mr. Hastings has repeatedly
offended against the rights and privileges of Asiatic government, if he was the faithful deputy of a power which
could not maintain itself for an hour without trampling upon
both ;—he may and must have offended against the laws of
God and nature, if he was the faithful viceroy of an empire
wrested in blood from the people to whom God and nature
had given it ;—he may and must have preserved that unjust
dominion over timorous and abject nations by a terrifying,
overbearing, and insulting superiority, if he was the faithful
administrator of your government, which, having no rest in
consent and affection, no foundation in similarity of interests,
nor support from any one principle that cements men together in society, could only be upheld by alternate strata-
gem and force. The unhappy people in India, feeble and
effeminate as they are from the softness of their climate,
and subdued and broken as they have been by the knavery
and strength of civilization, still occasionally start up in all

the vigour and intelligence of insulted nature :—to be governed at all, they must be governed with a rod of iron ; and our empire in the East would have been long since lost to Great Britain, if civil and military prowess had not united their efforts to support an authority, which Heaven never gave, by means which it can never sanction.

"Gentlemen, I think I can observe that you are touched with this way of considering the subject ; and I can account for it. I have not been considering it through the cold medium of books, but have been speaking of man and his nature, and of human dominion, from what I have seen of them myself, amongst reluctant nations submitting to our authority. I know what they feel, and how such feelings can alone be repressed. I have heard them in my youth from a naked savage in the indignant character of a Prince surrounded by his subjects, addressing the governor of a British colony, holding a bundle of sticks as the notes of his unlettered eloquence. 'Who is it,' said the jealous ruler over the desert encroached upon by the restless foot of English adventurers, 'who is it that causes this river to rise in the high mountains, and to empty itself into the ocean? Who is it that causes to blow the loud winds of winter, and that calms them again in the summer? Who is it that rears up the shade of those lofty forests, and blasts them with the quick lightning at his pleasure? The same Being who gave to you a country on the other side of the waters, and gave ours to us: and by this title we will defend it,' said the warrior, throwing down his tomahawk upon the ground, and raising the war-sound of his nation. These are the feelings of subjugated men all round the globe ; and, depend upon · it, nothing but fear will control where it is vain to look for affection.

" But under the pressure of such constant difficulties, so dangerous to national honour, it might be better, perhaps, to think of effectually securing it altogether, by recalling our troops and our merchants, and abandoning our Asiatic empire. Until this be done, neither religion nor philosophy can be pressed very far into the aid of reformation and punishment. If England, from a lust of ambition and dominion, will insist on maintaining despotic rule over distant and hostile nations, beyond all comparison more numerous and extended than herself, and gives commission to her viceroys to govern them, with no other instructions than to preserve them, and to secure permanently their revenues,—with what colour or consistency of reason can she place herself in the moral chair, and affect to be shocked at the execution of her own orders, adverting to the exact measure of wickedness and injustice necessary to their execution, and complaining only of the *excess* as the immorality ;—considering her authority as a dispensation for breaking the commands of God, and the breach of them as only punishable when contrary to the ordinances of man? Such a proceeding, gentlemen, begets serious reflections. It would be, perhaps, better for the masters and servants of all such governments to join in supplication that the great Author of violated humanity may not confound them together in one common judgment."

The author will conclude the extracts from this speech by giving Erskine's reasons for allowing that license of expression into which writers, warm with their subjects, may be betrayed :

" From minds thus subdued by the terrors of punishment there could issue no works of genius to expand the empire of human reason, nor any masterly compositions on the nature of government, by the help of which the great commonwealths of mankind have founded their establishments ; much less any of those useful applications of them to critical conjunctures, by which, from time to time, our own constitution, by the exertions of patriot citizens, has been brought back to its standard. Under such terrors all the great lights of science and civilisation must be extinguished ; for men cannot communicate their free thoughts to one another with the lash held over their heads. It is the nature of everything that is great and useful, both in the animate and inanimate world, to be wild and irregular ; and we must be contented to take them with the alloys which belong to them, or live without them. Genius breaks from the fetters of criticism; but its wanderings are sanctioned by its majesty and wisdom when it advances in its path; subject it to the critic and you tame it into dulness. Mighty rivers break down their banks in winter, sweeping to death the flocks which are fattened on the soil that they fertilise in the summer. Tempests occasionally shake our dwellings and dissipate our commerce; but they scourge before them the lazy elements which without them would stagnate into pestilence. In like manner, Liberty herself, the last and best gift of God to his creatures, must be taken just as she is. You might pare her down into bashful regularity, and shape her into a perfect model of severe scrupulous law, but she then would be Liberty no longer; and you must be content to die under the lash of this inexorable justice, which you had exchanged for the banners of freedom."

Lord Abinger, himself one of the greatest forensic orators of his day, heard this speech delivered, and he said that the effect on the audience was wholly unexampled: " that they all actually believed that they saw before them the Indian chief with his bundle of sticks and his tomahawk,—their breasts thrilled with the notes of his unlettered eloquence,— and they thought they heard him raise the war-sound of his nation." The jury returned a verdict of "Not Guilty."

Erskine's defence of Hardy is worthy of study by the advocate. Thomas Hardy was one of twelve persons indicted by the Grand Jury of Middlesex for treason. The prisoner had belonged to two societies having for their professed object Parliamentary Reform—the "Corresponding Society," and the "Society for Constitutional Information," —having branch societies in most of the largest cities of Great Britain. Hardy and his associates were indicted for attempting to bring about a revolution, the government seeking to make them responsible for the acts and utterances of indiscreet and zealous members of the societies mentioned. Hardy was tried alone. In this case Erskine gave the death-blow to the doctrine of constructive treason.

The trial of Hardy began on the 28th day of October,

1794, at the Old Bailey, before Lord Chief-Justice Eyre,
and several other judges, sitting under a special commission
of oyer and terminer. Sir John Scott, then Attorney-General, spoke nine hours in opening the case for the prosecution. It is said that no other trial for high treason in
England had ever occupied more than a day, but at midnight the case was only fairly begun. The principal evidence
for the Crown consisted, principally, of a large number of
speeches made, and resolutions passed, during several
months at London, Edinburgh, Norwich, and other places,
when the prisoner had been hundreds of miles away,—of
toasts at public dinners,—and of certain publications issued
by the societies mentioned, or which the societies had approved, or which had been written by members of the
society.

Erskine, ever ready to win the favour of the jury, expressed his willingness that they should separate and go to
their several homes, saying : " I am willing that they shall be
as free as air, with the single restriction that they will not
suffer themselves to be approached in the way of influence ;
and the gentlemen will not think it much that this should
be required, *considering the very peculiar nature of this case.*

An objection being made to their separation, it was agreed
that they should pass the night in a large room in a tavern
nearby, in the care of four bailiffs.

Erskine, however, with the great sagacity for which he was
justly noted, saw that the address of the Attorney-General
had affected them deeply, and he determined to give them
something else to think about. So before they retired he
said :

" My Lord, all this immense body of papers has been
seized, and been a long time in the hands of the officers of
the Crown. We applied to see them, but were refused—we
applied to the Privy Council, and were refused—we were referred to your Lordship, because they knew that your Lordship could not grant such a request. Here we are, therefore,
with all these papers tumbled upon our hands, without the
least opportunity of examining them ; and yet from this load

of papers, which the Attorney-General took nine hours to read, the act of compassing the King's death is to be collected. I trust your Lordships will be disposed to indulge me—indeed I shall expect, in justice to the prisoner, that I may have an opportunity, before I address the jury upon this mass of evidence, to know what is in it. I declare, upon my honour, as far as relates to myself and my friend who is assigned as counsel for the prisoner, we have no design whatever to trespass upon the patience of the Court, and your Lordships may have seen to-day how little of your time we have consumed. We have no desire upon earth but to do our best to save the man for whom your Lordships have assigned us to be counsel, and whom we believe to be innocent."

Erskine found it necessary to keep in check, without insulting, Lord Chief-Justice Eyre, who had leaned toward the prosecution from the beginning. While a witness for the Crown was writhing under a severe cross-examination, and prevaricating so as to revolt the jury, the Chief-Justice, interrupting, took him out of the counsel's hands, and in a coaxing manner repeated the question to him. *Erskine:* "I am entitled to have the benefit of this gentleman's deportment, if your Lordship will just indulge me for one moment." *L. C.-J. Eyre:* "Give him fair play." *Erskine:* "He has certainly had fair play. I wish *we* had as fair play,—but that is not addressed to the Court." *Attorney-General:* "Whom do you mean?" *Erskine:* "I say the prisoner has a right to fair play." *Garrow:* "But you declared that it was not said to the Court." *Erskine:* "I am not to be called to order by the Bar."

The following dialogue exhibits in a striking manner Erskine's occasional method of treating the Court and his adversary. A witness who pretended to relate, from notes he said he had taken of the proceedings of a reform society, having been asked for a date, and having answered that he *thought* it was about such a time. Erskine exclaimed: "None of your thinking when you have the paper in your hands!" *Witness:* "I have not a memorandum of the date." *Erskine:*

"What date have you taken, good Mr. Spy?" *Witness:* "I do not think on such an occasion being a spy is any disgrace." *Eyre, C.-J.:* "These observations are more proper when you come to address the jury." *Attorney-General:* "Really that is not a proper way to examine witnesses. Lord Holt held strong language to such sort of an address from a counsel to a witness who avowed himself a spy." *Erskine:* "I am sure I shall always pay that attention to the Court which is due from me; but I am not to be told by the Attorney-General how I am to examine a witness!" *Attorney-General:* "I thought you had not heard his Lordship." *Erskine:* "I am much obliged to his Lordship for the admonition he gave me. I heard his Lordship, and I heard you,—whom I should not have heard."

The celebrated Horne Tooke, in his copy of Hardy's trial, at the end of Erskine's argument, made the following note: "*This speech will live forever.*"

Erskine spoke seven hours in Hardy's case, and it is said that the time seemed too short to his hearers. For constitutional learning, wit, pathos, eloquence, and powerful reasoning, this speech must be considered one of Erskine's best efforts. The author will only give a few extracts from it, which should be studied as a whole by the reader. The speech was well calculated to win the affection and convince the understanding of the jury, as well as to excite their pity and indignation.

After having eulogised the constitution of England, and having referred to the state of affairs produced by the French Revolution, Erskine said:

"Let not *him* suffer under vague expositions of tyrannical laws more tyrannically executed. Let not *him* be hurried away to pre-doomed execution, from an honest enthusiasm for the public safety. I ask for him a trial by this applauded Constitution of our country: I call upon you to administer the law to *him* according to our own wholesome institutions, by its strict and rigid letter. However you may eventually disapprove of any part of his conduct, or, viewing it through a false medium, may think it even wicked, I claim for him as a subject of England that the law shall decide upon its criminal denomination. I protest in his name against all speculations respecting *consequences* when the law commands us to look only to *intentions*. If the state be threatened with evils, let Parliament administer a *prospective* remedy; but let the prisoner hold his life *under the law.* Gentlemen, I ask this solemnly of the Court, whose justice I am persuaded will afford it to me. I ask it more emphatically of you, the *jury*, who are called upon by your oaths to make a true deliverance of your countryman from this charge; but lastly and chiefly I implore it of Him in whose hands are all the issues of life, whose merciful eye expands itself over all the transactions of mankind, at whose command nations rise and fall and are regenerated. I implore it of God Himself, that He will fill your minds with the spirit of truth, so that you will be able to find your way through the labyrinth of matter laid before you—a labyrinth in which no man's life was ever before involved in the whole history of human justice or injustice."

Proceeding to consider the basis upon which the charge rested, he says:

"The unfortunate man whose innocence I am defending is arraigned before you of high treason, upon evidence not only repugnant to the statute, but such as never yet was heard in any capital trial—evidence which, even with all the attention you have given to it, I defy any one of you at this moment to say of what it consists—evidence (I tremble for my boldness, in standing up for the life of a man, when I am conscious I am incapable of understanding from it even what acts are imputed to him)—evidence which has consumed four days in the reading, made up from the unconnected writings of men unknown to one another, upon a hundred different subjects—evidence the very listening to which has filled my mind with unremitting distress and agitation, and which, from its discordant nature has suffered me to reap no advantage from your indulgence, but which, on the contrary, has almost set my brain on fire with the vain endeavour to analyse it. . . . But read these books over and over

again, and let us stand here a year and a day in discoursing
concerning them, still the question must return to what you,
and you only, can resolve—Is he guilty of that base, detestable intention to destroy the King?—not whether you suspect, nor whether it be probable—not whether he *may* be
guilty—no, but that '*provably*' he is guilty. If you can say
this upon the evidence, it is your duty to say so, and you
may with a tranquil conscience return to your families,
though by your judgment the unhappy object of it must
return no more to his. Alas! gentlemen, what do I say?
He has no family to return to; the affectionate partner of
his life has already fallen a victim to the surprise and horror
which attended the scene now transacting. But let that
melancholy reflection pass—it should not, perhaps, have
been introduced—it certainly ought to have no weight with
you who are to judge upon your oaths. I do not stand here
to desire you to commit perjury from compassion; but, at
the same time, my earnestness may be forgiven, since it proceeds from a weakness common to us all, I claim no merit
with the prisoner for my zeal; it proceeds from a selfish principle inherent in the human heart. I am counsel, gentlemen, for myself. In every word I utter, I feel that I am
pleading for the safety of my own life, for the lives of my
children after me, for the happiness of my country, and for
the universal condition of civil society throughout the
world."

Erskine, perceiving that the jury was with him, adverted
to the consequence of the principle on which the prosecution
was founded, in the following words:

"The delegates who attended the meetings could not be
supposed to have met with a different intention from those
who sent them; and if the answer to that is, that the constituents are involved in the guilt of their representatives, we
get back to the monstrous position from which I observed
you before to shrink with visible horror when I stated it—as
it involves in the fate of this single trial every man who corresponded with these societies, or who, as a member of societies in any part of the kingdom, consented to the meeting

which was assembled, or to the meeting which was in prospect. Upwards of forty thousand persons, upon the lowest
calculation, must alike be liable to the pains and penalties
of the law, and hold themselves as tenants at will of the crown.
The campaign of Judge Jeffreys, in the west was nothing to
what may follow. In whatever aspect, therefore, this prosecution is regarded, new difficulties and new uncertainties and
terrors surround it."

The manner in which Erskine handled one of the witnesses
for the prosecution—a government spy—is interesting as
illustrating his manner of commenting upon the testimony
of witnesses, one of the most important functions of an advocate before a jury:

" Mr. Grove professed to speak from notes, yet I observed
him frequently looking up to the ceiling whilst he was speaking—when I said to him : 'Are you now speaking from a note?
Have you got any note of what you are now saying?' He
answered : 'Oh no; this is from recollection.' Good God
Almighty! *Recollection* mixing itself up with *notes* in a case
of HIGH TREASON ! He did not even take down the words ;
nay, to do the man justice, he did not even affect to have
taken the words, but only the *substance*, as he himself expressed
it. Oh, excellent evidence! The substance of words taken
down by a spy, and supplied where defective by his memory !
But I must not call him a spy, for it seems he took them
bona fide as a delegate, and yet *bona fide* as a reformer.
What a happy combination of fidelity! faithful to serve and
faithful to betray!—correct to record for the benefit of the
society, and correct to dissolve and to punish it! In the
last precedent which could be cited of the production of
such testimony, the case of Lord Stafford, accused of being
concerned in the Popish Plot—all the proceedings were
ordered to be taken off the file and burnt, 'to the intent that
the same might no longer be visible to after ages,'—an order,
dictated, no doubt, by a pious tenderness for national honour
and meant as a charitable covering for the crimes of our fathers. But it was a sin against posterity ; it was treason against
society ; for instead of being burnt they should have been

directed to be blazoned in large letters upon the walls of our courts of justice, that, like the characters deciphered by the prophet of God to the Eastern tyrant, they might enlarge and blacken in your sight to terrify you from acts of injustice."

A few sentences from the peroration will conclude the extracts from this magnificent speech:

" My firmest wish is that we may not conjure up a spirit to destroy ourselves, nor set the example here of what in another country we deplore. Let us cherish the old and venerable laws of our forefathers. Let our judicial administration be strict and pure ; and let the jury of the land preserve the life of a fellow-subject, who only asks it from them on the same terms under which they hold their own lives, and all that is dear to them and their posterity for ever. Let me repeat the wish with which I began my address to you, and which proceeds from the very bottom of my heart ; may it please God, who is the author of all mercies to mankind, whose providence I am persuaded guides and superintends the transactions of the world, and whose guardian spirit has ever hovered over this prosperous island, to direct and fortify your judgments! I am aware I have not acquitted myself to the unfortunate man who has put his trust in me in the manner I could have wished ;—yet I am unable to proceed any farther—exhausted in spirit and in strength—but confident in the expectation of justice."

It is said that Erskine's exertions were so great that for ten minutes before he sat down he could only whisper to the jury, but the stillness was so intense that his faintest accents were heard in the remotest parts of the court-room.

When he finished his speech it is said that an irresistible acclamation, pervaded the court and was repeated to an immense distance around.

The streets were crowded with people, and it was some time before the judges were able to get to their carriages, Erskine went out, and addressed the multitude, asking them to confide in the justice of their country. He reminded them that the only security of Englishmen was under the laws, and that any attempt to overawe them would not only be an affront to public justice, but would probably endanger the lives of the accused. He then asked them to retire, and they immediately dispersed.

The jury shortly returned a verdict of "*Not-Guilty.*"

To the surprise of everybody, after Hardy's acquittal, John Horne Tooke was placed on trial. It had been the custom from time immemorial for the Government to abandon the prosecution after the acquittal of the first man tried of several jointly charged with high treason.

John Horne Tooke was a man of great ability, of popular manners, and of unrivalled powers of sarcasm. He was also perfectly fearless in court or out. For instance in a case where he was his own counsel in an action brought against him by Mr. Fox for the expenses of the Westminster election petition, he began his address to the jury as follows: " Gentlemen, there are here three parties to be considered— *You, Mr. Fox,* and *myself.* As for the *Judge* and the *crier,* they are sent here to preserve order, and they are both well paid for their trouble."

Tooke's health was bad at the time of his arraignment, but his mental faculties were unimpaired, as his opponents ascertained, to their cost, before the close of the trial. After the indictment was read, Tooke was asked how he would be tried. Campbell says that, although perfectly confident of an acquittal, he gave a foretaste of what might be expected during the trial, by putting on the aspect of a man weighed down by his oppressors, by looking around the court-room some seconds with an air of significant meaning, which few assumed better, and by answering while he emphatically shook his head, " I would be tried by God and my country ! But——" Here he paused, having intimated with sufficient distinctness that he feared much that he should not have this advantage.

Campbell says: " An application having been made that, on account of his infirmities, he might be permitted to sit by his counsel, he was told that ' this *indulgence* should be shown him.' Instead of humbly thanking the Judge in whose hands he was, and who was by and by to direct the jury on the question of his life or death, he observed, in a very quiet familiar tone, 'I cannot help saying, my Lord, that if I were a Judge, that word "*indulgence*" should never issue from my lips. My Lord, you have no indulgence to show; you are bound to be just; and to be just is to do that which is ordered.'"

Once seated at the table with the counsel, he was the most facetious and light-hearted of mortals, and seemed to have as much enjoyment in the proceeding as a young advocate who has unexpectedly got a brief with a good fee in a winning cause, which has excited great interest, and by which he expects to make his fortune. "Cool and prompt, ready at repartee and fond of notoriety, he trod the boards of the Old Bailey like some amateur actor pleased with his part, and resolved to make the most of it, even though the catastrophe should terminate in his death. After the acquittal of Hardy the reverend agitator would have deprecated his not being brought to trial as a personal misfortune. It is impossible to read this grave state prosecution without frequently indulging in an involuntary smile. From the constant merriment which rewarded his sallies, it might be guessed that a madder wag never stood at the bar; and yet he rarely laughed himself, but glanced around, from his keen and arch eyes, a satirical look of triumph. To the credit of Erskine be it stated, that he was not at all annoyed by the sallies of his client, although they were sometimes unseasonable, nor jealous of the *éclat* which they brought him; but, on the contrary, encouraged him to interpose, and rejoiced in the success of his hits. While the evidence for the prosecution was going on, he seemed content with the office of being second to one so perfect in the art of forensic duelling."

Campbell also gives the following quips of Tooke which Erskine highly applauded:

"Passages being read from pamphlets published by the Societies, abusing the King and the Lords, he offered to prove that much abuse of himself had been printed on *earthenware vessels*. A witness having said that a treasonable song had been sung at a public meeting, he proposed that it should be sung in court, so that the jury might ascertain whether there was anything treasonable, resembling *Ça ira* or the Marseillaise Hymn, in the tune. He not unfrequently succeeded in arguing questions of evidence, and if found out to be clearly wrong, he took a pinch of snuff, and quietly apologised, by saying, that ' he was only a student of forty years' standing.' On one occasion, when he objected to the admissibility of evidence of a particular fact, on the ground that he was not connected with it, Eyre reminded him, that if there were two or three links to make a chain, they must go to one first, and then to another, and see whether the chain was made. *Horne Tooke:* ' I beg your pardon, my Lord, but is not a chain composed of links? and may I not disjoin each link? and do I not thereby destroy the chain?' *Eyre, C.-J.:* ' I rather think not, till the links are put together and form the chain.' *Horne Tooke:* ' Nay, my Lord, with great submission to your Lordship, I rather think that I may, because it is my business to prevent the forming of that chain.' To prove him to be a republican, evidence was given that a society, of which he was a member, had approved of certain proceedings in the National Assembly. ' Egad,' said he, ' it is lucky we did not say there were some good things in the Koran, or we should have been charged to be Mahometans.' Having put questions to show that at public meetings they had often disapproved of his sentiments and his conduct, he gave a knowing nod to the jury, and said: ' My object, gentlemen, was to show that after I had deposed our Lord the King, I was likely to have very troublesome subjects, for I was constantly received with hisses." By putting the following question, he excited a roar of laughter against the solemn and empty Beaufoy, who pretended hardly to know him, and denied all recollection of a date to which he was interrogated: ' Now, witness, upon your oath, was it not the very day that you complained so bitterly to me you could not sleep because, notwithstanding all your services to Mr. Pitt, and all the money you had spent in his cause, he had refused to return your bow?' Few were aware at the time that this was pure invention, to expose a tuft-hunter. The

Attorney-General, in repelling some insinuations thrown out
against him for the manner in which he had instituted these
prosecutions, said, 'he could endure anything but an attack
on his *good name ;* it was the *little patrimony* he had to leave
to his children, and with God's help he would leave it unimpaired.' He then burst into tears, which, from his lachry-
mose habit, surprised no one ; but to the wonder of all, the
Solicitor-General, not known to be of the melting mood, became equally affected and sobbed in concert with his friend.
Tooke, afraid that this sympathy might extend to the jury,
exclaimed in a stage whisper : ' Do you know what Sir John
Mitford is crying about ? He is thinking of the destitute
condition of Sir John Scott's children, and the little patrimony they are likely to divide among them.' "

Erskine's speech, in defence, was excellent, almost as good
as that in behalf of Hardy. In commenting upon the authorities cited by his opponents, he said : " To give the case
of Lord Lovat any bearing upon the present, you must first
prove that our design was to arm, and I shall then admit the
argument and the conclusion. But has such proof been given
on the present trial ? It has not been attempted ; the abor-
tive evidence of arms has been abandoned. Even the solitary
pike that formerly glared rebellion from the corner of the
court, no longer makes its appearance, and the knives have
returned to their ancient office of carving. Happy was it
indeed for me that they were ever produced, for so perfectly
common were they throughout all England, and so notori-
ously in use for the most ordinary purposes, that public justice and benevolence, shocked at the perversion of truth in
the evidence concerning them, kept pouring them in upon
me from all quarters. The box before me is half full of them,
and if all other trades fail me, I might now set up a cutler's
shop."

He pointed out the improbability of the charge against
Tooke as follows : " Yet this gentleman, greatly advanced in
years, and broken in health, who was shut up then and long
before, within the compass of his house and garden at Wim-
bledon, where he used to wish that an act of Parliament

might confine him for life—who was painfully devoting the greatest part of his time to the advancement of learning—who was absorbed in researches which will hereafter astound the world—who was at that very moment engaged in a work such as the labour of man hardly ever undertook, nor perhaps his ingenuity ever accomplished—who never saw the Constitutional Society but in the courtesy of a few short moments after dining with some of the most respectable members, and who positively objected to the very measure which is the whole foundation of this prosecution,—is yet gravely considered to be .the master-spirit which was continually directing all the movements of a conspiracy as extensive as the island—the planner of a revolution in the government, and the active head of an armed rebellion. Gentlemen, is this a proposition to be submitted to the judgment of honest and enlightened men, upon a trial of life and death ? Why, there is nothing in the *Arabian Knights* or in the *Tales of the Fairies* which is not dull matter of fact compared with it. . . . Filled with indignation that an innocent man should be consigned to a prison for treading in the very steps which had conducted the Premier to his present situation, Mr. Horne Tooke did write ' that if ever that man should be brought to trial for his desertion of the cause of parliamentary reform, he hoped the country would not consent to send him to Botany Bay '; but whatever you may think of this sentiment, Mr. Tooke is not indicted for compassing and imagining the death of William Pitt."

The flimsy case against Horne Tooke rested chiefly upon the following letter addressed, to one Joyce, one of the alleged conspirators : " Dear Citizen :—This morning at six o'clock citizen Hardy was taken away by order from the Secretary of State's office : they seized everything they could lay hands on. *Query.—Is it possible to get ready by Thursday ?*" This evidence was disposed of by Erskine, as follows : " This letter being intercepted, was packed into the green box and reserved to establish the plot. It is another lesson of caution against vague suspicions. Mr. Tooke having undertaken to collect from the Court Calendar a list of the titles,

15

offices, and pensions bestowed by Mr. Pitt on his relations,
friends, and dependants, and being too correct to come out
with a work of that magnitude and extent upon a short notice, had fixed no time for it—which induced Mr. Joyce,
who was anxious for its publication, to ask if he could be
ready with it by Thursday—using the French designation of
'*citizen*' for the purpose of turning it into ridicule!"

Erskine then said : " To expose further the extreme absurdity of this accusation, if it be possible further to expose
it, let me imagine that we are again at peace with France,
while the other nations who are now our allies should continue to prosecute the war,—would it *then* be criminal to
congratulate France upon her success against them? When
that time arrives, might I not honestly wish the triumph of
the French armies? And might I not lawfully express that
wish? I know certainly that I might—and I know also that
I would! *I observe that this sentiment seems a bold one;* but
who is prepared to tell me that I shall not? I WILL assert
the freedom of an Englishman; I WILL maintain the dignity
of man. I WILL vindicate and glory in the principles which
raised this country to her pre-eminence among the nations
of the earth ; and as she shone the bright star of the morning to shed the light of liberty upon nations which now enjoy it, so may she continue in her radiant sphere to revive
the ancient privileges of the world, which have been lost,
and still to bring them forward to tongues and people who
have never yet known them, in the mysterious progression
of things."

Erskine's peroration was admirable: " I cannot conclude
without observing that the conduct of this abused and unfortunate gentleman throughout the whole of this trial has
certainly entitled him to admiration and respect. I had
undoubtedly prepared myself to conduct his cause in a manner totally different from that which I have pursued. It
was my purpose to have selected those parts of the evidence
only by which he was affected, and to have separated him
from the rest. By such a course I could have steered his
vessel safely through all perils, and brought her without

damage into a harbour of safety, while the other unfortunate prisoners were left to ride out this awful tempest. But he would not suffer his defence to be put upon the footing which discretion would have suggested. Though not implicated in the supposed conspiracy, he has charged me to waste and destroy my strength to prove that no such guilt can be brought home to others. I rejoice in having been made the humble instrument of so much good—my heart was never so much in any cause."

At the conclusion of the judge's charge, the jury immediately returned a verdict of " Not Guilty." The Government was not yet satisfied and, consequently, a third prisoner, Thelwall was put upon trial. Thelwall was a fool, and ought to have been hung two or three times, on general principles. He frequently interfered with Erskine during the progress of the trial, and at one time he was so much dissatisfied, that he wrote on a piece of paper, which he threw to Erskine, " I 'll be hanged if I don't plead my own cause "; upon which his counsel returned for answer: " You 'll be hanged if you do."

The Government endeavoured to make this case as short as possible, and it ended early on the third day. In the conduct of the cause Erskine displayed his usual zeal and ability. One passage of his speech, in which he sought to destroy the effect of very indiscreet and very intemperate language against the Government imputed to the prisoner by a spy, was admirable. After making an attack upon the credibility of the witness, Erskine proceeded as follows:

" Even if the very phrase had not been exaggerated, if the particular sentence had not been coloured or distorted, what allowance ought there not to be made for infirmity of temper, and the faults of the tongue, in a period of intense excitement. Let me ask, who would be safe, if every loose, word, if every vague expression, uttered in the moment of inadvertence or irritation, were to be admitted as sufficient evidence of a criminal purpose of the most atrocious nature? In the judgment of God we should, indeed, be safe, because He knows the heart—He knows the infirmities with which He

hath clothed us, and makes allowance for those errors which
arise from the imperfect state of our nature. From that
perfect acquaintance which He possesses with our frame, He
is qualified to regard in their proper point of view the involuntary errors of the misguided mind, and the intemperate
effusions of the honest heart. With respect to these, in the
words of a beautiful moral writer, 'the accusing angel, who
flies up to Heaven's chancery, blushes as he gives them in,
and the recording angel, as he writes them down, drops a
tear upon the words and blots them out for ever.' Who is
there that in the moment of levity or of passion has not
adopted the language of profaneness, and even trifled with
the name of the God whom he adores? Who has not in an
unguarded hour, from a strong sense of abuse, or a quick
resentment of public misconduct, inveighed against the
Government to which he is most firmly attached? Who has
not, under the impulse of peevishness and misapprehension,
made use of harsh and unkind expressions, even with respect
to his best and dearest relations—expressions which, if they
were supposed to proceed from the heart, would destroy all
the affection and confidence of private life? If there is such
a man present so uniformly correct in expression, so guarded
from mistake, so superior to passion, let him stand forth, let
him claim all the praise due to a character so superior to the
common state of humanity. For myself, I will only say,
I am not the man."

The jury returned a verdict of "*Not Guilty.*" The Attorney-General, after the acquittal of Thelwall, declined to proceed against the other prisoners, and they were acquitted
without any evidence being offered against them.

Erskine was employed, some time after the trial of Thelwall, to prosecute a bookseller by the name of Williams
for a blasphemous libel on the Christian religion. The
Government took the ground that a wider circulation
would only be given to the book by the notoriety of a public trial and abstained from prosecuting. "The Society for
the Suppression of Vice and Immorality," preferred the indictment.

A few extracts from his eloquent speech in this case will well repay an attentive perusal:

" ' For my own part, gentlemen, I have been ever deeply devoted to the truths of Christianity; and my firm belief in the Holy Gospel is by no means owing to the prejudices of education (though I was religiously educated by the best of parents), but has arisen from the fullest and most continued reflections of my riper years and understanding. It forms at this moment the great consolation of a life which as a shadow passes away; and without it I should consider my long course of health and prosperity (too long, perhaps, and too uninterrupted to be good for any man) only as the dust which the wind scatters, and rather as a snare than as a blessing.' Having read and commented on some of the most obnoxious parts of the book, he continued: ' In running the mind over the long list of sincere and devout Christians, I cannot help lamenting that Newton had not lived to this day to have had the darkness of his understanding illuminated by this new flood of light. But the subject is too awful for irony. I will speak plainly and directly. Newton was a Christian!—Newton, whose mind burst forth from the fetters fastened by nature upon our finite conceptions!—Newton, who carried the line and rule to the uttermost barriers of creation, and explained the principles by which all created matter exists and is held together!' In a similar strain he appealed to the testimony of Boyle, Locke, and Hale, and then introduced a still greater name: ' But it is said by the author that the Christian's fable is but the tale of the more ancient superstitions of the world, and may be easily detected by a proper understanding of the mythologies of the heathens. Did Milton understand these mythologies? Was HE less versed than Mr. Paine in the superstitions of the world? No! they were the subjects of his immortal song, and he poured them forth from the stores of a memory rich with all that man ever knew, and laid them in their order as the illustration of real and exalted faith—the unquestionable source of that fervid genius which has cast a shade on the other works of man:

> " He pass'd the flaming bounds of place and time,
>   The living throne, the sapphire blaze,
>   Where angels tremble while they gaze.
>   He saw—but, blasted with excess of light,
>   Closed his eyes in endless night."

But it was the light of the body only which was extinguished.   The celestial light shone inward, and enabled him to "*justify the ways of God to man.*" ' "

Before concluding, Erskine pays a tribute to the benefits of free and enlightened discussion :

" I do not dread the reasonings of Deists against the existence of Christianity itself, because, as was said by its Divine Author, *if it be of God it will stand.*   An intellectual book, however erroneous, addressed to the intellectual world, upon so profound and complicated a subject, can never work the mischief which this indictment is calculated to repress.   Such works will only incite the minds of men, cultivated by study, to a closer investigation of a subject well worthy of their deepest and continued contemplation. The changes produced by such reciprocations of lights and intelligences are certain in their progression, and make their way imperceptibly by the final and irresistible power of truth.   If Christianity be founded in falsehood, let us become Deists in this manner, and I am contented.   But this book has no such object, and no such capacity; it presents no arguments to the wise and the educated ; on the contrary, it treats the faith and opinion held sacred by the British people, with scoffing and ribaldry, and tends to make the thoughtless multitude view with contempt the obligations of law and the precepts of morality."

The jury instantly found a verdict of " Guilty."

Erskine thought very highly of his speech in this case. In a letter to Lord Campbell in reference to this prosecution he said : " My opening speech, correctly as it was uttered in court, is in Mr. Ridgway's collection of my speeches at the bar.   It was first printed by the Society and circulated to a very wide extent,—which gave me the greatest satisfaction ; as I would rather all my other speeches were committed to the flames, or in any manner buried in oblivion, than that a single page of it should be lost."

Erskine said that none of his speeches had been so much "admired and approved" as his speech in defence of Hadfield. This was the last case where he defended a prisoner accused by the Crown. James Hadfield was indicted for shooting at King George III. in Drury Lane Theatre. Erskine put in the plea of insanity. The case made out by the prosecution made a deep impression upon the minds of the court and jury.

It is said that Erskine began his address to the jury in a subdued and solemn tone, in order that he might win the sympathies of the jury, and to prepare them for the discussion of the important question arising from the distinction between the "insanity of passion, unaccompanied by delusion, and that total derangement of the intellectual faculties which ought to exempt from punishment acts the most atrocious." The few extracts which follow are all that will be given, but the whole speech should be studied by lawyers and physicians for its philosophical and accurate views of mental disease, as well as for its eloquence and touching appeals to human feeling. Erskine said :

"The scene which we are engaged in, and the duty which I am not merely *privileged* but *appointed* by the authority of the Court to perform, exhibits to the whole civilised world a perpetual monument of our national justice. The transaction, indeed, in every part of it, as it stands recorded in the evidence already before us, places our country and its government and its inhabitants upon the highest pinnacle of human elevation. It appears that upon the 15th of May last, His Majesty, after a reign of forty years, not merely in sovereign power, but spontaneously, in the very hearts of his people, was openly shot at (or to all appearance shot at) in a public theatre in the centre of his capital, and amidst the loyal plaudits of his subjects; YET NOT A HAIR OF THE HEAD OF THE SUPPOSED ASSASSIN WAS TOUCHED. In this unparalleled scene of calm forbearance, the King himself, though he stood first in personal interest and feeling, as

well as in command, was a singular and fortunate example.
The least appearance of emotion on the part of that august
personage must unavoidably have produced a scene quite
different and far less honourable than the Court is now witnessing : but his Majesty remained unmoved, and the person *apparently* offending was only secured, without injury
or reproach, for the business of this day." After the advocate had gracefully insinuated himself into the favour of
the jury, by an appeal to their loyal sympathies, he comes
to discuss the question on which their verdict was to
depend: "It is agreed by all jurists, and is established by
the law of this and every other country, that it is the reason
of man which makes him accountable for his actions, and
that the deprivation of reason acquits him of crime. This
principle is indisputable; yet so fearfully and wonderfully
are we made,—so infinitely subtle is the spiritual part of
our being,—so difficult is it to trace with accuracy the effect
of diseased intellect upon human action, that I may appeal
to all who hear me, whether there are any causes more difficult, or which indeed so often confound the learning of
the judges themselves, as when insanity, or the effects and
consequences of insanity, become the subjects of legal
consideration and judgment?· Your province, to-day, will
be to decide whether the prisoner, when he did the act,
was under the uncontrollable dominion of insanity, and was
impelled to do it by a morbid delusion, or whether it
was the act of a man who, though occasionally mad, or even
at the time not perfectly collected, was yet not actuated by
the disease, but by the suggestion of a wicked and malignant disposition. It is true, indeed, that in some, perhaps
in many cases, the human mind is stormed in its citadel, and
laid prostrate under the stroke of frenzy; these unhappy
sufferers, however, are not so much considered by physicians as maniacs, as in a state of delirium from fever.
There, indeed, all the ideas are overwhelmed, for reason
is not merely disturbed, but driven from her seat. Such
unhappy patients are unconscious, therefore, except at short
intervals, even of external objects, or at least are wholly

incapable of understanding their relations. Such persons, and such persons alone (except idiots), are wholly deprived of their understandings, in the Attorney-General's sense of that expression. But these cases are not only extremely rare, but can never become the subjects of judicial difficulty. There can be but one judgment concerning them. In other cases Reason is not driven from her seat, but Distraction sits down upon it along with her, holds her trembling upon it, and frightens her from her propriety. Such patients are victims to delusions of the most alarming description, which so overpower the faculties, and usurp so firmly the power of realities, as not to be dislodged and shaken by the organs of perception and sense : in such cases the images frequently vary, but in the same subjects are generally of the same terrific character. *Delusion*, therefore, when there is no frenzy or raving madness, is the true character of insanity ; and where it cannot be predicted on a man standing for life or death for a crime, he ought not, in my opinion, to be acquitted ; and if courts of law were to be governed by any other principle, every departure from sober rational conduct would be an emancipation from criminal justice. I shall place my claim to your verdict upon no such danger-ous foundation. I must convince you not only that the unhappy prisoner was a lunatic within my own definition of lunacy, but that the act in question was the IMMEDIATE UNQUALIFIED OFFSPRING OF THE DISEASE."

Erskine related, in the course of his speech, an extraordi-nary instance of monomania :

"A man of the name of Wood had indicted Dr. Monro, for keeping him as a prisoner, when he was sane. He under-went a most severe cross-examination from the defendant's counsel without exposing his infirmity : but Dr. Battye having come upon the bench by me, and having desired me to ask him ' what was become of the Princess with whom he had corresponded in cherry-juice,' he showed in a moment what he was. He answered, that ' there was nothing at all in that, because having been (as everybody knew) impris-oned in a high tower, and being debarred the use of ink, he had no other means of correspondence but by writing his letters in cherry-juice, and throwing them into the river which surrounded the tower, where the Princess received them in a boat.' There existed of course no tower, no imprisonment, no writing in cherry-juice, no river, no boat, no princess,—but the whole was the inveterate phantom of a morbid imagination. I immediately directed Dr. Monro to be acquitted. But this madman again indicted Dr. Monro, in the city of London, through a part of which he had been carried to his place of confinement. Knowing that he had lost his cause by speaking of the Princess, at Westminster, (such is the wonderful subtlety of madmen,) —when he was cross-examined on the trial in London, as he had successfully been before, in order to expose his madness, all the ingenuity of the Bar, and all the authority of the Court, could not make him say a single syllable upon that topic which had put an end to the indictment before, although he still had the same indelible impression upon his mind, as he signified to those who were near him ; but, conscious that the delusion had caused his former defeat, he obstinately persisted in holding it back. His evidence at Westminster was then proved against him by the short-hand writer ;—and I again directed an acquittal."

According to Lord Campbell :

" Erskine opened in the following affecting words, which are said to have drawn tears from almost all present,—the evidence he was to give of a recent attempt by the prisoner upon the life of a child whom he tenderly loved : 'To proceed to the proofs of his insanity down to the very period of his supposed guilt : This unfortunate man before you is the father of an infant of eight months, and I have no doubt whatever that, if the boy had been brought into court (but this is a grave place for the administration of justice, and not a theatre for stage effect),—I say, I have no doubt whatever that, if this poor infant had been brought into court, you would have seen the father writhing with all the emotions of parental affection ; yet upon the Tuesday preceding the Thursday when he went to the play-house, you will find his disease still urging him forward, with the impression that the time was come when he must be destroyed for the benefit of mankind ; and in the confusion, or rather delirium, of this wild conception, he came to the bed of the mother who had this infant in her arms, and, snatching it from her, was about to dash out its brains against the wall in her presence when his arm was arrested from the dreadful attempt."

Lord Kenyon stopped the trial after a few witnesses had been examined, on the ground that a case of insanity had been made out at the time when the pistol was fired. Hadfield was sent to the asylum, where he remained many years.

The author has said nothing of Erskine's career as a member of parliament, nor of his qualifications for the office of Lord Chancellor, neither will he do so, for the reason that he was not distinguished in either capacity. Erskine was returned to parliament for Portsmouth in 1783, and was made Lord Chancellor in 1806.

Erskine died on the 17th day of November, 1823.

The life of Lord Erskine should exercise a salutary influence on the younger members of the legal profession. It should constantly remind them of the noble objects of that noble profession, and impress indelibly upon their minds the great truth, that its highest rewards can only be attained by the advocate who is honest and strictly faithful to the interests of clients : He should be, as Erskine was, imbued, deeply, with the principles of patriotism and a passionate love of his highly honourable profession. He should ever be, too, keenly alive to human suffering, and reflect that it often becomes his duty to remember the forgotten, to attend the neglected, and visit the forsaken.

Lord Campbell says of Erskine:

" Many generations may pass away before his equal is presented to the admiration of mankind. Of course I do not refer to his qualifications as a judge: and can only say of him as a politician, that he was ever consistently attached to the principles of freedom, though by no means above the

prejudices of education and country. As a parliamentary
debater he was greatly inferior to several of his contemporaries; and even in our own degenerate age we could out-
match him. But as an advocate in the forum, I hold him
to be without an equal in ancient or in modern times.

"Notwithstanding the flippant observations of some who
can write and speak very fine sentences, without any notion
of the real business of life, and who pretend to despise that
for which they themselves would have been found utterly
unfit, I boldly affirm that there is no department of human
intellect in which the *mens divinior* may be more refulgently
displayed. I despise, as much as they can do, the man
wearing a gown, be it of bombasin or of silk, who is merely
'*præco actionum, cautor formularum, auceps syllabarum,*'—or
who sordidly thinks only of amassing money, and regulates
his attendance and his exertions according to the fee marked
on his brief. But let us imagine to ourselves an advocate
inspired by a generous love of fame, and desirous of hon-
ourably assisting in the administration of justice, by obtaining redress for the injured and defending the innocent,—who
has liberally studied the science of jurisprudence, and has
stored his mind, and refined his taste, by a general acquaintance with elegant literature,—who has an intuitive insight
into human character and the workings of human passion,—
who possesses discretion as well as courage, and caution
along with enthusiasm,—who is not only able by his powers
of persuasion to give the best chance of success to every
client whom he represents in every variety of private causes,
but who is able to defeat conspiracies against public liberty,
to be carried into effect by a perversion of the criminal law,
—and who, by the victories which he gains, and the principles which he establishes, places the free constitution of his
country on an imperishable basis! Such an advocate was
Erskine; and although he did creditably maintain his family
by professional *honoraries* voluntarily presented to him, he
was careless as to their amount, and he was ready on every
proper occasion to exert his best energies without any
reward beyond the consciousness of doing his duty. Such

an advocate, in my opinion, stands quite as high in the scale of true greatness as the parliamentary leader who ably opens a budget, who lucidly explains a new system of commercial policy, or who dexterously attacks the measures of the government. Certainly different qualities of mind as well as different acquirements are demanded for these two kinds of eloquence; and it may be admitted that in senatorial deliberations there is a greater scope for an enlarged view of human affairs, and that there only can be discussed the relative rights, duties, and interests of nations. But the forensic proceeding, though between private parties, or between the state and individual citizens, and though confined to a comparatively narrow field of investigation and of argument, has great advantages, from the intense and continued interest which it excites,—for, like a grand drama, it has often a well-involved plot, and a catastrophe which cannot be anticipated, rousing all the most powerful sympathies of our nature,—and sometimes, as on the impeachment of Lord Strafford, or the Treason Trials of 1794, the fate of the empire may depend upon the verdict. Look to the recorded efforts of genius in both departments. I will not here enter into a comparison of the respective merits of the different sorts of oratory handed down to us from antiquity, but I may be allowed to observe that, among ourselves, in the hundred and fifty volumes of Hansard, there are no specimens of parliamentary harangues which as literary compositions are comparable to the speeches of Erskine at the bar, with the exception of Burke's,—and they were delivered to empty benches. Do not, therefore, let it be assumed that Erskine is degraded into an inferior class of artists because he was not a skilful debater. He no doubt would have been a yet more wonderful creature if he had been as great in the senate as in the forum; but we should recollect that in the department of eloquence in which he did shine, he is allowed to have excelled, not only all his contemporaries, but all who have attempted it in this island, either in prior or in subsequent times,—while mankind are greatly divided as to the individual to whom the palm of parliamentary elo-

quence should be awarded ;—and there will again probably be
a debater equal to Pitt the father, Pitt the son, Fox, Sheridan,
Burke, or Grey, before there arises an advocate equal to
Erskine.

"Some have denied the possibility of his great pre-
eminence, on account of his limited stock of general
knowledge, but, although much culture is indispensable to
the development of the intellectual powers, and to the
refinement of taste, this culture may be applied, without
the knowledge of a great variety of languages, and without
any deep insight into science. No Greek knew any language but that which he learned from his nurse ; and Shakespeare could not have gone through an examination as hard
as that of many modern parish schools. Far be it from
me to discourage the acquisiton of classical and scientific
lore : this is delightful in itself, and it gives the best chance
of success in every liberal pursuit; but where true genius
exists, it may be brought into full operation and efficiency
by suitable discipline within very narrow limits ; and a man
may be superior to all others in his art, and be ignorant of
many things which it is .disgraceful to the common herd of
mortals not to know. Let it not be said, therefore, that
Erskine could not, better than any other man, lead the
understandings and control the passions of his audience
when arguing a point of constitutional law, or appealing to
the affections of domestic life, because he talked nonsense if
he indiscreetly offered an opinion upon a question of prosody
or of political economy. His moderate acquaintance with
the Latin poets, and his intense and unremitting study of
the best English writers, both in prose and verse, had taught
him to think, and had supplied him with a correct, chaste,
forcible, and musical diction, in which to express his
thoughts. Although, judged by his common conversation,
he was sometimes very lightly esteemed,—listen to his discourses when he is rescuing from destruction the intended
victim of arbitrary government, or painting the anguish of
an injured husband, and he appears to breathe celestial fire.

"In considering the characteristics of his eloquence, it is

observable that he not only was free from measured senten-
tiousness and tiresome attempts at antithesis, but that he
was not indebted for his success to riches of ornament, to
felicity of illustration, to wit, to humour, or to sarcasm. His
first great excellence was his devotion to his client, and in
the whole compass of his orations, there is not a single
instance of the business in hand—the great work of persuading—being sacrificed to raise a laugh or to excite admiration of his own powers. He utterly forgot himself in
the character he represented. Through life he was often
ridiculed for vanity and egotism,—but not for anything he
ever said, or did, in conducting a cause in a court of justice.
There, from the moment the jury were sworn, he thought of
nothing but the verdict, till it was recorded in his favour.
Earnestness and energy were ever present throughout his
speeches—impressing his argument on the mind of his
hearer with a force which seemed to compel conviction. He
never spoke at a tiresome length ; and throughout all his
speeches no weakness, no dulness, no flagging is discovera-
ble ; and we have ever a lively statement of facts,—or reasoning pointed, logical, and triumphant.

" I think I ought particularly to mention the familiar knowledge he displays of the most secret workings of the human
mind. How finely he paints the peril arising from the perversion of what is good ! ' Some of the darkest and most
dangerous prejudices of men arise from the most honourable principles. When prejudices are caught up from bad
passions, the worst of men feel intervals of remorse to soften
and disperse them ; but when they arise from a generous
though mistaken source, they are hugged closer to the bosom, and the kindest and most compassionate natures feel
a pleasure in fostering a blind and unjust resentment.' He
spoke as his clients respectively would have spoken, being
endowed with his genius. ' The dervise in the fairy tale,
who possessed the faculty of passing his own soul into the
body of any whom he might select, could scarcely surpass
Erskine in the power of impersonating for a time the feelings, wishes, and thoughts of others.'

"I must likewise mention the delight I feel from the exquisite sweetness of his diction, which is pure, simple, and mellifluous,—the cadences not being borrowed from any model, nor following any rule, but marked by constant harmony and variety. The rhythm of the Indian Chief is, I think, more varied, richer, and more perfect than that of any passage from any other composition in our language.

"When the great Lord Chatham was to appear in public, he took much pains about his dress, and latterly he arranged his flannels in graceful folds. It need not then detract from our respect for Erskine, that on all occasions he desired to look smart, and that when he went down into the country on special retainers he anxiously had recourse to all manner of innocent little artifices to aid his purposes. He examined the court the night before the trial, in order to select the more advantageous place for addressing the jury. On the cause being called, the crowded audience were perhaps kept waiting a few minutes before the celebrated stranger made his appearance; and when, at length, he gratified their impatient curiosity, a particularly nice wig and a pair of new yellow gloves distinguished and embellished his person beyond the ordinary costume of the barristers of the circuit.

"It may be more useful to hold up for imitation his admirable demeanour while engaged in business at the bar,—to which, perhaps, his success was not less due than to his talents. Respectful to the judges, although ever ready to assert his independence,—courteous to the jury, while he boldly reminded them of their duties,—free from asperity towards his opponents,—constantly kind and considerate to his juniors,—treating the witnesses as persons, generally speaking, reluctantly attending to assist in the investigation of truth,—looking benevolently even on the *circumstances*, and glad when he could accommodate them with a seat,—of a gay and happy temperament, enjoying uninterruptedly a boyish flow of animal spirits, and enlivening the dullest cause with his hilarity and good-humour,—he was a universal favourite—there was a general desire, as far as law and justice would permit, that he should succeed, and the *pres-*

tige of his reputation was considered the sure forerunner of victory. I have myself witnessed, from the student's box, towards the conclusion of his career at the bar, his daily skirmishes and triumphs; but it is vain to try by words to convey to others an idea of the qualities which he displayed, or the effect which he produced."

In justice to the reader, the writer thinks it incumbent on him to give other estimates of Erskine's eloquence and professional qualifications, some of which are not so flattering as Lord Campbell's. The magic of his eloquence cannot be appreciated by those who merely read his speeches. It is said that those who saw and heard him were not at a loss to account for the rapidity of his success.

Lord Brougham, an excellent judge of eloquence, and himself one of the most eloquent men of his day in the senate and the forum, paid the following just tribute to Erskine:

" Nor let it be deemed trivial, or beneath the historian's province, to mark that noble figure, every look of whose countenance is expressive, every motion of whose form graceful, an eye that sparkles, and pierces, and almost assures victory, while it speaks audience ere the tongue. Juries have declared that they felt it impossible to remove their looks from him, when he had riveted and, as it were, fascinated them by his first glance ; and it used to be a common remark among men, who observed his motions, that they resembled those of a blood horse, as light, as limber, as much betokening strength and speed, as free from all gross superfluity or incumbrance. Then hear his voice of surpassing sweetness, clear, flexible, strong, exquisitely fitted to strains of serious earnestness, deficient in compass indeed, and much less fitted to express indignation, or even scorn, than pathos, but wholly free from harshness or monotony. All these, however, and even his chaste, dignified, and appropriate action, were very small parts of this wonderful advocate's excellence. He had a thorough knowledge of men, of their passions, and their feelings—he knew every avenue to the heart, and could at will make all its chords vibrate to his

16

touch.   His fancy, though never playful in public, where he
had his whole faculties under the most severe control, was
lively and brilliant ; when he gave it vent and scope it was eminently sportive, but while representing his client it was wholly
subservient to that, in which his whole soul was wrapped up,
and to which each faculty of body and of mind was subdued
—the success of the cause.   His argumentative powers were
of the highest order, clear in his statements, close in his applications, unwearied, and never to be diverted in his deduc-.
tions, with a quick and sure perception of his point, and
undeviating in the pursuit of whatever established it ; endued
with a nice discernment of the relative importance and weight
of different arguments, and the faculty of assigning to each
its proper place, so as to bring forward the main body of the
reasoning in bold relief, and with its full breadth, and not
weaken its effects by distracting and disturbing the attention
of the audience among lesser particulars.   His understanding was eminently legal, though he had never made himself
a great lawyer, yet he could deliver a purely legal argument
with the most perfect success, and his familiarity with all the
ordinary matters of his profession was abundantly sufficient
for the purposes of the forum.   His memory was accurate,
and retentive in an extraordinary degree, nor did he ever
during the trial of a cause forget any matter, how trifling
soever, that belonged to it.   His presence of mind was perfect in action, that is, before the jury, when a line is to be
taken in the instant and a question risked to a witness, or a
topic chosen with the tribunal, on which the whole fate of
the cause may turn.   No man made fewer mistakes, none
left so few advantages unimproved ; before none was it so
dangerous for an adversary to slumber and be off his guard,
for he was ever broad awake himself, and was as adventurous
as he was skilful, and as apt to take advantage of any the
least opening, as he was cautious to leave none in his own
battle.   But to all these qualities he joined that fire, that
spirit, that courage, which gave vigour and direction to the
whole, and bore down all resistance.   No man, with all his
address and prudence, ever ventured upon more bold figures,

and they were uniformly successful, for his imagination was vigorous enough to sustain any flight ; his taste was correct, and even severe, and his execution felicitous in the highest degree."

" Adequately to estimate what Erskine was at this period," says a brother barrister, " we must forget all that the English bar has produced after him. They will afford no criterion by which he can be appreciated. They are all of inferior clay, the mere sweepings of the hall in comparison. Nor is it easy to form any tolerable idea of him, but by having seen him from day to day, from year to year, in the prime and manhood of his intellect, running with graceful facility through the chaos of briefs before him ; it is only by that personal experience that it is possible to form any notion of the admirable versatility with which he glided from one cause to another, the irony, the humour, the good nature with which he laughed down the adverse cause, and the vehemence and spirit with which he sustained his own."

" I never saw him grave," is the testimony of Espinasse, " but with a constant flow of animal spirits he enlivened those who surrounded him with whimsical conceits and jokes on what was passing. I had a full share of his *jeux d'esprit*, as my place in court was directly at his back." Erskine observed, how much confidence in speaking was acquired from habit and frequent employment. " I don't find it so," said Lamb, who happened to be present on one occasion, " for though I have a good share of business, I don't find my confidence increased ; rather the contrary." " Why," replied Erskine, " it is nothing wonderful that a Lamb should grow sheepish."

Erskine loved to play occasionally with the partialities of Lord Kenyon. It is said that when a question of law was started at a trial, the Chief-Justice pricked up his ears, and prepared his note-book to take down the point with great formality. In an action for assault, which was tried before him at Guildhall, the plaintiff, a giant in size and physical strength, kept a house of some notoriety, called " The Cock," at Temple Bar. The house was much frequented by country attorneys. It seems from the evidence that "a spruce little member of that profession came into the public room one evening, booted and spurred as if just off a journey. He took his seat in a box, but soon became so noisy and trouble-some that the other guests wished to have him turned out, and called on the landlord to do so. The lawyer demurred, and when pressed, assumed an attitude of defence. The landlord, acting under the authority of a habeas corpus of his own issuing, took possession of the person of his puny antagonist, by catching the little man up in his arms, and bearing him in triumph towards the door. The publican's embrace, which resembled the friendly hug of a bear, roused all the indignant energies of the lawyer; and being furnished with no weapons of defence except his spurs, he sprawled, kicked, and spurred so violently that the knees and shins of the host of The Cock were covered with blood. For this assault the action was brought, and the defendant pleaded that plaintiff had made the first assault on him, by forcibly taking him in his arms and turning him out of doors. Erskine defended him: he described the combat in the most ludicrous terms, and, with assumed gravity, appealed to the jury if instinct had not pointed out to every animal the best means of its defence; that his client had no weapon of any sort to oppose to the violence of the plaintiff, except his spurs, which he had therefore lawfully used for self-defence. The turn which Erskine's manner of treating it gave to the case, caused much laughter in the court, and he was not disposed to stop it. To the law cited on the other side, he said he would oppose a decisive authority from a book of long stand-ing, and entitled to the highest credit. Lord Kenyon, expecting that some text book or reporter was going to be cited, took up his pen, and put himself into the attitude for taking down the point. 'From what authority, Mr. Erskine?' said the Chief-Justice. 'From Gulliver's Travels, my lord,' was the reply. The whimsical contrast in appear-ance of plaintiff and defendant then on the floor presented the burlesque representation of Gulliver dandling in the arms of his Brobdignag friend. No other barrister would

have ventured to trifle so far with the gravity of the Chief;
but he knew that his anger was sheathed against himself,
and that if he did shake the head reproachfully, it was in
good-humour at the jest. The licensed joker of the court,
the petted school-boy of the robing-room, the gay oracle of
consultation,—he would follow his whim further than barristers in general feel inclined to pursue it, and would sport
with that privileged class, the attornies. He was aware that
they could not dispense with his talents of advocacy, and
that whether offended with his witticisms or not, the principal anxiety of each on the morrow would be, who should be
first with his retainer."

" He attached too little consequence," says Espinasse,
"to consultations: he relied solely on himself. As they
always took place in the evening, and his return from
court had not many hours preceded them, he had very
rarely read his brief, but reserved it for perusal at an early
hour in the morning. He therefore sought to relieve his
mind from the fatigues of the day by unbending it in conversation, or diverting it to something which amused him,
but which required little thought. I have often observed
the disappointment of his clients, who attended his consultations, expecting to hear their cases canvassed with some
degree of solemnity and attention, to find that he had not
read a line of his brief, but amused himself with talking
upon subjects either trifling or wholly unconnected with
them. I recollect accompanying a client to a consultation at
his house in Serjeants' Inn. We found on the table thirty
or forty phial bottles, in each of which was stuck a cutting
of geranium of different kinds. Our client was all anxiety
for the appearance of Erskine, and full of impatience for the
commencement of the consultation, sure that he should
hear the merits of his case and the objections to it accurately
gone into, and the law of it canvassed and well considered.
When Erskine entered the room, what was his disappointment at hearing the first words which he uttered! Erskine
—'Do you know how many kinds of geraniums there are?'
'Not I, truly,' was my reply. 'There are above one hun-

dred,' he said. He then proceeded with a detail and description of the different sorts, and indulged in a discussion
of their relative beauties and merits. This lecture on
geraniums evidently disconcerted our client. He listened
with patient anxiety till he had finished, hoping then to hear
something about his cause, when he heard him conclude.
Erskine—'Now state the case, as I have had no time to
read my brief.' With my statement of it the consultation
ended. But our client's disappointment of the evening he
found amply compensated by Erskine's exertions on the
following morning, when he heard every point of his case
put with accuracy and enforced with eloquence. To his
consultations, in fact, no feature of deliberation belonged.
If in the course of them any thought struck him, he
did not reserve the communication of it for a more fit
occasion, but uttered it as it occurred, though it broke in on
the subject under discussion, and was wholly foreign to and
unconnected with it." "At a consultation, in which I was
junior," says the same writer, "Christie, the auctioneer attended to give some information. In the middle of it Erskine
exclaimed, 'Christie, I want a house in the neighborhood of
Ramsgate, have you got such a one to dispose of?'
'What kind of a house do you want?' inquired the auctioneer.
Erskine described it. 'I have' said Christie, 'the very thing
that will suit you, and what is more, I'll put you into it as
Adam was put into Paradise, in a state of perfection.'
These playful humours the fortunate lawyer would sometimes
carry to an excess, bordering on burlesque. He had a large
and favourite dog, called Toss, which he had taught to sit
upon a chair with his paws placed before him on the table.
In that posture he would put an open book before it, with
one paw placed on each side, and one of his bands tied round
his neck. This ludicrous exhibition was presented to his
clients, who came to attend to his consultations. No one
would have ventured on such a childish experiment, but one
who felt that the indulgence of a trifling whim did not detract from the dignity of his professional character, and with
the perfect assurance of a superior mind, that his clients

could find no equal to him at the bar, or in fact do without him."

The auctioneering flourishes of this Christie, so " child-like and bland," in his manner to confiding purchasers enabled Erskine a favourable opportunity for obtaining verdict for his client by dint of laughter from the jury. He was conducting a case for the plaintiff in action to recover the deposit money for an estate which his client had foolishly purchased on Christie's representation of its beauties. According to the enchanting description given by Christie, the house commanded an extensive and beautiful lawn, with a distant prospect of the Needles, and as having amongst its numerous conveniences an excellent billiard-room. " To show you, gentlemen," said Erskine, " how egregiously my client has been deceived by the defendant's rhetoric, I will tell you what this exquisite and enchanting place actually turned out to be, when my client, who had paid the deposit on the faith of Mr. Christie's advertisement, went down in the fond anticipations of his heart to this earthly paradise. When he got there, nothing was found to correspond to what he had too unwarily expected. There was a house to be sure, and that is all—for it was nodding to its fall, and the very rats instinctively had quitted it. It stood, it is true, in a commanding situation, for it commanded all the winds and rains of heaven. As for lawn, he could find nothing that deserved the name, unless it was a small yard, in which, with some contrivance, a washerwoman might hang half a dozen shirts. There was, however, a dirty lane that ran close to it ; and perhaps Mr. Christie may contend that it was an error of the press, and therefore, for 'lawn,' we must read 'lane.' But where is the billiard room ? exclaimed the plaintiff, in the agony of disappointment. At last he was conducted to a room in the attic, the ceiling of which was so low that a man could not stand upright in it, and therefore must, perforce, put himself into the posture of a billiard player. Seeing this, Mr. Christie, by the magic of his eloquence, converted the place into a 'billiard room.' But the fine view of the Needles, gentlemen ; where was it ? No such thing was to be

seen, and my poor client might as well have looked for a
needle in a bottle of hay!"

From the preceding anecdotes and those which are to
follow it must not be thought that Erskine's occasional levity was disadvantageous to his client, or that he was lacking
in earnestness of purpose. He said on one occasion, on the
opening of the court, that he would do his duty, as if all the
angels in heaven were taking notes of whatever passed
through his mind on the subject.

If Justice Ashurst, long, lean, and lank as he was, had lived
in the days of Cervantes, he would have made an excellent
model for a pen picture of Don Quixote. On the visage of
the Justice before whom he daily practised, he penned the
following couplet:

> "Judge Ashurst, with his *lantern jaws,*
> Throws *light* upon the English laws."

He had a kindness for Park, one of his countrymen, who
afterwards became a judge of the Court of Common Pleas
but quizzed him occasionally, and he wrote upon him the
following lines:

> "James Allen Park
> Came naked stark
> From Scotland;
> But now wears clo'es,
> And lives with beaux
> In England."

Lord Campbell says, of his skill in examining witnesses:
"In describing his professional merits, I ought by no means
to omit his skill in examining witnesses, upon which the
event of a cause often depends, much more than upon fine
speaking. When he had to examine in chief,—not, as in
common fashion, following the order of the proofs as set
down in the brief,—seemingly without art or effort, he made
the witness lucidly relate, so as to interest and captivate the
jury, all the facts that were favorable to his client. In cross-
examination he could be most searching and severe; but he

never resorted to brow-beating, nor was gratuitously rude.
Often he carried his point by coaxing, and when the evidence could not be contradicted, he would try by pleasantry
to lessen the effect of it. Having to cross-examine a cox-
combical fellow, belonging to the self-important class of persons sent by the wholesale houses in London to scour the
country for orders,—formerly called ' Riders,' now styling
themselves 'Travellers,'—he began, ' You are a *Rider*, I
understand?' 'A Traveller, sir,' was the answer. ' I
might have discovered,' replied Erskine, 'that you considered yourself *licensed* to use all the privileges of a *Traveller.*' Another of the fraternity having long baffled him,
he suddenly remarked, ' You were born and bred in Manchester, I perceive?' The witness said he could not deny
it. ' I knew it,' said Erskine, carelessly, ' from the absurd
tie of your neckcloth.' The travelling dandy's weak point
was touched ; for he had been dressing after Beau Brummel ;
and, his presence of mind being gone, he was made to unsay
the greatest part of his evidence in chief. On the trial of an
action to recover the value of a quantity of whalebone, the
defence turning on the quality of the article, a witness was
called, of impenetrable stupidity, who could not be made to
distinguish between the two well-known descriptions of this
commodity—the 'long' and the 'thick.' Still confounding *thick* whalebone with *long*, Erskine exclaimed, in seeming despair, ' Why, man, you do not seem to know the
difference between what is *thick* and what is *long*! Now I
tell you the difference. You are *thick*-headed, and you are
not *long*-headed.' I myself remember, when a student,
being present when he was counsel for the plaintiff in an
action on a tailor's bill,—the defence being, that the clothes
were very ill-made, and, particularly, that the two sleeves of
a dress-coat were of unequal length. The defendant's witness accordingly swore, that 'one of them was longer than
the other'; upon which Erskine thus began : ' Now, sir, will
you swear that one of them was not *shorter* than the other.
The witness negativing this proposition, after an amusing
reply the plaintiff had the verdict.—The more difficult and

delicate task of re-examination he was in the habit of performing with equal dexterity,—not attempting clumsily to go over the same ground which he had before trod, but, by a few questions which strictly arose out of the cross-examination, restoring the credit of his witness, and tying together the broken threads of his case."

The professional life of Lord Erskine is useful as an example to, and worthy of imitation by, every lawyer. The undaunted and repeated refusal of Erskine to discontinue an address he felt it his duty to make, when haughtily and imperiously told by a tyrannical judge to sit down, the author hopes will never be forgotten. His conduct on that occasion has been commended by scores of the ablest lawyers of England and America. The bench has no right to overshadow the bar, and to expect servility and meanness from its members. The bar has rights which it has always vigorously maintained, and the author hopes it will ever maintain when encroached upon by judicial tyranny.

Erskine's life shows that a time-serving, base demeanour toward the judges is not the only road to preferment. By his patriotism and independence, united with the highest legal excellence, he has exalted, still higher, the useful profession to which he belonged. His life is extremely important as showing what one man, single-handed and alone, can do against the corruptions of the age in which he lived. In this country where, generally speaking, the administration of the law flows in such pure channels, where the vast majority of our judges are incorruptible, and watched by the scrutinising eyes of an enlightened bar, as well as the jealous public, where juries know and exercise their rights, where advocates of unimpeachable integrity and unquestioned ability can always be found to plead the cause of the oppressed—it is difficult to appreciate the great services performed by Erskine for the cause of civil liberty.

Eloquence is the offspring of knowledge and freedom, and can never flourish in the blighting shade of despotism. Her voice, sweet and entrancing, cannot be heard, when justice is surrounded by the hosts of corruption, armed with steel or with gold.

Upon the freedom, independence, knowledge, and eloquence of the American bar depend, in a great measure, the perpetuity of our most cherished institutions.

Erskine's alleged failure to support Fox as strenuously as he should have done, and his fear of Pitt in debate, his vanity, a weakness which he had in common with many great orators, his personal frailities, were all so outweighed by his noble qualities that they are hardly worthy of mention.

The writer cannot forbear giving Talfourd's opinion of Erskine, although he by no means approves of the whole of what he says:

" For that sphere, (the Court of King's Bench,) his powers, his acquisitions, and his temperament were exactly framed. He brought into it, indeed, accomplishments never displayed there before in equal perfection—glancing wit, rich humour, infinite grace of action, singular felicity of language, and a memory elegantly stored, yet not crowded, with subjects of classical and fanciful illustration. Above his audience, he was not beyond their sight, and he possessed rare facilities of raising them to his own level. In this purpose he was aided by his connection with a noble family, by a musical voice, and by an eloquent eye, which enticed men to forgive, and even to admire his natural polish and refined allusions. But his moral qualities tended even more to win them. Who could resist a disposition overflowing with kindness, animal spirits as elastic as those of a school-boy, and a love of gaiety and pleasure which shone out amidst the most anxious labours? His very weaknesses became instruments of fascination. His egotism, his vanity, his personal frailties, were all genial, and gave him an irresistible claim to sympathy. His warmest colours were drawn, not from the fancy, but the affections. If he touched on the romantic, it was on the little chapter of romance which belongs to the most hurried and feverish life. The unlettered clown and the assiduous tradesman understood him, when he revived some bright recollection of childhood, or brought back on the heart the enjoyments of old friendships, or touched the chord of domestic love and sorrow. He wielded with skill and power the weapons which precedent supplied, but he rarely sought for others. When he defended the rights of the subject, it was not by abstract disquisition, but by freshening up anew the venerable customs and immunities which he found sanctioned by courts and parliaments, and infusing into them new energy. He entrenched himself within the forms of pleading, even when he ventured to glance into literature and history. These forms he rendered dignified as a fence against oppression, and cast on them sometimes the playful hues of his fancy. His powers were not only adapted to his sphere, but directed by admirable discretion and taste. In small causes he was never betrayed into exaggeration, but contrived to give an interest to their details, and to conduct them at once with dexterity and grace. His jests told for arguments ; his digressions only threw the jury off their guard, that he might strike a decisive blow ; his audacity was always wise. His firmness was no less under right direction than his weaknesses. He withstood the bench, and rendered the bar immortal service ; not so much by the courage of the resistance, as by the happy selection of its time, and the exact propriety of its manner. He was, in short, the most consummate advocate of whom we have any trace ; he left his profession higher than he found it ; and yet beyond its pale, he was only an incomparable companion, a lively pamphleteer, and a weak and superficial debater."

It seems, from the concurrent testimony of those who were in a position to fairly judge of Erskine's ability, that he attained the highest intellectual eminence to which, under circumstances the most favourable, an advocate can reasonably aspire.

Sir James Scarlett—by which name he is better known to the legal profession than by the title of Lord Abinger, only held by him for the last few years of his life—was one of the most successful advocates of modern times. He gained more cases than any of his contemporaries.

Sir James Scarlett was born on the 13th day of December, 1769, in the Island of Jamaica. He was the descendant of an illustrious family on both sides. His father's ancestors had estates in Suffolk and Essex in the reign of Charles II. His grandfather, James Scarlett, married the daughter of a West Indian proprietor—a relative of General Wolfe, who fell at Quebec. Robert, the father of Lord Abinger, married Elizabeth Anglin, whose direct ancestor was President of Lord Protector Cromwell's Council during the Commonwealth.

Scarlett's parents, sensible of the corruption of morals incident to that unhappy state of slavery which existed in Jamaica, sent him, at an early age, to England to be educated. After his arrival there—having finished his preparatory studies—he entered himself a student of Trinity College, Cambridge. He took the degrees of Bachelor of Arts, and Master of Arts at that University. Having entered himself and studied law in the Temple, he was called to the Bar on the 28th day of July, 1791. Soon after his call to the Bar he was married to Miss Louise Henrietta Campbell, the daughter of Peter Campbell, Esq., of Kilmary, in Argyllshire. Scarlett says of her: "Her children lived to witness her sweet disposition, her divine temper, and consummate discretion. I lived with her in uninterrupted comfort and happiness from the time of our marriage to the month of March, 1829, and have lived ever since to lament her loss." For twenty-five years Scarlett remained a junior counsel, although he had a good practice. He joined the Northern Circuit, and also practiced in the court at Lancaster.

Scarlett's personal appearance was greatly in his favour, and he enjoyed the reputation of being "*the* handsome barrister" in the courts which he attended. His complexion was singularly clear, fresh, and delicate, and his countenance was redolent of health. His features were small, regular, and extremely pleasant. He was above the middle height, and late in life, Falstaffian in width.

It is said that Scarlett's handsome, contented, smiling countenance often deceived a witness into the belief that whether his answer was yes or no was a matter of very little importance. His replies, however, are said to have been his great *forte*. If the issue depended upon the balance of testimony, upon contradictory witnesses, no advocate had a happier faculty of displaying the weak points of his adversary's case and the strong points of his own. If it depended upon a deduction of inferences, upon the combination of many circumstances, upon reconciling evidence apparently discordant, he was sure to obtain attention in the commencement, and to hold it to the conclusion. He made few notes of what he intended to say, but arranged all the points in his memory, and when he arose his face expressed the certainty of a verdict in his favour. He was never tedious, and he always exhausted his subject, but never his hearers.

Scarlett always selected, with consummate judgment, the strongest points in his client's cause, and disregarding those of minor importance, he presented them to the court with unrivalled clearness. Stupid indeed, was the judge or juror who could not see the strongest features of his client's case, after it had been presented by him. In fact Scarlett was so skillful that he would allow them to look at nothing else, except what made against the other side. He would not allow them to glance at any other object. He presented, with surpassing skill, the leading facts and circumstances unfavourable to the opposite side, and it has been said, he was so remarkably clear and convincing in his reasonings that there was no chance to mistake his meaning.

Scarlett had the rare faculty of divesting legal technicalities of their repulsiveness to the mind of the average juror, and although he rarely indulged in rhetoric or oratory, as those terms are usually understood, juries rarely tired of listening to his speeches. He did more to enlighten the minds of the jury and the audience upon the principles of the common law, than any man of his time. An able professor, in a score of lectures, could not have done the work so effectively. By his talent for simplifying abstruse matters, and popularising technicalities, he invariably won the good-will and attention of the jury, and he rarely failed to make even a jury composed of the most ignorant labourers understand, fully, the law and the facts of every case.

Scarlett had the happy faculty of selecting the most talented man on the jury. His penetration in such cases amounted to a species of intuition. To the party thus singled out, Scarlett addressed himself almost as exclusively as if there had been no other juror in the box, and no other person in the court. The juror of course felt highly flattered at being thus distinguished from his fellows, and was consequently inclined to be favourably disposed to the advocate. He was very cheerful in his manner when he addressed a jury. He treated the jurors as if he had been upon terms of particular intimacy with them all his life. His style was conversational. His speeches were seldom laboured. He paid little attention to rounding his periods. His manner of addressing a jury was peculiar. His practice, ordinarily, is said to have been, to fold up the sides of his gown in his hands, and then, placing his arms on his breast, smile in the faces of the jury from the beginning to the end of his speech, talking at the same time to them as if they were engaged in a matter of mere friendly conversation.

The tone of his voice was usually low, but clear and distinct. Scarlett was a close observer, and he paid particular attention to the effect which the testimony both of his own witnesses, and those of his adversaries, had upon the jury.

It is said that Scarlett was extremely prudent in his management of a cause. He did not attempt to carry the feelings of the jury by storm before a torrent of eloquence as Brougham and some of his other contemporaries did. He confined himself closely to the facts of the case in every instance. He admitted some when they would n't hurt his case much, forgot to mention others that would, and explained those which were against him which he could not afford to pass in silence.

Scarlett's method of conducting his cases is well stated by Talfourd, himself an able advocate and an elegant writer:

" Mr. Scarlett, the present leader of the Court of King's Bench, has less brilliancy than his predecessor, (Erskine), but

is not perhaps essentially inferior to him in the management
of causes. He studiously disclaims imagination; he rarely
addresses the passions; but he now and then gives indications which prove that he has disciplined a mind of considerable elegance and strength to *Nisi Prius* uses. In the
fine tact of which we have already spoken—the intuitive
power of common sense sharpened within a peculiar circle—
he has no superior, and perhaps no equal. He never betrays
anxiety in the crisis of a cause, but instantly decides among
complicated difficulties, and is almost always right. He can
bridge over a non-suit with insignificant facts, and tread
upon the gulf steadily but warily to its end. What Johnson
said of Burke's manner of treating a subject is true of his
management of a cause, ' he winds himself into it like a great
serpent.' He does not take a single view of it, nor desert it
when it begins to fail, but throws himself into all its wind-
ings, and struggles in it while it has life. There is a lucid
arrangement and sometimes a light view of pleasantry and
feeling in his opening speeches; but his greatest *visible*
triumph is in his replies. These do not consist of a mere
series of ingenious remarks on conflicting evidence; still less
of a tiresome examination of the testimony of each witness
singly; but are as finely arranged on the instant, and thrown
into as noble and decisive masses, as if they had been prepared in the study. By a vigorous grasp of thought, he
forms a plan and an outline, which he first distinctly marks,
and then proceeds to fill up with masterly touches. When
a case has been spread over half a day, and apparently
shattered by the speech and witnesses of his adversary, he
will gather it up, condense, concentrate, and render it conclusive. He imparts a weight and solidity to all that he
touches. Vague suspicions become certainties, as he exhibits them; and circumstances light, valueless, and unconnected till then, are united together, and come down in
wedges which drive conviction into the mind. . . .
Scarlett, in the debate on the motion relative to the Chancellor's attack on Mr. Abercrombie, showed that he has felt
it necessary to bend his mind considerably to the routine of

his practice. He was then surprised into his own original nature; and forgetting the measured compass of his long-adopted voice and manner, spoke out in a broad northern dialect, and told daring truths which astonished the house. It is not thus, however, that he wins verdicts and compels the court to grant ' rules to show cause ! '

Notwithstanding Scarlett's usual mildness, when the occasion warranted, he could be extremely severe in his language, and he was once sued for slander. He called the plaintiff (the name of the case is Hodgson *v.* Scarlett, 1 B. and A, 232), ' a fraudulent and wicked attorney.' The court decided that a lawyer is not liable for words spoken in the argument of a cause, if they are pertinent to the issues involved.

Some of Scarlett's critics insist that he was haughty, supercillious, and arrogant to his inferiors, and that he was selfish, and unpatriotic. The writer is of the opinion that none of these charges are true ; on the contrary, while at the bar he was deservedly popular with all its members with very few exceptions, and he was always extremely desirous to aid in the enactment of laws which he deemed beneficial to his country. He did everything in his power to assist Sir Samuel Romilly and Sir James Mackintosh to mitigate the severities of the English criminal law. It is true he was quiet and unostentatious in his efforts to reform abuses ; others often obtained credit which was due him. Various conjectures have been made as to the cause of Sir James Scarlett's success at the bar, and many of them are very plausible, but the cause of his success is better stated by himself than by any of his critics. He says in his *Autobiography*: "From these remarks it will appear that my success did not in the least depend on those tirades of declamation which make the reputation of a speaker. Nor in the most considerable and difficult cases in which I have carried the verdict, can any one who reads the printed speech either take any interest in it or even understand it without reading over and understanding the whole of the evidence. I never made a speech with a view to my own

17

reputation, nor for any other object but to serve my client. The general audience, therefore, which crowded to hear popular speakers took little interest in my performances. But the judge and the jury, on the contrary, gave me their profound attention, and I believe I may say that no advocate in my time possessed a greater influence with them. Upon this subject, perhaps, I may be excused for relating an anecdote which is an illustration of it. On the Northern Circuit at certain periods there used to be a grand supper, at which all the members were assembled, and the expenses of which were paid by fines and congratulations that resulted in contributions to which the principal leaders were subject. These were introduced, in general, in a ceremonious speech by one of the body who bore the office of Attorney-General of the Circuit. Upon the occasion to which I allude, the present Lord Chief-Justice Tindal held that office. I was leader of the Circuit both in rank and business. He introduced my name for the purpose of a congratulation, by stating that his friend Mr. Scarlett had for many years been employing his genius in the invention of a machine which he had brought to perfection. The operation, the whole Circuit were in the habit of witnessing, with astonishment at his success. He, the Attorney-General, had at length discovered the secret, which was no other than a machine which he dexterously contrived to keep out of sight, but by virtue of which he produced a surprising effect on the head of the judge. 'You have all noticed, gentlemen, that when my learned friend addresses the court he produces on the judge's head a motion angular to the horizon, like this,' he then made a movement of his head which signified a nod of approbation. When he had carried his motion by a unanimous vote of congratulation, he proceeded to another leader of the Circuit, a gentleman of more popular and much higher reputation as a speaker than myself. He said: 'This gentleman, as you all know, has for years been devoting his illustrious talents to surpass Mr. Scarlett. This he endeavours to accomplish by various means, and amongst others by imitating his example in the invention of a machine to operate on the head of the judge. In this he has at length, after much labour and study, succeeded. But you have observed that the motion he produces is of a different character. It is parallel to the horizon, in this fashion,' he then moved his head in a manner denoting dissent. The contrast and the joke occasioned much laughter, in which the gentleman last alluded to most heartily joined, his good-nature being not less remarkable than his talents.

"I avoided every topic that I observed made an unfavourable impression upon them, and when I discovered the strings that vibrated in their bosoms, I often by a single touch on the true card, in the course of my address or sometimes in an incidental remark on the evidence as it was given, saw that I had carried the verdict. I recollect that early in my career I was junior counsel for the sitting member upon an election petition. The case was one of very great interest from many exaggerated and false accounts that had been published before the meeting of parliament. The petitioner was a strong supporter of ministers, and the great majority of the committee was formed of persons actually in office, or of his own partisans. I soon perceived from the petitioner's evidence and the manner in which it was received, that to retain the seat was hopeless, and that even to avoid seating the petitioner was a task of considerable difficulty. My leader was a learned sergeant, who opened his case for the sitting member something too high. The evidence on both sides, however, satisfied me that the true conclusion was to make it a void election, but, that to lead the committee to that conclusion required very close and exact reasoning on the evidence. I determined to try my powers. It was the first election committee on which I was concerned. I began my address by stating that I should add nothing to the arguments of my leader in support of the seat, because I felt that if he had not satisfied them upon that point, it would be vain for me to attempt it. I should therefore confine myself strictly to the question whether the petitioner had established a right to the seat,

or whether it was a void election, and though I did not disguise to myself the difficulties that lay in my way even upon
that question, I entertained a strong hope that if they
would honour me with their attention whilst I brought
before them such parts of the evidence on both sides as appeared to me material, it would be in my power to convince
them that they ought to take the same view of the case
which induced me to entertain that hope; the more especially as I did not doubt that much of the prejudice that had
been excited, and which gave so strong an interest in the
case, had already been dispelled by the evidence.

"Confining their attention to a single point, I omitted all
facts that might be doubted, selected only those which
could not be disputed, and made my remarks as concisely
and as perspicuously as I was able to do. In the course of
the first half hour I found that the majority of the committee were listening to me with the most profound attention,
which was preserved to the end of a speech of two hours and
a half, much the shortest that had been delivered. The result was that the committee came to the conclusion I had
desired, namely, that the election was void, by a small
majority, in which I considered it a great enhancement of
my victory to find the nominee of the petitioner. This
nominee was no other than Mr. Bond the king's counsel
and at that time judge advocate. A friend of mine who
took an interest in my success, asked this gentleman how
Scarlett had acquitted himself. He replied, ' he made a very
masterly dissection of the evidence, and certainly convinced
me.' *There was the whole secret, to make a masterly dissection of evidence when the cause depended on a correct judgment of the facts.*"

Scarlett obtained a seat in the House of Commons in 1818,
but his parliamentary career did not altogether satisfy his
friends. In the year 1822 he was returned for the University
of Cambridge, and subsequently represented Maldon and
Cockermouth; and after the Reform Bill, he was member
for the city of Norwich.

In 1827 he was made attorney-general and was knighted.

On December 24, 1834, Scarlett was made Chief Baron of the Court of Exchequer, and in the following month he was elevated to the House of Peers by the title of Lord Abinger, of Abinger, in Surrey, an estate which he had purchased. Scarlett did not distinguish himself while on the bench. It is conceded, however, that he was a lover of learning and of learned men, a patron of art and artists, and a man of liberal thoughts and acquirements.

A very high compliment was paid Sir James Scarlett by Sir James Coleridge, who, while speaking of his legal attainments, said, in the year 1859, that his place at the bar, twenty-five years after his leaving it, was yet unfilled. Scarlett was struck with a fit of paralysis while attending the Norfolk Circuit as a judge in 1844, and died soon thereafter at the age of seventy-five years.

Bright.—John Bright was born November 16, 1811, at Greenbank, Rochdale, England. He was placed in his father's counting-house after an ordinary school-training. During the discussion of the Reform Bill of 1831–32, he distinguished himself. He was also an ardent and eloquent supporter, along with Richard Cobden, of the Anti-Corn Law League. This body was dissolved at Manchester in 1846, after the legislature established free trade.

Mr. Bright entered parliament in the year 1843. He soon became one of the most popular speakers in the house. One writer says of his published speeches, "We doubt if our language possesses a record of any speeches really spoken, which are superior to them." The following account has been given of his oratory. "During three years Mr. Bright has been an involuntary absentee from parliamentary life. 'I shall not know the House of Commons without Sir Robert Peel,' said Macaulay, when his election for Edinburgh restored him to his old place there. The Reformed House of Commons has scarcely been itself without Mr. Bright. His accustomed seat below the gangway has lacked him, and his absence was even less conspicuous when his place was empty than when it was filled by some veteran Leaguer, or some preferred home ruler from the upper benches. The portly

figure and the lion-like head caught the glance of all
strangers ; and ' Bright ' was pointed out with pride by the
habitués or the attendants of the place. The time is probably
approaching when he will be seen there again ; when visitors
will comment on the sharp decision with which the member
for Birmingham accompanied his talk to his neighbour ; and
watch for the quick, nervous glance towards the chair, and
the slight movement which seldom failed to catch at once
the eye of the Speaker, and to arrest the attention of the
House, as he rose to take part in the debate. Whatever
differences of opinion might exist in the House of Commons
with respect to Mr. Bright as a politician, there never was
any question as to his consummate ability as an orator.
The emptiest house—if perchance he rose in an empty house,
which he was seldom prone to do—speedily filled when he
was known to be on his legs. Beginning in low and
measured tones, with a sort of conversational hesitation
in the opening sentences, he speedily rose to animation.
The first condition of his success was this : that business
was the backbone of his speeches. They were always animated by a purpose which was clear to himself, and which
he never failed to make clear to his hearers. No one could
fail to know what he was driving at.

" Though essentially a plain speaker, both in the literary
and moral meaning of the phrase, there can be no greater
mistake than that he is (if one may still speak in the present
tense) a rude or unpolished one. In one sense, he is the
most cultivated speaker in the House of Commons, inas-
much as he has most elaborately and successfully trained
his natural gifts of eloquence. A presence which fills the
eye, a voice which at once takes the ear, and a slow and deliberate utterance which seems to choose the best word, and to
watch its effect in order that he may so choose and place the
next as to heighten, or, if need be, to soften and qualify the
impression of the first, compel attention and interest. Mr.
Bright's power of convincing does not lie so much in strict
logic—he does not often affect the forms of logic, though his
speeches never want the substance of it—as in the submis-

sion of the essential elements of a question to sagacious common sense and right feeling. Nothing can be better fitted than his words to his thought. The best answer to the imputation that he is un-English in character might, perhaps, be found in his language, which is more thoroughly and racily English than that of any speaker in either House. It combines in happy blending, alike the simple and dignified elements of our tongue. Mr. Bright, if he has not as much talent as Mr. Disraeli, has a great deal more humor; he has as much earnestness as Mr. Gladstone, with more self-possession; and he has a simplicity of pathos, and an occasional grandeur, scorn, and indignation, which belong to neither. No orator has contributed more to the public stock—more images and phrases that will live—than Mr. Bright. Mr. Disraeli as the mountebank, with a pill for the earthquake, and Mr. Lowe and Mr. Horsman as the Scotch terrier party of which no one could tell the head from the tail, belong now to history as completely as the Adullamites and the fancy franchises to our political vocabulary. Few things finer have ever been uttered by any orator than Mr. Bright's appeal to the rival leaders to lay aside their animosities in order to seek a remedy for the wrongs of Ireland, than the passage in which he described the angel of death visiting the homes to be desolated by the Crimean war, or than the moral dignity of the sentences in which he vindicated his own career at Birmingham."

Although there is a great diversity of opinion as to Mr. Bright's rank as a statesman, posterity will unhesitatingly say that he was one of the greatest orators of his time. Those who have heard him speak most frequently, and those most capable of passing judgment upon his oratory, are loudest in their praise of it. Mr. Bright, in one of his speeches at Birmingham, described himself as having, during the quarter of a century over which his public life then extended, endured measureless insult, and passed through hurricanes of abuse.

While Mr. Bright was alive, the following graphic and able account of his manner of speaking was written by Mr. T. W.

Reid : " His manner, when speaking, is quiet and subdued, but it is the apparent subjugation which a bar of iron undergoes when it passes from the red-hot stage to the condition of white-heat. The red-hot bar splutters and sends forth sparks, and is, on the whole, the more imposing to the passing glance. But there are more heat and power in the quiet-looking bar that steadfastly burns, content, without calling attention to the process, by occasionally spluttering forth an ineffectual shower of sparks. In the course of a speech Mr. Bright generally manages to say something damaging to his opponents and helpful to the cause he advocates. But when he sits down, there is invariably a feeling amongst his audience that he has by no means exhausted himself, but could, if he pleased, have said a great deal more that would have been equally effectual. To this end his quiet, self-possessed manner greatly tends. He has himself well in hand throughout his orations, and therefore maintains his hold upon his audience. His gestures are of the fewest ; but unlike Mr. Disraeli's, they always seem appropriate and natural. A simple wave of the right hand, and the sentence is emphasized. Nature has gifted him with a fine presence, and a voice the like of which has but rarely rung through the rafters of St. Stephen's. 'Like a bell' is the illustration usually employed in the endeavour to convey by words an impression of its music. But I think it were better to say 'like a peal of bells,' for a single one could not produce the varied tones in which Mr. Bright suits his expressions to his theme. On the whole, the dominant note is one of pathos. Possibly because nearly all Mr. Bright's great speeches have been made when he has been pleading the cause of the oppressed, or denouncing a threatened wrong, a tone of melancholy can be heard running through all. And for the expression of pathos, there are marvelously touching tones in his voice, tones which carry right to the listener's heart the tender thoughts that come glowing from the speaker's and are clad in simple words as they pass his tongue.

" We have seen him thrill to tears, or rouse to shouts of applause the like of which we never heard before, a rough

Lancashire audience of eight or nine thousand persons, packed within one of the great mills at Rochdale; and in the House of Commons we have heard him speak for an hour at a stretch, whilst every man in the building listened with breathless attention, and the cheers that broke out at the end of every sentence came almost as much from the one side of the House as from the other.   Nay, we have watched the faces of the men to whom is committed the government of the British Empire, and of the 'strangers' permitted to join with them, strangers including princes of the blood, peers of long descent, the ministers of foreign countries, and the leaders of the Church ; we have watched them, as slowly, word by word, he was rolling forth the magnificent peroration of one of his great speeches, and we have seen upon their countenances such a rapt, and almost awe-stricken expression, as—to return to the simile we mentioned at the beginning of this sketch—one might have expected to see on the faces of a Hebrew congregation before whom an Isaiah was delivering himself of his heaven-born visions.

" We cannot resist the temptation of transcribing this one ' vision ' of the member for Birmingham, in 1862, on the subject of the American war, and the delivery of which will ever dwell, in the memories of those who heard it uttered, as one of the most wonderful incidents in their lives.   ' The leaders of this revolt,' said he, after speaking nearly two hours with regard to the war, ' propose this monstrous thing —that, over a territory forty times as large as England the blight of slavery shall be forever perpetuated. I cannot believe, for my part, that such a fate will befall that fair land, stricken though it now is with the ravages of war.   I cannot believe that civilisation, in its journey with the sun, will sink into endless night, in order to gratify the ambition of the leaders of this revolt, who seek to

> " Wade through slaughter to a throne,
>   And shut the gates of mercy to mankind."

" ' I have another and a far brighter vision before my gaze. It may be but a vision, but I will cherish it.   I see one vast confederation, stretching from the frozen North in unbroken line to the glowing South, and from the wild billows of the Atlantic, westward to the calmer waters of the Pacific main —and I see one people, and one language, and one law, and one faith, and over all that wide continent the home of free-dom, and a refuge for the oppressed of every race and of every clime.'

"And yet, whilst the effect produced by Mr. Bright upon those who listen to him is wonderful, the first impression of those who hear him for the first time is one of disappoint-ment. When he begins to speak to any audience, he gen-erally opens his address in a low tone, pauses occasionally, as though to find a suitable word, and seems to have no idea whatever of rousing the enthusiasm of those who listen to him. Those who have taken with them pre-conceived notions of Mr. Bright, presenting him to their imaginations as a reckless demagogue, full of sound and fury, will hardly be able to recognise the great orator in the quiet and unim-passioned speaker who stands motionless before them, pour-ing forth a stream of noble Saxon words, the very simplicity and appropriateness of which rob the orator of a portion of the credit which is due to him.

"But presently, while the stranger is wondering at the infatuation of those who have placed upon the brows of this man the crown of eloquence, he is himself drawn within the circle of his influence, and, forgetting his pre-conceived notions, his subsequent disappointment and his whole the-ory of the art of oratory, he listens enchanted to the man who can put the most difficult questions so plainly before his audience, and in whose hands the dryest subject becomes so interesting.

"Then, when the speaker has drawn the whole of his hearers into sympathy with him, he begins to work on their emotions like a skilful player on the harp. And first he rouses the scorn of scorn in their hearts by a few simple words, which, when we read them in the morning, appear altogether innocent, but which, as he utters them, scathe the object of his wrath more terribly than the bitterest or most violent invective. Perhaps in nothing has Mr. Bright so much power as in his use of sarcasm. The manner in which, by a mere inflection of his voice, he can express the intensest scorn, and so express it as to make his feelings more completely known to his audience than if he spent an hour in trying to explain them, is simply marvellous. We remember one or two instances in which the mere tone of his voice has conveyed an impression of his boundless contempt for his adversary which no language could have expressed half so well.

"But almost directly after the audience has been stirred by the orator's sarcasm, he begins in the calmest and most deliberate manner to tell some story. Mr. Bright is a wonderful story-teller, and some of the best anecdotes and illustrations that have been given to us in modern times have come from him. The story of the old gentleman, for instance, who used to say that a 'hole wore longer than a patch,' is worthy of being placed beside the history of Dame Partington ; . . . and the Syrian monk, to whom 'tears were as natural as perspiration,' are good examples of the ready wit with which he supplies every argument he employs with an appropriate illustration.

"More notable examples of the same quality are to be found in that speech in which he christened the Adullamites, and added a new phrase—'the Cave '—to the vocabulary of party politics. The speech itself was a triumph of humour, nothing in it being more grotesquely irresistible than that never-to-be-forgotten of the 'party of two,' which bore so striking a resemblance to the young ladies' terrier, 'which was so covered with hair that you could not tell which was the head and which was the tail of it.'

"Perhaps none of Mr. Bright's qualities does so much to render him popular, as a speaker, both in the House of Commons and in the provinces, as his humour. And one peculiarity of his humour is, that it always appears to be unconscious. When he is telling one of his best stories, or uttering one of his best sayings, he hardly moves a muscle of his face, and seemingly takes no share in the merriment of his audience."

Mr. Bright rarely indulged in classical quotations, for the reason, probably, that he received his education at Quaker schools and colleges, where the classics were not taught. But his knowledge of English literature was very considerable, and his quotations from the greatest authors were frequent and felicitous.

When Mr. Bright desired to cover with ridicule the faction of which Mr. Lowe was the head, he thought of the escape of David from Achish, King of Gath, and the people who subsequently gathered with him in the Cave of Adullam.

On another occasion when speaking complainingly of the Conservatives, he said that if that party "had been in the wilderness, they would have complained of the Ten Commandments as a harassing piece of legislation."

He called Mr. Disraeli the "mystery man of the ministry." And he said of Sir Charles Adderly in a letter to a friend, "I hope he thought he was speaking the truth, but he is rather a dull man, and is liable to make blunders." Of another man, who boasted that his ancestors came over with the Conqueror, he said, "I never heard that they did anything else."

Mr. Bright was unable to attend to his parliamentary duties for a short time on account of sickness; a nobleman impudently remarked in public, that, by way of punishment for the use he had made of his talents, Providence had inflicted upon Mr. Bright a disease of the brain. Mr. Bright said, when he resumed his duties: "It may be so, but in any case, it will be some consolation to the friends and family of the noble lord to know that the disease is one which even Providence could not inflict upon him."

One of the most striking passages to be found in any of Mr. Bright's speeches is the following one, taken from his speech against the prosecution of the Crimean war:

"I do not suppose that your troops are to be beaten in actual conflict with the foe, or that they will be driven into the sea; but I am certain that many homes in England in which there exists a fond hope that the distant one may return—many such homes may be rendered desolate when the next mail shall arrive. The angel of death has been abroad throughout the land; you may almost hear the beating of his wings. There is no one, as when the first-born was slain of old, to sprinkle with blood the lintel and the two side-posts of our doors, that he may spare and pass on; he takes his victims from the castle of the noble, the mansion of the wealthy, and the cottage of the poor and lowly, and it is in behalf of all these classes that I make this solemn appeal. . . . I would ask, I would entreat the noble lord (Palmerston) to take a course which, when he looks back upon his whole political career—whatever he may find therein to be pleased with, whatever to regret—cannot but be a source of gratification to him. By adopting that course he would have the satisfaction of reflecting that, having obtained the laudable object of his ambition—having become the foremost subject of the crown, the director of, it may be, the destinies of his country, and the presiding genius of her councils—he had achieved a still higher and nobler ambition; that he had returned the sword to its scabbard—that at his words torrents of blood had ceased to flow—that he had restored tranquillity to Europe, and saved this country from the indescribable calamities of war."

On November 3, 1868, Mr. Bright was presented with the freedom of the city of Edinburgh, and in 1869 he accepted office as president of the Board of Trade. He was appointed to the Chancellorship of the Duchy of Lancaster in August, 1873, and held that post till the dissolution of the Liberal Government, February, 1874. Mr. Bright's name was also identified with a scheme for the reform of the electoral representation.

Mr. Bright was robust of frame, broad-shouldered, broad-chested, and of graceful manners. He had a broad, full, decidedly Saxon face. His forehead was broad and high. His brows were dark and heavy. His eyes were a keen, tender blue, full of "sweet gravity, and wonderfully intellectual." They could flash fire, or melt into tears, and captivated all who came within the sphere of their influence.

" His mouth," says a writer, who gave a description of him
·before his death, " though large, is firm and indicative of the
greatness of his heart, and has an expression of good
humour. The lips have, in their fleshy and massive outline,
abundant marks of habitual reflection and intellectual occupation. The streak of the unfaded rose still enlivens his
cheeks. When animated during a speech his comely Saxon
features brighten into unmistakable beauty, and when seen
in the profile are even finer than when viewed from the
front. The whole has an expression of fine intellectual dignity, candour, serenity, and lofty, gentlemanly repose."

Mr. Bright was a philanthropist in the true sense of that
term. He devoted the best years of his life to the study of
the causes of human misery and degradation, and he honestly advocated such measures as he deemed best calculated
to ameliorate the condition of the poor and oppressed. But,
he at the same time, recognised the fact that property
owners have rights which should be respected. As to the
wisdom of the legislative remedies which he proposed for
the cure of the diseases of the body politic, which he conceived to exist, there is a wide difference of opinion, but all
agree that Mr. Bright was sincere in his convictions.

Patriotism, and deep earnestness, were the chief features
of Mr. Bright's strength as an orator, but his oratorical success was due not to one or two qualities, but to a combination of qualities like the light and shade of a picture. His
speeches had fervor, force, reason and passion, and touched
the heart, conscience, and intellect, of his hearers.

His memory was extraordinarily tenacious, and allowed
nothing to escape which he had once given due consideration. His information upon subjects with which a statesman
should be familiar is said to have been wide and accurate.

Although, usually, his style was chaste and simple, yet
when the subject permitted, his poetical diction imparted
warmth and brilliancy to facts, which would have been dull
if treated by a less skilful speaker. At times, however, his
language was, to the objects of his attacks, distressingly
plain. The following extract from a speech delivered in

1868 is an example in point. Mr. Bright said: " One of the
candidates for the inferior position of minority member for
Birmingham complained on a recent occasion that I had not
read the speeches of his colleague in the candidature, and
that I had not, in duty bound, undertaken to answer him.
The fact is I am too busy in these days to dwell very much
on works of fiction. The speeches of Mr. Lloyd are what I
call dull fiction, and the speeches of his colleague, though
not less fiction, are certainly of a more sparkling and
sensational character."

Soon after his death, which took place on the 7th day of
March, 1889, the following tribute was paid to Mr. Bright, by
his political associate and personal friend, Hon. W. E. Gladstone:

Mr. Gladstone, upon rising, was received with cheers. He
said :

" Mr. Bright has been, to a very remarkable degree, happy
in the moment of his removal from among us. He lived to
see the triumph of almost every great cause to which he
specially devoted his heart and mind. He has established a
special claim to the admiration of those from whom he differed through his long political life by marked concurrence
with them upon the prominent and dominant question of
the hour. ('Hear! hear!') While he has in that way
opened the minds and hearts of those with whom he differed to appreciation of his merits he has lost nothing by
that concord with them on the particular subjects we so
much represent. Though Mr. Bright came to be separated
from the great bulk of the liberals on the Irish question, on
no single occasion has there been any word of disparage-
ment. I acknowledge that I have not, through my whole
political life, fully embraced the character of Mr. Bright and
the value of that character to the country. I say this because it was at the particular epoch of the Crimean war that
I came more to understand than before the position held by
him and some of his friends and the hold they had laid upon
the confidence of the people. I was one of those who did
not agree with the particular views he took of the Crimean

contest, but felt profoundly, and never ceased to feel what must have been the moral elevation of men, who, nurtured all their lives in the temple of popular approval, could at a moment's notice consent to part with the whole of that favour they enjoy, which opponents might think the very breath of their nostrils. ('Hear! hear!') They accepted undoubted unpopularity, for that war commanded the enormous approval of the people. It was at that time that, although we had known much of Mr. Bright, we learned more. We had known of his great mental gifts, his courage, his consistency, and his splendid eloquence. We had not known how high was the moral tone of those popular leaders, and what splendid examples they could set their contemporaries.

"Among other gifts Mr. Bright was delighted to be one of the chief guardians of the purity of the English tongue. ('Hear! hear!') He knew how the character of a nation is associated with its language. He was enabled, as an Englishman professedly attached to his country, the tongue of the people being to him almost an object of worship, to preserve the purity of the language of Shakespeare and Milton. (Cheers.)

"Another circumstance of his career is better known to me than to any other person present. Everybody is aware that office had no attraction for him. But few can be aware what extra efforts were required to induce him to become a servant of the Crown. In the crisis of 1868, when the fate of the Irish Church hung in the balance, it was my duty to propose to Mr. Bright that he become a Minister. I never undertook so difficult a task. From 11 o'clock at night until 1 o'clock in the morning we steadily debated the subject. It was only at the last moment that he found it possible to set aside the repugnance he felt at doing anything that might in the eyes of any one, even of the more ignorant class of his countrymen, appear to detract in the slightest degree from that lofty independence of character which I have mentioned, and which never throughout his career was held in doubt.

" It was a happy lot to unite so many attractive qualities. If I had to dwell upon them alone I should present a dazzling picture to the world. It was a happier lot to teach moral lessons by simplicity, consistency, unfailing courage, and constancy of life, thus presenting a combination of qualities that carried us to a higher atmosphere. (' Hear! hear! ') His sympathies were not strong only, but active ; not sympathies awaiting calls to be made upon them, but sympathies of a man seeking objects upon which to bestow the inestimable advantages of eloquence and courage. In Ireland, when support of the Irish cause was rare ; in India, when support of the native cause was rarer still; in America, at the time when Mr. Bright, foreseeing the ultimate issue of the great struggle of 1861, stood as the representative of an exceedingly small portion of the educated community of the country, although undoubtedly representing a large part of the national sentiment (' Hear! hear! ') ; in all these cases Mr. Bright went far outside the necessities of his calling. Whatever touched him as a man of the great Anglo-Saxon race, whatever touched him as a subject, obtained, unasked, his sincere, earnest, and enthusiastic aid. (' Hear! hear! ') All causes having his powerful advocacy made a distinct advance in the estimation of the world and distinct progress toward triumphant success. Thus it has come about that he is entitled to a higher eulogy than is due to success. Of mere success, indeed, he was a conspicuous example. In intellect he might claim a most distinguished place. But his character lies deeper than intellect, deeper than eloquence, deeper than anything that can be described or that can be seen upon the surface. The supreme eulogy that is his due is that he elevated political life to the highest point—to a loftier standard than it had ever reached. He has bequeathed to his country a character that can not only be made a subject for admiration and gratitude, but—and I do not exaggerate when I say it — that can become an object of reverential contemplation. In the encomiums that come from every quarter there is not a note of dissonance. I do not know of any statesman of my time who had the happi-

18

ness of receiving, on removal from this passing world, the
honour of approval at once so enthusiastic, so universal, and
so unbroken. ('Hear! hear!') Yet none could better dispense with the tributes of the moment, because the triumphs
of his life were recorded in the advance of his country and
of its people. His name is indelibly written in the annals of
Time and on the hearts of the great and overspreading race
to which he belonged, whose wide extension he rejoiced to
see, and whose power and prominence he believed to be full
of promise and glory for the best interests of mankind."

Mr. Bright's death made a profound impression in all
circles of society. He was respected and beloved by men
of all parties.

Disraeli.—Volumes have been, and many more will be,
filled with criticisms upon the character and public life, of
that remarkable statesman—Mr. Benjamin Disraeli. It is
the author's purpose, however, to treat of him merely as
a political orator. He was undoubtedly gifted with the
highest oratorical talents.

His writings and speeches added new treasures to English
literature. They did something more than amuse. Many
things that he said, posterity will not willingly let die.

Mr. Disraeli was born in London, December 21, 1805.
He was taught chiefly by private tutors.

It was his original intention to study law, but after spending three years in the office of an eminent solicitor in London, he decided to devote his life to politics and literature.

When only twenty years of age, his novel, *Vivian Grey*,
was published. It immediately brought him into notice, and
won for him many flattering social attentions. Lady Bless-
ington's description to Mr. Willis of Mr. Disraeli's first appearance in her drawing-room, is thus given by that author:

"Disraeli, the elder, came here with his son the other
night. It would have delighted you to see the old man's
pride in him, and the son's respect for his father. Disraeli,
the elder, lives in the country, about twenty miles from
town; seldom comes up to London, and leads a life of
retired leisure, each day hoarding up and dispensing forth

treasures of literature. He is courtly, yet urbane, and impresses one at once with confidence in his goodness. In his manner, Disraeli, the younger, is quite the character of *Vivian Grey*, full of genius and eloquence, with extreme good nature and perfect frankness of character."

After travelling in the East for a considerable length of time, young Disraeli gave his attention almost exclusively to politics for some years.

Disraeli was an extremely courageous man, and when he got into a controversy with his political opponents, and strong language was applied to him, he usually clothed his replies in vigorous English. In 1835, while making a canvass for a seat in parliament, as a conservative, he publicly denounced the celebrated Daniel O'Connell as a " bloody traitor." To this O'Connell replied that Disraeli was a " lineal descendant of the blasphemous thief who died upon the cross." Mr. Disraeli, immediately, challenged Morgan O'Connell, but the challenge was not accepted, Disraeli was bound over to keep the peace, and the controversy ended.

A few years later when he obtained a seat in parliament, he gave the following description of Sir Robert Peel's speeches: " They are dreary pages of interminable talk ; full of predictions falsified, pledges broken, calculations that had gone wrong, and budgets that had blown up. And this not relieved by a single original thought, a single generous impulse, or a single happy expression."

When Lord Beaconsfield made his first speech, in the House of Commons, it was met by opposition and ridicule, and at last drowned in uproar. Stopping in the middle of a sentence, he lifted his hand and said, in the full tones of a voice which rose above the tumult:

" I have begun several times many things, and yet have often succeeded at last. I will sit down now, but the time will come when you *shall* hear me ! "

Afterward when speaking of this incident to his constituents he said :

" Was I to yield to this insulting derision like a child or a poltroon ? No. When I sat down I sent them my defiance.

There are emergencies when it becomes necessary to show
that a man will not be crushed. I trust I showed, under
unparalleled interruption, the spirit of a man, and the generosity of a combatant who does not soon lose his temper."

At the death of Lord G. Bentinck he became the acknowledged leader of the Conservatives in the House of Commons. Under Lord Derby, he acted for a short period as
Chancellor of the Exchequer. In 1868 he became First
Lord of the Treasury, which position he held also for a few
months. In 1874, Disraeli became Prime Minister at the
head of the Conservative Government, for the first time.

Disraeli's face was inscrutable. At critical moments hundreds of keen eyes were turned towards that face to read, if
possible, something of his thoughts, but never once, not
even in the most exciting crisis of personal or political conflict, did the face unwittingly relax, so that friend or foe
could read aught there. His face was truly remarkable,
sphinx-like, and unfathomable. His courage in the parliamentary contests in which he was engaged was of the highest order. He was a most excellent leader. He had perfect
command of his temper, and he knew how to encourage his
followers and to arouse them to enthusiasm.

As an orator Mr. Disraeli was, in some respects, superior
to any of his contemporaries. His self-possession, which
nothing could disturb ; his terse, epigrammatic replies, when
interrupted by questions ; his keen, mercilessly sarcastic
attacks upon his assailants when provoked ; his wonderful
command of language, and fluency of speech rendered him
one of the most effective parliamentary orators of any age
or nation.

It has been said by some of his critics that the weakest
points in his oratory were a lack of earnestness and sincere
conviction, but judging from the fairest and most impartial
accounts which have been given of his speeches the accusation is not well-founded, when applied to matter, or manner.

His speeches were instructive, convincing, and persuasive,
and had a prodigious effect upon the people of England as
long as he remained in public life.

Mr. Disraeli, when the occasion demanded it, was not only a powerful, and logical speaker, but exceedingly pathetic, as well. When President Lincoln was so foully assassinated, the speech of Mr. Disraeli, of all those made, the world over, was the most pathetic and touching, by far, and brought tears to the eyes of thousands.

The following remarks upon Mr. Disraeli's oratory by a writer in the *Gentleman's Magazine* are interesting :

" When he rises to speak he generally rests his hand for a moment upon the table, but it is only for a moment, for he invariably endeavors to gain the ear of his audience by making a point, at the outset, and the attitude which he finds most conducive to the happy delivery of points is to stand balancing himself upon his feet with his hand in his coat-tail pockets. In this position, with his head hung down as if he were mentally debating how best to express a thought that had just occurred to his mind, Mr. Disraeli slowly utters the polished and poisoned sentence over which he has spent laborious hours in the closet.

" But the merest tyro in the House knows a moment beforehand when Mr. Disraeli is approaching what he regards as a convenient place in his speech for dropping in the phrase-gem he pretends to have just found in an odd corner of his mind. They see him leading up to it; they note the disappearance of his hands in the direction of the coat-tail pockets, sometimes in search of the pocket-handkerchief, which is brought out and shaken with a light and careless air, but most often to extend the coat-tails, whilst with body gently rocked to and fro, and an affected hesitancy of speech, the speaker produces his *bon mot.* For the style of repartee in which Mr. Disraeli indulges—which may be described generally as a sort of solemn chaffing, varied by strokes of polished sarcasm—this manner is admirable, in proportion as it has been seldom observed. But it is monotonous to a degree perhaps exceeded only by that of Mr. Cardwell, who, during his last speech on the Army Estimates, was timed with a watch, and found to go through the following series of oratorical performances with the regularity of a pendu-

lum, preserving throughout an hour the exact time allotted
at the outset to each manœuvre : First, he advanced to the
table and rested upon it, leaning his left arm upon the edge ;
secondly, he stood bolt upright and retired half a pace from
the table, letting his arms hang stiffly by his side ; thirdly,
he put both hands out and arranged the papers before him ;
fourthly, he retired a full pace, folded his hands behind him
under his coat-tails, and again stood bolt upright, looking
like an undertaker who had called for orders.   This latter
was his favourite position, and he remained in it for the
longest period.   But when the time came to forsake it, he
advanced, leaned his arm upon the table, and again went
through the full round of graceful action.   Mr. Disraeli is
not as this, etc.''   This account, and many others of a similar
character, have done Mr. Disraeli great injustice, and were
evidently penned by his political enemies, who hoped to
lessen his influence by attacking him with the keen weapon
of satire.   But he was more than a match for any of his
assailants when he chose to answer their attacks.   It is
greatly to be regretted that public men should be subjected
to such unfair criticisms.   Critics, though hostile, should
have too much self-respect to lie outright in order to bring
unmerited reproach and public contempt upon the object
of their envenomed assaults ; but the discriminating few,
the wisest and best men, always loathe and detest such
malignancy.   Nothing has impaired, to a greater extent, the
influence of the press than the publication of scurrilous articles which secretly aim to compass the ruin or injury of
those who have incurred the enmity of the writers.

Few statesmen of ancient or modern times have been
more witty and humourous than Mr. Disraeli was when he
chose to be.   In a speech to the conservatives at Glasgow,
November, 1873, alluding to the Abyssinian war he said :
" I should myself from my own individual experience be
most careful not to follow the example which one of the
most distinguished members of the present Administration
pursued with respect to us when we had to encounter the
Abyssinian difficulty.   When I introduced the necessity of

interference in order to escape from difficulties which we had inherited and not made, Mr. Lowe rose in parliament and violently attacked the Government of the day for the absurdity, the folly, the extreme imprudence of attempting any interference in the affairs of Abyssinia. . . . He described the horrors of the country, and the terrors of the clime. He said there was no possibility by which any suc-cess could be obtained, and the people of England must prepare themselves for the most horrible catastrophe. He described not only the fatal influence of the climate, *but, I remember, he described one pink fly alone which* he said would eat up the whole British army. He was as vituperative as the insects of Abyssinia."

When Lords Beaconsfield and Salisbury returned from Berlin in 1878, a dinner in their honour was given at Knightsbridge by members of the conservative party, more than five hundred being present. On this occasion, Lord Beaconsfield, in the course of his speech, referred as follows to some criticisms of Mr. Gladstone : " I was astonished to learn that the Convention of Constantinople has been de-scribed as ' an insane convention.' That is a strong epithet, but I do not pretend to be as competent a judge of insanity as the right honourable gentleman who used it. I will not say to the right honourable gentleman what I had occasion to say in the House of Lords this year, *Naviget Auticyram ;* but I would put this issue to an intelligent English jury—which do you believe most likely to enter into an insane convention, a body of English gentlemen, honoured by the favour of their sovereign and the confidence of their fellow subjects, managing your affairs for five years, I hope with prudence and not altogether without success, or a sophistical rhetorician, inebriated with the exuberance of his own ver-bosity, and gifted with an egotistical imagination, that can at all times command an interminable and inconsistent series of arguments to malign his opponents and to glorify himself."

Young men should learn from the life of Lord Beacons-field that " Never despair " is a good motto, and that diffi-culties " ought to be no more than the threads of gossamer, sparkling with dew-drops, which we break away by thousands as we stride through the morning fields."

Even from boyhood Lord Beaconsfield determined, if possible, to become Prime Minister of England.

He loved to encourage young men, and at Manchester, speaking to youths, he said :

" I give to them that counsel which I have ever given to youth. I tell them to aspire. I believe that the youth who does not *look up*, will *look down*; and that the spirit which does not *dare* to *soar*, is *destined* perhaps, to *grovel.*"

He did not urge them, however, to a selfish ambition. He said : " You will be called to great duties. Remember what has been done for you. Remember that when the inheritance devolves upon you, you are not only to enjoy, but to improve. You will one day succeed to the high places of this great community. Recollect those who lighted the way for you; and when you have wealth, when you have authority, when you have power, let it not be said that you were deficient in public virtue or public spirit. When the torch is delivered to *you*, do you also light the path of human progress to educated man."

Lord Beaconsfield delivered an address to the members of the Manchester Athenæum on the 23d of October, 1844. In that address occurs the following beautiful and striking passage upon knowledge: " It is knowledge that equalises the social condition of man—that gives to all, however different their political position, passions which are in common, and enjoyments which are universal. Knowledge is like the mystic ladder in the patriarch's dream. Its base rests on the primeval earth, its crest is lost in the shadowy splendour of the empyrean ; while the great authors, who, for traditionary ages have held the chain of science and philosophy, of poesy and erudition, are the angels ascending and descending the sacred scale, and maintaining as it were, the communication between man and heaven. This feeling is so universal that there is no combination of society in any age in which it has not developed itself. It may, indeed, be partly restrained under despotic governments, under peculiar systems of retarded civilisation ; but it is a consequence as incidental to the spirit and the genius of the Christian civilisation of Europe, as that the day shall follow night and the stars should shine according to their laws and order."

The author believes that the passage above quoted, is alone sufficient proof of the great Disraeli's goodness of heart, and of his ardent love of all mankind, and his earnest wish that their condition should be improved socially, mentally, morally, and materially. Disraeli's ambition was a noble one. He did not covet fame or fortune. He was always indifferent to money, and neglectful of his pecuniary interests. He played a great part in the history of his country, and he played it well. When we think of it, his career was wonderful. His rise from comparative poverty and obscurity to the greatest height to which a subject can attain in England, and the qualities he displayed in prosperity and adversity,—these are things which must command the sympathy and admiration of the wise and the good of all future ages. His career was romantic, but it is a romance that teaches many noble and useful lessons, and that will have power to fire many a young soul with the highest ambition.

Gladstone.—It is not the author's purpose to treat of Mr. Gladstone as a man of letters, nor as a statesman. He has been more highly praised, and more severely censured, than any statesman of this century. His friends call him the grand old man, and his enemies the grand old woman. By many of his admirers, his political sagacity is thought to be phenomenal, and he is considered by them the prince of modern statesmen. He is undoubtedly one of the ablest men of modern times.

Mr. Gladstone is an earnest Christian, while recognising the prophetic element in Homer, and enraptured by his exquisite creations, and no one has described them with a more vivid and brightly tinctured pencil, he yet bows before the higher poetic genius of Isaiah, and sees in the marvellous ideals of Christian poets, from Dante to Tennyson, a more perfect bloom of the human mind, and character.

The Right Hon. William Ewart Gladstone was born at

Liverpool, on the 29th of December, 1809. He is the fourth son of the late Sir John Gladstone, a Liverpool merchant. He studied at Eton and Christ Church, Oxford, and he entered the House of Commons as member for Newark in the Conservative interest. Sir Robert Peel, in 1834, appointed him Under-Secretary for the Colonies. In the revision of the British tariff, in 1842, his defence of the policy of the government, and his complete mastery of its details led to its being passed almost without alteration in both Houses. In 1851 he left the Conservatives, and has ever since appeared on the Liberal side.

He has held office as follows : Vice-President of the Board of Trade, and Master of the Mint, from September, 1841, to May, 1843 ; President of the Board of Trade, from May, 1843, to February, 1845 ; Secretary of State for the Colonies, 1846 ; appointed Chancellor of the Exchequer, in Lord Aberdeen's ministry, 28th December, 1852 ; resigned along with the Aberdeen ministry, 30th January, 1855 ; held the same office under Lord Palmerston 5th February, resigned 21st February, 1855 ; held office as Chancellor of the Exchequer, from 18th June, 1859, to 5th July, 1866 ; represented South Lancashire in parliament from, 1865 to 1868 ; was elected for Greenwich in November, 1868, and was elected First Lord of the Treasury on 8th December, of the same year. On March 1, 1869, he introduced his measure for the disestablishment of the Irish Church, unfolding in a speech, which even Disraeli praised, the details of his comprehensive scheme. The passage of the bill which was carried through the House in less than five months, mainly by the energy of Mr. Gladstone, has been pronounced one of the most important legislative achievements of modern times.

During his leadership of the Liberal party other measures of great importance were passed, the Elementary Education Act, the abolition of purchase in the army, the removal of the University tests, and the Trades-Union bill.

Mr. Gladstone resigned the leadership of his party after forty-two years of public life, but in 1879, he accepted the invitation of the Liberal electors of Mid-Lothian, to stand as their candidate, though the district was a stronghold of Conservatism and his opponent the son of the Duke of Buccleugh. His aggressive campaign astonished the United Kingdom ; the result of the elections of 1880 proved that his resistless eloquence had reached the popular heart. The Liberal majority in the new parliament was 114, and the great commoner, to whom the revolution was due, was justly called to be prime minister.

In 1883 Gladstone had given up the office of Chancellor of the Exchequer, but the government in every crisis was obliged to depend on his oratory. In 1886 Mr. Gladstone became prime minister a third time, and his course since that time is familiar to the world.

In his life of Gladstone, an interesting work, which every person should read, Mr. G. R. Emerson gives the following sketch of his career at Eton and Oxford: "Mr. John Gladstone, we may be tolerably certain, was not slow to discover the early promise of ability given by his fourth son, who, in September, 1821, as yet wanting three months of completing his twelfth year, was sent to Eton. He was a robust and active, as well as a clever boy, and made light of many of the hardships which have made public school life very unpleasant to weak or timid lads. Gladstone soon showed that he was well able to take his own part ; and when it was found that he was not only one of the most active and successful in all school sports, but also one of the very cleverest of the boys, his popularity was assured.

"He remained about six years at Eton, and there formed some lasting friendships. One of his school-fellows, of the same age as himself, was George Augustus Selwyn, afterwards the famous missionary bishop of New Zealand, and who died Bishop of Lichfield. Francis Hastings Doyle, who in after life became Professor of Poetry at Oxford, was also at school at the time ; and another of the Eton boys of Gladstone's time, but two years younger than he, was the modern Lycidas, Arthur Henry Hallam, whose friendship with Tennyson and early death produced one of the noblest poems of our time, *In Memoriam*. Gladstone soon distin-

guished himself in the school by his success in Latin versifi-
cation; and it was not likely that he would remain unaffected
by the literary traditions of the school.   George Canning— .
in the estimation of all the Gladstone family a very Admirable Crichton—had, when he was an Eton boy, contributed
to a school magazine; so had John Hookham Frere—the
author of the *Whistlecraft Papers* (which suggested to Byron
the style of *Beppo* and *Don Juan*), and father of Sir Bartle
Frere—and Winthrop Mackworth Praed.   The *Etonian*, to
which the latter contributed, was published at Windsor by
Charles Knight, at that time a bookseller and printer in the
royal town; and so much talent was brought to light in its
pages, that it was made the basis of another magazine, to
which Macaulay and others who did not belong to Eton contributed.   In the last year of Gladstone's residence at the
school, he was one of the projectors of the *Eton Miscellany*,
and certainly the most prolific contributor, young Selwyn
ranking next.   Thirteen papers from the pen of William
Ewart Gladstone appeared in the first volume; among them
a poem in well balanced heroic couplets, celebrating the
achievements of Richard Cœur de Lion, and *Gnatimozin's
Death Song*, for the suggestion of which he was probably indebted to his mother's relative, Principal Robertson, in his
account of the conquest of Mexico by Cortez.   To the second
volume of the *Miscellany* he made seventeen contributions.
Classical literature was, of course, among the subjects of the
papers.   At a very early period the Homeric poems appear
to have powerfully attracted his attention; but there were
also articles, professedly humorous, in which we imagine he
was less successful.   The title of one paper was *Eloquence*,
and if the youth's oratorical powers in any adequate degree
indicated those of the man, he was assuredly competent to
write effectively on such a topic.   Probably he felt a confidence that he possessed the power, 'the applause of listening senates to command,' and, indeed, there is in the essay
an indication of an ambition which is not unlike Benjamin
Disraeli's day-dreams of his *Vivian Grey* period.   Both
youths were prophets, inspired by the consciousness of great

abilities and faith in themselves. ' A successful *debut*,' wrote Gladstone (in his eighteenth year, at school at Eton), ' an offer from the minister, a Secretaryship of State, and even the premiership itself, are the objects which form the vista along which a young visionary loves to look.'

" In 1827 he bade farewell to Eton, its school-room and playing fields. Few of the pupils at that famous school were so well grounded in the classical learning chiefly valued there. He continued his studies for about two years as private pupil of Dr. Turner, who was afterwards appointed Bishop of Calcutta, and then entered as student, Christ Church College, Oxford. Here his industry was enormous, and even in the vacation he scarcely relaxed his ardour. One writer, describing his career at this period, says: ' No matter where he was, whether in college rooms or country mansion, from 10 A.M. to 2 P.M. no one ever saw William Ewart Gladstone. During this interval he was invariably locked up with his books. From the age of eighteen till that of twenty-one, he never neglected studying during these particular hours, unless he happened to be travelling; and his evening ordeal was scarcely less severe. Eight o'clock saw him once more engaged in a stiff bout with Aristotle, or plunged deep in the text of Thucydides.'

" In one respect the industrious student was more prudent than many of his fellows and competitors. Throughout his long life he has recognised the natural alliance of the physical and intellectual portions of our compound being. Naturally hardy and muscular, he cultivated his bodily powers by regular, active exercise, and his high moral nature preserved him from the temptation to indulge enervating luxuriousness. Temperate and active, trained to muscular exertion, he could probably have outwalked any of the undergraduates of his college as easily as he could have surpassed most of them in mental acquirements. A brisk walk of thirty or forty miles was a small matter to the handsome, well-knit young student, who returned from it with a refreshed brain and renewed vitality to his studies. The Oxford Union, that renowned debating society where so many of our

greatest statesmen, lawyers, and divines trained their oratorical powers and learned their first lessons in practical
politics and philosophy, offered great attractions to Gladstone. The position of President of the Union was justly
looked upon as conferring a high honour, due to acknowledged intellectual power and oratorical ability ; and it is
worth noting that seven presidents were at one time united
in one of the administrations of which Mr. Gladstone was
the chief. He had only been a member of the university
for a few months when he made his first speech at the Union
on the 11th of February, 1830. He was afterwards a frequent speaker, taking the Tory view of public questions.
That his style was rather rhetorically ornate, and that he
made frequent reference to classical examples and freely resorted to classical quotations, we can readily suppose ; and
that he was fluent, enthusiastic, and excitable is equally
probable. He opposed the removal of Jewish disabilities
and Parliamentary Reform, but supported Catholic Emancipation. A few years since, he referred to the opinions he
had held in these Oxford days : ' I trace,' he said, ' in the
education of Oxford of my own time one great defect.
Perhaps it was my own fault ; · but I must admit that I did
not learn when at Oxford that which I have learned since,
namely, to set a due value on the imperishable and inestimable principles of human liberty. The temper which
I think too much prevailed in academic circles was to regard
liberty with jealousy.' "

Mr. Gladstone has given much of his time to " inter-
viewers." An American who called on Mr. Gladstone gives
a very interesting account of his visit. He chose Sunday as
the best day on which to make the call, because Mr. Gladstone is always at home on that day. He says :

" I was profoundly surprised and impressed when I was
shown into the library at Hawarden to find Mr. Gladstone
reading the Sermon on the Mount. During the˙few hours
I had the advantage of spending in his company I was more
than once reminded of the deep piety and absolute faith of
this greatest living Englishman, whose pure and simple life

is an example for the so-called latter-day philosophers who spend their lives in attempting to pull down the Temple of God. Like all English gentlemen, Mr. Gladstone is thoroughly well bred, and, like all really great men, he is perfectly simple and natural in his manners. He bore his seventy-five years remarkably well. His voice was full, strong, and rich; his hair, although white, was abundant, with little signs of baldness. A slight stoop in his shoulders was the only indication of advanced age that the great commoner exhibited. In conversing with an American visitor, Mr. Gladstone would naturally speak of the United States, for which country he has a decided admiration.

" 'America has a magnificent future,' he said, 'if the American people are only true to their possibilities. Before the close of the twentieth century the vast continent embraced within the limits of the United States, stretching from the Atlantic to the Pacific and from the Gulf of Mexico to the great lakes of the North, will be the home of 300,000,000 of freemen, representing every nation upon earth; vaster in extent and population than the Roman Empire in its palmiest days, but free from the danger that attended the extension of that empire among barbarous peoples, which was the primary and potent cause of the decline and fall of the greatness of Rome. Every true Englishman should be proud of the progress of the United States, for the Americans are our kith and kin, and having the same literature, the same language, and the same sturdy love for political independence. The wrestling of Magna Charta from King John prepared the way for the battle of Bunker Hill and the Declaration of Independence.'

" ' It is strange you have never visited the United States that you might see the practical working of Republican institutions, Mr. Gladstone.' 'Nothing would give me more pleasure,' was his reply, ' but I have never been able to find the time. I have been in public life almost uninterruptedly since 1832, and for the last thirty-five years I have either been in office or one of the leaders of the opposition.'

" I was deeply impressed with Mr. Gladstone from a per-

sonal point of view. He is tall, his eyes are blue, his hands
large, his feet English, you know; his manners gentle but
dignified, and, while absolutely free from affectation, he displays an ease and polish which we expect to find in an English gentleman of his political and social position.   William
E. Gladstone is not like his great rival, Disraeli, a dashing
political acrobat, but he is a great statesman, possessing a
genius capable of guiding his country successfully through
one of the most critical periods of her history.   When he
leaves the scene where he has shone so long and so bril-
liantly, England will find it difficult to select from her public
men one capable of taking the place of this Great Old Man."

This sketch of Mr. Gladstone would be incomplete without the following interesting account of his oratorical ability :

Mr. Gladstone as an Orator.[1]

" When the armies of political parties are set in battle
array, Mr. Gladstone's transcendent abilities as an orator
alone have full play.   When, before rising to speak, he has
definitely made up his mind which of three or more courses
he shall take, and has nothing to do but declare his colours, build around them a rampart of argument, and seek
to rally to them halting friends, then the marvellous clearness of his perception and his unusual ability for making
dark places light is disclosed.   After purporting to answer a
simple question, and taking a quarter of an hour to do it in,
Mr. Gladstone has sometimes sat down leaving the House
in a condition of dismayed bewilderment, hopelessly attempting to grope its way through the intricacies of the
sonorous sentences it has been listening to. But if he desires
to make himself understood, there is no one who can better
effect the purpose.   There are few instances of a Government measure which met with more determined and di-
versely motived opposition than the Irish University Act,
introduced in the session of 1873.   It is a matter of history
that it broke the power of the strongest ministry that has

[1] *Men and Manner in Parliament.* By the Member for the Chiltern Hundreds.

ruled England in these latter days. The provisions of the measure were singularly intricate, but when Mr. Gladstone sat down after speaking for upwards of three hours in explanation of the measure, he had not only made it clear from preamble to schedule, but he had momentarily talked the House of Commons over into the belief that this was a bill it would do well to accept. Mr. Horsman has been much laughed at because, whilst the glamour of this great speech was still strong upon him, he wrote an enthusiastic letter to the *Times* hailing Mr. Gladstone and his bill as among the most notable of recent dispensations of a benefi-cent Providence, words which he subsequently ate in the presence of a crowded House. But Mr. Horsman differed from seven-eighths of the House of Commons only in this, that he put pen to paper whilst he was yet under the influ-ence of the orator's spell, whereas the rest of the members contented themselves by verbal and private expressions of opinion. Mr. Gladstone's oratorical manner is much more strongly marked by action than is Mr. Bright's. He empha-sises by smiting his right hand in the open palm of his left; by pointing his finger straight out at his adversary, real or representative; and, in his hottest moments, by beating the table with his clenched hand. Sometimes in answer to cheers he turns right round to his immediate supporters on the benches behind him, and speaks directly to them; where-upon the Conservatives, who hugely enjoy a baiting of the emotionable ex-Premier, call out 'Order! order!' This call seldom fails in the desired effect of exciting the right honourable gentleman's irascibility, and when he loses his temper his opponents may well be glad. Mr. Bright always writes out the peroration of his speeches, and at one time was accustomed to send the slip of paper to the reporters. Mr. Disraeli sometimes writes out the whole of his speeches. The one he delivered to the Glasgow students in Novem-ber, 1873, was in type in the office of a London newspaper at the moment the right honourable gentleman was speaking at the university. Mr. Gladstone never writes a line of his speeches, and some of his most successful ones have been

19

made in the heat of debate, and necessarily without preparation. His speech in winding up the debate on the Irish
University Bill has rarely been excelled for close reasoning,
brilliant illustration, and powerful eloquence; yet if it be
referred to it will be seen that it is for the greater and best
part a reply to the speech of Mr. Disraeli, who had just sat
down, yielding the floor to his rival half an hour after midnight. Evidence of the same swift reviewing of a position,
and of the existence of the same power of instantly mar-
shalling arguments and illustrations, and sending them forth
clad in a panoply of eloquence, is apparent in Mr. Gladstone's
speech when commenting on Mr. Disraeli's announcement
of the withdrawal of the main portion of the Endowed
Schools Act Amendment Bill. The announcement, and
especially the manner in which it was made, was a surprise
that almost stunned and momentarily bewildered the House
of Commons. Mr. Gladstone was bound to speak, and to
speak the moment Mr. Disraeli resumed his seat. He had
no opportunity to take counsel, and no time to make preparations for his speech; but the result of his masterly oration
at this crisis was that the unpopularity and dissatisfaction
created by the course he had taken in the matter of the
Regulation of Public Worship Bill melted like snow in the
firelight."

The description of Mr. Gladstone's oratory by Mr. G. W.
Smalley, the English correspondent of the *New York Tribune*, who accompanied Mr. Gladstone to Mid-Lothian in
1884, is interesting: "The first note of his voice was listened for with something like anxiety. Is it possible, that,
after five years, that marvellous organ should be still in its
full perfection of visible, of flexible strength? The curious
in such details may note that a bottle of yellow fluid, from
which a tumbler has been half-filled, stands on the table.
The yellow fluid is egg-flip, a beverage, which, on this occasion, may be described as purely medicinal in character and
purpose, and is compounded of the yolk of two or three
eggs and two glasses of sherry. This is to keep throat and
voice in order; and, before the orator has made an end, he

has sipped a tumblerful. But the first note of the voice, and the first half-dozen sentences of the first day, were re-assuring. There is no longer any fear that Mr. Gladstone is overtaxing his energies. I heard one of his friends say that he himself could take an accurate measure of his capacities, and of the precise demands a particular hall and audience would make upon them. He feels, as the rest of us feel, that the voice is all right. Yet he does not once try its full compass. The speech is didactive, argumentative, expository, anything you like but passionate or pathetic ; and you never know the full resources of this all but unequalled voice till you have heard it used in anger, in pity, in ridicule (for which he keeps one or two very subtle semi-notes), —above all, in one of those appeals to principle, and to what I must call religious conviction, which so often and so nobly close some of his greatest speeches.

" I can well imagine that a stranger, hearing Mr. Gladstone on Saturday for the first and only time, should go away with a certain sense of incompleteness in his experience. He would have heard a speech which nobody else could have made, but he would by no means have heard the orator at his best. What I have said about the little call he made on his voice may be applied to the speech itself. He has not asked himself to do all he can. It is a speech with a definite purpose ; and he has deliberately sacrificed everything to the one great end of impressing on the country the supreme importance of the Franchise Bill, and on the lords the supreme advisability of yielding, without force, to the will of the people. But let the stranger come again on Monday. The place is the same, the scene is the same, the same orator stands on the same platform. But he is no longer in the same mood of sweet reasonableness, and nothing else. The very face has changed. On Saturday it wore a look of resolute placidity. On Monday the features are allowed their natural play, and if you sit near enough to look into those onyx-hued eyes, you will vainly try to sound their luminous depths. Anybody who has seen Mr. Gladstone often, will discover at once, that, for this second ad-

dress, he feels himself—to use again his own memorable
expression—unmuzzled.   There is no longer the dread of
rousing popular passion against an institution, which, in his
heart of hearts, the prime minister is more anxious to support than to assail.   The inexorable necessity of caution
weighs him down no longer.   He approaches this new task
with a buoyant delight in the easy triumph he is about to
win.   The five years have rolled off his brow.   Erect, elastic,
exultant, he can hardly wait till the five thousand in front
have done cheering,—indeed, but for his obvious impatience
to begin, they might be cheering till now.   In the first sentence on Monday, you really hear his voice for the first time.
No trace of fatigue from the long effort on Saturday.   None
of the hardness of tone which was to be heard then.   Compass, range, and quality are all enlarged and lettered.

" His task now is, to retort upon his opponents the charges
they have been heaping up against him.   For five years the
Tories have gone about insisting, with vague but emphatic
assertion and re-assertion, that the prime minister had falsified the pledges which Mr. Gladstone had given in the first
Mid-Lothian speeches.   Three-fourths of his speech on
Monday are one triumphant cry, ' Prove it !' or, rather,
' You have tried to prove it.   You have had the text.   You
have piled accusation upon accusation, you have years to
get up your case.   I challenge you to put your finger on
one count of this long indictment which you have supported
by one syllable of evidence.'   He goes over the record.   He
reviews the situation.   He passes from topic to topic, perhaps too rapidly ; perhaps with a too comprehensive ambition, and with too much eagerness to survey, in one single
statement, the whole course of his administration, and to
condense into this hour and a half a complete epitome of all
he said in a week, in 1879, and all that his enemies have said
in five years since ; and to set in a halo of light all the glaring
contradictions, the baseless inventions of his critics, and the
perfect and absolute harmony between his own pledges and
the accomplished facts of his subsequent career.   But what
a scope such a programme gives him !   How he revels in it !

How he heaps irony upon sarcasm! and how his defense rises to white-heat, and the steel you thought he was shaping into a shield suddenly flashes before you a two-edged sword, and cleaves asunder, in one blinding stroke, the unhappy foe!

"Oh, yes! this indeed is oratory; and in the two hours, less ten minutes, during which it lasts, you may find examples of nearly every charm which it is possible for an orator to work upon his hearers. The effect he produces does not owe much to gesture. There is gesture, but it often lacks expressiveness. The arms are used pretty constantly; but the same movement of the same muscles is made to signify, or meant to signify, very different things. It wants what on the French stage is called largeness or amplitude; and it is sometimes violent, sometimes deficient in the grace and suavity which the admirable smoothness of voice leads you to expect. The shoulders rise and fall with what I am afraid must at times be described as jerkiness. Indeed, at such moments, the voice itself sometimes loses its purity, and harsh notes are heard. The rather frequent passage of the right forefinger across the lips, and the curious touch of the thumb on a particular spot at the summit of the broad arch of the forehead, are peculiarities which I only mention for the sake of fidelity, and with every apology to the orator for taking note of such specks upon the general splendour of his delivery. So of the quick bending and straightening of the knees. The impression one gets from these exceptional things is but momentary. They are incidents due to the overmastering intensity of thought and aim,—nature in her cruder moods, getting the better of the consummate art which is the prevailing, and all but continuous, condition with the orator. If there be any deficiencies of this sort, you will hardly observe them unless after long familiarity with the speaker. It is the face which will rivet your gaze, —the play of features, alike delicate and powerful, and the ever-restless, far-searching glance. Never was such a tell-tale countenance. Expression after expression sweeps across it, the thought pictures itself to you almost before it is uttered;

and if your eyes by chance meet his, it is a blaze of sunlight which dazzles you. Nor do the little blemishes really matter. What masters, what impresses, you, and what you will carry away with you as a permanent and precious memory is, above all other things, the nobleness of presence, the beautiful dignity, the stateliness of bearing, the immense sincerity, which are visible to the eyes of the most careless spectator, and which fill the hall with their influence, and place the whole multitude wholly at the mercy of the one fellow-being who stands before them."

The charm of Hawarden is its park, as it is of every other noted European house. Mr. Gladstone delights chiefly in his trees, and he likes them too well to let them fall into decay. When a tree has reached its perfect growth, he rejoices to cut it down with a good American axe. He has a collection of thirty axes, many of which have been sent to him by persons sympathizing with his love of the woodsman's craft. For his own chopping he never uses an axe not made in New England.

There is a great deal of entertaining information about the daily life of the Grand Old Man in a recent issue of one of the English papers. Mr. Gladstone lives a very regular life at his home, we are told. He breakfasts lightly about seven o'clock in the morning, and shortly before eight walks to the Hawarden Church for prayers. Upon his return he retires to his study, where he peruses and answers his enormous mass of daily correspondence. Luncheon at the Castle is conducted in a homely manner. The "lunch is on the hob" at Hawarden Castle for an hour or two during the day, and is partaken of by those at home at various times. In the afternoon Mr. Gladstone takes a walk in the grounds and dines at eight o'clock. He retires early, and shortly after ten o'clock his day's labours are over. He drinks bitter beer with his luncheon. A glass or two of claret at dinner, and sometimes a glass of port, that nectar of orators, satisfy his very moderate requirements for stimulant.

Like General Ignatieff, he has never smoked. He belongs to the older school, which acquired its habits at a time when tobacco smoking was regarded as somewhat vulgar. Hence, neither pipe, cigar nor cigarette is ever to be seen between his lips. But Mr. Gladstone is not in any sense ascetic; he is a generous liver and is a great believer in the virtues of a glass of good port wine. When speaking, his fillip is a compound of sherry and egg, which is carefully prepared by Mrs. Gladstone, who attends to its manufacture with as much anxiety as if it were the elixir of life.

Mr. Gladstone usually has three books in reading at the same time, and changes from one to another when his mind has reached the limit of absorption. This is a necessary corrective to the tendency to think only of one thing at one time, which sometimes in politics leads him to neglect that all-round survey of the situation which is indispensable to a Prime Minister. During the beginning of the Irish question in 1880 he was so absorbed in the question of the coercion of Turkey that he could hardly be induced to spare a thought for Ireland; now it is just as difficult to get him to think of any political question but that of Ireland.

He complains sometimes that his memory is no longer quite so good as it used to be, but, although that may be true, it is still twice as good as anybody else's, for Mr. Gladstone has an extraordinary faculty of not only remembering those things he ought to remember but for forgetting those things it is useless for him to remember.

He possesses the enormous gift of being able to sleep. All his life long he has been a sound sleeper. It used to be said that he had a faculty which was possessed by Napoleon Bonaparte of commanding sleep at will, and, what is perhaps still rarer, of waking up instantly in full possession of every faculty. Some people can go to sleep soon, but they take some time to wake. Mr. Gladstone, it used to be said, was capable of sitting down in a chair, covering his face with a handkerchief and going to sleep in thirty seconds, and after sleeping for thirty minutes or an hour, as the case might be, waking up as bright as ever, all drowsiness disappearing the moment he opened his eyes. During all Mr. Gladstone's career he has never lost his sleep, except once and that was

during the troubles that arose about Egypt and General
Gordon. Then he slept badly and for the first time, it was
feared that he would not be able to maintain the burden of
office. He has, however, got over the effect of that period
of stress and strain and he is still able to count confidently
upon at least five consecutive hours of sound and refreshing
sleep every night. But for that he would long ago have
broken down.

Although Mr. Gladstone is pre-eminently a talker in
society, yet he does not disdain the other arts by which
people who dine out contrive to spend the time. In his
younger days he used to be quite noted for singing either
solos or part-songs, and even down to the present time the
musical bass of his voice is often heard to great advantage
in family worship at Hawarden on Sunday nights. Whether
he still keeps up the practice of singing in company is doubtful, but there are legends of the wonderful effect with which
he was wont to render a favourite Scotch song, and irrever-
ent gossips have even declared that on one occasion Mr.
Gladstone brought down the drawing-room by the vivacity
and rollicking spirit with which he rendered the well-known
Camptown Races with its familiar refrain :

> " Gwine to ride all night,
> Gwine to ride all day ;
> I bet my money on the bob-tail nag,
> And somebody bet on the bay.
> O du-dah-day ! "

His high spirits break out at every moment, and he used
to rejoice to play a comedy part on his own or his son's
lawn. It would be incorrect to say that on the occasion of
popular celebrations, of local fancy fairs and cottage gardening
shows, Mr. Gladstone plays down to the level of his audience.
On the contrary, he exhibits just sufficient sympathy to raise
them to enthusiasm, and no more. Of Mr. Gladstone's lieutenant, Mr. Morley, it may be said that he has no amusements whatever. He neither boats, nor rides, nor cuts down
trees, nor, as one veracious chronicler asserted, does he spend

his leisure time in catching butterflies. He indulges in none of the ordinary dissipations by which the statesman and the man of letters can unbend his bow. Mr. Gladstone, as might be expected, is most catholic in his tastes, but, except for wood-cutting and pedestrianism, he can hardly be said to be much of an athlete. He has played cricket and other games, but he has never thrown himself into them with that passion which is necessary for success, although one could imagine Mr. Gladstone being the champion cricketer of England, if he gave his mind to it, even now. But in out-of-door sports he prefers Shank's pony to any other means, excepting the cutting down of trees, of amusing himself. He is a great pedestrian, and is able to distance any ordinary walker, although he will soon be in his 80th year. Mrs. Gladstone is also a good pedestrian, and one Summer they amused themselves one afternoon by ascending a hill some 3000 feet above the sea-level without appearing to feel the exertion arduous. At indoor games Mr. Gladstone used to enjoy a rubber at whist, but he is now more devoted to back-gammon, a game which he plays with the same concentration of energy and attention that he devotes to the preparation of a Budget or the course of a parliamentary debate. He occasionally plays at draughts, but is a very bad hand at the chequers.

Mr. Gladstone's society has always been an immense addition to the company to which he was invited. No one could be more humble and more simple, or more ready to "take a back seat," but he never takes airs upon himself, and falls in harmoniously with anything that is going on. The account published some time ago of Mr. Gladstone as a conversationalist is singularly incorrect in representing him as monopolising all the conversation. Mr. Gladstone no doubt takes his fair share, which is a very large one, but no one is less given to monopolising talk than he. He can talk about anything, and pours out a flood of information, of anecdote and of illustration, upon any theme that may be started in a fashion which makes the ordinary visitor feel that the best service he can render is to listen, merely throw-

ing in, from time to time, a remark necessary to start Mr.
Gladstone along on a fresh track, or to force him to draw
still more deeply from the immense reservoir of hoarded
knowledge which he has under his command.

Not that Mr. Gladstone is a man whom you can lightly
contradict, or one before whom you would care to hazard
any observation which you had not carefully considered.
The promptitude with which he comes down upon any unhappy wretch who may have happened to hazard an observation which Mr. Gladstone does not believe to have been
founded on fact is like the swoop of an eagle on its prey.
The eye flashes and the unfortunate interlocutor is compelled to "stand and deliver" his facts, his references, and
his "justificatory pieces" in a fashion which once experienced is never forgotten. The peculiar flash in Mr.
Gladstone's eye as he turns upon anyone whose remarks or
acts have slightly ruffled the equanimity of his soul, was
very marked ten years ago! Of late he requires more rousing than he used to, but even still there are times when
those who know him can well understand the remark of the
West-countryman who once wrote to Mr. Gladstone saying:
"You do not know me, and have forgotten that we ever met.
I have not forgotten you, nor can I ever forget the flash of
your eagle eye on Frome platform, which went through
me."

Mr. Gladstone has been one of England's most wonderful statesmen. His influence has been world-wide, and
will last until the end of time. Many years have elapsed
since Macaulay described Mr. Gladstone as the "rising hope
of the stern and unbending Tories, who follow reluctantly
and mutinously a leader whose experience and eloquence
are indispensable to them, but whose cautious temper and
moderate opinions they abhor." How completely his career
has disappointed the "stern and unbending Tories," it is
unnecessary to say.

The purity of Mr. Gladstone's motives no one has ever
dared to question. His public and private character are
beyond reproach. The generosity and magnanimity with

which he treats his political adversaries; his fidelity to his colleagues and constituents; the earnestness with which he throws himself into any cause which he believes to be right —are traits which should not be forgotten in estimating his character. Mr. Gladstone is a singularly great and noble man, and has honestly won the admiration with which he is universally regarded.

CHAPTER V.

ORATORY IN FRANCE.

THE legal profession in France has achieved for itself a proud position. The forensic orators of France have always been justly noted for their great humanity, their chivalrous courage, profound knowledge of the law, their varied accomplishments, and their powerful eloquence. They have always discharged their duties to their clients with the greatest boldness and fidelity. Not only has the French bar been remarkably free from corruption, but judicial corruption has always been punished there with great severity. As a proof of the strict severity with which corruption on the part of any member of the court, in France, was punished, it is said, that, as long ago as 1348, one of the judges, named Alani de Ourdery, was hanged by order of the parliament for corruption in office.

Another instance of the same impartial justice occurred in 1496, when Claude de Chamvreux, a judge and formerly a councillor, was convicted of corruption in regard to certain matters which had been referred to him. A strong effort was made to save him, but the guilty judge was not allowed to escape. "He was deprived of his office, and openly stripped of his scarlet gown and furred cap ; and then with naked feet and bare head, and holding in his hand a lighted torch, he fell upon his knees upon the floor, and begged aloud for mercy from God, and the king, and justice, and the parties whom he had injured. The report which he had falsified was then torn to pieces by an officer of the court ;

and the culprit was conducted to the quadrangle of the
Palais de Justice, and, being consigned over to the public
executioner, was forced to mount upon a cart, and conducted
to the pillory, where he stood for three hours. He was afterwards branded on the forehead by a hot iron with a *fleur de
lis*, and banished forever from the realm." It is a great pity
that all unjust judges in every country could not be treated
in a similar manner, and when our civilisation becomes
higher they will be.

The order of advocates in France bore some analogy to
the order of knighthood, as may be seen by the following
rules, to which, with many others, the advocate promised
obedience upon his admission to the bar:

" 1. He shall not undertake just and unjust causes alike
without distinction, nor maintain such as he undertakes,
with trickery, fallacies, and misquotations of authorities.

" 2. He was not, in his pleadings, to indulge in abuse of
the opposite party or his counsel.

" 3. He was not to compromise the interests of his clients,
by absence from court when the cause in which he was retained was called on.

" 4. He was not to violate the respect due to the court, by
either improper expressions, or unbecoming gestures.

" 5. He was not to exhibit a sordid avidity of gain, by
putting too high a price upon his services.

" 6. He was not to make any bargain with his client for a
share in the fruits of the judgment he might recover.

" 7. He was not to lead a dissipated life, or one contrary
to the gravity of his calling.

" 8. He was not, under pain of being debarred, to refuse
his services to the indigent and oppressed."

The last rule, it will be noticed, breathes the very spirit of
chivalry.

" Purity of life and disinterested zeal in the cause of the
poor and friendless were enjoined upon the chevalier and
the advocate alike; and doubtless the resemblance between
the two professions, of which the latter was thus reminded,
had a powerful effect in producing a tone of high-minded

feeling which ought ever to be the characteristic of the bar. But sometimes the resemblance was carried farther than was either safe or agreeable, and the advocate had to perform a warlike office, not in a figurative, but a literal sense. I allude to the appeal or wager of battel, whereby the sword was made the arbiter of disputes, and sanguinary duels were sanctioned by courts of law."

M. Berryer has drawn an interesting picture of one of the French advocates of the olden time in the performance of his daily duties: " We see him, dressed in his robes of black satin, set out at an early hour, on a summer morning, from one of the picturesque houses, with peaked turrets and high gable ends, which rose above the banks of the Seine in old Paris, and hurrying forward to the court, because the clock of the Holy Chapel had just struck six, at which the judges are obliged to take their seats, under pain of losing their salary for the day. He is busy thinking over the cause which he has to plead, and taxes his ingenuity to compress his speech into as brief a compass as possible ; for he remembers that an ordinance of Charles VIII., issued in 1493, imposes a fine upon long-winded advocates who weary the court with their prolixity. Look at his countenance. The furred hood which covers his head, and the ample grey cloak, the collar of which hides half his face, cannot so far conceal it as to prevent you from seeing an expression of anger there, which is no doubt excited by the recollection of the arguments used by his opponent on the preceding evening. But think not that when he reaches the court and rises to reply, he will retort by any abusive language ; for by another regulation of the same king, counsel are expressly forbidden to use any opprobrious words towards their antagonists. The judges are seated on their chairs ; the parties are before them ; and now he, whose portrait we are sketching, rises to address the court. He speaks under the solemn sanction of an oath, for he has sworn to undertake only such causes as, in his conscience, he believes to be just ; he has also sworn not to spin out his pleadings by any of the tricks of his profession, but make them as concise as possible. If, in the course of his harangue, he touches on any question which he thinks may affect the interests of the crown, he suddenly stops and gives formal notice of it to the court. Twelve o'clock strikes just after the cause is over and judgment pronounced, and the court rises. His client has been successful, and he now takes his counsel aside to settle with him the amount of his fees; and it is not without an effort that he grudgingly gives him the sum which the royal ordinance permits him to receive."

Every nation has its standard of eloquence—nay, even in different sections of the same country—the standards are different, as, for instance, in the United States—the orators of the South and West are more demonstrative than the orators of the North. But a finished speaker would be listened to by an intelligent audience with pleasure in any country, notwithstanding the differences in the standards of oratory.

To the comparatively cold English or American audiences, the eloquence of many of the French orators would appear too declamatory in character, while a French audience would think an English or American orator lacking in warmth and animation.

It is not the author's purpose to give a history of the French bar, and the limits of the present work forbid more than a glance at some of the greatest of the modern forensic and political orators of France.

The reader is doubtless familiar with the history of the French Revolution, and knows that the Convention of the States-General, and the final organisation of the National Assembly, fixed it irretrievably. The deputies of the people, after they assembled from every quarter of France, found themselves opposed by a corrupt Court and aristocracy, and, although the nation was on the brink of ruin, they were obliged to spend months in contending for the plainest principles of civil liberty. The reformations which were demanded by the exigencies of the times might not have been carried, had it not been for Mirabeau,—the great orator of the Assembly. He hurled defiance and scorn on the nobility and the King, from the very beginning, and inspired the Convention with his own boldness. "No matter what vacillation or fears might agitate the members, when his voice of thunder shook the hall in which they sat, every heart grew determined and resolute. With his bushy black hair standing on end, and his eyes flashing fire, he became at once the hope of the people and the terror of the aristocracy. Incoherent and unwieldy in the commencement of his speech, steady and strong when fairly under motion, he carried resistless powers in his appeals. As a huge ship in a dead calm rolls and rocks on the heavy swell, but the moment the wind fills its sails stretches proudly away, throwing the foam from its front,—so he tossed irregular and blind upon the sea of thought, until caught by the breath of passion, when he moved majestically, irresistibly onward."

"Slave, go tell your master that we are here by the will of the people, and that we will depart only at the point of the bayonet." These words, spoken to the emissary of Lewis by Mirabeau, sealed the fate of despotism in France.

The Constituent Assembly sat from 1789 to 1791. The overthrow of the Bastile, and triumph of the people, caused the aristocrats to fly from France in crowds. Theretofore they had constituted the chief opponents of the deputies of the people, and after their departure, there being no longer any opposition, the deputies split into two parties among themselves.

The Girondists, at first, were the Republicans, and favoured the establishment of a government founded on the principles of the republics of Greece and Rome, but a party springing up, more radical than their own, and pushing the state toward anarchy, they became Conservatives. Mirabeau, in the meantime, full of gloomy forebodings, died. The Mirabeau family was Etruscan. It retained in all its members for many generations, not alone its Latin origin, but the aristocratic pride, the talent for oratory, the rich imagination, the war-like spirit, the cultivated tastes, for which the family was famous.

Mirabeau.—Honoré Gabriel Riquette, Compte de Mirabeau, was born at Bignon, in France, on the 9th of March,
1749. He was the greatest of the French political orators.
Mirabeau was one of the most extraordinary men of his age.
In intellect he far surpassed all the great luminaries of that
brilliant period. With all his vices, Mirabeau had many redeeming traits. A more ardent patriot than Mirabeau never
lived. The love of France never ceased in his heart but with
his last breath, and the good of his country was mingled even
with his dying aspirations. If his life had been spared it is
thought by many writers that the Revolution would have
taken another direction. The following graphic sketch of
his oratorical character, which will afford the reader some
idea of his vehemence as a public speaker, is furnished by a
distinguished French writer, author of *Noted French Orators.*

"Mirabeau in the tribune was the most imposing of orators; an orator so consummate, that it is harder to say what
he wanted than what he possessed.

"Mirabeau had a massive and square obesity of figure,
thick lips, a forehead broad, bony, prominent; arched eyebrows, an eagle eye, cheeks flat and somewhat flabby,
features full of pock-holes and blotches, a voice of thunder,
an enormous mass of hair, and the face of a lion.

"His manner as an orator is that of the great masters of
antiquity, with an admirable energy of gesture, and a vehemence of diction which perhaps they had never reached.

"Mirabeau in his premeditated discourses was admirable.
But what was he not in his extemporaneous effusions? His
natural vehemence, of which he repressed the flights in his
prepared speeches, broke down all barriers in his improvisations. A sort of nervous irritability gave then to his whole
frame an almost preternatural animation and life. His
breast dilated with an impetuous breathing. His lion face
became wrinkled and contorted. His eyes shot forth flame.
He roared, he stamped, he shook the fierce mass of his hair,
all whitened with foam; he trod the tribune with the supreme
authority of a master, and the imperial air of a king. What
an interesting spectacle to behold him, momently, erect and

exalt himself under the pressure of obstacle! To see him display the pride of his commanding brow! To see him, like the ancient orator, when, with all the powers of his unchained eloquence, he was wont to sway to and fro in the forum the agitated waves of the Roman multitude! Then would he throw by the measured notes of his declamation, habitually grave and solemn. Then would escape him broken exclamations, tones of thunder, and accents of heartrending and terrible pathos. He concealed with the flesh and colour of his rhetoric the sinewy arguments of his dialectics. He transported the Assembly, because he was himself transported. And yet—so extraordinary was his force—he abandoned himself to the torrent of his eloquence without wandering from his course; he mastered others by its sovereign sway, without losing for an instant his own self-control." Throughout his strange career, Mirabeau bore with him the remembrance of an unnatural father's hate.

"I have nothing to tell you of my prodigious son," writes his father a few months after the child's birth, "except that he battles with his nurse." A year later he adds: "He is as ugly as a child of the devil." When the boy is five years old, he says: "He is as sand on which no impression remains. I have placed him in Poisson's hands, who is as devoted as a spaniel to me. Thank him much for the education he is giving the brat. Let him form him into a steady citizen, and that is all that is necessary. Possessing those qualities, he can make the pigmy race who play fine at court tremble! . . . To-night a little monster that they say is my son is to perform a part in a play; but were he the son of our greatest comedian he could not be a more perfect buffoon, mimic, and actor. His body increases, his chattering increases, his face grows marvellously ugly, ugly as if by preference and intent, and, further, he declaims perfectly at random. He is a sickly child; if it were necessary for me to produce another, where the devil should I find a pattern of the same material? He is turbulent, yet gentle and amenable, indeed so much so that it approaches to stupid

ity. Like Punch, all belly and all back, but very ready on
the occasion to imitate the tortoise, presenting the shell,
and allowing himself to be struck. This big, ungainly
Gabriel goes about everywhere soliciting alms in order to
give charity to beggars; following in that respect the example of his mother, notwithstanding all I say about its
being contrary to my principles. The other day at one of
those fêtes given at my house when races are run, and
prizes won, he gained a hat, and then turning to a child
who had a cap on, he put his own on him, saying to the little peasant, ' Here; take it, I have not two heads!' That
youth appeared to me then emperor of the world! I don't
know what godlike expression passed over his face at the
moment, but it haunted me in my dreams, and brought
tears to my eyes. The lesson did me good."

As a fine specimen of his burning eloquence, we quote his
beautiful eulogium on our immortal Franklin, pronounced
on the 11th of June, 1790:

"Franklin is dead! Restored to the bosom of the divinity
is that genius which gave freedom to America and rayed
forth torrents of light upon Europe. The sage whom two
worlds claim—the man whom the history of empires and the
history of science alike contend for—occupied, it cannot be
denied, a lofty rank among his species. Long enough have
political cabinets signalised the death of those who were
great in their funeral eulogies only. Long enough has the
etiquette of courts prescribed hypocritical mournings. For
their benefactors only should nations assume the emblems
of grief; and the representatives of nations should commend
only the heroes of humanity to public veneration.

"In the fourteen states of the confederacy, Congress has
ordained a mourning of two months for the death of Franklin; and America is at this moment acquitting herself of
this tribute of honour to one of the Fathers of her Constitution. Would it not become us, gentlemen, to unite
in this religious act; to participate in this homage, publicly
rendered, at once to the rights of man, and to the philosopher who has contributed most largely to their vindication

throughout the world? Antiquity would have erected altars
to this great and powerful genius, who, to promote the
welfare of mankind, comprehending both the heavens
and the earth in the range of his thought, could at once
snatch the bolt from the cloud and the scepter from
tyrants. France, enlightened and free, owes at least the ac-
knowledgement of her remembrance and regret to one of
the greatest intellects that ever served the united cause of
philosophy and liberty. I propose that it be now decreed
that the national Assembly wear mourning, during three
days, for Benjamin Franklin."   ▸

Mirabeau's capacity for hard work was simply marvellous.
It is said that he did more in a day than the majority of
men would do in a month. He carried on a prodigious
amount of business simultaneously. No time was lost from
his conception of a project to its execution. To-day, not
to-morrow, seems to have been his motto. Conversation
alone could seduce him from his work, and even that he
converted into a means of labour.

He read.very little, but with great rapidity. He discovered at a glance what was useful to him in a book. As fast
as a speech was changed, he had fresh copies of it made.
He was very impatient of delays. His secretary one day
said to him, "The thing you require is impossible." Said
Mirabeau, passionately starting from his chair, "*Impossible!*
never again use that foolish word in my presence!"

Carmenin, an eloquent French writer says of Mirabeau :

"Everywhere, in every thing, already Mirabeau reveals
himself ;—in his letters, in his pleadings, in his memorials,
in his treatises on arbitrary imprisonments, on the liberty of
the press, on the privileges of the nobility, on the inequality
of distinctions, on the financial affairs and the situation of
Europe: enemy of every abuse, vehement, polemic, bold
reformer ; more remarkable, it is true, for elevation, hardi-
hood, and originality of thought, for sagacity of observation,
and vigour of reasoning, than for the graces of form ; verbose,
even loose, incorrect, unequal, but rapid and picturesque in
style,—*a spoken, not a written style, as is that of most orators.*

With what masculine eloquence he objurgates the King of Prussia! " Do but what the son of your slave will have done ten times a day, ten times better than you, the courtiers will tell you you have performed an extraordinary action. Give full reign to your passions, they will tell you, you do well. Squander the sweat and the blood of your subjects like the waters of the rivers, they will say you do well. If you descend to avenge yourself,—you so powerful —they will say you do well. They have said so, when Alexander, in his drunkenness, tore open with his piognard the bosom of his friend. They have said so, when Nero assassinated his mother."

Is not this in the oratorical style?

The following picture of a legal constitution must have thrilled the popular heart :

" Too often are bayonets the only remedy applied to the convulsions of oppression and want. But bayonets never re-establish but the peace of terror, the silence of despotism. Ah! the people are not a furious herd which must be kept in chains! Always quiet and moderate, when they are truly free, they are violent and unruly but under those governments where they are systematically debased in order to have a pretext to despise them. When we consider what must result to the happiness of twenty-five millions of men, from a legal constitution in place of ministerial caprices,— from the consent of all the wills and the co-operation of all the lights of the nation in the improvement of our laws, from the reform of abuses, from the reduction of taxes, from economy in the finances, from the mitigation of the penal laws, from regularity of procedure in the tribunals, from the abolition of a multitude of servitudes which shackle industry and mutilate the human faculties, in a word, from that grand system of liberty, which, planted on the firm basis of freely-elected municipalities, rises gradually to the provincial administrations, and receives its completion from the annual recurrence of the States-General—when we weigh all that must result from the restoration of this vast empire, who does not feel that the greatest of crimes, the darkest

outrage against humanity, would be to offer opposition to
the rising destiny of our country and thrust her back into
the depths of the abyss, there to hold her oppressed beneath
the burthen of all her chains."

When he proposed that the thanks of the Assembly be
voted to Bailly and Lafayette, he enumerated the difficulties of their civil and military administration with great
accuracy and nicety of observation :

" What an administration ! what an epoch, where all is to be
feared and all to be braved ! when tumult begets tumult, when
an affray is produced by the very means taken to prevent it ;
—when moderation is unceasingly necessary, and moderation
appears pusillanimity, timidity, treason, when you are beset
with a thousand counsels, and yet must take your own—
when all persons are to be dreaded, even citizens whose intentions are pure, but whom distrust, excitement, exaggeration, render almost as formidable as conspirators—when one
is obliged, even in critical circumstances, to yield up his
wisdom, to lead anarchy in order to repress it, to assume an
employment glorious, it is true, but environed with the most
harassing alarms—when it is necessary besides, in the midst
of such and so many difficulties, to show a serene countenance, to be always calm, to enforce order even in the smallest details, to offend no one, to heal all jealousies, to serve
incessantly and seek to please, but without the appearance
of being a servant."

When M. Necker, minister of finance, asked the Assembly for a vote of confidence, Mirabeau, in order to carry
it by storm, displayed all the irony of his eloquence and all
the might of his logic ; and when he saw the auditory
shaken, he hurled against bankruptcy the following fulmi-
nations :

" Oh ! if declarations less solemn did not guarantee our
respect for the public faith, our horror of the infamous
word bankruptcy, I should say to those who familiarise
themselves perhaps with the idea of repudiating the public
engagements, through fear of excessive sacrifices, through
terror of taxation : What, then, is bankruptcy, if it is not the

cruelest, the most iniquitous, the most disastrous of imposts?
My friends, listen to me, a word, a single word!

"Two centuries of depredation and robbery have ex-
cavated the abyss wherein the kingdom is on the verge of
being engulfed. This frightful gulf it is indispensable to fill
up. Well, here is a list of the proprietors. Choose from
among the richest, so as to sacrifice the smallest number of
the citizens. But choose! for is it not expedient that a
small number perish to save the mass of the people? Come
—these two thousand notables possess wherewith to supply
the deficit. Restore order to our finances, peace and prosperity to the kingdom. Strike, and immolate pitilessly these
melancholy victims, precipitate them into the abyss; it is
about to close. . . . What, you recoil with horror! . . .
Inconsistent, pusillanimous men! And do you not see that
in decreeing bankruptcy—or, what is more odious still, in
rendering it inevitable without decreeing—you disgrace
yourselves with an act a thousand times more criminal; for,
in fact, that horrible sacrifice would remove the deficiency.
But do you imagine, that because you refuse to pay, you
shall cease to owe? Do you think the thousands, the millions of men who will lose in an instant by the dreadful explosion or its revulsions, all that constituted the comfort of
their lives, and perhaps their sole means of subsistence, will
leave you in the peaceable enjoyment of your crime!
Stoical contemplators of the incalculable woes which this
catastrophe will scatter over France; unfeeling egotists, who
think these convulsions of despair and wretchedness will
pass away like so many others, and pass the more rapidly as
they will be the more violent, are you quite sure that so
many men without bread will leave you tranquilly to luxuri-
ate amid the viands which you will have been unwilling to
curtail in either variety or delicacy? . . . No, you will
perish; and in the universal conflagration, which you do not
tremble to kindle, the loss of your honour will not save you
a single one of your detestable luxuries! Vote, then, this
extraordinary subsidy, and may it prove sufficient! Vote it,
because the class most interested in the sacrifice which the

government demands, is you yourselves! Vote it, because
the public exigencies allow of no evasion, and that you will
be responsible for every delay! Beware of asking time;
misfortune never grants it. What! gentlemen, in reference
to a ridiculous movement of the Palais-Royal, a ludicrous
insurrection which had never any consequence except in the
weak imaginations or the wicked purposes of a few designing men, you have heard not long since these insane cries:
Cataline is at the gates of Rome, and you deliberate. And
assuredly, there was around you neither Cataline, nor danger,
nor factions, nor Rome. . . . But to-day, bankruptcy,
hideous bankruptcy, is there before you. It threatens to
consume you, your country, your property, your honour!
. . . And you deliberate!"

This is as beautiful as it is antique.

Dumont, in his *Recollections of Mirabeau*, gives the following account of that great man as an orator:

" In the tribune he was impenetrable; those who have
seen him know that the waves rolled around him without
moving him, and that even in the midst of all the abuse he
remained master of his passions. I remember hearing him
deliver a report on the town of Marseilles; every word was
interrupted by those sitting on the right side by abuse; he
heard the words calumniator, liar, assassin, scoundrel, and
all the eloquence of a Billingsgate, echo around him. He
stopped a moment, and addressing himself to the most
furious, in a soft sweet voice, said: ' I will wait, gentlemen;
till this pleasantness shall have exhausted itself,' and he remained perfectly tranquil as if they had given him the most
favourable reception. He never looked on himself as sufficiently provoked to forget oratorical decorum. But what
was wanting in him as a political orator was the art of discussion on subjects which were exacted from him; he did
not know how to embrace a series of arguments and proofs;
he did not understand refuting with method; also he was induced to abandon important motions whenever he had read
his speech, and after a brilliant beginning he disappeared,
leaving the field to his adversary. Barnave had better

reasoning powers, and followed step by step the arguments
of his antagonists, but he had no imagination, gave no colour-
ing to anything, had no style, and consequently no eloquence.
One day when a parallel was drawn between his talent for
argument and Mirabeau's talent for oratory, some one said,
' How can you compare that artificial, stiff hedge to a tree
in an open space displaying all its natural beauty?' It is
certain these two men were not of the same temperament;
but Mirabeau well knew his weak point, and one day when
he had been speaking with that description of refutation
with some little success, he said to us, ' I see well enough
that in order to extemporise on a subject, one must commence by well understanding it.' It was, moreover, the wise
habit of Mirabeau to give himself leisure for reflection whenever he had to reply on important subjects. He called reflection, with much reason, man's greatest power. He took
care not to neglect it. More a thinker than an extemporiser,
he never spoke without first writing or dictating his speeches.
Resembling Cicero and Demosthenes in this respect, he read
them over, put finishing strokes, gave them solidity by
lengthened arguments, lightened them by touches of eloquence, recalled them to his memory, sometimes read them,
but more often spoke them, adding, to that which he had
meditated on, the abrupt unforeseen fire of inspiration. At
the sittings when he was going to speak, he always made
his secretaries and compilers follow him, such as Dumont,
Duroveray, Pellene, and de Comps.

" He kept them shut into a small room near the tribune,
behind the president's office, waiting his orders. These
confidants of his thoughts were desired to follow the dis-
cussions in which he took part, and to note all the ideas and
all the refutations that the circumstance and debate suggested to them. If he was obliged to re-ascend the tribune
for a reply, however short, he went first and consulted this
intimate council.

" He dictated to them the terms in which he proposed
answering his adversaries, he listened to their remarks,
he noted their arguments, he wrote down his reply, he

read it over to his friends, he made, so to speak, the trial of
his inspiration in their presence before doing so in the
presence of his auditory. He had too much respect for the
tribune to present himself as a rhetorician simply, with
words. The sense and the manner were of more importance
with him than the useless facility of stringing words together. It was from this meeting he used to come out
laden with ideas for his improvisations, as also for his
speeches.

" The statesman and man of eloquence left nothing to
chance that he could himself keep for reflection. He felt
himself speaking before posterity, and he watched from afar
over his renown."

" Mirabeau's voice," says Dumont, " was full, manly, and
sonorous; it filled the ear and pleased it; always sustained
but flexible, he made himself as well heard when lowering it
as when he raised it; he could run over comments pronouncing the final words with so much care that not one
was ever lost. His usual manner was rather lagging; he
began with a little embarrassment, often hesitated, but in a
way that called forth interest; one saw him, so to speak,
seeking the expression most apt; discarding, choosing,
weighing the words, till he became animated, and the
bellows of the forge were in full play. In the moments of
greatest excitement, the feeling that made him lay stress on
certain words to express their force prevented his being
rapid; he had a great dislike to French volubility, and the
false zeal which he called the thunder and storms of the
opera. He never lost the gravity of a senator, and at his
first beginning his fault perhaps was a little preparation, and
a little pretention; he lifted his head with too much pride,
and sometimes his contempt amounted to insolence. What
is almost beyond belief is, that they managed little pencilled
notes to reach him at the foot of the tribune, and sometimes
in the very tribune itself (as he wrote an infinite number in
the Assembly), and that he had the power of reading these
notes whilst speaking, and introducing them into his speech.
He felt himself beautiful in his ugliness; when preparing his

speeches he would proudly display and contemplate in the glass his bust, his great size, and his strongly marked features, pitted with small-pox.

"'The great power of my ugliness,' he said, 'is not known': and that ugliness he thought beautiful. He was very carefully and well dressed; he had an enormous head of hair, artistically arranged, and which increased the size of his head. 'When I shake my terribly wild-looking head,' he used to say, 'there is no one that dares to interrupt me.' He very willingly placed himself before a large glass, looking at himself with the greatest pleasure whilst speaking, throwing his head back and squaring his shoulders. He had that peculiarity of vain men, that the very sound of their names strikes on them pleasantly, and who can like even to repeat it themselves.

"But in looking for the characteristic trait of his genius, I find it after mature reflection in the political sagacity, the foreseeing of events, and the knowledge of mankind which he appeared to me to possess in a more rare and eminent degree than all the other qualities of the mind. In this respect, he left far behind him the most distinguished of his colleagues. There were moments when, he said, he felt as if he were a prophet, and he seemed in fact as if he had inspiration of the future. He was not believed, because others could not see as far as he did, and because his depression was often attributed to his self-love; but I know at the time he prognosticated the greatest ill to the monarchy he had the most exalted idea of the nation's destiny in the future."

He said Necker was the pigmy of the Revolution. "Malebranche," he added, "saw everything through God, Necker sees everything through Necker!" He called d'Espremenil, Crispin-Catilina; Lafayette, Cromwell-Grandisson, or Giles-Cæsar. Like Voltaire, by reconciling the two names which contrasted, he gave the double signification of the pretention and helplessness of a living man. He had caricature medals struck and put in circulation against those he did not esteem, or that he esteemed sufficiently to fear. He could not suffer praise to be decreed to men of

small genius.   These praises seemed to him robberies from
the men to whom legitimately belonged true glory.

" Doubts have been raised as to his personal courage,"
again says Dumont.   " His youth proved that these doubts
were calumnies.   But he very wisely formed the resolution
to refuse all single combat during the session of the Northern
Assembly.   ' Our enemies,' he said, ' can find as many bravos
as they like, and can, by duels, release themselves of all who
give them umbrage, for were I to kill even ten, I should myself fall as the eleventh.'   He was always armed with pistols,
and his servants also, like himself.   He often feared being
assassinated.   He was adored by those who served him : exceedingly particular in his dress, he spun out the time by a
thousand trifles with his valets-de-chambre ; he read little
and very rapidly ; by a glance he discovered in those thousands of pages what was new and interesting.   He wrote a
great deal and with great rapidity—a cramped hand ; his
hand-writing resembled hieroglyphic characters.

" Copies of his manuscripts and speeches were made in his
house, with a promptitude which, however, did not satisfy
his impatience.   They were copied one after the other ten or
twelve times to attain the beauty of style he sought to give
his discourses.   His hours were seized on by the public, who
beset his doors.   His levees were those of a prince.   They
commenced at seven in the morning, and continued without
interruption up to the hour of his going to the Assembly.
Even then, his stairs, the court-yard, the entrance to his
house, the street, were all filled with groups assembled from
admiration and curiosity.   The people perceived in him,
through instinct, the royalty of human intellect and the only
true genius of the revolution and the country."

Although France has produced some excellent orators
since the days of Mirabeau, she has had none of extraordinary merit, and in order to avoid swelling the size of the
present volume, the author has not given a sketch of the
French orators since the Revolution.

CHAPTER VI.

ORATORY IN AMERICA.

IT is unquestionably true that forensic eloquence should be more diligently cultivated by the American bar than it is. Framed by the wisest men, cemented by the concurrence of succeeding generations, and strengthened by the lapse of time, our laws have at length been erected into a beautiful system, that embraces almost every imaginable point of the personal security of the citizen, but, extended as they are, and calculated for this beneficial purpose, such is the variety of circumstances that daily demand its attention, and such consequently are its numerous and intricate ramifications, that it requires a peculiar learning, and a distinct mode of eloquence, to pursue and apply them to the wrongs they are intended to redress.

It is true that the advocate should not indulge too often in flights of the imagination. He is addressing the court to protect the injured, and to punish the oppressor, by the due administration of known and settled laws; and therefore those meretricious arts, whereby the unsteady vulgar alone are moved, will be of little avail. But when he considers that his auditory are freemen, fulfilling the most awful office of free laws; that their decision may affect the future prosperity of thousands; that they whose life, liberty, or prosperity is at stake are citizens, by their birthright entitled to a clear and impartial distribution of justice; that the eyes of many, interested in these rights, are upon the court and himself, should not his mind be animated to the dignified fervour of a plain and manly eloquence, that seems to feel the importance of its own exertions, and that seeks not its own elevation in forms and phrases of speech?

Immense fortunes are at stake in the cases tried every day in our courts ; in other cases the more sacred and valuable rights of life, liberty, and reputation must be adjudicated. What a fine field is here for the unselfish, the conscientious, and enlightened advocate, to stand between oppressor and oppressed!

The earliest specimens of American oratory are chiefly characterised by sublimity and patriotism.

The erection of the magnificent fabric of liberty in this country called forth the best efforts of the greatest orators.

An ample theme was afforded by the Revolutionary contest, for the exhibition of all that is indignant, touching, daring, grand, and overwhelming in eloquence, consequently some of the most vehement passages that ever stirred the human soul are to be found in the speeches of the Revolutionary orators. Then it was that the orators of freedom fearlessly raised their thunder tones against oppression. It was, the brightest period in the history of British and American oratory.

The period of our Colonial and Revolutionary history was, in fact, an era of great superiority in eloquence, at home and abroad. England then presented an array of orators such as she had known at no other time. In Westminster Hall the accomplished Mansfield was constantly heard in support of kingly power, while the philosophic and argumentative Camden exercised his mighty intellect in defence of popular rights. Burke had awoke with all his wealth of fancy, daring imagination, and comprehensive learning. Fox had entered the arena of forensic and senatorial gladiatorship, with his great, glowing heart, and titanic passions, all kindled into volcanic heat. Junius, by his sarcasm and audacity, stung the loftiest circles into desperation. Erskine embellished the dark heavens by the rainbow tints of his genius; and Chatham, worthily succeeded by his "cloud-compelling" son, ruled the billowy sea of excited mind with the majesty of a god.

James Otis, Patrick Henry, Samuel Adams, Josiah Quincy, Joseph Warren, John Hancock, John Adams, and Richard Henry Lee, were among the most renowned American patriots and orators who flourished during the period of which we are speaking.

In order to exhibit the style of oratory prevalent in those days, a few short extracts from the speeches of our Revolutionary patriots and orators will be given.

While the glorious banner of Liberty shall continue to spread its folds over our Republic, the patriotic sentiments of our forefathers cannot be repeated without thrilling emotions.

No true American can read the eloquent speech of General Warren on the Boston massacre without being deeply moved:

" The voice of your father's blood cries to you from the ground, ' My sons, scorn to be slaves!' In vain we met the frowns of tyrants; in vain we crossed the boisterous ocean, found a New World, and prepared it for the happy residence of liberty ; in vain we toiled, in vain we fought, we bled in vain, if you our offspring want valor to repel the assaults of her invaders!—stain not the glory of your worthy ancestors ; but, like them, resolve never to part with your birthright. Be wise in your deliberations, and determined in your exertions for the preservation of your liberties. Follow not the dictates of passion, but enlist yourselves under the sacred banner of reason. Use every method in your power to secure your rights. At least, prevent the curses of posterity from being heaped upon your memories.

" If you, with united zeal and fortitude, oppose the torrent of oppression ; if you feel the true fire of patriotism burning in your breasts; if you from your souls despise the most gaudy dress that slavery can wear ; if you really prefer the lowly cottage (whilst blessed with liberty) to gilded palaces, surrounded with the ensigns of slavery,—you may have the fullest assurance that tyranny, with her whole accursed train, will hide their hideous heads in confusion, shame, and despair. If you perform your part, you must have the strongest confidence that the same Almighty Being, who protected your pious and venerable forefathers, who enabled them to turn a barren wildernesss into a fruitful field, who so often made bare his arm for their salvation, will still be mindful of you, their offspring.

" May this Almighty Being graciously preside in all our councils. May He direct us to such measures as He Himself shall approve, and be pleased to bless. May we ever be a people favored of God. May our land be a land of liberty, the seat of virtue, the asylum of the oppressed, a name and a praise in the whole earth, until the last shock of time shall bury the empires of the world in one common, undistinguished ruin."

The language of Quincy is similar to this. Just before the Revolutionary war he addressed his townsmen in an eloquent speech, from which the following is an extract : " Oh, my countrymen ! what will our children say when they read the history of these times, should they find we tamely gave way, without one noble struggle, the most invaluable of earthly blessings? As they drag the galling chain, will they not execrate us ? If we have any respect for things sacred ; any regard to the dearest treasure on earth ; if we have one tender sentiment for posterity ; if we would not be despised by the world, let us, in the most open, solemn manner, and with determined fortitude swear, —we will die,—if we cannot live freemen ! "

John Hancock, on the 5th of March, 1774, made a stirring speech to the citizens of Boston, which was concluded with the following elevated sentiments : " I have the most animating confidence, that the present noble struggle for liberty will terminate gloriously for America. And let us play the man for our God, and for the cities of our God ; while we are using the means in our power, let us humbly commit our righteous cause to the great Lord of the Universe, who loveth righteousness and hateth iniquity. And having secured the approbation of our hearts, by a faithful and unwearied discharge of our duty to our country, let us joyfully leave our concerns in the hands of Him who raiseth up and pulleth down the empires and kingdoms of the world."

The denunciations which he poured forth in his oration on the Boston Massacre are a striking example of Hancock's style: "Let this sad tale of death never be told without a tear; let not the heaving bosom cease to burn with a manly indignation at the relation of it through the long tracts of future time; let every parent tell the shameful story to his listening children till tears of pity glisten in their eyes, or boiling passion shakes their tender frames.

"Dark and designing knaves, murderers, parricides! how dare you tread upon the earth which has drunk the blood of slaughtered innocence, shed by your hands? How dare you breathe that air which wafted to the ear of heaven the groans of those who fell a sacrifice to your accursed ambition. But if the laboring earth does not expand her jaws—if the air you breathe is not commissioned to be the minister of death—yet, hear it, and tremble. The eye of heaven penetrates the secret chambers of the soul; and you, though screened from human observation, must be arraigned—must lift your hands, red with the blood of those whose death you have procured, at the tremendous bar of God."

Such was the impassioned oratory which fell from the lips of the first orators of freedom in this country.

Hamilton.—Alexander Hamilton was born January the 11th, 1757, in the island of Nevis, the most beautiful of the British West Indies.

He was early left to buffet the storms of adversity, his parents having died when he was very young. In 1769 he was placed as a clerk in the counting-house of Mr. Nicholas Cruger, a wealthy and highly respected merchant of Santa Cruz.

Hamilton had an aspiring mind, and when only thirteen years old, he wrote to a young friend at school as follows: "I contemn the grovelling condition of a clerk, to which my fortune condemns me, and would willingly risk my life, though not my character, to exalt my station; I mean to prepare the way for futurity."

The sentiments which Hamilton expressed in his letter were those of a noble youth, eagerly desirous of achieving

21

fame, but with the strongest attachment to untarnished integrity, — guarantees of the splendid success which he achieved in after years.

Hamilton prosecuted his studies, while with Mr. Cruger, with the greatest diligence, giving all his spare time to his books. Some of his youthful compositions were published, and the talent which he displayed in writing them, induced his friends to send him to New York for the purpose of completing his education. He arrived in this country in October, 1772, and was placed at a grammar school in Elizabeth, N. J., under the instruction of Francis Barber, afterward a distinguished officer in the American army.

Hamilton entered King's (now Columbia) College, where he soon " gave extraordinary displays of genius and energy of mind."

Here, while a student, Hamilton began his glorious political career, performing services for his country which will cause his name to shine forever in the annals of our country.

In college, Hamilton pursued with the greatest assiduity those studies which his natural tastes and glowing ambition required. His powerful mind, versatile pen, and eloquent voice were from the first employed in defending colonial opposition to the acts of the British Parliament.

He wrote, anonymously, in December, 1774, and February, 1775, several pamphlets in favor of the pacific measures of defence recommended by Congress.

At that early day Hamilton suggested the policy of giving encouragement to domestic manufactures, as a sure means of lessening the needs of external commerce. " He anticipated ample resources at home, and, among other things, observed that several of the southern colonies were so favorable in their soil and climate to the growth of cotton, that such a staple alone, with due cultivation, in a year or two would afford products sufficient to clothe the whole continent. He insisted upon our unalienable right to the steady, uniform, unshaken security of constitutional freedom ; to the enjoyment of trial by jury ; and to the right of freedom from taxation, except by our own immediate representatives, and that colonial legislation was an inherent right, never to be abandoned or impaired."

"Freedom or Death," was the motto inscribed on the leathern caps which he and his fellow-students wore as members of the military corps which he organised while at college. Hamilton was not only busy promoting measures of resistance, but at the same time he mastered the science of political economy, the laws of commerce, the balance of trade, and the circulating medium, so that when these topics came afterward to be discussed, Hamilton was fully prepared to take his part in the discussion.

The author regrets that he is not permitted by the nature of this work to record all the achievements of the great Hamilton in the Cabinet, the Field and the Forum. He can only say that Hamilton entered the army in 1776, and became the inseparable companion of the peerless Washington, and continued with him till 1781. He took part in the battles of Brandywine, Germantown, and Monmouth; and he led, at his own request, at the siege of Yorktown, the detachment which carried by assault one of the strongest outworks of the foe.

The first political speech to a popular assembly was delivered by Hamilton at "the great meeting in the fields," as it was called. The object of it was to choose delegates to the first Congress. He was at that time a student in King's College, and was very juvenile in appearance. As Hamilton was unexpectedly called upon, his effort was unpremeditated, and at first he hesitated and faltered, being awed by the immense audience before him. His youthful countenance, slender form, and novel aspect, awakened curiosity and excited universal attention. The "infant orator," as they called him, astonished and electrified the vast multitude.

After discussing in an able and striking manner the important principles involved, he depicted in glowing colours the long-continued and constantly aggravated oppressions of the mother country. In speaking upon this topic he burst forth in a strain of bold and thrilling eloquence. He said, in part: " The sacred rights of mankind are not to be rumaged for among old parchments or musty records; they are written as with a sunbeam in the whole volume of human nature, by the hand of Divinity itself, and can never be erased or obscured by mortal power."

Hamilton insisted on the duty of resistance, pointed out the means and certainty of success, and described " the waves of rebellion sparkling with fire, and washing back on the shores of England the wrecks of her power, her wealth, and her glory." Under this spontaneous burst of mature eloquence from lips so youthful, the vast multitude first sank in awe and surprise, and then arose with irrepressible astonishment. The death-like silence ceased as he closed, and repeated huzzas resounded to the heavens.

At the age of thirty-eight, in 1795, Hamilton resumed the practice of the law, in New York, where he continued in active professional pursuits until the tragical close of his life.

At that time Hamilton was under the middle size, thin in person, but remarkably erect and dignified in his deportment. His hair was turned back from his forehead, powdered, and collected in a club behind. His complexion was exceedingly fair, and varying from this only by the delicate rosiness of his cheeks. In form and tint his face was considered uncommonly handsome. When in repose, it bore a serene and thoughtful expression; but when engaged in conversation, it immediately assumed an attractive smile. His ordinary costume was a blue coat with bright buttons, the skirts being unusually long; he wore a white waistcoat, black silk small clothes, and white silk stockings. His appearance and deportment accorded with the exalted distinction which, by his stupendous public services, he had attained. His voice was engagingly pleasant, and his whole mien commanded the respect due to a master-mind. His natural frankness inspired the most affectionate attachment; and his splendid talents, as is usual, elicited the firmest love and the most furious hate. One of the ablest writers of modern times pays him the following high compliment as a statesman:

" Hamilton must be classed among the men who have best known the vital principles and the fundamental conditions of a government ; not of a government such as this (France) but of a government worthy of its mission and of its name. There is not in the Constitution of the United States an element of order, of force, or of duration, which he has not powerfully contributed to introduce into it and caused to predominate."

The following account has been given of Hamilton's eloquence : " The eloquence of Hamilton was said to be persuasive and commanding ; the more likely to be so, as he had no guide but the impulse of a great and rich mind, he having had little opportunity to be trained at the bar or in popular assemblies.

Those who could speak of his manner from the best opportunities to observe him, in public and in private, concurred in pronouncing him to be a frank, amiable, high-minded, open-hearted gentlemen. He was capable of inspiring the most affectionate attachment ; but he could make those whom he opposed, fear and hate him cordially.

He was capable of intense and effectual application, as is abundantly proved by his public labours. But he had a rapidity and clearness of perception in which he may not have been equalled. One, who knew his habits of study, said of him, that when he had a serious object to accomplish, his practice was to reflect on it previously ; and when he had gone through his labour, he retired to sleep without regard to the hour of the night, and having slept six or seven hours, he rose, and having taken strong coffee, seated himself at his table, where he would remain six, seven, or eight hours ; and the product of his rapid pen required little correction for the press. He was among the few, alike excellent, whether in speaking or in writing. In private and friendly intercourse, he is said to have been exceedingly amiable, and to have been affectionately beloved.

It has been said that he " was the most sagacious and laborious of our Revolutionary orators. He anticipated time and interrogated history with equal ease and ardour.

He explored the archives of his own land, and drew from
foreign courts the quintessence of their ministerial wisdom.
He illuminated the councils where Washington presided,
and with him guarded our youthful nation with the eyes of
a lynx, and the talons of a vulture."

Hamilton's political writings will be read with interest
while time lasts. Aside from the seductive charms of his
style, the comprehensive and valuable thoughts upon the
science of government, which they contain, render them
invaluable to the statesman earnestly desirous of promoting
the public welfare.

Fisher Ames said : " That writer would deserve the fame
of a public benefactor who could exhibit the character of
Hamilton, with the truth and force that all who intimately
knew him conceived it; his example would then take the
same ascendant as his talents. The portrait alone, however exquisitely finished, could not inspire genius where it
is not; but if the world should again have possession of so
rare a gift, it might awaken it where it sleeps, as by a spark
from Heaven's own altar; for surely if there is anything like
divinity in man, it is in his admiration for virtue.

" The country deeply laments when it turns its eyes back
and sees what Hamilton was; but my soul stiffens with
despair when I think what Hamilton *would have been.* It
is not as Apollo, enchanting the shepherds with his lyre,
that we deplore him; it is as Hercules, treacherously slain
in the midst of his unfinished labours, leaving the world
over run with monsters."

It is unnecessary to give an account of the fatal duel by
which Hamilton lost his life in 1804. The facts are universally known.

The following extract will serve to illustrate the style of
Hamilton's political oratory. It is on the Constitution of
the United States:

" After all our doubts, our suspicions, and speculations, on
the subject of Government, we must return, at last, to this
important truth,—that, when we have formed a Constitution
upon free principles, when we have given a proper balance

to the different branches of Administration, and fixed Representation upon pure and equal principles, we may, with
safety, furnish it with the powers necessary to answer, in the
most ample manner, the purposes of Government. The
great desiderata are a free Representation, and mutual
checks. When these are obtained, all our apprehensions of
the extent of powers are unjust and imaginary. What, then,
is the structure of this Constitution? One branch of the
Legislature is to be elected by the People,—by the same
People who choose your State Representatives. Its members are to hold their office two years, and then return to
their constitutents. Here, Sir, the People govern. Here
they act by their immediate Representatives. You have
also a Senate, constituted by your State Legislatures,—by
men in whom you place the highest confidence,—and forming another Representative branch. Then, again, you have
an Executive Magistrate, created by a form of election
which merits universal admiration.

" In the form of this Government, and in the mode of Legislation, you find all the checks which the greatest politicans
and the best writers have ever conceived. What more can
reasonable men desire? Is there any one branch in which
the whole Legislative and Executive powers are lodged?
No! The Legislative authority is lodged in three distinct
branches, properly balanced; the Executive authority is
divided between two branches; and the Judicial is still
reserved for an independent body, who hold their office
during good behaviour. This organisation is so complex, so
skilfully contrived, that it is next to impossible that an
impolitic or wicked measure should pass the great scrutiny
with success. Now, what do Gentlemen mean, by coming
forward and declaiming against this Government? Why
do they say we ought to limit its powers, to disable it, and
to destroy its capacity of blessing the People? Has philosophy suggested, has experience taught, that such a Government ought not to be trusted with everything necessary
for the good of society? Sir, when you have divided and
nicely balanced the departments of Government ; when you

have strongly connected the virtue of your rulers with their
interests; when, in short, you have rendered your system
as perfect as human forms *can* be,—you *must* place confidence; you *must* give power."

Hamilton won for himself, the most imperishable renown.
He will always be affectionately remembered by the lovers
of liberty throughout the world, as the soldier of the revolution—the friend and confidant of Washington—the founder
of the American system of finance—the enlightened statesman—the great counsellor—the magnificent orator—and the
man of probity, tried and spotless.

Henry.—Patrick Henry was born on the 29th day of May,
1736, in the County of Hanover, and Colony of Virginia.

Mr. Henry's youth gave no presage of his future greatness.
He was idle and lazy, and spent most of his time in fishing,
hunting, and playing the violin. At the age of sixteen he
was established in trade by his father, but through idleness,
the love of music and the charms of the chase and a readiness to trust every one, he soon became bankrupt. While a
merchant he studied human nature continually. Not in
reference to the honesty and solvency of his customers, but
in relation to the structure of their minds and opinions.

By endeavouring, constantly, to make political, and other
subjects understood by his illiterate hearers, he became a
master of that clear and simple style which forms the best
vehicle of thought to a popular assembly. He was also instructed by these exercises in those topics of persuasion by
which men are most certainly to be moved, and in the kind
of imagery and structure of language which were the best
fitted to strike and agitate their hearts.

Mr. Henry studied law and was admitted to the bar at
the age of twenty-four.

The controversy in 1763, between the clergy, and the
Legislature of Virginia, touching the stipend of the former,
was the occasion when Mr. Henry made his first public
appearance, as a lawyer.

Says Mr. Wirt: "On this first trial of his strength, he
rose very awkwardly, and faltered much in his exordium.

The people hung their heads at so unpromising a commencement, the clergy were observed to exchange sly looks with each other, and his father is described as having almost sunk , with confusion from his seat. But these feelings were of short duration, and soon gave place to others, of a very different character. For, now were these wonderful faculties which he possessed for the first time developed ; and now was first witnessed that mysterious and almost supernatural transformation of appearance, which the fire of his own eloquence never failed to work in him. For, as his mind rolled along and began to glow from its own action, all the *exuviæ* of the clown seemed to shed themselves spontaneously. His attitude by degrees became erect and lofty. The spirit of his genius awakened all his features. His countenance shone with a nobleness and grandeur which it had never before exhibited. There was a lightning in his eyes which seemed to rive the spectator. His action became bold, graceful, and commanding; and in the tones of his voice, but more especially in his emphasis, there was a peculiar charm, a magic, of which any one who ever heard him will speak as soon as he is named, but of which no one can give any adequate description. They can only say that it struck upon the ear and upon the heart, *in a manner which language cannot tell.* Add to all these his underworking fancy, and the peculiar phraseology in which he clothed its images; for he painted to the heart with a force that almost petrified it. In the language of those who heard him on this occasion, ' he made their blood run cold, and their hair to rise on end.'

"It will not be difficult for any one who ever heard this most extraordinary man, to believe the whole account of this transaction which is given by his surviving hearers ; and from their account, the court-house of Hanover County must have exhibited, on this occasion, a scene as picturesque as has ever been witnessed in real life. They say that the people, whose countenance had fallen as he arose, had heard but a very few sentences before they began to look up; then to look at each other in surprise, as if doubting the evidence of their own senses ; then attracted by some strong

gesture, struck by some majestic attitude, fascinated by the
spell of his eye, the charm of his emphasis, and the varied
and commanding expression of his countenance, they could
look away no more. In less than twenty minutes they
might be seen in every part of the house, on every bench, in
every window, stooping forward from their stands, in death-
less silence; their features fixed in amazement and awe; all
their senses listening and riveted upon the speaker, as if to
catch the last strain of some heavenly visitant. The mock-
ery of the clergy was soon turned into alarm; their triumph
into confusion and despair; and at one burst of his rapid
and overwhelming invective, they fled from the bench in
precipitation and terror. As for the father, such was his
surprise, such his amazement, such his rapture, that, forgetting where he was, and the character which he was
filling, tears of ecstacy streamed down his cheeks, without
the power or inclination to repress them. The jury seemed
to have been completely bewildered; for, thoughtless even
of the admitted right of the plaintiff, they had scarcely left
the bar when they returned with a verdict of *one penny
damages*. A motion was made for a new trial; but the court,
too, had now lost the equipose of their judgment, and over-
ruled the motion by a unanimous vote. The verdict and
judgment overruling the motion, were followed by redoubled
acclamations from within and without the house. The
people, who had with difficulty kept their hands off their
champion, from the motion of closing his harangue, no
sooner saw the fate of the cause finally sealed, than they
seized him at the bar, and in spite of his own exertions, and
the continued cry of ' order ' from the sheriffs and the court,
they bore him out of the court-house, and raising him upon
their shoulders, carried him about the yard in a kind of
electioneering triumph."

As a member of the House of Burgesses in 1765, Mr.
Henry introduced his resolutions against the Stamp Act,
which proved the opening of the American Revolution in
the colony of Virginia. It was in the midst of the debate
upon those resolutions that he " exclaimed, in a voice of

thunder and with the look of a god, ' Cæsar had his Brutus
—Charles the First his Cromwell—and George the Third—
[" Treason " cried the Speaker; " treason ! treason ! " echoed
from every part of the house. Henry faltered not for an
instant, but rising to a loftier attitude, and fixing on the
Speaker an eye of the most determined fire, finished his sen-
tence with the firmest emphasis]—*may profit by their example.*
If this be treason, make the most of it.' "

At Philadelphia, in Carpenter's Hall, the first Congress
met on the 4th of September, 1774. This assembly was
composed of the most prominent men of the several colonies, on the wisdom of whose councils was staked the
liberties of the colonists, and their posterity. The first
meeting is described as " awfully solemn. They had been
called together to consider a subject of incalculable magnitude." Mr. Henry rose slowly, as if borne down with the
weight of the subject, and, after faltering, according to his
habit, through a most impressive exordium, he launched
gradually into a recital of colonial wrongs. Rising, as he
advanced, with the grandeur of his subject, and glowing at
length with all the majesty and expectation of the occasion,
his speech seemed more than that of mortal man. There
was no rant, no rhapsody, no labour of the understanding, no
straining of the voice, no confusion of the utterance. His
countenance was erect, his eye steady, his action noble, his
enunciation clear and firm, his mind poised on its centre, his
views of his subject comprehensive and great, and his imagination coruscating with a magnificence and a variety
which struck even that assembly with amazement and awe.
He sat down amid murmurs of astonishment and applause,
and as he had been proclaimed the greatest orator of Virginia, he was now, on every hand, admitted to be the first
orator of America.

Mr. Henry in his youth was indifferent to dress, but he
became more refined as he rose in experience and influence
His appearance, however, was at all times wonderfully impressive. " He was nearly six feet high, spare and raw-
boned, with a slight stoop of his shoulders. His complexion

was dark and sallow; his natural expression grave, thoughtful and penetrating. He was gifted with a strong and musical voice, often rendered doubly fascinating by the mild splendours of his brilliant blue eyes. When animated he spoke with the greatest variety of manner and tone. . . .

"Gleams of passion inter-penetrating the masses of his logic, rendered him a spectacle of delight to the friendly spectator, or of dread to his antagonist. He was careless in dress, and sometimes intentionally and extravagantly awkward in movement; but always, like the phosphorescent stone at Bologna, he was less rude than glowing. He could be vehement, insinuating, humorous and sarcastic by turns, and to every sort of style he gave the highest effect. He was an orator by nature and of the highest class, combining all those traits of figure and intellect, action and utterance, which have indissolubly linked his brilliant name with the history of his country's emancipation."

Patrick Henry had great moral courage, and moral courage is the true basis of oratorical success. In order to be effective, the orator must think vigorously, and say what he thinks, fearlessly. When the welfare of his country demands it, he must exhibit the courage of the soldier on the field of battle, and express his opinions on all subjects at the hazard of his life, or of his earthly possessions. He is not worthy to be called an orator, in the true sense of the word, unless he has this patriotic heroism and firmness.

Mr. Henry was happily endowed with that rich imagination which gives vitality to the body of thought, and which is essential to the success of the great orator. He was deeply imbued with that vehemence of conviction, that oratorical action, which modulates the tones, tinges the visage with irresistible power, and suggests to the hearer more than articulated language can express.

From his magnificent speech advising resistance to British aggression, delivered on the 23d of March, 1775, in the old church at Richmond, the following is an extract:

" MR. PRESIDENT : It is natural to man to indulge in the illusions of Hope. We are apt to shut our eyes against a painful truth, and listen to the song of that siren, till she transforms us into beasts. Is this the part of wise men, engaged in a great and arduous struggle for liberty. Are we disposed to be of the number of those, who, having eyes, see not, and having ears, hear not, the things which so nearly concern our temporal salvation? For my part, whatever anguish of spirit it may cost, I am willing to know the whole truth,—to know the worst and to provide for it!

"I have but one lamp, by which my feet are guided; and that is the lamp of experience. I know of no way of judging of the future but by the past. And, judging by the past, I wish to know what there has been in the conduct of the British ministry, for the last ten years, to justify those hopes with which gentlemen have been pleased to solace themselves and the House? Is it that insidious smile with which our petition has been lately received? Trust it not, sir; it will prove a snare to your feet! Suffer not yourselves to be betrayed with a kiss! Ask yourselves how this gracious reception of our petition comports with those warlike preparations which cover our waters and darken our land. Are fleets and armies necessary to a work of love and reconciliation? Have we shown ourselves so unwilling to be reconciled, that force must be called in to win back our love?

"Let us not deceive ourselves, sir. These are the implements of war and subjugation;—the last arguments to which kings resort. I ask gentlemen, sir, what means this martial array, if its purpose be not to force us to submission? Can gentlemen assign any other possible motive for it? Has Great Britain any enemy in this quarter of the world, to call for all this accumulation of navies and armies? No, sir, she has none. They are meant for us; they can be meant for no other. They are sent over to bind and rivet upon us those chains which the British ministry have been so long forging. And what have we to oppose to them?—Shall we try argument? Sir, we have been trying that for the last ten years. Have we anything new to offer upon the subject? Nothing. We have held the subject up in every light of which it is capable; but it has been all in vain.

"Shall we resort to entreaty and humble supplication? What terms shall we find which have not already been exhausted? Let us not, I beseech you, sir, deceive ourselves longer. Sir, we have done everything that could be done, to avert the storm which is now coming on. We have petitioned, we have remonstrated, we have supplicated, we have prostrated ourselves before the throne, and have implored its interposition to arrest the tyrannical hands of the ministry and parliament. Our petitions have been slighted, our remonstrances have produced additional violence and insult, our supplications have been disregarded, and we have been spurned, with contempt, from the foot of the throne.

"In vain, after these things, may we indulge the fond hope of peace and reconciliation? There is no longer any reason for hope. If we wish to be free, if we mean to preserve inviolate those inestimable privileges for which we have been so long contending,—if we mean not basely to abandon the noble struggle in which we have been so long engaged, and which we have pledged ourselves never to abandon until the glorious object of our contest shall be obtained,—we must fight; I repeat it, sir, we must fight! An appeal to arms, and to the God of Hosts, is all that is left us!"

Otis.—James Otis descended in the fifth generation from John Otis, who came over from England at a very early period and was one of the first settlers of Hingham, Massachusetts. He took the freeman's oath on the 3d of March, 1635. By his mother's side he was connected with the first founders of Plymouth Colony, who arrived in the *Mayflower* in 1620.

He was born at Great Marshes, in what is now called West Barnstable, February 5, 1725. Says one of his biographers: "During the first two years of his college life, his natural ardour and vivacity made his society much courted by the elder students, and engaged him more in amusement than in study; but he changed his course in the junior year, and began thenceforward to give indications of great talent and power of application." Although at times grave and sedate, sometimes he would discover the wit and humour which formed afterwards striking ingredients in his character. A small party of young people having assembled one day at his father's house, when he was at home during a college vacation, he had taken a slight part in their sports, when, after much persuasion, they induced him to play a country dance for them with his violin, on which instrument he then practised a little. The set was made up, and after they were fairly engaged, he suddenly stopped, and holding up his fiddle and bow, exclaimed: 'So Orpheus fiddled, and so danced the brutes!' and then tossing the instrument aside, rushed into the garden, followed by the disappointed revellers, who were obliged to convert their intended dance into a frolicsome chase after the fugitive musician.

The important events preceding and connected with the American Revolution attracted the attention of Mr. Otis. In 1760, George the Second died, and his grandson reigned in his stead. The conquest of Canada was completed, and it was rumoured that the colonists were to be deprived of their charters and formed into royal governments. Edicts were issued by the sovereign which enabled the king's collectors to compel all sheriffs and constables to attend and aid them in breaking open houses, stores, cellars, ships' trunks, etc., to search for goods which it was supposed had not paid the unrighteous tax imposed by parliament. The good-will of the colonists was wanted no longer to advance the prosecution of the war, and *Writs of Assistance* were undertaken through the influence of the royal governor and others. Application was first made for those writs at Salem, Massachusetts. Stephen Sewall, who was then Chief-Justice of the Superior Court, expressed great doubt of the legality of such writs, and of the authority of the court to grant them. The other judges were of the same opinion. The matter, however, was postponed until the next term of the court at Boston, in February, 1761. Mr. Otis undertook to argue against the writs at the request of the colonists, and met in conflict his law-teacher, Mr. Gridley, then Attorney-General. Mr. Otis was Advocate-General of the Colony of Massachusetts when the order relating to Writs of Assistance

came from England. Deeming them illegal, he refused to
enforce them. This was the case when Mr. Otis first became
famous in history. "The fire in the flint shines not till it
be struck." James Otis distinguished himself as the bold,
brilliant, victorious champion of Colonial rights. He gave
free rein to his oratorical powers and soared into regions of
patriotic principles, new both to himself and the world.

Says John Adams, in his sketch of the scene: "Otis was a
flame of fire. With a promptitude of classical allusions, and
a depth of research, a rapid summary of historical events and
dates, a profusion of legal authorities, a prophetic glance of
his eyes into futurity, and a rapid torrent of impetuous eloquence, he hurried away all before him. The seeds of patriots
and heroes were then and there sown. Every man of an
immensely crowded audience appeared to me to go away,
as I did, ready to take arms against Writs of Assistance.
Then and there was the first scene of the first act of opposition to the arbitrary claims of Great Britain. Then and
there the child Independence was born. In fifteen years,
that is in 1776, he grew up to manhood and declared himself
free." The principles laid down by Otis with such profound
learning could not be subverted. The decision of the court
was as follows: "The court has considered the subject of
Writs of Assistance, and can see no foundation for such a
writ; but as the practice in England is not known, it has
been thought best to continue the question to the next term,
that in the meantime opportunity may be given to know the
result." No judgment was pronounced at the next term,
and nothing was said about Writs of Assistance. Few of
the rhetorical productions of Mr. Otis are now extant. None
of his speeches were fully recorded. As an orator his memorials are rather traditionary than actual. The admiration
which his countrymen had for him was boundless, and his
memory will always be revered.

His eloquence was bold, witty, pungent, and practical. He
communed with other minds, but more with his own. He
was learned, and yet original, courteous in debate, and always treating the opinions of his adversaries with the respect

they deserved; but he was bold and daring in his own inves-
tigations. He always listened to appeals which were conciliating, and motives that were just. In the presence,
however, of arrogance and oppression, he was as firm as a
rock. The following extract from his *Vindication of the
Colony of Massachusetts in 1762,* will illustrate both the boldness and wit of Mr. Otis:

"In order to excuse, if not altogether justify, the offensive passage, and clear it from ambiguity, I beg leave to
premise two or three *data :* 1. God made all men naturally
equal. 2. The ideas of earthly superiority, pre-eminence, and
grandeur, are educational, at least, acquired, not innate. 3.
Kings were, (and plantation governors should be), made for
the good of the people, and not the people for them. 4. No
government has a right to make hobby-horses, asses, and
slaves of the subject; nature having made sufficient of the
two former for all the lawful purposes of man, from the
harmless peasant in the field, to the most refined politician
in the cabinet, but none of the last, which infallibly proves
that they are unnecessary."

Mr. Otis always forgot himself in the subjects he discussed. He explored all the resources at his command, and
was tireless in preparation. He appeared to be completely
absorbed by his theme while speaking, and thought as little
of the skill he should display as an orator, as one fighting
for his life thinks of the grace he shall exhibit in the flourish
of his weapons. He was enthusiastic, sincere, forceful,
natural, and spoke the language of a powerful mind under
high but well regulated excitement.

It may be said of Otis as it was of John Marshall: "He
was one of those rare beings that seem to be sent among
men from time to time, to keep alive our faith in humanity."
He was finely formed, and had an intelligent countenance;
his eye, voice, and manner were very impressive. The elevation of his mind and the known integrity of his purposes,
enabled him to speak with decision and dignity, and commanded the respect as well as the admiration of his audience. His eloquence showed but little imagination, yet it

was instinct with the fire of passion. His oratory was extremely serviceable to the Colonists. He charmed the timid
and inspired the weak, boldly attacked and subdued the
haughty, and enthralled the prejudiced.

John Adams said of him: " I have been young, and now
am old, and I solemnly say, I have never known a man
whose love of his country was more ardent and sincere ;
never one who suffered so much ; never one, whose services
for any ten years of his life, were so important and essential
to the cause of his country, as those of Mr. Otis, from 1760
to 1770."

A few weeks previous to his death Otis said to his sister,
" I hope when God Almighty in his righteous providence,
shall take me out of time into eternity, that it will be by a
flash of lightning." His prayer was heard and answered.
On the 28th of May, 1783, during a heavy thunder-storm,
he, with a greater part of the family with which he resided
had entered the house to wait until the shower should have
passed. Otis, with his cane in one hand, stood in the front
entry near a door, and was telling a story to the assembled
group when a terrible explosion took place, which seemed
to shake the solid earth, and he fell without a struggle, or
an utterance, instantaneously dead. He had often expressed
a desire to die as he did.

Ames.—Fisher Ames was born at Dedham, in Norfolk
County, Massachusetts, on the 9th of April, 1758. He was
descended from one of the oldest families in the province. ·

Ames exhibited an ardent fondness for classical literature
at an early age. He commenced the study of Latin when
he was only six years of age. At Harvard College to which
he was admitted in the year 1770, and from which he graduated in 1774, shortly after the completion of his twelfth
year, he was noted for his application and industry. His
vivacity and animation, and his geniality and modesty made
him a general favourite.

He joined a debating society while at college and it
was early observed that he coveted the glory of eloquence.
In his declamation before this society, he was remarked for

the energy and propriety with which he delivered such specimens of impassioned oratory as his genius led him to select. His compositions at this time bore the characteristic stamps which has always marked his speaking and writing. They were sententious and full of ornament.

After his graduation Mr. Ames devoted himself to teaching, giving his leisure to the study of the classics, ancient and modern history, and English literature, especially poetry. Milton and Shakespeare were his favourite authors. He was attentive, also, to the cultivation of his talents in composition and oratory. He laid his favourite authors under heavy contributions for the purpose of enriching and ornamenting his mind. Nearly all of the splendid passages which they contain, he committed to memory, and would sometimes recite them for the entertainment of his friends.

This course of reading enabled him to furnish that fund of materials for speaking and writing which he possessed in singular abundance, his remarkable fertility of allusion, and his ability to evolve a train of imagery adapted to every subject of which he treated.

Mr. Ames was admitted to the bar in 1781.

Mr. Ames, soon after his admission to the bar, wrote several articles on political topics which attracted the attention of the leading men in his state.

He was elected in 1789 a member of the First Congress under the Constitution, and remained a member of that body during the eight years of Washington's administration.

He delivered his celebrated speech on the appropriation for Jay's Treaty in 1796—a production of the deepest pathos and richest eloquence.

Dr. Charles Caldwell thus speaks of Ames's oratory : " He was decidedly one of the most splendid rhetoricians of the age. Two of his speeches, in a special manner—that on Jay's Treaty, and that usually called the ' Tomahawk Speech ' (because it included some resplendent passages on Indian massacres)—were the most brilliant and fascinating specimens of eloquence I have ever heard ; yet have I list-

ened to some of the most celebrated in the British Parliament—among others to Wilberforce, and Mackintosh,
Plunket, Brougham, and Canning; and Dr. Priestly who
was familiar with the oratory of Pitt the father, and Pitt the
son, and also with that of Burke and Fox, made to myself the
acknowledgment that, in his own words, ' the speech of Ames,
on the British treaty, was the most bewitching piece of
parliamentary oratory he had ever listened to.' "

In person Mr. Ames was above middle stature and well
formed. His countenance was very handsome, and his eye
blue in colour, and expressive. His features were not strongly
marked. His forehead was neither high nor broad. His
mouth was beautifully shaped, and was one of his finest
features; his hair was black, and he wore it short, and in the
latter years of his life unpowdered. He was exceedingly
erect in walking, and when speaking he raised his head
slightly. It is said that his expression was usually mild and
complacent when in debate, and if he meant to be severe, it
was seen in good-natured sarcasm, rather than in acrimonious
words.

Mr. Ames died in 1808.

On the sanctity of treaties, Mr. Ames said:

" We are either to execute this treaty or break our faith.
To expatiate on the value of public faith may pass with
some men for declamation; to such men I have nothing to
say. To others, I will urge, can any circumstance mark
upon a people more turpitude and debasement? Can anything tend more to make men think themselves mean,—or
to degrade to a lower point their estimation of virtue, and
their standard of action? It would not merely demoralise
mankind; it tends to break all the ligaments of society; to
dissolve that mysterious charm which attracts individuals to
the nation; and to inspire, in its stead, a repulsive sense of
shame and disgust.

" What is patriotism? Is it a narrow affection for the
spot where a man was born? Are the very clods where we
tread entitled to this ardent preference, because they are
greener? No, sir; this is not the character of the virtue.

It soars higher for its object. It is an extended self-love, mingling with all the enjoyments of life, and twisting itself with the minutest filaments of the heart. It is thus we obey the laws of society, because they are the laws of virtue. In their authority we see, not the array of force and terror, but the venerable image of our country's honour. Every good citizen makes that honour his own, and cherishes it, not only as precious, but as sacred. He is willing to risk his life in its defense, and is conscious that he gains protection while he gives it; for what rights of a citizen will be deemed inviolable, when a State renounces the principles that constitute their security? Or, if his life should not be invaded, what would its enjoyments be, in a country odious in the eye of strangers, and dishonoured in his own? Could he look with affection and veneration to such a country as his parent? The sense of having one would die within him: he would blush for his patriotism, if he retained any,—and justly, for it would be a vice. He would be a banished man in his native land. I see no exception to the respect that is paid among nations to the law of good faith. It is the philosophy of politics, the religion of governments. It is observed by barbarians. A whiff of tobacco-smoke, or a string of beads, gives not merely binding force, but sanctity, to treaties. Even in Algiers, a truce may be bought for money; but, when ratified, even Algiers is too wise, or too just, to disown and annul its obligation."

On the British treaty in 1796, Mr. Ames said:

"Are the posts of our frontier to remain forever in the possession of Great Britain? Let those who reject them, when the treaty offers them to our hands, say, if they choose, they are of no importance. Will the tendency to Indian hostilities be contested by any one? Experience gives the answer. Am I reduced to the necessity of proving this point? Certainly the very men who charged the Indian war on the detention of the posts will call for no other proof than the recital of their own speeches. 'Until the posts are restored,' they exclaimed, 'the treasury and the frontiers must bleed.' Can gentlemen now say that an Indian peace, without the posts, will prove firm? No, sir, it will not be peace, but a sword; it will be no better than a lure to draw victims within the reach of the tomahawk.

"On this theme my emotions are unutterable. If I could find words for them, if my powers bore any proportion to my zeal, I would swell my voice to such a note of remonstrance, it should reach every log-house beyond the mountains. I would say to the inhabitants, Wake from your false security! Your cruel dangers, your more cruel apprehensions, are soon to be removed. The wounds, yet unhealed, are to be torn open again. In the daytime, your path through the woods will be ambushed. The darkness of midnight will glitter with the blaze of your dwellings. You are a father,—the blood of your sons shall fatten your corn-fields! You are a mother,—the war-whoop shall wake the sleep of the cradle!

"Who will say that I exaggerate the tendencies of our measures? Will any one answer, by a sneer, that all this is idle preaching? Will any one deny that we are bound, and, I would hope, to good purpose, by the most solemn sanctions of duty, for the vote we give? Are despots alone to be reproached for unfeeling indifference to the tears and blood of their subjects? Are republicans irresponsible? Can you put the dearest interest of society at risk, without guilt, and without remorse? It is vain to offer, as an excuse, that public men are not to be reproached for the evils that may happen to ensue from their measures. This is very true, where they are unforeseen or inevitable. Those I have depicted are not unforeseen; they are so far from inevitable, we are going to bring them into being by our vote. We choose the consequences, and become as justly answerable for them as for the measure that we know will produce them.

"By rejecting the posts, we light the savage fires, we bind the victims. This day we undertake to render account to the widows and orphans whom our decision will make; to the wretches that will be roasted at the stake; to our country, and, I do not deem it too serious to say, to con-

science and to God, we are answerable ; and, if duty be anything more than a word of imposture, if conscience be not
a bugbear, we are preparing to make ourselves as wretched
as our country. There is no mistake in this case. There
can be none. Experience has already been the prophet of
events, and the cries of our future victims have already
reached us. The Western inhabitants are not a silent and
uncomplaining sacrifice. The voice of humanity issues from
the shade of the wilderness. It exclaims that, while one
hand is held up to reject this treaty, the other grasps a
tomahawk. It summons our imagination to the scenes that
will open. It is no great effort of the imagination to conceive that events so near are already begun. I can fancy
that I listen to the yells of savage vengeance and the shrieks
of torture ! Already they seem to sigh in the Western
wind ! Already they mingle with every echo from the
mountains ! "

Randolph.—John Randolph, of Roanoke, one of the
most remarkable men that ever lived in any age, was born
on the 2d day of June, 1773, near Petersburg, Virginia.
His extraordinary eloquence early fastened the attention of
his countrymen upon him.

Mr. Randolph made his first appearance, in public life, in
1799, as a candidate for Congress. He was indebted, for his
success, to his ability, as he was without family influence in
his district, and a mere boy in appearance. Patrick Henry,
the popular statesman and orator, was his opponent. An
anecdote is related, which is characteristic of both combatants. Mr. Randolph was addressing the populace in
answer to Mr. Henry, when a friend said to the latter :
" Come, Henry, let us go ; it is not worth while to listen to
that boy." Mr. Henry generously said in reply : " Stay, my
friend, there is an old man's head on that boy's shoulders."

Although John Randolph was devoted to America, he
also loved England. Speaking of Randolph's opposition to
war between England and this country Baldwin says :

" But, more especially, Randolph did not desire war with
England. He had no prejudices against England. He saw

and condemned her faults. He did not justify her conduct
toward us. But he remembered that we were of the blood
and bone of her children. He remembered that we spoke
her language, and that we were connected with her by the
strongest commercial ties and interests ; that, though we
had fought her through a long and bloody war, yet we had
fought her by the light of her own principles ; that her own
great men had cheered us on in the fight ; and that the
body of the English nation were with us against a corrupt
and venal ministry, when we took up arms against their and
our tyrants. He remembered that from England we had
inherited all the principles of liberty which lie at the basis
of our government—freedom of speech and of the press ;
the *Habeas Corpus ;* trial by jury ; representation *with*
taxation ; and the great body of our laws. He reverenced
her for what she had done in the cause of human progress,
and for the Protestant religion ; for her achievements in arts
and arms ; for her lettered glory ; for the light shed on the
human mind by her master writers ; for the blessings show-
ered by her great philanthropists upon the world.

"He saw her in a new phase of character. Whatever
was left of freedom in the old world, had taken shelter in
that island, as man, during the deluge, in the ark.

"She opposed the only barrier now left to the sway of
unlimited empire, by a despot, whom she detested as one of
the most merciless and remorseless tyrants that ever scourged
this planet. Deserted of all other men and nations, she
was not dismayed. She did not even seek—such was the
spirit of her prodigious pride—to avoid the issue. She defied it. She dared it—was eager—fevered—panting for it.
She stood against the arch-conqueror's power, as her own
sea-girt isle slants in the ocean—calm amidst the storm and
the waves that blow and break harmlessly on the shore.
She was largely indebted, but she poured out money like
water. Her people were already heavily taxed, but she
quadrupled the taxes. She taxed everything that supports
or embellishes life, all the elements of nature, everything of
human necessity or luxury, from the cradle to the coffin.

The shock was about to come. The long guns of the cinque ports were already loaded, and the matches blazing, to open upon the expectant enemy, as he descended upon her coasts. We came as a new enemy into the field. It was natural to expect her, in the face of the old foe, thought by so many to be himself an over-match for her, to hasten to make terms with us, rather than have another enemy upon her. No! She refused, in the agony and stress of danger, to do what she refused in other times. She turned to us the same look of resolute and imperturbable defiance—with some touch of friendly reluctance in it, it may be—which she turned to her ancient foe. As she stood in her armour, glittering like a war-god, beneath the lion banner, under which we had fought with her at the Long Meadows, at Fort Du Quesne, and on the Heights of Abraham, Randolph could not—for his soul, he could not find it in his heart to strike her then."

His sentiments cost him his seat in Congress, but, says Mr. Baldwin: "Without a murmur he bowed his head to the stroke and went into retirement."

Randolph was one of the most brilliant orators .that America has produced. He was sometimes bitter and sarcastic to his foes, but he was an open foe. His severest attacks were made in public—in the face of day and in the presence of his enemies.

In polite learning he was accomplished beyond the most of the *literati* of his country. He was, beyond question, the wittiest man of his time.

He made the resources of others subservient to his purposes, but he gave a new value to the sentence quoted, and there was as much genius in the selection and application, as in the conception and expression of the idea. He usually spoke without preparation, and it is said his speeches depended much upon the state of his nervous system. He was, therefore, an unequal speaker, sometimes speaking with the greatest felicity, and sometimes with diminished power.

He was an honest and a conscientious man, and his mind

was pure and elevated.   His principles,—he never deserted. He never pandered to the passions of the mob.

Mr. Randolph was a descendant, in the seventh generation, from the celebrated Pocahontas, the daughter of Powhatan, the great Indian chief.

Mr. Randolph died in 1833, in Philadelphia.

As a specimen of his style, the following extract from his speech on British influence, delivered in 1811, is given:

"Imputations of British influence have been uttered against the opponents of this war.   Against whom are these charges brought?   Against men who, in the war of the Revolution, were in the Councils of the Nation, or fighting the battles of your country!   And by whom are these charges made?   By runaways, chiefly from the British dominions, since the breaking out of the French troubles. The great autocrat of all the Russias receives the homage of our high consideration.   The Dey of Algiers and his divan of pirates are very civil, good sort of people, with whom we find no difficulty in maintaining the relations of peace and amity.   'Turks and Infidels,'—Melimelli or the Little Turtle,—barbarians and savages of every clime and colour, are welcome to our arms.   With chiefs of banditti, negro, or mulatto, we can treat and can trade.   Name, how-ever, but England, and all our antipathies are up in arms against her.   Against whom?   Against those whose blood runs in our veins; in common with whom we claim Shake-speare, and Newton, and Chatham, for our countrymen ; whose form of government is the freest on earth, our own, only, excepted ; from whom every valuable principle of our own institutions has been borrowed,—representation, jury trial, voting system, writ of *habeas corpus*, our whole civil and criminal jurisprudence;—against our fellow-Protestants, identified in blood, in language, in religion, with ourselves.

"In what school did the worthies of our land—the Wash-ingtons, Henrys, Hancocks, Franklins, Rutledges, of America —learn those principles of civil liberty which were so nobly asserted by their wisdom and valour?   American resistance to British usurpation has not been more warmly cherished by these great men and their compatriots,—not more by Washington, Hancock, and Henry,—than by Chatham and his illustrious associates in the British Parliament. It ought to be remembered, too, that the heart of the English people was with us. It was a selfish and corrupt ministry, and their servile tools, to whom *we* were not more opposed than *they* were. I trust that none such may ever exist among us; for tools will never be wanting to subserve the purposes, however ruinous or wicked, of kings and ministers of state. I acknowledge the influence of a Shakespeare and a Milton upon my imagination; of a Locke, upon my understanding; of a Sidney, upon my political principles; of a Chatham, upon qualities which would to God I possessed in common with that illustrious man! of a Tillotson, a Sherlock, and a Porteus, upon my religion. This is a British influence which I can never shake off."

Pinkney.—William Pinkney was born at Annapolis, Maryland, on the 17th of March, 1764. He was admitted to the bar in 1786, and the same year removed to Hartford County and commenced practice. Wheaton says: " His very first efforts seem to have given him a commanding attitude in the eye of the public. His attainments in the law of real property and the science of special pleading, then the two great foundations of legal distinction, were accurate and profound ; and he had disciplined his mind by the cultivation of that species of logic, which, if it does not lead to the brilliant results of inductive philosophy, contributes essentially to invigorate the reasoning faculty, and to enable it to detect those fallacies which are apt to impose upon the understanding in the warmth and hurry of forensic discussion. His style in speaking was marked by an easy flow of natural eloquence and a happy choice of language. His voice was very melodious, and seemed a winning accompaniment to his pure and effective diction. His elocution was calm and placid—the very contrast of that strenuous, vehement, and emphatic manner which he subsequently adopted."

Mr. Pinkney for many years stood at the head of the bar

of Maryland, and for the last ten years of his life he did not
have a superior as a lawyer, perhaps, in the United States.

In person he was strong and muscular, square-shouldered
and firm-set, exhibiting great vigour of action, with much
grace and ease of movement. His countenance was intelligent and open, and was capable of the most powerful and
various expression. His forehead was rather low, and his
head oval in shape. Few men have equalled Mr. Pinkney
in the power to invent, select, illustrate, and combine topics
for the purposes of argument.

But he did not rely on the resources of his genius. He
improved it by constant and laborious study. From early
life he was a diligent student, not only of law, but of general
literature. His knowledge of the law was extensive, deep,
and accurate. It is not the author's design to present even
an outline of Mr. Pinkney's character as a statesman or a
scholar, but chiefly as a forensic orator. The sketch of Mr.
Pinkney as an orator, drawn by the distinguished Judge
Story, is worthy of insertion here :

"The celebrity of Mr. Pinkney, as a public speaker, requires some notice in this place of the nature and character
of his oratory. It was, in manner, original, impressive, and
vehement. He had some natural and some acquired defects,
which made him, in some degree, fall short of that exquisite
conception of the imagination, a perfect orator. His voice
was thick and gutteral. It rose and fell with little melody
and softening of tones, and was occasionally abrupt and
harsh in its intonations, and wanting in liquidness and
modulation. At times his utterance was hurried on to an
excess of vehemence; and then, as it were, *per saltum*, he
would suffer it to fall, at the close of the sentence, to a low
and indistinct whisper, which confused, at once, the sense and
the sound. This inequality of elocution did not seem so
much a natural defect as a matter of choice or artificial
cultivation. But the effect, from whatever cause it arose,
was unpleasing; and sometimes gave to his speeches the air
of too much study, measured dignity, or dramatic energy.
These, however, were venial faults, open to observation, in-

deed, but soon forgotten by those, who listened to his instructive and persuasive reasoning ; for no man could hear
him, for any length of time, without being led captive by his
eloquence. His imagination was rich and inventive ; his
taste, in general, pure and critical ; and his memory uncommonly exact, full, and retentive. He attained to a complete
mastery of the whole compass of the English language ; and,
in the variety of use, as well as the choice of diction, for all
the purposes of his public labours, he possessed a marvellous
felicity. It gave to his style an air of originality, force,
copiousness, and expressiveness, which struck the most careless observer. His style was not, indeed, like that of Junius ;
but it stood out, among all others, with that distinct and
striking peculiarity which has given such fame to that truly
great, unknown author. His powers of amplification and
illustration, whenever these were appropriate to his purpose,
seemed almost inexhaustible ; though he possessed, at the
same time, the power of condensation, both of thought and
language, to a most uncommon degree. He never used his
powers of amplification and illustration for mere ornament ;
but as auxiliaries to the main purposes of his argument,
artfully interweaving them with the solid materials of the
fabric. Occasionally, indeed, he would indulge himself in
digressions of such singular beauty and brilliancy, such a
magnificence of phrase, and an appropriateness of allusion,
that they won applause, even from those whose functions
demand a severe and scrutinising indifference to everything,
but argument. In general, his speeches did not abound with
rhetorical flourishes, or sparkle with wit, or scorch with sarcasm ; though he possessed the faculty of using each of
them ·with great skill and promptitude. But when the
occasion seemed to him, from its extraordinary interest, or
the state of public excitement, to require it, his speeches
abounded with poetical imagery, and ambitious ornaments,
and were elaborated with all the studied amplitude of phrase
of Burke and Bolingbroke.

"But the principal and distinguishing faculty of Mr.
Pinkney's mind, (in which few, if any, have ever excelled

him,) and which gave such solid weight to his arguments, and carried home conviction to the doubting and the reluctant, was the closeness, acuteness, clearness, and vigour of his power of ratiocination. His luminous analysis of the merits of his case, his severe and searching logic, his progressive expansion of the line of argument, sustaining itself at every step, by a series of almost impregnable positions, and his instantaneous perception of the slightest infirmity in the arguments or concessions of his adversary, gave him, in most debates, a captivating, if not a dangerous superiority, and made him, at the bar, a formidable antagonist, always to be watched with jealousy, and always to be approached with caution.

"Mr. Pinkney entertained the loftiest notions of the dignity and utility of the profession ; and he endeavoured, on all occasions, to diffuse among the members of the bar the deepest sense of its importance, and responsibility to the public. He was desirous of fame, of that fame, which alone is enduring, the fame which reposes on sound learning, exalted genius, and diligent, nay, incessant study. Whatever might be the success of his oratory in the estimate of other persons, it never seemed to reach his own standard of excellence. He was, therefore, engaged in a constant struggle, not merely to excel others, but to excel himself ; and thus, his orations, (for such many of his speeches were,) and his juridical arguments, were perpetually enriched by the last accumulations of a mind, whose ambition never tired, and whose industry never slackened, in its professional meditations and readings. In these respects, his example may fitly be propounded to all who seek solid reputation at the bar. He knew well that genius without labour· could accomplish little ; and that he who would enlighten others, or be foremost in the race of life, must quicken his own thoughts, by giving his days and nights, not to the indulgences of pleasure, or the soft solicitudes of literary ease, but to severe discipline, and the study of the great instructors of mankind in learning and science. His loss, in this edifying and cheering career, will long be felt. It has cast a gloom over the profession, which can be dissipated only by the rise of some other master spirit, to guide, to cheer, and to instruct us."

Wirt.—On the 8th of November, 1772, William Wirt was born at Bladensburg, Md. He was admitted to the bar in 1792. He made considerable reputation in the trial of Aaron Burr in 1807, against whom he appeared in aid of the prosecution. He wrote the *Life of Patrick Henry*, in 1817. In the same year he was appointed Attorney-General of the United States by President Monroe. He died at Washington on the 18th day of February, 1834.

Mr. Wirt was not only a student of the law, but he was an author and a diligent student of oratory. In a letter to a young man engaged in the study of the law, Mr. Wirt shows how thorough he was in his methods of study. The extract is well worthy of insertion here:

"You may ask for instructions adapted to improvement in eloquence. This is a subject for a treatise, not for a letter. Cicero, however, has summed up the whole art in a few words; it is '*apte—distincte—ornate—dicere*'—to speak to the purpose—to speak clearly and distinctly—to speak gracefully ;—to be able *to speak to the purpose,* you must understand your subject and all that belongs to it :—and then your *thoughts and methods* must be *clear in themselves, and clearly and distinctly enunciated;*—and lastly, your voice, style of delivery and gesture must be *graceful, and delightfully impressive.* In relation to this subject I would strenuously advise you two things: *Compose much and often and carefully with reference to this same rule,* 'apte, distincte, ornate,' and let your conversation have reference to the same objects. I do not mean that you should be *elaborate* and *formal* in your ordinary conversation. Let it be *perfectly simple and natural,* but *always in good time,* (to speak as the musicians,) and well enunciated.

"With regard to the style of eloquence that you shall adopt, that must depend very much on your own taste and genius. You are not disposed, I presume, to be a humble imitator

of any man. If you are you may bid farewell to the hope
of eminence in this walk. None are mere imitators to
whom Nature has given original powers. If you are endowed with such a portion of the spirit of oratory as can
advance you to a high rank in this walk, you manner *will be*
your own. I can only tell you that the *florid and Asiatic
style* is not the taste of the age. The *strong*, and the *rugged
and abrupt* are far more successful. Bold propositions,
boldly and briefly expressed—pithy sentences—nervous
common sense—*strong phrases*—the *feliciter audax*, both in
language and conception—well-compacted periods—sudden
and strong masses of light—an apt adage—a keen sarcasm—
a merciless personality—a mortal thrust—these are the
beauties and deformities that now make a speaker the most
interesting. A gentleman and a Christian will conform to
the reigning taste so far only as his principles and habits of
decorum will permit. We require that a man should *speak
to the purpose, and come to the point*—that he should *instruct
and convince*. To do this, his mind must move with great
strength and power; reason should be manifestly his master
faculty—argument should predominate throughout ; but
these great points secured, wit and fancy may cast their
lights around his path, provided the wit be courteous, as
well as brilliant, and the fancy chaste and modest. But they
must be kept well in the background, for they are dangerous
allies ; and a man had better be without them, than to show
them in front, or to show them too often."

These precepts are excellent, and it would be difficult to
find a better code for the student of oratory of the same
length.

Mr. Wirt had in his personal appearance much about him
to win public favour. " He possessed a fine person, manners
remarkably conciliating, and coloquial powers of the highest
order. The most casual glance upon him in repose or
action, impressed the beholder with an instinctive sense
of his superiority. His natural air was dignified and commanding ; his countenance was broad, open, manly and expressive ; his eye was full of fire and feeling ; his mouth

denoted mingled humour and firmness; and his whole appearance was truly oratorical. His frame was large, but
agile; his nose was Roman, his complexion pale and marked
with lines of thought; his forehead was not high, but broad;
his hair was sandy, and his head bald on the top. He had
great original powers of action, but spoke with a chastened
dignity which commanded respect bordering on awe. Of
him it might have been said, as Dryden in his time declared
of Harte, that 'kings and princes might have come to him,
and taken lessons how to comport themselves with dignity.'
Wirt's impressiveness resulted from the aggregate of a Ciceronian person, a Chatham face, the voice of Anthony, and
the mental qualities of Irving and Bowditch,—a model of
grace and a master of dialectics,—poetry and philosophy combined. He had much of the acuteness of Marshall, and all
the intrepidity of Pinkney; but in his composition, there.
was no want of fluency, and no insolence or exultation of
manner. Judgment and imagination lay in the balance of
his mind in such delicate and equal proportions that the scale
seldom trembled, and the splendours that encompassed the
glorious combination in his mature life was never obscured.

"Such an advocate will be heard. The envious and fastidious may pronounce him vague, impalpable or diffuse,
yet all are compelled to listen to him with that spell-bound
emotion which is always produced by noble and harmonious
eloquence emanating from an honest and impassioned heart.
Wirt was not a stranger to the popular esteem which such
talents command.

"His pathos was refined and thrilling. He could subdue
all his admirable powers of mind and voice to those delicate
tones which go directly to the heart, like zephyrs changed
to angelic strains as they traverse Æolian strings. Such was
his power when he described female innocence and beauty
abandoned by him who had basked in her smiles, and who
should have prevented the winds of heaven from visiting her
too roughly, now left ' shivering at midnight on the winter
banks of the Ohio, and mingling her tears with the torrent,
which froze as they fell.' "

23

Another description of Mr. Wirt and of his oratory, will be found interesting: " His manner in speaking was singularly attractive. His manly form, his intellectual countenance and musical voice, set off by a rare gracefulness of gesture, won, in advance the favour of his auditory. He was calm, deliberate, and distinct in his enunciation, not often rising into any high exhibition of passion, and never sinking into tameness. His key was that of earnest and animated argument, frequently alternated with that of a playful and sprightly humour. His language was neat, well chosen, and uttered without impediment or slovenly repetition. The tones of his voice played, with a natural skill, through the various cadences most appropriate to express the flitting emotions of his mind, and the changes of his thought. To these external properties of his elocution we ·may ascribe the pleasure which persons of all conditions found in listening to him. Women often crowded the court-rooms to listen to him, and as often astonished him, not only by the patience, but the visible enjoyment with which they were wont to sit out his argument to the end,—even when the topic was too dry to interest them, or too obstruse for them to understand his discourse. It was the charm of manner, of which the delicate tact of women is ever found to be the truest gauge and the most appreciative judge. His oratory was not of that strong, bold and impetuous nature which is often the chief characteristic of the highest eloquence, and which is said to sway the senate with absolute dominion, and to imprison or set free the storm of human passion in the multitude, according to the speaker's will. It was smooth, polished, scholar-like, sparkling with pleasant fancies, and beguiling the listener with its varied graces, out of all note or consciousness of time.

" Without claiming for Mr. Wirt the renown of the most powerful orator or the profoundest lawyer in the country, it is sufficent to say, that he stood beside the first men of his day, equal in rank and repute, and superior to most, if not all, in the various accomplishments which he brought to the adornment of his profession."

Mr. Wirt's sensibility was acute and his imagination refined. In his earlier years his style was, at times, too florid, but as he grew older it became more chaste and elegant. He was never content to rest on his laurels. He continued to improve as he advanced in life, and to the last he always invested legal, political, or other topics with a graceful and charming spirit, and yet he was one of the most practical men of his day.

He improved to the last not only as an advocate, but as a counsellor and scholar. The young candidate for forensic fame or political honours would do well to imitate his example.

Mr. Wirt devoted his whole soul to the interests of his clients, and in this he was wise, for a lawyer who does not sincerely believe that his client ought to have a verdict will be apt to lose his case. His own unbelief will certainly be noticed by the jury, and will prove fatal to his case. No protestations which do not come from the heart will prevent it.

Swedenborg, who could see more than any man of his day, both in this world and in the realm of disembodied spirits, professed to have seen in the spiritual world a number of persons endeavouring in vain to express a proposition which they did not believe; but it was impossible, though in repeated attempts their faces were distorted with rage, and their lips quivered with indignation.

Mr. Wirt's account of a sermon he heard preached by a blind minister gives a fair specimen of his narrative style:

"It was one Sunday, as I was travelling through the county of Orange, that my eye was caught by a cluster of horses tied near a ruinous old wooden house, in the forest, not far from the roadside. Having frequently seen such objects before in travelling through these states, I had no difficulty in understanding that this was a place of religious worship.

"Devotion, alone should have stopped me to join the duties of the congregation; but I must confess that curiosity to hear the preacher of such a wilderness was not the least of my motives. On entering I was struck with his preter-

natural appearance. He was a tall and very spare old man;
his head, which was covered with a white linen cap, his
shrivelled hands, and his voice, were all shaking under the
influence of a palsy; and a few moments ascertained to me
that he was perfectly blind.

"The first emotions which touched my breast were those
of mingled pity and veneration. But how soon were all
my feelings changed! It was a day of the administration
of the sacrament; and his subject, of course, was the passion of our Saviour. I had heard the subject handled a
thousand times. I had thought it exhausted long ago.

"Little did I suppose that in the wild woods of America
I was to meet with a man whose eloquence would give to
this topic a new and more sublime pathos than I had ever
before witnessed. As he descended from the pulpit to dis-
tribute the mystic symbols, there was a peculiar—a more
than human solemnity in his air and manner, which made
my blood run cold, and my whole frame shiver.

"He then drew a picture of the sufferings of our Saviour
—his trial before Pilate—his ascent up Calvary—his crucifixion—and his death. I knew the whole history; but
never, until then, had I heard the circumstances so selected,
so arranged, so coloured! It was all new; and I seemed to
have heard it for the first time in my life.

"But when he came to touch on the patience, the forgiv-
ing meekness of our Saviour; when he drew, to the life, his
blessed eyes streaming in tears to heaven, his voice breathing to God a soft and gentle prayer of pardon on his enemies,
'Father, forgive them, for they know not what they do,'
the voice of the preacher, which had all along faltered, grew
fainter and fainter, until, his utterance being entirely obstructed by the force of his feelings, he raised his hander-
chief to his eyes, and burst into a loud and irrepressible
flood of grief. The effect was inconceivable. The whole
house resounded with the mingled groans, and sobs, and
shrieks of the congregation.

"It was some time before the tumult had subsided so far
as to permit him to proceed. Indeed, judging by the usual

but fallacious standard of my own weakness, I began to be
very uneasy for the situation of the preacher; for I could
not conceive how he would be able to let his audience
down from the height to which he had wound them, without impairing the solemnity and dignity of his subject, or
perhaps shocking them by the abruptness of the fall. But .
the descent was as beautiful and sublime as the elevation `
had been rapid and enthusiastic.

" The first sentence with which he broke the awful silence
was a quotation from Rosseau. ' Socrates died like a philosopher, but Jesus Christ—like a God.' I despair of giving
you any idea of the effect produced by this short sentence,
unless you could perfectly conceive the whole manner of
the man, as well as the peculiar crisis in the discourse.
Never before did I completely understand what Demosthenes meant by laying such stress on delivery.

"You are to call to mind the pitch of passion and enthusiasm to which the congregation were raised ; and then, the
few minutes of portentous, death-like silence which reigned
throughout the house ; the preacher, removing his white
handkerchief from his aged face (even yet wet from the
recent torrent of his tears), and slowly stretching forth the
palsied hand which holds it, as he begins the sentence,
'Socrates died like a philosopher,' then pausing, raising
his other hand, pressing them both, clasped together, with
warmth and energy to his breast, lifting his 'sightless balls'
to heaven, and pouring his whole soul into his tremulous
voice as he continues, 'but Jesus Christ—like a God!' If
he had been in deed and in truth an angel of light, the effect
could scarcely have been more divine."

Everett.—Edward Everett was born in Dorchester, Mass.,
on the 11th day of April, 1794. He began his education at
the public schools of Dorchester and Boston. He graduated
at Harvard University in his seventeenth year, and was
a tutor there until his twentieth year. About this time he
was called to the ministry. He spent four years in Europe
in order to prepare himself for the Greek professorship at
Harvard. He filled various positions of honour and trust,

having been member of Congress, United States Senator, Governor of his native state, and Secretary of State of the United States, and the candidate on the Union ticket for the Vice-Presidency in 1860. He died January 15, 1865.

Mr. Everett was one of the most graceful and polished speakers of modern times. He was called the " golden-mouthed orator " by his friends and contemporaries, Choate, Webster and Phillips.

In preparing his speeches no detail was too minute to escape his care—invention, arrangement of matter, expression, intonation and gesture — all received the greatest attention.

Mr. Everett's eloquence was of the Ciceronian order—copious, graceful, and flowing. He also resembled Cicero in the variety—and extent of his knowledge. His memory was very retentive.

His sensibilities were refined. His imagination rich and sparkling. His gestures were graceful, and appropriate, and the tones of his voice clear, sweet and melodious. His manner was elegant and persuasive. It is said that no one could listen to him without being moved, instructed, and delighted.

The following extracts from his magnificent orations, the author trusts, will prove interesting to his readers.

Speaking of the " Advantages of Adversity to the Pilgrim Fathers," he said:

"From the dark portals of the star-chamber, and in the stern text of the acts of uniformity, the pilgrims received a commission, more efficient than any that ever bore the royal seal. Their banishment to Holland was fortunate ; the decline of their little company in the strange land was fortunate ; the difficulties which they experienced in getting the royal consent to banish themselves to this wilderness were fortunate ; all the tears and heart-breakings of that ever memorable parting at Delfthaven[1] had the happiest influence on the rising destinies of New England.

---

[1] Delft ha'ven, a fortified town in South Holland (now Belgium), between Rotterdam and Schiedam. At this place the Pilgrims of New England took their last farewell of their European friends.

" All this purified the ranks of the settlers. These rough touches of fortune brushed off the light, uncertain, selfish spirits. They made it a grave, solemn, self-denying expedition, and required of those who engaged in it to be so too. They cast a broad shadow of thought and seriousness over the cause; and, if this sometimes deepened into melancholy and bitterness, can we find no apology for such a human weakness?

" It is sad, indeed, to reflect on the disasters which the little band of Pilgrims encountered ; sad to see a portion of them, the prey of unrelenting cupidity, treacherously embarked in an unsound, unseaworthy ship, which they are soon obliged to abandon, and crowd themselves into one vessel ; one hundred persons, besides the ship's company, in a vessel of one hundred and sixty tons. One is touched at the story of the long, cold, and weary autumnal passage ; of the landing on the inhospitable rocks at this dismal season ; where they are deserted, before long, by the ship which had brought them, and which seemed their only hold upon the world of fellow-men, a prey to the elements and to want, and fearfully ignorant of the numbers, the power, and the temper of the savage tribes, that filled the unexplored continent, upon whose verge they had ventured.

" But all this wrought together for good. These trials of wandering and exile, of the ocean, the winter, the wilderness, and the savage foe, were the final assurances of success. It was these that put far away from our father's cause all patrician softness, all hereditary claims to pre-eminence. No effeminate nobility crowded into the dark and austere ranks of the Pilgrims. No Carr nor Villiers would lead on the ill-provided band of despised Puritans. No well-endowed clergy were on the alert to quit their cathedrals, and to set up a pompous hierarchy in the frozen wilderness. No craving governors were anxious to be sent over to our cheerless El Dorados of ice and snow.

" No ; they could not say they had encouraged, patronized, or helped the Pilgrims : their own cares, their own labours, their own councils, their own blood, contrived all, bore all, sealed all. They could not afterward fairly pre-

tend to reap where they had not strewn ; and, as our fathers
reared this broad and solid fabric with pains and watchfulness, unaided, barely tolerated, it did not fall when the
favour, which had always been withholden, was changed into
wrath ; when the arm, which had never supported, was
raised to destroy.

" Methinks I see it now, that one solitary, adventurous
vessel, the Mayflower of a forlorn hope, freighted with the
prospects of a future state, and bound across the unknown
sea. I behold it pursuing, with a thousand misgivings, the
uncertain, the tedious voyage. Suns rise and set, and weeks
and months pass, and winter surprises them on the deep,
but brings them not the sight of the wished-for shore.

" I see them now scantily supplied with provisions ;
crowded almost to suffocation in their ill-stored prison :
delayed by calms, pursuing a circuitous route,—and now
driven in fury before the raging tempest, on the high and
giddy waves. The awful voice of the storm howls through
the rigging. The labouring masts seem straining from their
base ; the dismal sound of the pumps is heard ; the ship
leaps, as it were, madly, from billow to billow ; the ocean
breaks, and settles with ingulfing floods over the floating
deck, and beats, with deadening, shivering weight, against
the staggered vessel.

" I see them, escaped from these perils, pursuing their all
but desperate undertaking, and landed at last, after a five
months' passage, on the ice-clad rocks of Plymouth,—weak
and weary from the voyage, poorly armed, scantily provi-
sioned, depending on the charity of their shipmaster for a
draught of beer on board, drinking nothing but water on
shore,—without shelter, without means,—surrounded by
hostile tribes.

" Shut now the volume of history, and tell me, on any principle of human probability, what shall be the fate of this
handful of adventurers. Tell me, man of military science,
in how many months were they all swept off by the thirty
savage tribes, enumerated within the early limits of New
England ? Tell me, politician, how long did this shadow of

a colony, on which your conventions and treaties had not smiled, languish on the distant coast? Student of history, compare for me the baffled projects, the deserted settlements, the abandoned adventures of other times, and find the parallel of this.

"Was it the winter's storm, beating upon the houseless heads of women and children ; was it hard labour and spare meals; was it disease; was it the tomahawk; was it the deep malady of a blighted hope, a ruined enterprise, and a broken heart, aching in its last moments at the recollection of the loved and left beyond the sea ;—was it some or all of these united, that hurried this forsaken company to their melancholy fate? And is it possible that neither of these causes, that not all combined, were able to blast this bud of hope? Is it possible that, from a beginning so feeble, so frail, so worthy not so much of admiration as of pity, there has gone forth a progress so steady, a growth so wonderful, an expansion so ample, a reality so important, a promise, yet to be fulfilled, so glorious?"

From an "Address on the Uses of Astronomy," the following beautiful passage, descriptive of sunrise and early dawn, is taken :

"Much as we are indebted to our observatories for elevating our conceptions of the heavenly bodies, they present, even to the unaided sight, scenes of glory which words are too feeble to describe. I had occasion, a few weeks since, to take the early train from Providence to Boston, and for this purpose rose at two o'clock in the morning. Everything around was wrapped in darkness and hushed in silence, broken only by what seemed at that hour the unearthly clank and rush of the train. It was a mild, serene, midsummer's night ; the sky was without a cloud, the winds were hushed.

"The moon, then in the last quarter, had just risen, and the stars shone with a spectral lustre but little affected by her presence. Jupiter, two hours high, was the herald of the day ; the Pleiades, just above the horizon, shed their sweet influence in the east ; Lyra sparkled near the zenith ; Andromeda veiled her newly discovered glories from the naked eye in the south; the steady Pointers, far beneath the pole, looked meekly up, from the depths of the north, to their sovereign. Such was the glorious spectacle as I entered the train. As we proceeded, the timid approach of twilight became more perceptible; the intense blue of the sky began to soften; the smaller stars, like little children, went first to rest; the sister beams of the Pleiades soon melted together; but the bright constellations of the west and north remained unchanged. Steadily the wondrous transfiguration went on. Hands of angels, hidden from mortal eyes, shifted the scenery of the heavens; the glories of night dissolved into the glories of the dawn.

"The blue sky now turned more softly gray; the great watch-stars shut up their holy eyes; the east began to kindle. Faint streaks of purple soon blushed along the sky; the whole celestial concave was filled with the inflowing tides of the morning light, which came pouring down from above in one great ocean of radiance; till at length, as we reached the Blue Hills, a flush of purple fire blazed out from above the horizon, and turned the dewy tear-drops of flower and leaf into rubies and diamonds. In a few seconds, the everlasting gates of the morning were thrown wide open, and the lord of day, arrayed in glories too severe for the gaze of man, began his state.

"I do not wonder at the superstition of the ancient Magians, who, in the morning of the world, went up to the hilltops of Central Asia, and, ignorant of the true God, adored the most glorious work of His hand. But I am filled with amazement when I am told that, in this enlightened age, and in the heart of the Christian world, there are persons who can witness the daily manifestation of the power and wisdom of the Creator and yet say in their hearts, ' There is no God.' "

The following passage contains Mr. Everett's celebrated panegyric on England :

"No character is perfect among nations, more than among men; but it must needs be conceded, that of all the states of Europe, England has been, from an early period, the most favoured abode of liberty; the only part of Europe where, for any length of time, constitutional liberty can be said to have a stable existence. We can scarcely contemplate with patience the idea, that we might have been a Spanish colony, a Portuguese colony, or a Dutch colony. What hope can there be for the colonies of nations which possess themselves no spring of improvement, and tolerate none in the regions over which they rule; whose administration sets no bright examples of parliamentary independence; whose languages send out no reviving lessons of sound and practical science, of manly literature, of sound philosophy, but repeat, with every ship that crosses the Atlantic, the same debasing voice of despotism, bigotry, and antiquated superstition?

"What citizen of our Republic is not grateful in the contrast which our history presents? Who does not feel, what reflecting American does not acknowledge, the incalculable advantages derived to this land out of the deep fountains of civil, intellectual, and moral truth, from which we have drawn in England? What American does not feel proud that his fathers were the countrymen of Bacon, of Newton, and of Locke? Who does not know that, while every pulse of civil liberty in the heart of the British empire beat warm and full in the bosom of our ancestors, the sobriety, the firmness, and the dignity, with which the cause of free principles struggled into existence here, constantly found encouragement and countenance from the friends of liberty there?

"Who does not remember that, when the Pilgrims went over the sea, the prayers of the faithful British confessors, in all the quarters of their dispersion, went over with them, while their aching eyes were strained till the star of hope should go up in the western skies? And who will ever forget that, in that eventful struggle which severed these youthful republics from the British crown, there was not heard, throughout our continent in arms, a voice which spoke louder for the rights of America, than that of Burke or of Chatham within the walls of the British Parliament, and at the foot of the British throne?

"No; for myself, I can truly say that, after my native
land, I feel a tenderness and a reverence for that of my
fathers. The pride I take in my own country makes me
respect that from which we are sprung. In touching the
soil of England, I seem to return, like a descendant, to the
old family seat ; to come back to the abode of an aged and
venerable parent. I acknowledge this great consanguinity
of nations. The sound of my native language beyond the
sea is a music to my ear, beyond the richest strains of Tus-
can softness or Castilian majesty. I am not yet in a land of
strangers, while surrounded by the manners, the habits, and
the institutions under which I have been brought up.

"I wander delighted through a thousand scenes, which the
historians and poets have made familiar to us, of which the
names are interwoven with our earliest associations. I tread
with reverence the spots where I can retrace the footsteps
of our suffering fathers ; the pleasant land of their birth has
a claim on my heart. It seems to me a classic, yea, a holy
land ; rich in the memory of the great and good, the cham-
pions and the martyrs of liberty, the exiled heralds of
truth ; and richer as the parent of this land of promise in
the West.

"I am not—I need not say I am not—the panegyrist of
England. I am not dazzled by her riches, nor awed by her
power. The sceptre, the mitre, and the coronet,—stars,
garters, and blue ribbons,—seem to me poor things for
great men to contend for. Nor is my admiration awakened
by her armies mustered for the battles of Europe, her navies
overshadowing the ocean, nor her empire grasping the farthest East. It is these, and the price of guilt and blood by
which they are too often maintained, which are the cause
why no friend of liberty can salute her with undivided affections.

"But it is the cradle and the refuge of free principles,
though often persecuted ; the school of religious liberty, the
more precious for the struggles through which it has passed ;
the tombs of those who have reflected honour on all who
speak the English tongue ; it is the birthplace of our fathers,

the home of the Pilgrims;—it is these which I love and venerate in England. I should feel ashamed of an enthusiasm for Italy and Greece, did I not also feel it for a land like this. In an American, it would seem to me degenerate and ungrateful to hang with passion upon the traces of Homer and Virgil, and follow without emotion the nearer and plainer footsteps of Shakespeare and Milton. I should think him cold in his love for his native land who felt no melting in his heart for that other native country which holds the ashes of his forefathers."

The following eloquent passage, on knowledge, is taken from one of Mr. Everett's addresses on "Education Favourable to Liberty, Morals, and Knowledge," delivered at Amherst College, August 25, 1835:

"What is human knowledge? It is the cultivation and improvement of the spiritual principle in man. We are composed of two elements: the one, a little dust caught up from the earth, to which we shall soon return; the other, a spark of that divine intelligence, in which and through which we bear the image of the great Creator. By knowledge the wings of the intellect are spread; by ignorance, they are closed and palsied, and the physical passions are left to gain the ascendancy. Knowledge opens all the senses to the wonders of creation; ignorance seals them all up, and leaves the animal propensities unbalanced by reflection, enthusiasm, and taste. To the ignorant man the glorious pomp of day, the sparkling mysteries of night, the majestic ocean, the rushing storm, the plenty-bearing river, the salubrious breeze, the fertile field, the docile animal tribes, the broad, the various, the unexhausted domain of nature, are a mere outward pageant, poorly understood in their character and harmony and prized only so far as they minister to the supply of sensual wants. How different the scene to the man whose mind is stored with knowledge! For him the mystery is unfolded, the veils lifted up, as one after another he turns the leaves of that great volume of creation, which is filled in every page with the characters of wisdom, power, and love; with lessons of truth the most exalted ; with images of unspeakable loveliness and wonder ; arguments of Providence ; food for meditation ; themes of praise. One noble science sends him to the barren hills, and teaches him to survey their broken precipices. Where ignorance beholds nothing but a rough, inorganic mass, instruction discerns the intelligible record of the primal convulsions of the world ; the secrets of ages before man was ; the landmarks of the elemental struggles and throes of what is now the terraqueous globe. Buried monsters, of which the races are now extinct, are dragged out of deep strata, dug out of eternal rocks, and brought almost to life, to bear witness to the power that created them. Before the admiring student of nature has realised all of the wonders of the elder world, thus, as it were, re-created by science, another delightful instructress, with her microscope in her hand, bids him sit down and learn at last to know the universe in which he lives, and contemplate the limbs, the motions, the circulations of races of animals, disporting in *their* tempestuous ocean—a drop of water. Then, while his whole soul is penetrated with admiration of the power which has filled with life, and motion, and sense these all but non-existent atoms, oh! then, let the divinest of the muses, let Astronomy approach, and take him by the hand ; let her

> ' Come, but keep her wonted state,
> With even step and musing gait,
> And looks commercing with the skies,
> Her rapt soul sitting in her eyes.'

Let her lead him to the mount of vision ; let her turn her heaven-piercing tube to the sparkling vault ; through that let him observe the serene star of evening, and see it transformed into a cloud-encompassed orb, a world of rugged mountains and stormy deeps ; or behold the pale beams of Saturn, lost to the untaught observer amidst myriads of brighter stars, and see them expand into the broad disk of a noble planet,—the seven attendant worlds, the wondrous rings,—a mighty system in itself, borne at the rate of twenty-two thousand miles an hour on its broad pathway through the heavens ; and then let him reflect that our great solar system, of which Saturn and his stupendous retinue is but a small part, fills itself, in the general structure of the universe, but the space of one fixed star; and that the power which filled the drop of water with millions of living beings is present and active throughout this illimitable creation !— Yes, yes,

' An undevout astronomer is mad ! ' "

Corwin.—Thomas Corwin, one of the greatest natural orators that ever lived in America, was born in Bourbon County, Kentucky, July 29, 1794. In the year 1798, his parents went to Ohio.

Mr. Corwin, as a young man, was studious in his habits, and was fitted at an early day to exert a decided influence upon those around him, in concerns of a general public interest.

He was well grounded in the principles calculated to make a public man eminently useful, before he entered public life.

In Congress, his appearance in debate was rare, but when he spoke he commanded the greatest attention.

He who is destined to become a great orator must not only understand thoroughly the laws which govern the human mind, but by critical observations in the outward world, and through self-analysis, he should master those traits by which various classes are individualised, and hence can palpably portray the hopes and feelings of all bosoms,— " like the Arabian Magician, he holds a polished mirror to our gaze, wherein we behold not ourselves and the present only, but the thoughts and emotions of the past, scenes the most remote, and characters the most diversified. Men thus endowed will touch most sensibly a mixed audience, as well as interest to the greatest degree the most refined. Not only his graver productions will the erudite enjoy, but, in common with the unsophisticated masses, they will keenly relish his lighter and more homely strains."

Said Michael Angelo to the young sculptor: "Do not trouble yourself too much about the light on your statue, the light of the public square will test its value." So candidates for public favour are sure to be most successful who seek rather to deserve public favour than to forestall it.

These truths Mr. Corwin thoroughly understood and appreciated. His chief study was man, and his school society at large. Therein he learned to draw the subtle discriminations of mental action in every stage of life, and amongst every class of mankind. He was powerful because he was true. He expressed, frankly and fearlessly, what he distinctly saw and acutely felt.

Mr. Corwin was usually very courteous in debate, but when he or his friends were attacked he usually replied to his adversary with effect. His vindication of the patriotic Harrison from the attack of General Crary, of Michigan, is an example in point. General Crary, on the 14th of February, 1840, in a debate on the *Cumberland Road* in Congress, endeavoured to enlighten mankind with his views of General Harrison's deficiencies as a military commander, his mistakes at Tippecanoe, etc. Mr. Corwin replied in a speech replete with sarcasm, humour, and ridicule. Crary was completely overwhelmed, and John Quincy Adams a few days after referred to him as "the late Mr. Crary." The following passage will give some idea of the scathing wit with which the speech abounds:

"In all other countries, and in all former times, a gentleman who would either speak or be listened to on the subject of war, involving subtle criticisms and strategy, and careful reviews of marches, sieges, battles, regular and casual, and irregular onslaughts, would be required to show, first, that he had studied much, investigated fully, and digested the science and history of his subject. But here, sir, no such painful preparation is required; witness the gentleman from Michigan! He has announced to the House that he is a militia general on the peace establishment! That he is a lawyer we know, tolerably well read in Tidd's *Practice* and Espinasse's *Nisi Prius*. These studies, so happily adapted to the subject of war, with an appointment in the militia in time of peace, furnish him at once with all the knowledge necessary to discourse to us, as from high authority, upon all the mysteries of the 'trade of death.' Again, Mr. Speaker, it must occur to every one, that we, to whom these questions are submitted and these military criticisms are addressed, being all colonels at least, and most of us, like the gentleman himself, brigadiers, are, of all conceivable tribunals, best qualified to decide any nice points connected with military science. I hope the House will not be alarmed with the impression that I am about to discuss one or the other of the military questions now before us at length, but I wish to submit a remark or two, by way of preparing us for a proper appreciation of the merits of the discourse we have heard. I trust as we are all brother-officers, that the gentleman from Michigan, and the two hundred and forty colonels or generals of this honourable House, will receive what I have to say as coming from an old brother in arms, and addressed to them in a spirit of candour,

'Such as becometh comrades free,
Reposing after victory.'

" Sir, we all know the military studies of the military gentleman from Michigan before he was promoted. I take it to be beyond a reasonable doubt that he had perused with great care the title-page of *Baron Steuben.* Nay, I go further ; as the gentleman has incidentally assured us that he is prone to look into musty and neglected volumes, I venture to assert, without vouching in the least from personal knowledge, that he has prosecuted his researches so far as to be able to know that the rear rank stands right behind the front. This, I think, is fairly inferable from what I understood him to say of the two lines of encampment at Tippecanoe. Thus we see, Mr. Speaker, that the gentleman from Michigan, being a militia general, as he has told us, his brother officers, in that simple statement has revealed the glorious history of toils, privations, sacrifices, and bloody scenes, through which, we know from experience

24

and observation, a militia officer, in time of peace, is sure to
pass. We all in fancy now see the gentleman from Michigan in that most dangerous and glorious event in the life of
a militia general on the peace establishment—a parade day!
That day, for which all the other days of his life seem to
have been made. We can see the troops in motion—um-
brellas, hoes, and axe-handles, and other like deadly implements of war, overshadowing all the fields when lo! the
leader of the host approaches!

' Far off his coming shines ! '

His plume which, after the fashion of the great Bourbon, is of awful length, and reads its doleful history in the
bereaved necks and bosoms of forty neighbouring hen-
roosts. Like the great Suwaroff, he seems somewhat careless in forms or points of dress ; hence his epaulettes may
be on his shoulders, back, or sides, but still gleaming, gloriously gleaming, in the sun. Mounted he is, too, let it not
be forgotten. Need I describe to the colonels and generals
of this honourable House the steed which heroes bestride
on these occasions ? No ! I see the memory of other days
is with you. You see before you the gentleman from Michigan, mounted on his crop-eared, bushy-tailed mare, the singular obliquity of whose hinder limbs is best described by
that most expressive phrase, 'sickle hams'—for height just
fourteen hands, 'all told'; yes, sir: there you see his
'steed that laughs at the shaking of the spear'; that is his
war horse, 'whose neck is clothed with thunder.' Mr.
Speaker, we have glowing descriptions in history of Alexander the Great and his war horse Bucephalus, at the head of
the invincible Macedonian phalanx ; but, sir, such are the
improvements of modern times, that every one must see
that our militia general, with his crop-eared mare with bushy
tail and sickle hams, would totally frighten off a battle-field
a hundred Alexanders. But, sir, to the history of the parade
day. The general, thus mounted and equipped, is in the
field and ready for action. On the eve of some desperate
enterprise, such as giving order to shoulder arms, it may be,

there occurs a crisis, one of those accidents of war, which
no sagacity could foresee nor prevent. A cloud rises and
passes over the sun! Here is an occasion for the display of
that greatest of all traits in the history of a commander—
the tact which enables him to seize upon and turn to good
account unlooked-for events as they arise. Now for the
caution wherewith the Roman Fabius foiled the skill and
courage of Hannibal! A retreat is ordered, and troops and
general, in a twinkling, are found safely bivouacked in a
neighbouring grocery. But even here the general still has
room for the execution of heroic deeds. Hot from the field,
and chafed with the heroic events of the day, your general
unsheathes his trenchant blade, eighteen inches in length, as
you will remember, and with energy and remorseless fury
he slices the water-melons that lie in heaps around him, and
shares them with his surviving friends. Others of the sinews
of war are not wanting here. Whiskey, Mr. Speaker, that
great leveller of modern times, is here also, and the shells of
the water-melons are filled to the brim. Here, again, Mr.
Speaker, is shown how the extremes of barbarism and civilisation meet. As the Scandinavian heroes of old, after the
fatigues of war, drank wine from the skulls of their slaughtered enemies in Odin's halls, so now our militia general and
his forces, from the skulls of the melons thus vanquished, in
copious draughts of whiskey assuage the heroic fire of their
souls after a parade day. But, alas for this short-lived race
of ours! all things will have an end, and so it is even with
the glorious achievements of our general. Time is on the
wing, and will not stay his flight; the sun, as if frightened
at the mighty events of the day, rides down the sky, and
' at the close of day, when the hamlet is still,' the curtain of
night drops upon the scene,

> ' And Glory, like the phœnix in its fires,
> Exhales its odours, blazes, and expires.' "

Mr. Corwin was not an office-seeker. He did not compromise his self-respect, as is often done by over-anxious
candidates for public positions. He had aspirations, it is

true, but they were of the loftiest and purest kind. He was never desirous of promoting his own selfish schemes at the public expense. His knowledge of our political and civil institutions was extensive and accurate, and he was animated with the sentiment of patriotism that would administer and maintain them in their true strength and purity.

As an orator, Mr. Corwin was pre-eminently gifted by nature, and his elocutionary powers were highly cultivated. He was perfectly self-possessed in manner, and always spoke with great fluency. His language was pure and chaste. He always received the best attention from his audiences and held it unbroken to the end. One of the secrets of his power was that he knew when he had exhausted a subject, and when to stop. Unlike the great English orator, Charles James Fox, he rarely repeated his arguments. This was due to the clearness of his conceptions, and his exact arrangement of them—hence he rarely offended, as many of our best speakers do, by occasional indications of a want of thorough understanding of their own minds.

On momentous occasions Mr. Corwin often exhibited oratorical powers which could hardly be excelled.

His amiable and gentlemanly temper saved him from the hazard of giving personal offence to the victims of his wit and ridicule. In this respect he was fortunate, for his quick perception of the weak points in an opponent's position, and, if open to ridicule, his ready association of them with the most grotesque forms of exposure, give often, even to his grave speeches, a force and influence which the severest logic would utterly fail to give.

Mr. Corwin allowed no doubt in his auditory of the sincerity of what he said, and this was one of the most striking features of his oratory.

Prentiss.—Sergeant S. Prentiss was born at Portland, Maine, on the 30th day of September, 1808.

Prentiss was always fond of reading, and before he had reached his tenth year he had read all the books that he could "lay hands on." The Bible and the *Pilgrim's Progress* were two of his favourite books even in childhood.

He entered Bowdoin College in 1824. At college his course was brilliant. On leaving college he commenced the study of law, and in the summer of 1827 he went to Natchez, Mississippi. He was admitted to the bar in June, 1829, and soon after formed a partnership with General Felix Huston. His first appearance at the bar is thus described by one of his biographers : " He was a slight-made, beardless boy, extremely youthful-looking, by no means physically imposing, and a stranger to all at the court. It was a case he was appearing in for Mr. Huston ; and when it was called he responded to it, and stated the nature of the case, and that it stood on demurrer to some part of the proceedings which he desired to argue. The judge with some nonchalance told him he did not wish to hear argument on the subject, as he had made up his mind adversely to the side Mr. Prentiss appeared for ; upon this Mr. Prentiss modestly, but firmly, insisted on his client's constitutional right to be heard, by himself or counsel, before his case was adjudged against him. His right was recognised, and he was heard, and made a speech that astonished both court and bystanders; and the judge, to his honour be it spoken, was not only convinced of the error of his previous opinion, but had the manliness to acknowledge it." Few young men, in a strange place, with a cause prejudged and the decision announced, would have so boldly asserted and maintained their client's rights.

Mr. Prentiss appeared before the Supreme Court of the United States in 1833, and made a speech which consumed three or four hours. His propositions were so well fortified by authorities, and his speech was so gracefully delivered, that he instantly attracted the attention of Chief Justice Marshall, and called forth from that eminent jurist involuntary praise.

As a political orator Mr. Prentiss was always heard with the deepest interest. His self-possession, under the most trying circumstances, was remarkable. He was a warm admirer of Henry Clay, and an active opponent of General Jackson. On one occasion his speech was a powerful invective against General Jackson, for his removal of the members of his first Cabinet. While he was summing up the excuses of the Democratic party alleged for the act, he was suddenly confronted by a fellow holding up a large flag with nothing on it but the words " Hurrah for Jackson ! " inscribed with large letters. The man advanced slowly towards the speaker, whose eye no sooner caught the pennant than he exclaimed, without the slightest perturbation—" In short, fellow-citizens, you have now before you the sum and substance of all the arguments of the party— *Hurrah for Jackson !* " The effect was electrical, and the poor man slunk away trailing his banner after him.

In 1837, Mr. Prentiss canvassed his State and was elected to Congress. On his arrival at Washington his seat was contested, and a day was set apart for him to address the House in support of his claims. When the appointed time arrived, " nearly all the members were in their seats, the galleries were crowded, and every eye and ear were fixed in eager expectation. His first sentence riveted the attention of the whole audience, and each succeeding sentence increased the surprise and pleasure awakened by the first. Some, anticipating an outburst of fervid but unpolished declamation, were charmed to find themselves listening to an orator, whose logic was as accurate and subtle as that of a schoolman, while the fairest gems of literary culture adorned his rhetoric. Others, expecting a violent party harangue, were no less astonished to find themselves in the presence of a statesman and jurist discussing, with patriotic zeal, a great principle of constitutional law. His peroration was short, but it thrilled the immense assemblage like an electric touch. Much of its force was owing to the tones of his voice, the glow of his eye and countenance, his peculiarly earnest manner, and the high-wrought feelings of his hearers ; but no one can read it even now without admiring its skill and beauty."

" Nobody could equal it," Mr. Webster briefly remarked to a friend, as he left the hall.

Mr. Prentiss received enthusiastic congratulations from

friends and political foes upon the conclusion of his speech. President Fillmore was a member of the House when the speech was delivered, and he said of it in a letter, written in 1853: "I can never forget that speech. It was, certainly, the most brilliant that I ever heard, and, as a whole, I think it fully equalled, if it did not exceed, any rhetorical effort to which it has been my good fortune to listen in either House of Congress. It elevated him at once to the front rank of Congressional orators, and stamped his short but brilliant parliamentary career with the impression of undoubted genius and the highest oratorical powers. I have never read the published speech, but I apprehend it is not possible that it should convey to the reader any adequate idea of the effect produced by its delivery."

When the vote was taken on the question of his right to a seat, it was a tie, and the vote of the Speaker, James K. Polk, being cast against him, Mr. Prentiss returned home, but was soon after elected to Congress and served with great credit to himself his term.

Mr. Prentiss was distinguished as a lawyer for the remarkable analytical power of his mind, and his acute and discerning logical faculty, as well as for his sound learning, his eloquence, and his extraordinary memory. Although his reading was full and general, it is said that he never forgot, and had always at command all that he had ever read.

As an extemporaneous speaker Mr. Prentiss has had few equals, and no superiors.

Mr. Prentiss removed to New Orleans in 1845. The following address was delivered by him before the New England Society of New Orleans, on the 22d of December, 1845 :

Address on the Landing of the Pilgrims.

" This is a day dear to the sons of New England, and ever held by them in sacred remembrance. On this day, from every quarter of the globe, they gather in spirit around the rock of Plymouth, and hang upon the urns of their Pilgrim Fathers the garlands of filial gratitude and affection. We

have assembled for the purpose of participating in this honourable duty; of performing this pious pilgrimage. To-day
we will visit that memorable spot. We will gaze upon the
place where a feeble band of persecuted exiles founded a
mighty nation; and our hearts will exult with proud gratification as we remember that on that barren shore our
ancestors planted not only empire, but Freedom. We will
meditate upon their toils, their sufferings, and their virtues,
and to morrow return to our daily avocations, with minds
refreshed and improved by the contemplation of their high
principles and noble purposes.

" The human mind cannot be contented with the present.
It is ever journeying through the trodden regions of the
past, or making adventurous excursions into the mysterious
realms of the future. He who lives only in the present is
but a brute, and has not attained the human dignity. Of
the future but little is known; clouds and darkness rest upon
it; we yearn to become acquainted with its hidden secrets;
we stretch out our arms towards its shadowy inhabitants;
we invoke our posterity, but they answer us not. We wander
in its dim precincts till reason becomes confused and at last
start back in fear, like mariners who have entered an unknown ocean, of whose winds, tides, currents, and quick-
sands they are wholly ignorant. Then it is we turn for
relief to the past, that mighty reservoir of men and things.
There we have something tangible to which our sympathies
can attach; upon which we can lean for support; from
whence we can gather knowledge and learn wisdom. There
we are introduced into Nature's vast laboratory and witness
her elemental labours. We mark with interest the changes
in continents and oceans by which she has notched the centuries. But our attention is still more deeply aroused by
the great moral events which have controlled the fortunes
of those who have preceded us, and still influence our own.
With curious wonder we gaze down the long aisles of the
past, upon the generations that are gone. We behold, as in
a magic glass,. men in form and feature like ourselves, actuated by the same motives urged by the same passions,

busily engaged in shaping both their own destinies and ours. We approach them and they refuse not our invocation. We hold converse with the wise philosophers, the sage legislators, and the divine poets. We enter the tent of the general, and partake of his most secret counsels. We go forth with him to the battle-field, and behold him place his glittering squadrons; then we listen with a pleasing fear to the trumpet and the drum, or the still more terrible music of the booming cannon and the clashing arms. But most of all, among the innumerable multitudes who peopled the past, we seek our own ancestors, drawn towards them by an irresistible sympathy. Indeed, they were our other selves. With reverent solicitude we examine into their character and actions, and as we find them worthy or unworthy, our hearts swell with pride, or our cheeks glow with shame. We search with avidity for the most trivial circumstances in their history, and eagerly treasure up every memento of their fortunes. The instincts of our nature bind us indissolubly to them and link our fates with theirs. Men cannot live without a past; it is as essential to them as a future. Into its vast confines we still journey to-day, and converse with our Pilgrim fathers. We will speak to them and they shall answer us.

" Two centuries and a quarter ago, a little tempest-tost, weather-beaten bark, barely escaped from the jaws of the wild Atlantic, landed upon the bleakest shore of New England. From her deck disembarked a hundred and one care-worn exiles. To the casual observer no event could seem more insignificant. The contemptuous eye of the world scarcely deigned to notice it. Yet the famous vessel that bore Cæsar and his fortunes carried but an ignoble freight compared with that of the *Mayflower*. Her little band of Pilgrims brought with them neither wealth nor power, but the principles of civil and religious freedom. They planted them for the first time in the Western Continent. They cherished, cultivated, and developed them to a full and luxuriant maturity; and then furnished them to their posterity as the only sure and permanent foundations for a free government.

Upon those foundations rests the fabric of our great Republic; upon those principles depends the career of human liberty. Little did the miserable pedant and bigot who then wielded the sceptre of Great Britain imagine that from this feeble settlement of persecuted and despised Puritans, in a century and a half, would arise a nation capable of coping with his own mighty empire in arts and arms.

" It is not my purpose to enter into the history of the Pilgrims; to recount the bitter persecutions and ignominious sufferings which drove them from England; to tell of the eleven years of peace and quiet spent in Holland, under their beloved and venerated pastor; nor to describe the devoted patriotism which prompted them to plant a colony in some distant land, where they could remain citizens of their native country and at the same time be removed from its oppressions; where they could enjoy liberty without violating allegiance. Neither shall I speak of the perils of their adventurous voyage; of the hardships of their early settlement; of the famine which prostrated, and the pestilence which consumed them.

" With all these things you are familiar, both from the page of history and from the lips of tradition. On occasions similar to this, the ablest and most honoured sons of New England have been accustomed to tell, with touching eloquence, the story of their sufferings, their fortitude, their perseverance, and their success. With pious care, they have gathered and preserved the scattered memorials of those early days, and the names of Carver, Bradford, Winslow, Standish, and their noble companions have long since become with us venerated household words.

" There were, however, some traits that distinguished the enterprise of the Pilgrims from all others and which are well worthy of continued remembrance. In founding their colony they sought neither wealth nor conquest, but only peace and freedom. They asked but for a region where they could make their own laws, and worship God according to the dictates of their own consciences. From the moment they touched the shore, they laboured with orderly, systematic, and persevering industry. They cultivated, without a murmur, a poor and ungrateful soil, which even now yields but a stubborn obedience to the dominion of the plough. They made no search for gold, nor tortured the miserable savages, to wring from them the discovery of imaginary mines. Though landed by a treacherous pilot upon a barren and inhospitable coast, they sought neither richer fields nor a more genial climate. They found liberty, and for the rest it mattered little. For more than eleven years they had meditated upon their enterprise, and it was no small matter could turn them from its completion. On the spot where first they rested from their wanderings, with stern and high resolve, they built their little city and founded their young republic. Their honesty, industry, knowledge, and piety grew up together in happy union. There, in patriarchal simplicity and republican equality, the Pilgrim fathers and mothers passed their honourable days, leaving to their posterity the invaluable legacy of their principles and example.

" How proudly can we compare their conduct with that of the adventurers of other nations who preceded them. How did the Spaniard colonise? Let Mexico, Peru, and Hispaniola answer. He followed in the train of the great Discoverer, like a devouring pestilence. His cry was gold! gold!! gold!!! Never in the history of the world had the *sacra fames auri* exhibited itself with such fearful intensity. His imagination maddened with visions of sudden boundless wealth, clad in mail, he leaped upon the New World, an armed robber. In greedy haste he grasped the sparkling sand, then cast it down with curses, when he found the glittering grains were not of gold.

" Pitiless as the bloodhound by his side, he plunged into the primeval forests, crossed rivers, lakes, and mountains, and penetrated to the very heart of the continent. No region, however rich in soil, delicious in climate, or luxuriant in production, could tempt his stay. In vain the soft breeze of the tropics, laden with aromatic fragrance, wooed him to rest ; in vain the smiling valleys, covered with spontaneous fruits and flowers, invited him to peaceful quiet. His search was still for gold ; the accursed hunger could not be appeased. The simple natives gazed upon him in superstitious wonder, and worshipped him as a god ; and he proved to them a god, but an infernal one—terrible, cruel, and remorseless. With bloody hands he tore the ornaments from their persons, and the shrines from their altars ; he tortured them to discover hidden treasure, and slew them that he might search, even in their wretched throats, for concealed gold. Well might the miserable Indians imagine that a race of evil deities had come among them, more bloody and relentless than those who presided over their own sanguinary rites.

"Now let us turn to the Pilgrims. They, too, were tempted ; and had they yielded to the temptation how different might have been the destinies of this continent—how different must have been our own ! Previous to their undertaking, the Old World was filled with strange and wonderful accounts of the New. The unbounded wealth, drawn by the Spaniards from Mexico and South America, seemed to afford rational support for the wildest assertions. Each succeeding adventurer, returning from his voyage, added to the Arabian tales a still more extravagant story. At length Sir Walter Raleigh, the most accomplished and distinguished of all those bold voyageurs, announced to the world his discovery of the province of Guiana and its magnificent capital, the far-famed city of El Dorado. We smile now at his account of the 'great and golden city,' and 'the mighty, rich, and beautiful empire.' We can hardly imagine that anyone could have believed, for a moment, in their existence. At that day, however, the whole matter was received with the most implicit faith. Sir Walter professed to have explored the country, and thus glowingly describes it from his own observation :

" 'I never saw a more beautiful country, nor more lively prospects ; hills so raised here and there over the valleys— the river widening into divers branches—the plains adjoining, without bush or stubble—all fair green grass—the deer crossing in every path—the birds, towards the evening, singing on every tree with a thousand several tunes—the air fresh, with a gentle easterly wind ; and every stone that we stopped to take up promised either gold or silver by its complexion. For health, good air, pleasure, and riches, I am resolved it cannot be equalled by any region either in the East or West.'

" The Pilgrims were urged, in leaving Holland, to seek this charming country, and plant their colony among its Arcadian bowers. Well might the poor wanderers cast a longing glance towards its happy valleys, which seemed to invite to pious contemplation and peaceful labour. Well might the green grass, the pleasant groves, the tame deer, and the singing birds allure them to that smiling land beneath the equinoctial line. But while they doubted not the existence of this wondrous region, they resisted its tempting charms. They had resolved to vindicate, at the same time, their patriotism and their principles, to add dominion to their native land, and to demonstrate to the world the practicability of civil and religious liberty. After full discussion and mature deliberation, they determined that their great objects could be best accomplished by a settlement on some portion of the northern continent, which would hold out no temptation to cupidity—no inducement to persecution. Putting aside, then, all considerations of wealth and ease, they addressed themselves with high resolution to the accomplishment of their noble purpose. In the language of the historian, ' Trusting to God and themselves,' they embarked upon their perilous enterprise.

" As I said before, I shall not accompany them on their adventurous voyage. On the 22d day of December, 1620, according to our present computation, their footsteps pressed the famous rock which has ever since remained sacred to their venerated memory. Poets, painters, and orators have tasked their powers to do justice to this great scene. Indeed, it is full of moral grandeur ; nothing can be more beautiful, more pathetic, or more sublime. Behold the Pilgrims, as they stood oh that cold December day—stern men, gentle women, and feeble children—all uniting in singing a hymn of cheerful thanksgiving to the good God, who had con-

ducted them safely across the mighty deep, and permitted
them to land upon that sterile shore. See how their upturned faces glow with a pious confidence which the sharp
winter winds cannot chill, nor the gloomy forest shadows
darken.

> ' Not as the conqueror comes,
>   They, the true-hearted came ;
>   Not with the roll of the stirring drum,
> .   Nor the trumpet, that sings of fame
>   Nor as the flying come,
>   In silence and in fear—
>   They shook the depths of the desert gloom
>   With their hymns of lofty cheer.'

" Noble and pious band ! your holy confidence was not in
vain, your ' hymns of lofty cheer ' find echo still in the
hearts of grateful millions. Your descendants, when pressed
by adversity, or when addressing themselves to some high
action, turn to the ' Landing of the Pilgrims,' and find heart
for any fate—strength for any enterprise.

" How simple, yet how instructive, are the annals of this
little settlement. In the cabin of the *Mayflower* they settled
a general form of government, upon the principles of a pure
democracy. In 1636 they published a declaration of rights
and established a body of laws. The first fundamental
article was in these words : ' That no act, imposition, law,
or ordinance be made, or imposed upon us, at present or to
come, but such as has been or shall be enacted by the consent of the body of freemen or associates, or their representatives legally assembled,' etc.

" Here we find advanced the whole principle of the Revolution—the whole doctrine of our republican institutions.
Our fathers, a hundred years before the Revolution, tested
successfully, as far as they were concerned, the principle of
self-government, and solved the problem, whether law and
order can co-exist with liberty. But let us not forget that
they were wise and good men who made the noble experi-

ment, and that it may yet fail in our hands, unless we imitate their patriotism and virtues.

" There are some who find fault with the character of the Pilgrims, who love not the simplicity of their manners, nor the austerity of their lives. They were men, and of course imperfect ; but the world may well be challenged to point out, in the whole course of history, men of purer purpose or braver action—men who have exercised a more beneficial influence upon the destinies of the human race, or left behind them more enduring memorials of their existence.

" At all events, it is not for the sons of New England to search for the faults of their ancestors. We gaze with profound veneration upon their awful shades; we feel a grateful pride in the country they colonised—in the institutions they founded—in the example they bequeathed. We exult in our birthplace and in our lineage.

" Who would not rather be of the Pilgrim stock than claim descent from the proudest Norman that every planted his robber blood in the halls of the Saxon, or the noblest paladin that quaffed wine at the table of Charlemagne ? Well may we be proud of our native land, and turn with fond affection to its rocky shores. The spirit of the Pilgrims still pervades it, and directs its fortunes. Behold the thousand temples of the Most High, that nestle in its happy valleys and crown its swelling hills ! See how their glittering spires pierce the blue sky, and seem like so many celestial conductors, ready to avert the lightning of an angry Heaven. The piety of the Pilgrim patriarchs is not yet extinct, nor have the sons forgotten the God of their fathers.

" Behold yon simple building near the crossing of the village road ! It is small and of rude construction, but stands in a pleasant and quiet spot. A magnificent old elm spreads its broad arms above and seems to lean towards it, as a strong man bends to shelter and protect a child. A brook runs through the meadow near, and hard by there is an orchard— but the trees have suffered much and bear no fruit, except upon the most remote and inaccessible branches. From within its walls comes a busy hum, such as you may hear in a disturbed bee-hive. Now peep through yonder window and you will see a hundred children, with rosy cheeks, mischievous eyes, and demure faces, all engaged, or pretending to be so, in their little lessons. It is the public school—the free, the common school—provided by law; open to all; claimed from the community as a right, not accepted as a bounty. Here the children of the rich and poor, high and low, meet upon perfect equality, and commence under the same auspices the race of life. Here the sustenance of the mind is served up to all alike, as the Spartans served their food upon the public table. Here young Ambition climbs his little ladder, and boyish Genius plumes his half-fledged wing. From among these laughing children will go forth the men who are to control the destinies of their age and country—the statesman whose wisdom is to guide the Senate —the poet who will take captive the hearts of the people and bind them together with immortal song—the philosopher who, boldly seizing upon the elements themselves, will compel them to his wishes, and, through new combinations of their primal laws, by some great discovery, revolutionise both art and science.

" The common village school is New England's fairest boast —the brightest jewel that adorns her brow. The principle that society is bound to provide for its members' education as well as protection, so that none need be ignorant except from choice, is the most important that belongs to modern philosophy. It is essential to a republican government. Universal education is not only the best and surest, but the only sure foundation for free institutions. True liberty is the child of knowledge; she pines away and dies in the arms of ignorance.

" Honour, then, to the early fathers of New England, from whom came the spirit which has built a schoolhouse by every sparkling fountain, and bids all come as freely to the one as to the other. All honour, too, to this noble city, who has not disdained to follow the example of her northern sisters, but has wisely determined that the intellectual thirst of her children deserves as much attention as their physical, and that it is as much her duty to provide the means of assuaging the one as of quenching the other.

"But the spirit of the Pilgrims survives, not only in the knowledge and piety of their sons, but, most of all, in their indefatigable enterprise and indomitable perseverance.

"They have wrestled with nature till they have prevailed against her, and compelled her reluctantly to reverse her own laws. The sterile soil has become productive under their sagacious culture, and the barren rock, astonished, finds itself covered with luxuriant and unaccustomed verdure.

"Upon the banks of every river they build temples to industry, and stop the squanderings of the spendthrift waters. They bind the naiads of the brawling stream. They drive the dryads from their accustomed haunts, and force them to desert each favourite grove; for upon river, creek, and bay they are busy transforming the crude forest into staunch and gallant vessels. From every inlet or in-denture along the rocky shore swim forth these ocean birds —born in the wildwood, fledged upon the wave. Behold how they spread their white pinions to the favouring breeze, and wind their flight to every quarter of the globe—the carrier pigeons of the world! It is upon the unstable element the sons of New England have achieved their greatest triumphs. Their adventurous prows vex the waters of every sea. Bold and restless as the old northern Vikings, they go forth to seek their fortunes in the mighty deep. The ocean is their pasture, and over its wide prairies they follow the monstrous herds that feed upon its azure fields. As the hunter casts his lasso upon the wild horse, so they throw their lines upon the tumbling whale. They 'draw out Leviathan with a hook.' They 'fill his skin with barbed irons,' and in spite of his terrible strength they 'part him among the merchants.' To them there are no pillars of Hercules. They seek with avidity new regions, and fear not to be 'the first that ever burst' into unknown seas. Had they been the companions of Columbus, the great mariner would not have been urged to return, though he had sailed westward to his dying day.

25

"Glorious New England! thou art still true to thy ancient fame and worthy of thy ancestral honours. We, thy children, have assembled in this far-distant land to celebrate thy birthday. A thousand fond associations throng upon us, roused by the spirit of the hour. On thy pleasant valleys rest, like sweet dews of morning, the gentle recollections of our early life; around thy hills and mountains cling, like gathering mists, the mighty memories of the Revolution; and far away in the horizon of thy past gleam, like thine own Northern Lights, the awful virtues of our Pilgrim sires! But while we devote this day to the remembrance of our native land, we forget not that in which our happy lot is cast. We exult in the reflection that, though we count by thousands the miles which separate us from our birthplace, still our country is the same. We are no exiles meeting upon the banks of a foreign river, to swell its waters with our home-sick tears. Here floats the same banner which rustled above our boyish heads, except that its mighty folds are wider and its glittering stars increased in number.

"The sons of New England are found in every State of the broad Republic. In the East, the South, and the unbounded West, their blood mingles freely with every kindred current. We have but changed our chamber in the paternal mansion; in all its rooms we are at home, and all who inhabit it are our brothers. To us the Union has but one domestic hearth; its household gods are all the same. Upon us, then, peculiarly devolves the duty of feeding the fires upon that kindly hearth; of guarding with pious care those sacred household gods.

"We cannot do with less than the whole Union; to us it admits of no division. In the veins of our children flows Northern and Southern blood; how shall it be separated; who shall put asunder the best affections of the heart, the noblest instincts of our nature? We love the land of our adoption, so do we that of our birth. Let us ever be true to both; and always exert ourselves in maintaining the unity of our country, the integrity of the Republic.

"Accursed, then, be the hand put forth to loosen the golden

cord of Union ; thrice accursed the traitorous lips, whether of Northern fanatic or Southern demagogue, which shall propose its severance! But, no, the Union cannot be dissolved ; its fortunes are too brilliant to be marred ; its destinies too powerful to be resisted. Here will be their greatest triumph, their most mighty development. And when, a century hence, this Crescent City shall have filled her golden horns, when within her broad-armed port shall be gathered the products of the industry of a hundred millions of freemen, when galleries of art and halls of learning shall have made classic this mart of trade, then may the sons of the Pilgrims, still wandering from the bleak hills of the North, stand upon the banks of the Great River, and exclaim with mingled pride and wonder: ' Lo! this is our country ; when did the world ever witness so rich and magnificent a city—so great and glorious a Republic!' "

Webster.—Daniel Webster was one of the greatest political and forensic orators that ever lived in any age or country. He was born in the town of Salisbury, New Hampshire, on the 18th of January, 1782, the last year of the revolutionary war. He came of a patriotic ancestry. Ebenezer Webster, his father, was a captain in that war. He participated in the battle of White Plains, and was in the thickest of the fight at Bennington. He was elected a representative from Salisbury to the Legislature of New Hampshire, and was afterward State Senator, and was finally chosen as a judge of the Court of Common Pleas. He died in 1806, at the age of sixty-seven. Ebenezer Webster was married twice. His second wife, the mother of Daniel Webster, was a woman of remarkably great mental endowments.

Daniel Webster was reared amidst the rugged, majestic scenery of New Hampshire. It is the opinion of some writers that scenery which is grand and sublime contributes to the formation of character—intellectual and moral; and it has been said that nearly all the heroism, moral excellence, and ennobling literature of the world has been produced by those who, in infancy and in youth, were fostered by the inspiration of exalted regions, where the turf is covered with a rude beauty, rocks and wilderness are piled in bold and inimitable shapes of savage grandeur, tinged with the hues of untold centuries, and over which awe-inspiring storms often sweep with thunders in their train. This is the influence which more than half created the Shakespeares, Miltons, Spensers, Wordsworths, Scotts, Coleridges, Shelleys, Irvings, Coopers, Bryants, and Websters of the world. An eloquent speaker said of him : " Born upon the verge of civilisation,—his father's house the farthest by four miles on the Indian trail to Canada,—Mr. Webster retained to the last his love for that pure fresh nature in which he was cradled. The dashing streams, which conduct the waters of the queen of New Hampshire's lakes to the noble Merrimac ; the superb group of mountains (the Switzerland of the United States), among which those waters have their sources ; the primeval forest, whose date runs back to the twelfth verse of the first chapter of Genesis, and never since creation yielded to the settler's axe ; the gray buttresses of granite which prop the eternal hills ; the sacred alternation of the seasons, with its magic play on field and forest and flood ; the gleaming surface of lake and stream in summer ; the icy pavement with which they are floored in winter ; the verdure of spring, the prismatic tints of the autumnal woods, the leafless branches of December, glittering like arches and corridors of silver and crystal in the enchanted palaces of fairy-land—sparkling in the morning sun with winter's jewelry, diamond and amethyst, and ruby and sapphire ; the cathedral aisles of pathless woods—the mournful hemlock, the ' cloud-seeking ' pine,—hung with drooping creepers, like funeral banners pendant from the roof of chancel or transept over the graves of the old lords of the soil ; —these all retained for him to the close of his life an undying charm."

As an agricultural labourer Daniel Webster, in his youth at least, was not greatly distinguished, except for inefficiency, and he said on one occasion that his father sent him to college to make him equal to the other children. At one time, Daniel was put to mowing, but he made bad work of it. His scythe was sometimes in the ground, and sometimes over the tops of all the grass. He complained to his father that his scythe was not hung right. Various attempts were made to hang it better, but with no success. His father told him, at length, he might hang it to suit himself, and he therefore hung it upon a tree, and said, " There, that 's right." His father laughed, and told him to let it hang there.

When he reached his fourteenth year, Webster was taken by his father, whom he always so tenderly loved, to the Phillips Academy, Exeter, and placed under the care of the good Dr. Benjamin Abbott.

Webster mastered in a short time the principles of English grammar, and made some progress with his other studies.

Diffident speakers should note the fact that early in life Webster had the strongest antipathy to public declamation, and when he first declaimed at school he became greatly embarrassed, and even burst into tears.

Mr. Webster was graduated at Dartmouth College in August, 1801. He was admitted to the bar in 1805.

When he was thirty years of age, he was elected to Congress, and took his seat at the extra session in May, 1813. In the following June of the same year, he made his first speech in Congress on the Berlin and Milan decrees. This speech placed Webster at once in the front rank of parliamentary orators. Chief Justice Marshall, and many other eminent men who heard it, were greatly pleased with it, and the learned Chief Justice predicted that he would become one of the " very first statesmen in America, and perhaps the first "; and the celebrated Mr. Lowndes remarked that the North had not his equal, nor the South his superior.

In a letter dated June 24, 1839, Thomas Carlyle writes to his friend Ralph Waldo Emerson, as follows, of Webster: ". . . Not many days ago I saw at breakfast the notablest of all your Notabilities, Daniel Webster. He is a magnificent specimen ; you might say to all the world: This is your Yankee Englishman, such limbs we make in Yankeeland ! As a logic-fencer, Advocate, or Parliamentary Hercules, one would incline to back him at first sight against the extant world. The tanned complexion, that amorphous crag-like face; the dull black eyes under the precipice of brows, like dull anthracite furnaces, needing only to be *blown;* the mastiff-mouth, accurately closed:—I have not traced as much of *silent Berserkir-rage,* that I remember of, in any other man. 'I guess I should not like to be your nigger!' Webster is not loquacious, but he is pertinent, conclusive; a dignified, perfectly bred man, though not English in breeding: a man worthy of the best reception from us; and meeting such, I understand. He did not speak much with me that morning, but seemed not at all to dislike me. . . ."

The following graphic and interesting description of Webster was written by Miss Mary Russell Mitford to one of her friends in 1839:

" Daniel Webster is himself not more than fifty-five now— the first lawyer, orator, and statesman of America, certainly, and the next, or next but one, President. He is the noblest-looking man I ever saw, both in face and person. The portrait prefixed to his *Speeches* does him great injustice, for his countenance is delightfully gracious—such a smile! and he is a broad, muscular, splendid figure. His manner, too, is all that one can imagine of calm, and sweet, and gracious —as charming as the Duke of Devonshire; as courteous even as that prince of courtesy, and equally free from conde-scension—whilst amidst the perfect simplicity and gentle-ness there is great conversational power. His wife and daughters seem to adore his very footsteps; and he has conquered for himself a degree of real consideration and respect in London never shown before to any transatlantic personage; least of all to a lion. My father adores him. I think he liked him even better than I did; and he says that he promised him to come again, and that he is sure to keep his word.

" I should like you to see Daniel Webster! When I tell you that expecting from him what I did, and hearing from twenty people, accustomed to see in perfect intimacy all distinguished people, that he alone gave them the idea of a

truly great man—when I say that he exceeded our expectations by very far, you may imagine what he is. I am to
send them all my flower-seeds, and they are to send me all
theirs. I chose the Murder-Speech (is it not wonderfully
fine? like Sheil, without the tawdriness, I think,) to read to
my father, because that is free from the alloy, to an English
ear, of allusions intelligible across the water, but not to us.
Two very clever friends of ours went to Oxford to hear him
speak, and they say that they would walk there again and
back, to hear him only speak the same speech over again!
Is not that praise?"

His speech in the Dartmouth College case established his
reputation as a lawyer upon a firm basis. It was one of the
finest forensic efforts on record. The profound legal knowledge and the overpowering eloquence he displayed on that
occasion placed him in the front rank of jurists and forensic
orators. It is said that its effects upon the audience were
prodigious, and that the concluding remarks of his argument were uttered in tones of the deepest pathos which
thrilled his hearers. When he ceased to speak there was a
death-like stillness throughout the court-room which lasted
for some moments. The dignified Chief Justice Marshall was
overcome by this manly burst of eloquence—his furrowed
cheeks trembled with emotion, and his eyes were suffused
with tears. Said Rufus Choate: "Well, as if of yesterday,
I remember how it was written home from Washington, that
'Mr. Webster closed a legal argument of great power by a
peroration which charmed and melted his audience.'"

One of Mr. Webster's most eloquent speeches in Congress
was that which he made on the Revolution in Greece. The
exordium contains a striking and happy allusion to Greece
as the mistress of the world in the arts and sciences. The
author will give this passage:

"I am afraid, Mr. Chairman, that, so far as my part in this
discussion is concerned, those expectations which the public
excitement existing on the subject, and certain associations
easily suggested by it, have conspired to raise, may be disappointed. An occasion which calls the attention to a spot

so distinguished, so connected with interesting recollections, as Greece, may naturally create something of warmth and enthusiasm. In a grave political discussion, however, it is necessary that those feelings should be chastised. I shall endeavour properly to repress them, although it is impossible that they should be altogether extinguished. We must, indeed, fly beyond the civilised world ; we must pass the dominion of law and the boundary of knowledge ; we must, more especially, withdraw ourselves from this place, and the scenes and objects which here surround us,—if we would separate ourselves entirely from the influence of all those memorials of herself which ancient Greece has transmitted for the admiration and the benefit of mankind. This free form of government, this popular assembly, the common council held for the common good —where have we contemplated its earliest models? This practice of free debate and public discussion, the contest of mind with mind, and that popular eloquence which, if it were now here, on a subject like this, would move the stones of the Capitol,—whose was the language in which all these were first exhibited? Even the edifice in which we assemble, these proportioned columns, this ornamental architecture, all remind us that Greece has existed, and that we, like the rest of mankind, are greatly her debtors."

In this speech of Mr. Webster occurs one of the finest passages in the English language on the power of public opinion over mere physical force. He was asked what kind of aid this country should give Greece, whether we should declare war on her account, or furnish her armies and navies. He replied in the following eloquent language :

" Sir, this reasoning mistakes the age. The time has been, indeed, when fleets, and armies, and subsidies were the principal reliances even in the best cause. But, happily for mankind, there has arrived a great change in this respect. Moral causes come into consideration, in proportion as the progress of knowledge is advanced ; and the *public opinion* of the civilised world is rapidly gaining an ascendancy over mere brutal force. It may be silenced by military power, but it

cannot be conquered. It is elastic, irrepressible, and invul-
nerable to the weapons of ordinary warfare. It is that
impassable, inextinguishable enemy of mere violence and
arbitrary rule, which, like Milton's angels,

> 'Vital in every part, .   .   .
> Can not, but by annihilating, die.'

"Unless this be propitiated or satisfied, it is in vain for
power to talk either of triumph or repose. No matter
what fields are desolated, what fortresses surrendered, what
armies subdued, or what provinces overrun, there is an enemy
that still exists to check the glory of these triumphs. It
follows the conqueror back to the very scene of his ovations;
it calls upon him to take notice that the world, though silent,
is yet indignant; it shows him that the sceptre of his victory
is a barren sceptre; that it shall convey neither joy nor honour,
but shall moulder to dry ashes in his grasp. In the midst of
his exultation, it pierces his ear with the cry of injured justice; it denounces against him the indignation of an enlightened and civilised age; it turns to bitterness the cup of his
rejoicing; and wounds him with the sting which belongs to
the consciousness of having outraged the opinion of mankind."

Mr. Webster was called upon to deliver an address at the
laying of the corner-stone of the Bunker Hill Monument on
the 17th day of June, 1825—the fiftieth anniversary of the
battle. It is said that on this occasion Mr. Webster thrilled
the hearts of his immense audience by a strain of eloquence
as lofty and majestic as ever flowed from the lips of an
orator. The following passage, the writer thinks, is particularly worthy of quotation:

"We come, as Americans, to mark a spot which must
forever be dear to us and to our posterity. We wish that
whosoever, in all coming time, shall turn his eye hither, may
behold that the place is not undistinguished where the first
great battle of the Revolution was fought. We wish that
this structure may proclaim the magnitude and importance

of that event to every class and every age. We wish that
infancy may learn the purpose of its erection from maternal
lips, and that weary and withered age may behold it, and be
solaced by the recollections which it suggests. We wish
that labour may look up here, and be proud, in the midst of
its toil. We wish that in those days of disaster, which, as
they come upon all nations, must be expected to come upon
us also, desponding patriotism may turn its eyes hitherward
and be assured that the foundations of our national power
are still strong. We wish that this column, rising towards
heaven among the pointed spires of so many temples dedi-
cated to God, may contribute also to produce, in all minds,
a pious feeling of dependence and gratitude. We wish,
finally, that the last object to the sight of him who leaves
his native shore, and the first to gladden his who revisits it,
may be something which shall remind him of the liberty and
glory of his country. *Let it rise ! let it rise ! till it meet the
sun in his coming ! let the earliest light of the morning gild it,
and parting day linger and play on its summit.*"

What can be more eloquent than the following passage
proclaiming the immortality of Adams and Jefferson, taken
from the funeral discourse, the most eloquent ever pronounced in any language or in any country, upon those
distinguished patriots, delivered in Faneuil Hall on the
2d day of August, 1826, in the presence of an immense
audience :

"Although no sculptured marble should rise to their
memory, nor engraved stone bear record of their deeds, yet
will their remembrance be as lasting as the land they honoured. Marble columns may, indeed, moulder into dust,
time may erase all impress from the crumbling stone, but
their fame remains, for with American liberty it rose, and
with American liberty only can it perish. It was the last
swelling peal of yonder choir, ' *Their bodies are buried in
peace, but their name liveth evermore.*' I catch that solemn
song, I echo that lofty strain of funeral triumph ' Their name
liveth evermore.' "

One of the greatest subjects which enlisted the attention

of Mr. Webster was the Bank question. President Jackson, on the 18th day of September, 1833, ordered the removal of the public deposits from the Bank of the United States. The business of the country suffered greatly by this step. About two months after this removal had taken place, Congress met, and Mr. Clay introduced a resolution, which passed the Senate (March 28, 1834), censuring the President for assuming power not warranted by the Constitution. General Jackson communicated his protest against this resolution on the 17th of April. This drew from Mr. Webster, on the 7th of May, a speech of great power.

The most eloquent passage in this speech is the one in which Mr. Webster referred to the extent of the power of England.

Mr. Webster properly regarded the act of the President as unconstitutional, and a dangerous encroachment upon the liberties of the people, and one which should not be allowed to pass unnoticed.

He felicitously adverted in the course of his speech to the fundamental principles of civil liberty, and to the resistance made by the Revolutionary patriots to the claim of England that she had the right to tax them. He said:

" We are not to wait till great public mischiefs come, till the government is overthrown, or liberty itself put into extreme jeopardy. We should not be worthy sons of our fathers were we so to regard great questions affecting the general freedom. Those fathers accomplished the Revolution on a strict question of principle. The Parliament of Great Britain asserted a right to tax the Colonies in all cases whatsoever; and it was precisely on this question that they made the Revolution turn. The amount of taxation was trifling, but the claim itself was inconsistent with liberty; and that was, in their eyes, enough. It was against the recital of an act of Parliament, rather than against any suffering under its enactments, that they took up arms. They went to war against a preamble. They fought seven years against a declaration. They poured out their treasures and their blood like water in a contest against an assertion which those less sagacious and not so well schooled in the principles of civil liberty would have regarded as barren phraseology, or mere parade of words. They saw in the claim of the British Parliament a seminal principle of mischief, the germ of unjust power, they detected it, dragged it forth from underneath its plausible disguises, struck at it ; nor did it elude either their steady eye or their well-directed blow till they had extirpated and destroyed it, to the smallest fibre. *On this question of principle, while actual suffering was yet afar off, they raised their flag against a power, to which, for purposes of foreign conquest and subjugation, Rome, in the height of her glory, is not to be compared ; a power which has dotted* over the surface of the whole globe with her possessions and military posts, whose morning drum-beat, following the sun, and keeping company with the hours, circles the earth with one continuous and unbroken strain of the martial airs of England."

This speech was well received throughout the country. Chancellor Kent, soon after the speech was delivered, wrote Mr. Webster to the following effect:

" You never equalled this effort. It surpasses everything in logic, in simplicity and beauty and energy of diction ; in cleverness, in rebuke, in sarcasm, in patriotic and glowing feeling, in just and profound constitutional views, in critical severity, and matchless strength. It is worth millions to our liberties."

In the opinion of many writers, Webster's reply to Hayne was his greatest speech. Undoubtedly Mr. Webster's well-timed speech did much to save the Union. His defence of the Constitution was admirable, and his attack upon the pernicious doctrine of nullification was unanswerable. Colonel Hayne was a foeman worthy of his steel. The following account has been given of him: " Robert Y. Hayne, the great antagonist of Daniel Webster, and one of the most brilliant orators of the South, was born near Charleston, South Carolina, on the 10th of November, 1791. The Senate of the United States was the theatre of his greatest glory. Here he acquired a reputation which will last forever. In 1832, Mr. Hayne was elected Governor of South Carolina. He died on the 24th of September, 1841, in the 48th year of his age.

" Colonel Hayne possessed some of the highest characteristics of eloquence. He was often vehement and impassioned. His invectives were unsparing. His voice was full and melodious, and his manner earnest and impressive. Full of ingenuous sensibility, his eyes were as expressive as his tongue, and as he poured out his thoughts or feelings, either in a strain of captivating sweetness or of impetuous and overbearing passion, every emotion of his soul was distinctly depicted in the lineaments of his countenance. His mind was active, energetic, and aggressive. He was full of enthusiasm, altogether in earnest ; when he spoke, every limb of his body, and every feature of his countenance, sympathised with the action of his mind.

" Hayne dashed into debate like the Mameluke cavalry upon a charge. There was a gallant air about him that could not but win admiration. He never provided for retreat ; he never imagined it. He had an invincible confidence in himself, which arose partly from constitutional temperament, partly from previous success. His was the Napoleonic warfare ; to strike at once for the capitol of the enemy, heedless of danger or cost to his own forces. Not doubting to overcome all odds, he feared none, however seemingly superior. Of great fluency and no little force of expression, his speech never halted, and seldom fatigued.

" His oratory was graceful and persuasive. An impassioned manner, somewhat vehement at times, but rarely if ever extravagant ; a voice well modulated and clear ; a distinct, though rapid enunciation ; a confident but not often offensive address ; these, accompanying and illustrating language well selected, and periods well turned, made him a popular and effective speaker."

On Monday, the 25th January, 1830, Colonel Hayne in concluding his argument made several allusions to the Eastern States and to Mr. Webster personally which bordered on the offensive. After Haynes's speech. Mr. Iredell, a

Senator from North Carolina, speaking to a friend, said :
" He has started the lion ; but wait till we hear his roar, or
feel his claws." Colonel Hayne soon after did hear the roar
of the lion, and did feel his claws.

The day on which Mr. Webster delivered his great speech
on Foot's resolution—the 26th day of January, 1830—was a
memorable one in the history of Mr. Webster and of this
country. The scene in the Senate-chamber as well as the
circumstances connected with this speech are graphically
described by Mr. March :

" It was on Tuesday, January the 26th, 1830,—a day to
be hereafter forever memorable in senatorial annals,—that
the Senate resumed the consideration of Foot's resolution.
There never was before, in the city, an occasion of so much
excitement. To witness this great intellectual contest, multitudes of strangers had for two or three days previous been
rushing into the city, and the hotels overflowed. As early
as 9 o'clock of this morning, crowds poured into the Capitol,
in hot haste ; at 12 o'clock, the hour of meeting, the Senate-
chamber—its galleries, floor, and even lobbies—was filled to
its utmost capacity. The very stairways were dark with
men, who hung on to one another, like bees in a swarm.

" The House of Representatives was early deserted. An
adjournment would have hardly made it emptier. The
Speaker, it is true, retained his chair, but no business of
moment was or could be attended to. Members all rushed
in to hear Mr. Webster, and no call of the House or other
parliamentary proceedings could compel them back. The
floor of the Senate was so densely crowded, that persons
once in could not get out, nor change their position ; in the
rear of the Vice-Presidential chair, the crowd was particularly
dense. Dixon H. Lewis, then a Representative from Ala-
bama, became wedged in here. From his enormous size, it
was impossible for him to move without displacing a vast
portion of the multitude. Unfortunately, too, for him, he
was jammed in directly behind the chair of the Vice-President, where he could not see, and could hardly hear, the
speaker. By slow and laborious effort, pausing occasionally

to breathe, he gained one of the windows which, constructed of painted glass, flanked the chair of the Vice-President on either side. Here he paused, unable to make more headway. But, determined to see Mr. Webster as he spoke, with his knife he made a large hole in one of the panes of the glass, which is still visible as he made it. Many were so placed as not to be able to see the speaker at all. The courtesy of Senators accorded to the fairer sex room on the floor—the most gallant of them their own seats. The gay bonnets and brilliant dresses threw a varied and picturesque beauty over the scene, softening and embellishing it.

"Seldom, if ever, has a speaker in this or any other country had more powerful incentives to exertion : a subject the determination of which involved the most important interests, and even duration, of the Republic ; competitors, unequalled in reputation, ability, or position ; a name to be made still more glorious, or lost forever ; and an audience, comprising not only persons of this country most prominent in intellectual greatness, but representatives of other nations, where the art of eloquence had flourished for ages. All the soldier seeks in opportunity was here.

"Mr. Webster perceived, and felt equal to, the destinies of the moment. The very greatness of the hazard exhilarated him. His spirits rose with the occasion. He awaited the time of onset with a stern and impartial joy. He felt, like the war-horse of the Scriptures,—who ' paweth in the valley, and rejoiceth in his strength ; who goeth on to meet the armed men,—who sayeth among the trumpets, Ha, ha ! and who smelleth the battle afar off, the thunder of the captains, and the shouting.'

"A confidence in his own resources, springing from no vain estimate of his power, but the legitimate offspring of previous severe mental discipline, sustained and excited him. He had gauged his opponents, his subject, and himself.

"He was, too, at this period, in the very prime of manhood. He had reached middle age—an era in the life of man when the faculties, physical or intellectual, may be supposed to attain their fullest organisation and most per-

fect development. Whatever there was in him of intellectual energy and vitality, the occasion, his full life and high
ambition, might well bring forth.

"He never rose on an ordinary occasion to address an
ordinary audience more self-possessed. There was no tremu-
lousness in his voice nor manner ; nothing hurried, nothing
simulated. The calmness of superior strength was visible
everywhere ; in countenance, voice, and bearing. A deep-
seated conviction of the extraordinary character, of the
emergency, and of his ability to control it, seemed to possess him wholly. If an observer, more than ordinarily keen-
sighted, detected at times something like exultation in his
eye, he presumed it sprang from the excitement of the moment, and the anticipation of victory.

"The anxiety to hear the speech was so intense, irrepressible, and universal, that no sooner had the Vice-President assumed the chair, than a motion was made and
unanimously carried, to postpone the ordinary preliminaries
of senatorial action, and to take up immediately the consideration of the resolution.

"Mr. Webster rose and addressed the Senate. His exordium is known by heart, everywhere : 'Mr. President,
when the mariner has been tossed, for many days, in thick
weather, and on an unknown sea, he naturally avails himself of the first pause in the storm, the earliest glance of the
sun, to take his latitude, and ascertain how far the elements
have driven him from his true course. Let us imitate this
prudence ; and before we float farther on the waves of this
debate, refer to the point from which we departed, that we
may, at least, be able to form some conjecture where we
now are. I ask for the reading of the resolution.'

"There wanted no more to enchain the attention. There
was a spontaneous, though silent, expression of eager approbation, as the orator concluded these opening remarks.
And while the clerk read the resolution, many attempted
the impossibility of getting near the speaker. Every head
was inclined closer towards him, every ear turned in the
direction of his voice—and that deep, sudden, mysterious

silence followed, which always attends fulness of emotion. From the sea of upturned faces before him, the orator beheld his thoughts reflected as from a mirror. The varying countenance, the suffused eye, the earnest smile, and ever-attentive look assured him of his audience's entire sympathy. If among his hearers there were those who affected at first an indifference to his glowing thoughts and fervent periods, the difficult mask was soon laid aside, and profound, undisguised, devoted attention followed. In the earlier part of his speech, one of his principal opponents seemed deeply engrossed in the careful perusal of a newspaper he held before his face; but this, on nearer approach, proved to be *upside down.* In truth, all, sooner or later, voluntarily, or in spite of themselves, were wholly carried away by the eloquence of the orator.

" Those who had doubted Mr. Webster's ability to cope with and overcome his opponents were fully satisfied of their error before he had proceeded far in his speech. Their fears soon took another direction. When they heard his sentences of powerful thought, towering in accumulative grandeur, one above the other, as if the orator strove, Titan-like, to reach the very heavens themselves, they were giddy with an apprehension that he would break down in his flight. They dared not believe that genius, learning, any intellectual endowment however uncommon, that was simply mortal, could sustain itself long in a career seemingly so perilous. They feared an Icarian fall.

" Ah! who can ever forget, that was present to hear, the tremendous, the *awful* burst of eloquence with which the orator spoke of the *Old Bay State!* or the tones of deep pathos in which the words were pronounced.

" ' Mr. President, I shall enter on no encomium upon Massachusetts. There she is—behold her, and judge for yourselves. There is her history; the world knows it by heart. The past, at least, is secure. There is Boston, and Concord, and Lexington, and Bunker Hill—and there they will remain forever. The bones of her sons fallen in the great struggle for independence, now mingle with the soil

26

of every State, from New England to Georgia; and there
they will lie forever. And, sir, where American Liberty
raised its first voice; and where its youth was nurtured and
sustained, there it still lives, in the strength of its manhood
and full of its original spirit. If discord and disunion shall
wound it—if party strife and blind ambition shall hawk at
and tear it—if folly and madness—if uneasiness, under salutary and necessary restraint—shall succeed to separate it
from that Union by which alone its existence is made sure,
it will stand, in the end, by the side of that cradle in which
its infancy was rocked; it will stretch forth its arm with
whatever of vigour it may still retain, over the friends who
gather round it; and it will fall at last, if fall it must, amidst
the proudest monuments of its own glory, and on the very
spot of its origin.'

"What New England heart was there but throbbed with
vehement, tumultuous, irrepressible emotion, as he dwelt
upon New England sufferings, New England struggles, and
New England triumphs during the war of the Revolution?
There was scarcely a dry eye in the Senate; all hearts were
overcome; grave judges and men grown old in dignified
life turned aside their heads, to conceal the evidences of
their emotion.

"In one corner of the gallery was clustered a group of
Massachusetts men. They had hung from the first moment
upon the words of the speaker, with feelings variously but
always warmly excited, deepening in intensity as he proceeded. At first, while the orator was going through his
exordium, they held their breath and hid their faces, mindful of the savage attacks upon him and New England, and
the fearful odds against him, her champion;—as he went
deeper into his speech, they felt easier; when he turned
Haynes's flank on Banquo's ghost, they breathed freer and
deeper. But now, as he alluded to Massachusetts, their
feelings were strained to the highest tension; and when the
orator, concluding his encomium upon the land of their
birth, turned, intentionally or otherwise, his burning eye full
upon them—*they shed tears like girls !*

" No one who was not present can understand the excitement of the scene. No one, who was, can give an adequate
description of it. No word-painting can convey the deep,
intense enthusiasm, the reverential attention, of that vast
assembly—nor limner transfer to canvas their earnest, eager,
awe-struck countenances. Though language were as subtile
and flexible as thought, it still would be impossible to represent the full idea of the scene. There is something intangi-
ble in an emotion, which cannot be transferred. The nicer
shades of feeling elude pursuit. Every description, therefore, of the occasion, seems to the narrator himself most
tame, spiritless, unjust.

" Much of the instantaneous effect of the speech arose, of
course, from the orator's delivery, the tones of his voice, his
countenance and manner. These die mostly with the occasion
that calls them forth—the impression is lost in the attempt
at transmission from one mind to another. They can only
be described in general terms. ' Of the effectiveness of Mr.
Webster's manner, in many parts,' says Mr. Everett, ' it
would be in vain to attempt to give any one not present the
faintest idea. It has been my fortune to hear some of the
ablest speeches of the greatest living orators on both sides
of the water, but I must confess I never heard anything
which so completely realised my conception of what Demosthenes was when he delivered the Oration for the Crown.'
The variety of incident during the speech, and the rapid
fluctuation of passions, kept the audience in continual expectation and ceaseless agitation. There was no chord of
the heart the orator did not strike, as with a master-hand.
The speech was a complete drama of comic and pathetic
scenes : one varied excitement ; laughter and tears gaining
alternate victory.

" A great portion of the speech is strictly argumentative ;
an exposition of constitutional law. But grave as such portion necessarily is, severely logical, abounding in no fancy or
episode, it engrossed throughout the undivided attention of
every intelligent hearer. Abstractions, under the glowing
genius of the orator, acquired a beauty, a vitality, a power

to thrill the blood and enkindle the affections, awakening into earnest activity many a dormant faculty. His ponderous syllables had an energy, a vehemence of meaning in them that fascinated, while they startled. His thoughts in their statuesque beauty merely would have gained all critical judgment ; but he realised the antique fable, and warmed the marble into life. There was a sense of power in his language, —of power withheld and suggestive of still greater power,— that subdued, as by a spell of mystery, the hearts of all. For power whether intellectual or physical, produces in its earliest development a feeling closely allied to awe. It was never more felt than on this occasion. It had entire mastery. The sex which is said to love it best and abuse it most, seemed as much or more carried away than the sterner one. Many who had entered the hall with light, gay thoughts, anticipating at most a pleasurable excitement, soon became deeply interested in the speaker and his subject, surrendered him their entire heart ; and, when the speech was over, and they left the hall, it was with sadder, perhaps, but, surely, with far more elevated and ennobling emotions.

" The exulting rush of feeling with which he went through the peroration threw a glow over his countenance, like inspiration. Eye, brow, each feature, every line of the face, seemed touched as with a celestial fire.

" The swell and roll of his voice struck upon the ears of the spell-bound audience in deep and melodious cadence, as waves upon the far-resounding sea. The Miltonic grandeur of his words was the fit expression of his thought and raised his hearers up to his theme. His voice, exerted to its utmost power, penetrated every recess or corner of the Senate, penetrated even the ante-rooms and stairways, as he pronounced, in deepest tones of pathos, these words of solemn significance : ' When my eyes shall be turned to behold, for the last time, the sun in heaven, may I not see him shining on the broken and dishonoured fragments of a once glorious Union ; on States dissevered, discordant, belligerent ; on a land rent with civil feuds, or drenched, it may be, in fraternal blood ! Let their last feeble and lingering glance rather behold the glorious ensign of the Republic, now known and honoured throughout the earth, still full high advanced, its arms and trophies streaming in their original lustre, not a stripe erased or polluted, not a single star obscured, bearing for its motto no such miserable interrogatory as, What is all this worth? nor those other words of delusion and folly : Liberty first and Union afterwards ; but everywhere, spread all over in characters of living light, blazing on all its ample folds, as they float over the sea and over the land, and in every wind under the whole heavens, that other sentiment, dear to every American heart : *Liberty and Union, now and forever, one and inseparable.*'

" The speech was over, but the tones of the orator still lingered upon the ear, and the audience, unconscious of the close, retained their positions. The agitated countenance, the heaving breast, the suffused eye, attested the continued influence of the spell upon them. Hands that in the excitement of the moment had sought each other, still remained closed in an unconscious grasp. Eye still turned to eye, to receive and repay mutual sympathy ;—and everywhere around seemed forgetfulness of all but the orator's presence and words."

Mr. Webster in the course of his speech paid a glowing tribute to the patriotism of the South during the war of the Revolution. He was earnestly desirous of preserving the Union. He had a just horror of the vices of the slave system, but he was afraid that the Union could not be preserved if the question was agitated, and he preferred the preservation of the Union at all hazards. But the friends of Mr. Webster always regretted the position he assumed on the slave question in the great speech he delivered on the 7th of March, 1850, about two years before his death.

No well-informed statesman either North or South would have the brazen effrontery at the present time to advocate the mischievous doctrine of secession or nullification. No one who has a logical mind can fail to be convinced, after reading the Constitution of the United States and the political history of this country, that the secession notions were nonsensical. All great questions which have heretofore divided the North and South have happily been settled. It is an error, commonly made, that the doctrine of secession originated in South Carolina, and that it was first conceived by John C. Calhoun, the great Disunionist, the great Secessionist, the great Nullifier, and the great bad man generally.

The writer is not a defender of Calhoun's political principles, on the contrary he has always opposed them, but he certainly did not originate the doctrine of secession, and no well-informed statesman will contend that he did. It is difficult to trace the origin of secession views. Statesmen North, South, and West have held them at various times. One of the first traces of the secession doctrine is to be found in the *Abridged Congressional Debates*, vol. iv., page 327. According to the *Record*, Mr. Josiah Quincy, of Massachusetts, while discussing, (1811) a bill for the admission of what was then called the Orleans Territory, now Louisiana into the Union as a State, said, with the approval of many of his colleagues, that Congress did not have the power to admit into the Union a foreign state, whose territory was not a part of the original domain at the time of the adoption of the Constitution and the formation of the Union consummated. Mr. Quincy said, that if the bill was passed and Orleans (what is now Louisiana) was admitted, the act would be subversive of the Union, and each State would be freed from its federal bonds and obligations, " and that as it will be, the right of all (the States) so it will be the duty of some, to prepare definitely for a separation—amicably if they can, violently if they must." Afterward he committed what he had said to writing, in order to avoid mistake, in the following language :

"If this bill passes, it is my deliberate opinion that it is virtually a dissolution of the Union ; that it will free the States from their moral obligation, and as it will be the right of all, so it will be the duty of some, definitely to prepare for a separation—amicably if they can, violently if they must."

Doctrines of a similar character were advocated a few

years afterward at the famous Hartford Convention. Even prior to Quincy's time the doctrine had doubtless been enunciated.

Webster's magnificent speech, the greatest, in many respects, ever made by an orator in ancient or modern times, did incalculable service to his country.

The same year Mr. Webster made an eloquent forensic address on the trial of John Francis Knapp, for the murder of Captain Joseph White, of Salem, Mass.

When reminding the jury of the obligation they were under to discharge their duty, he said in part:

"Gentlemen : Your whole concern should be to do your duty, and leave consequences to take care of themselves. You will receive the law from the court. Your verdict 't is true may endanger the prisoner's life ; but then it is to save other lives. If the prisoner's guilt has been shown and proved, beyond all reasonable doubt, you will convict him. If such reasonable doubt of guilt remain, you will acquit him. You are the judges of the whole case. You owe a duty to the public, as well as to the prisoner at the bar. You cannot presume to be wiser than the law. Your duty is a plain straightforward one. Doubtless, we would all judge him in mercy. Towards him, as an individual, the law inculcates no hostility ; but towards him, if proved to be a murderer, the law, and the oaths you have taken, and public justice, demand that you do your duty.

"With consciences satisfied with the discharge of duty, no consequences can harm you. There is no evil that we cannot either face or fly from, but the consciousness of duty disregarded.

"A sense of duty pursues us ever. It is omnipresent, like the Deity. If we take to ourselves the wings of the morning and dwell in the utmost parts of the seas, duty performed, or duty violated, is still with us, for our happiness or our misery. If we say the darkness shall cover us, in the darkness, as in the light our obligations are yet with us. We cannot escape their power, nor fly from their presence. They are with us in this life, will be with us at its close ; and in

that scene of inconceivable solemnity, which lies yet farther
onward—we shall still find ourselves surrounded by the consciousness of duty, to pain us wherever it has been violated,
and to console us so far as God may have given us grace to
perform it."

Mr. Webster in his picture of the self-betrayal of
the murderer, shows a profound knowledge of human
nature :

"Ah! gentlemen, that was a dreadful mistake. Such a
secret can be safe nowhere. The whole creation of God has
neither nook nor corner where the guilty can bestow it, and
say it is safe. Not to speak of that eye which glances through
all disguises, and beholds everything as in the splendour of
noon—such secrets of guilt are never safe from detection,
even by men. True it is, generally speaking, that 'murder
will out.' True it is, that Providence hath so ordained, and
doth so govern things, that those who break the great law of
heaven, by shedding man's blood, seldom succeed in avoiding discovery. Especially, in a case exciting so much attention as this, discovery must come, and will come sooner or
later. A thousand eyes turn at once to explore every
man, every thing, every circumstance, connected with the
time and place; a thousand ears catch every whisper; a thousand excited minds intensely dwell on the scene, shedding
all their light, and ready to kindle the slightest circumstance
into a blaze of discovery. Meantime the guilty soul cannot
keep its own secret. It is false to itself; or rather it feels
an irresistible impulse of conscience to be true to itself. It
labours under its guilty possession, and knows not what to do
with it. The human heart was not made for the residence of
such an inhabitant. It finds itself preyed on by a torment,
which it dares not acknowledge to God or man. A vulture is
devouring it, and it can ask no sympathy or assistance, either
from heaven or earth. The secret which the murderer possesses soon comes to possess him; and, like the evil spirits
of which we read, it overcomes him, and leads him whither-
soever it will. He feels it beating at his heart, rising to his
throat, and demanding disclosure. He thinks the whole

world sees it in his face, reads it in his eyes, and almost hears
its workings in the very silence of his thoughts. It has become his master. It betrays his discretion, it breaks down
his courage, it conquers his prudence. When suspicions,
from without, begin to embarrass him, and the net of circumstance to entangle him, the fatal secret struggles with still
greater violence to burst forth. It must be confessed, it will
be confessed, there is no refuge from confession but suicide,
and suicide is confession."

And in the same speech, with what great ability does he
set forth his theory of the murderer's plan:

"Let me ask your attention, then, in the first place,
to those appearances on the morning after the murder,
which have a tendency to show that it was done in pursu-
ance of a preconcerted plan of operation. What are they?
A man was found murdered in his bed. No stranger had
done the deed—no one acquainted with the house had done
it. It was apparent, that somebody from within had opened,
and somebody from without had entered. There had been
there, obviously and certainly, concert and co-operation.
The inmates of the house were not alarmed when the murder was perpetrated. The assassin had entered, without
any riot, or any violence. He had found the way prepared
before him. The house had been previously opened. The
window was unbarred, from within, and its fastenings un-
screwed. There was a lock on the door of the chamber in
which Mr. White slept, but the key was gone. It had been
taken away, and secreted. The footsteps of the murderer
were visible, out-doors, tending toward the window. The
plank by which he entered the window still remained. The
road he pursued had been thus prepared for him. The victim was slain, and the murderer had escaped. Everything
indicated that somebody from within had co-operated with
somebody from without. Everything proclaimed that some
of the inmates, or somebody having access to the house, had
had a hand in the murder. On the face of the circumstances, it was apparent, therefore, that this was a premeditated,
concerted, conspired murder. Who, then, were the conspir-

ators? If not now found out, we are still groping in the dark, and the whole tragedy is still a mystery."

When the Bunker Hill Monument was completed in 1843, Mr. Webster was invited to deliver an oration on the occasion.

At least one hundred thousand people were present.

The eloquence of the following remarkable passage compels its insertion here. Mr. Webster said:

"A *duty* has been performed. A work of gratitude and patriotism is completed. This structure, having its foundations in soil which drank deep of early Revolutionary blood, has at length reached its destined height, and now lifts its summit to the skies.

"The Bunker Hill Monument is finished. Here it stands. Fortunate in the high natural eminence in which it is placed, higher, infinitely higher, in its objects and purpose, it rises over the land and over the sea; and, visible, at their homes, to three hundred thousand of the people of Massachusetts, it stands a memorial of the last, and a monitor to the present and to all succeeding generations. I have spoken of the loftiness of its purpose. If it had been without any other design than the creation of a work of art, the granite of which it is composed would have slept in its native bed. It has a purpose, and that purpose gives it character. That purpose enrobes it with dignity and moral grandeur. That well-known purpose it is which causes us to look up to it with a feeling of awe. *It is itself the orator of this occasion.* It is not from my lips, it could not be from any human lips, that that strain of eloquence is this day to flow most competent to move and excite the vast multitudes around me. *The powerful speaker stands motionless before us.* It is a plain shaft. It bears no inscriptions, fronting to the rising sun, from which the future antiquary shall wipe the dust. Nor does the rising sun cause tones of music to issue from its summit. But at the rising of the sun, and at the setting of the sun, in the blaze of noonday, and beneath the milder effulgence of lunar light, it looks, it speaks, it acts, to the full comprehension of every American mind, and the awakening of glowing enthusiasm in every American heart. Its silent, but awful utterance; its deep pathos, as it brings to our contemplation the 17th of June, 1775, and the consequences which have resulted to us, to our country, and to the world, from the events of that day, and which we know must continue to rain influence on the destinies of mankind to the end of time; the elevation with which it raises us high above the ordinary feeling of life, surpass all that the study of the closet, or even the inspiration of genius, can produce. To-day it speaks to us. Its future auditories will be the successive generations of men, as they rise up before it and gather around it. Its speech will be of patriotism and courage; of civil and religious liberty; of free government; of the moral improvement and elevation of mankind; and of the immortal memory of those who, with heroic devotion, have sacrificed their lives for their country."

In this connection, the writer is of the opinion, that the following beautiful and eloquent passage from the speech of Kossuth, the Hungarian patriot, cannot fail to prove interesting to the intelligent reader:

"My voice shrinks from the task to mingle with the awful pathos of that orator [pointing to the monument]. Silent like the grave, and yet melodious like the song of immortality upon the lips of cherubim,—senseless, cold granite, and yet warm with inspiration like a patriot's heart,—immovable like the past, and yet stirring like the future, which never stops,—it looks like a prophet, and speaks like an oracle. And thus it speaks:

"'The day I commemorate is the rod with which the hand of the Lord has opened the well of Liberty. Its waters will flow; every new drop of martyr blood will increase the tide. Despots may dam its flood, but never stop it. The higher its dam, the higher the tide; it will overflow, or break through.

"'Bow, and adore, and hope!'

"Such are the words which come to my ears; and I bow, I adore, I hope!

"In bowing, my eyes meet the soil of Bunker Hill—that

awful opening scene of the eventful drama to which Lexington and Concord had been the preface.

"The spirits of the past rise before my eyes. I see Richard Gridley hastily planning the entrenchments. I hear the dull, cold, blunt sound of the pickaxe and spade in the hands of the patriot band. I hear the patrols say that 'all is well.' I see Knowlton raising his line of rail fence, upon which soon the guns will rest, that the bullets may prove to their message true. I see the tall, commanding form of Prescott marching leisurely around the parapet, inflaming the tired patriots with the classical words that those who had the merit of the labour should have the honour of the victory. I see Asa Pollard fall, the first victim of that immortal day; I see the chaplain praying over him; and now the roaring of cannon from ships and from batteries, and the blaze of the burning town, and the thrice-renewed storm, and the persevering defence, till powder was gone, and but stones remained. And I see Warren telling Elbridge Gerry that it is sweet and fair to die for the fatherland. I see him lingering in his retreat, and, struck in the forehead, fall to the ground; and Pomeroy with his shattered musket in his brave hand, complaining that he remained unhurt when Warren had to die; and I see all the brave who fell unnamed, unnoticed, and unknown, the nameless corner-stones of American independence!"

The last of Mr. Webster's patriotic addresses was delivered on the 4th of July, 1851, at the magnificent ceremonial of the laying of the corner-stone of the addition to the Capitol. It was one of the greatest of his orations. It was natural that the orator should refer to the illustrious Washington, who, in 1793, had laid the corner-stone of the original Capitol. "The allusion and apostrophe to Washington will be rehearsed by the generous youth of America as long as the English language is spoken on this side of the Atlantic Ocean," said Everett. In the following lines we have the beautiful allusion and apostrophe:

"Fellow-citizens, what contemplations are awakened in our minds as we assemble here to re-enact a scene like that performed by Washington! Methinks I see his venerable form now before me, as presented in the glorious statue by Houdon, now in the Capitol of Virginia. He is dignified and grave, but concern and anxiety seem to soften the lineaments of his countenance. The government over which he presides is yet in the crisis of experiment. Not free from troubles at home, he sees the world in commotion and in arms all around him. He sees that imposing foreign powers are half disposed to try the strength of the recently established American government. We perceive that mighty thoughts, mingled with fears as well as with hopes, are struggling within him. He heads a short procession over these then naked fields; he crosses yonder stream on a fallen tree; he ascends to the top of this eminence, whose original oaks of the forest stand as thick around him as if the spot had been devoted to Druidical worship, and here he performs the appointed duty of the day.

" And now, fellow-citizens, if this vision were a reality ; if Washington actually were now amongst us, and if he could draw around him the shades of the great public men of his own day, patriots and warriors, orators and statesmen, and were to address us in their presence, would he not say to us: 'Ye men of this generation, I rejoice and thank God for being able to see that our labours and toils and sacrifices were not in vain. You are prosperous, you are happy, you are grateful ; the fire of liberty burns brightly and steadily in your hearts, while *duty* and the *law* restrain it from bursting forth in wild and destructive conflagration. Cherish liberty, as you love it ; cherish its securities, as you wish to preserve it. Maintain the Constitution which we laboured so painfully to establish, and which has been to you such a source of inestimable blessings. Preserve the union of the States, cemented as it was by our prayers, our tears, and our blood. Be true to God, to your country, and to your duty. So shall the whole eastern world follow the morning sun to contemplate you as a nation ; so shall all generations honour you, as they honour us; and so shall that Almighty Power which so graciously protected us, and which now protects you, shower its everlasting blessings upon you and your posterity.'

"Great Father of your Country! we heed your words; we feel their force as if you now uttered them with lips of flesh and blood. Your example teaches us, your affectionate addresses teach us, your public life teaches us, your sense of the value of the blessings of the Union. Those blessings our fathers have tasted, and we have tasted, and still taste. Nor do we intend that those who come after us shall be denied the same high fruition. Our honour as well as our happiness is concerned. We can not, we dare not, we will not, betray our sacred trust. We will not filch from posterity the treasure placed in our hands to be transmitted to other generations. The bow that gilds the clouds in the heavens, the pillars that uphold the firmament, may disappear and fall away in the hour appointed by the will of God; but until that day comes, or so long as our lives may last, no ruthless hand shall undermine that bright arch of Union and Liberty which spans the continent from Washington to California."

Mr. Webster's standard of American citizenship was high, and he had a just notion of the mental and moral qualifications necessary to fit a statesman for the discharge of his duties as a Representative in Congress. He was unremitting in his endeavours to cultivate his great intellectual faculties, and to develop his latent energies. His golden words as to the responsibility of an American citizen should ever be held in remembrance by all patriots:

"Let us cherish, fellow-citizens, a deep and solemn conviction of the *duties* which have devolved upon us. This lovely land, this glorious liberty, these benign institutions, the dear purchase of our fathers, are ours; ours to enjoy, ours to preserve, ours to *transmit*. Generations past, and generations to come, hold us *responsible* for this sacred trust. Our fathers, from behind, admonish us, with their anxious paternal voices; posterity calls out to us, from the bosom of the future; the world turns hither its solicitous eyes—all, *all* conjure us to act wisely, and faithfully, in the relation which we sustain. We can never, indeed, pay the *debt* which is upon us; but by virtue, by morality, by religion, by the cultivation of every good principle and every good habit, we may hope to *enjoy* the blessing, through our day, and to leave it unimpaired to our children. Let us feel deeply how much of what we are and of what we possess, we owe to this *liberty*, and these institutions of government. Nature has, indeed, given us a soil, which yields bounteously to the hands of industry; the mighty and fruitful ocean is before us, and the skies over our heads shed health and vigour. But what are lands, and seas, and skies, to civilised men, without *society*, without *knowledge*, without *morals*, without *religious culture;* and how can these be enjoyed, in all their extent, and all their excellence, but under the protection of wise institutions and a free government? Fellow-citizens, there is not *one* of us, there is not one of us *here present*, who does not, at this moment, and at *every* moment, experience in his own condition, and in the condition of those most near and dear to him, the *influence* and the *benefit* of this liberty and these institutions. Let us then acknowledge the blessing, let us feel it deeply and powerfully; let us cherish a strong affection for it, and resolve to maintain and perpetuate it. The blood of our fathers—let it not have been shed *in vain;* the great hope of posterity—let it not be *blasted.*"

On the 23d day of February, 1852, Mr. Webster delivered, before the New York Historical Society, an exceedingly interesting and instructive address from which we take the following extract which deserves careful attention:

" Unborn ages and visions of glory crowd upon my soul, the realisation of all which, however, is in the hands and good pleasure of Almighty God; but, under his Divine blessing, it will be dependent on the character and the virtues of ourselves and of our posterity. If classical history has been found to be, is now, and shall continue to be, the concomitant of free institutions and of popular eloquence, what a field is opening to us for another Herodotus, another Thucydides, and another Livy!

" And let me say, gentlemen, that if we and our posterity shall be true to the Christian religion,—if we and they shall live always in the fear of God, and shall respect his commandments,—if we and they shall maintain just, moral sentiments, and such conscientious convictions of duty as shall control the heart and life, we may have the highest hopes of the future fortunes of our country; and if we maintain those institutions of government and that political union, exceeding all praise as much as it exceeds all former examples of political associations, we may be sure of one thing—that, while our country furnishes materials for a thousand masters of the historic art, it will afford no topic for a Gibbon. It will have no Decline and Fall. It will go on prospering and to prosper.

" But, if we and our posterity reject religious instruction and authority, violate the rules of eternal justice, trifle with the injunctions of morality, and recklessly destroy the political constitution which holds us together, no man can tell how sudden a catastrophe may overwhelm us, that shall bury all our glory in profound obscurity. Should that catastrophe happen, let it have no history! Let the horrible narrative never be written! Let its fate be like that of the lost books of Livy, which no human eye shall ever read; or the missing Pleiad, of which no man can ever know more, than that it is lost, and lost forever!

" But, gentlemen, I will not take my leave of you in a tone of despondency. We may trust that Heaven will not forsake us, nor permit us to forsake ourselves. We must strengthen ourselves, and gird up our loins with new resolution; we must counsel each other; and, determined to sustain each other in the support of the Constitution, prepare to meet, manfully, and united, whatever of difficulty or of danger, whatever of effort or of sacrifice, the providence of God may call upon us to meet.

" Are we of this generation so derelict, have we so little of the blood of our revolutionary fathers coursing through our veins, that we cannot preserve what they achieved? The world will cry out ' SHAME ' upon us, if we show ourselves unwoithy to be the descendants of those great and illustrious men, who fought for their liberty, and secured it to their posterity, by the Constitution of the United States.

"Gentlemen, inspiring auspices, this day, surround us and cheer us. It is the anniversary of the birth of Washington. We should know this, even if we had lost our calendars, for we should be reminded of it by the shouts of joy and gladness. The whole atmosphere is redolent of his name; hills and forests, rocks and rivers echo and re-echo his praises. All the good, whether learned or unlearned, high or low, rich or poor, feel, this day, that there is one treasure common to them all, and that is the fame and character of Washington. They recount his deeds, ponder over his principles and teachings, and resolve to be more and more guided by them in the future.

"To the old and the young, to all born in the land, and to all whose love of liberty has brought them from foreign shores to make this the home of their adoption, the name of Washington is this day an exhilarating theme. Americans by birth are proud of his character, and exiles from foreign shores are eager to participate in admiration of him; and it is true that he is, this day, here, everywhere, all the world over, more an object of love and regard than on any day since his birth.

"Gentlemen, on Washington's principles, and under the guidance of his example, will we and our children uphold the Constitution. Under his military leadership our fathers conquered; and under the outspread banner of his political and constitutional principles will we also conquer. To that standard we shall adhere, and uphold it through evil report and through good report. We will meet danger, we will meet death, if they come, in its protection; and we will struggle on, in daylight and in darkness, ay, in the thickest darkness, with all the storms which it may bring with it, till

> 'Danger's troubled night is o'er
> And the star of Peace return.'"

Mr. Webster died on the quiet Sabbath morning of the 24th of October, 1852.

An account of the last hours of Mr. Webster has been given by an able speaker, which the writer will quote:

" Among the many memorable words which fell from the lips of our friend just before they were closed forever, the most remarkable are those which have been quoted by a previous speaker: '*I still live.*' They attest the serene composure of his mind; the Christian heroism with which he was able to turn his consciousness in upon himself, and explore, step by step, the dark passage (dark to us, but to him, we trust, already lighted from above) which connects this world with the world to come. But I know not what words could have been better chosen to express his relation to the world he was leaving—' I still live.' This poor dust is just returning to the dust from which it was taken, but I feel that I live in the affections of the people to whose services I have consecrated my days. ' I still live.' The icy hand of death is already laid on my heart, but I shall still live in those words of counsel which I have uttered to my fellow-citizens, and which I now leave them as the last bequest of a dying friend.

" In the long and honoured career of our lamented friend, there are efforts and triumphs which will hereafter fill one of the brightest pages of our history. But I greatly err if the closing scene—the height of the religious sublime—does not, in the judgment of other days, far transcend in interest the brightest exploits of public life. Within that darkened chamber at Marshfield was witnessed a scene of which we shall not readily find the parallel.

" The serenity with which he stood in the presence of the King of Terrors, without trepidation or flutter, for hours and days of expectation; the thoughtfulness for the public business, when the sands were so nearly run out; the hospitable care for the reception of the friends who came to Marshfield; that affectionate and solemn leave separately taken, name by name, of wife and children and kindred and friends and family, down to the humblest members of the household; the designation of the coming day, then near at hand, when 'all that was mortal of Daniel Webster should cease to exist!' the dimly recollected strains of the funeral poetry of Gray; the last faint flash of the soaring intellect; the feebly murmured words of Holy Writ repeated from the lips of the good physician, who, when all the resources of human art had been exhausted, had a drop of spiritual balm for the parting soul; the clasped hands; the dying prayers. Oh! my fellow citizens, this is a consummation over which tears of pious sympathy will be shed ages after the glories of the forum and the senate are forgotten.

> ' His sufferings ended with the day,
>   Yet lived he at its close ;
> And breathed the long, long night away,
>   In statue-like repose.' "

Mr. Webster was very fond of the study of geology, astronomy, and the classics. One of his biographers says: " At one time, while conversing on the subject of reading, and of topics worth the attention of men, he said he wished he could live three lives, while living this:

" One he would devote to the study of Geology, or, to use his own words, ' to reading the earth's history of itself.'

" Another life he would devote to Astronomy; he said he had lately been reading the history of that science, written so clearly, that he, although no mathematician, could understand it, and he was astonished at seeing to what heights it had been pushed by modern intellects.

" The other life he would devote to the Classics."

The following is an interesting account of the reception of Mr. Webster, and of the effect of one of his speeches on a popular assembly in New Hampshire, given by a stranger who happened to be present :

" At early candle-light he went to the caucus room ; it was filled to overflowing, but some persons, seeing that he was a stranger, gave way, and he found a convenient place to stand ; no one could sit. A tremendous noise soon announced that the orator had arrived ; but as soon as the meeting was organised, another arose to make some remarks on the object of the caucus; he was heard with a polite apathy; another and another came, and all spoke well, but this would not do, and if Chatham had been among them, or St. Paul, they would not have met the expectations of the multitude. The beloved orator at length arose, and was for a while musing upon something which was drowned by a constant cheering; but when order was restored he went on, with great serenity and ease, to make his remarks without apparently making the slightest attempt to gain applause. The audience was still, except now and then a murmur of delight which showed that the great mass of the hearers were ready to burst into a thunder of applause, if those who generally set the example would have given an intimation that it might have been done; but they, devouring every word, made signs to prevent any interruption. The harangue was ended; the roar of applause lasted long, and was sincere and heartfelt. It was a strong, gentlemanly, and appropriate speech, but not a particle of the demagogue about it; nothing like the speeches on the hustings to catch attention. He drew a picture of the candidates on both sides of the question, and proved, as far as reason could prove, the superiority of those of his own choice; but the gentleman traveller, who was a very good judge, has often said that the most extraordinary part of it was, that a promiscuous audience should have had good sense enough to relish such sound, good reasoning in a place where vague declamation is best received."

The traveller pursued his journey toward the east, but to his great surprise the speech of Webster had preceded him, and was the common theme of conversation in every hotel and other public place.

The following picture of Mr. Webster is well drawn:

" The person of Mr. Webster is singular and commanding; his height is above the ordinary size, but he cannot be called tall; he is broad across the chest, and stoutly and firmly built, but there is nothing of clumsiness either in his form or gait. His head is very large, his forehead high, with good shaped temples. He has a large, black, solemn-looking eye that exhibits strength and steadfastness, and which sometimes burns but seldom sparkles. His hair is of a raven black, and both thick and short, without the mark of a grey hair. His eyebrows are of the same colour, thick and strongly marked, which gives his features the appearance of sternness; but the general expression of his face, after it is properly examined, is rather mild and amiable than otherwise. His movements in the house and in the street are slow and dignified; there is no peculiar sweetness in his voice, its tones are rather harsh than musical, still there is a great variety in them, and some of them catch the ear and chain it down to the most perfect attention. He bears traces of great mental labour, but no marks of age; in fact, his person is more imposing now, in his forty-eighth year, than it was at thirty years of age."

A talented English writer who saw Mr. Webster in London in 1839 gives the following portrait of the great statesman:

" Mr. Webster's personal appearance is particularly striking. He has a very large, massive head; his forehead is, I think, the most ample in its proportions of all the foreheads I have ever witnessed. It is remarkably striking on various accounts. It is, first of all, exceedingly broad; and, though of a sloping or receding shape towards the summit, it prominently protrudes at the eyebrows. A little above the eyes it is quite flat. The level part is the more observable, from the circumstance of its being so full in all other places. Its unusual loftiness is displayed to greater advantage owing to the comparative absence of hair in the front. Let no one infer from this that Mr. Webster is bald-headed; he is nothing of the kind; he has as ' fine a head of hair,' to use the favourite phraseology of perruquiers, as the great admirers of that commodity could wish to possess. It is of a jet-black hue if seen some yards distant, but a nearer inspection will discern an incipient darkish grey in some of its tufts. It is carelessly arranged on the learned gentleman's head. . . . Mr. Webster's head, large as it is in every department, has a peculiarly full development in the locality of the temples.

His eyebrows are quite black; and, between their extraordinary size and the amazing quantity of hair on them, are
perhaps the most prominent ever seen on the face either of
an Englishman or a native of the United States. They
overlap the eyes (which, I should observe, are unusually
deeply set) in a very marked manner. Mr. Webster's large
dark eyes are full of expression. His features are generally
prominent, but his nose is particularly so, in consequence of
its narrow ridge and aquiline conformation. His face has a
copper complexion; and though Mr. Webster is a man who
has performed herculean labours for many years past, both
at the bar and in the senate, there is not on it the slightest
appearance of wrinkles, nor any other indication of anxiety
or over-exertion. His countenance has a fresh and healthful
appearance; its habitual expression is that of thoughtfulness;
at times it would indicate a reserve amounting to taciturnity.
It is in other respects in perfect accordance with what we
know to be the leading attributes of his mental character.
No one could look on the countenance of Daniel Webster
without coming to the conclusion that he is a man of great
energy of mind, and of indomitable moral courage—a person
whom no power in the world could dismay—a man who is
not to be diverted from his purpose by any earthly consideration. And in happy keeping with his mental decision is his
outward frame. Though not above the ordinary height, he
·is evidently a man of great muscular power; he is broad and
firmly built, especially about the shoulders. His frame altogether has an unusual appearance of robustness about it.
He is such a man as would, had his destiny placed him in the
humbler ranks of life, been singled out from a hundred others
for his assumed capabilities for performing hard manual
labour. . . . His appearance and manners are plain. He
has more the aspect of a farmer living in the country than of
one whose time is principally spent among judges, lawyers,
legislators, and the commercial aristocrats of the leading
cities of the United States. He wears a brown coat with a
velvet collar, a buff waistcoat, dark small-clothes, and Wellington boots."

When Mr. Webster arose to address the Senate the description given by Milton of one of his characters could have been fittingly applied to him :

> " With grave
> Aspect he rose, and in his rising seemed
> A pillar of state ; deep on his front engraven
> Deliberation sat, and public care. . . . .
> His look
> Drew audience and attention still as night
> Or summer's noontide air."

It may be of interest to young men desirous of studying Mr. Webster's methods of preparing his speeches to know that he did not depend altogether upon the inspiration of the moment for the language or the thoughts which he meant to use. The impression has been current that his great speeches were unstudied. He said on one occasion that he would as soon think of appearing before an audience half-clothed as half-prepared, and at another time he told one of his friends that he would as soon stand up and tell his audience that he had garments enough at home, but did not think it worth while to put them on, as to tell them that he could have made a satisfactory speech, perhaps, if he had taken the requisite pains. Mr. Webster was always a laborious student, and in the early part of his career he expended much time in the preparation of his public addresses.

An entertaining writer, General Lyman, says : " He happened to be dining with a company of friends a few years since, when the first message of an eminent public man, then Governor of the State of New York, was issued and became the subject of conversation. 'Governor W——,' said Mr. Webster, on being appealed to for his opinion, ' is a very able man and a very able writer—the only thing he needs to learn is how to *scratch out.*' A Senator of the United States expressed some surprise at this remark, and said that no one who read Mr. Webster's addresses, or listened to his speeches, could suppose that he ever had occasion to alter or amend anything that came from his pen. ' However that may be now,' replied Mr. Webster, ' a very large part of my life has been spent in "scratching out." When I was a young man, and for some years after I had acquired a respectable degree of eminence in my profession, my style was bombastic and pompous in the extreme. Some kind friend was good enough to point out that fact to me, and I determined to correct it, if labour could do it. Whether it has been corrected or not, no small part of my life has been spent in the attempt.' "

Clay.—" I would rather be right than be President." The utterance of these words alone would have immortalised the subject of this sketch. Henry Clay was born in Hanover County, Virginia, on the 12th day of April, 1777. He was the son of John Clay, a Baptist minister, poor but highly respected. Mr. Clay's father died when he was four years old, leaving a widow and eight children. Clay's mother was affectionate, devoted, intelligent, and heroic, and by carefully husbanding her small resources she succeeded in sending Clay to school. The teacher, to whom Clay was sent, Peter Deacon, was more noted for his love of liquor than his love of learning, but if he did not teach his pupils very much, he did thrash the most of them soundly on the slightest provocation, and about the only thing which Clay remembered after he left Mr. Deacon's school was the severe drubbings which that gentleman had from time to time given him.

Clay, when he had nothing else to do, after his graduation from the seat of learning presided over by the irascible Mr. Deacon, spent his time in going to mill, mounted on a horse without a saddle, guided by a rope bridle, with a bag of corn or meal to sit on; ploughing, chopping wood, and other light and enjoyable work of a similar character. His neighbours called him " the mill-boy of the Slashes," and when in after years the great man was nominated for the presidency the nickname became a term of endearment to his hundreds of thousands of enthusiastic admirers and supporters.

Having early in life been compelled to buffet continually the storms of adverse fortune, he always sympathised warmly with the poor in their privations.

Clay's friends succeeded in getting a position for him in the office of the Clerk of the High Court of Chancery in Richmond, Va. While in the office Clay became acquainted with Hon. George Wythe, then the Chancellor of the High Court of Chancery. Mr. Wythe was a man of ability and culture, and became much attached to Clay. He advised Clay to study law, and selected him as his amanuensis in writing out his official decisions. Clay and his patron spent much of their time together. Mr. Wythe directed Clay's grammatical, legal, and historical studies.

While in the Clerk's office, Clay became acquainted with the most distinguished men in the State, and attracted their attention strongly by his talents and amiable qualities.

After studying law for one year he was admitted to the bar. He removed soon after to Lexington, Ky., where he resided till his death. When Mr. Clay entered on the duties of his profession at Lexington, his prospects were not very flattering. Afterward, referring to this period of his life, he said: " I was without patrons, without friends, and destitute of the means of paying my weekly board. I remember how comfortable I thought I should be if I could make £100 Virginia money, per annum, and with what delight I received the first fifteen-shilling fee. My hopes were more than realised ; I immediately rushed into a lucrative practice."

As a lawyer and as a politician Mr. Clay was justly celebrated for his tact. He was perfectly familiar with the manners and customs of the farmers, mechanics, and labourers, and always had a pleasant word for them, not because he hoped to be benefited by them, but because he loved them sincerely, devotedly, and hoped to aid them by the passage of beneficent legislative measures, and by the improvement of their respective conditions. Mr. Clay was a warm-hearted philanthropist, and his life was spent in continual labour for the public welfare. He knew how to win the affections of the people, by entering into their sports and pastimes as well as by taking an interest in their occupations and business pursuits.

An incident is related by one of his biographers which

illustrates his tact in seizing and turning to good account circumstances comparatively trivial : " He had been engaged in speaking some time, when a company of riflemen who had been performing military exercise, attracted by his attitude, concluded to go and hear what that fellow had to say, as they termed it, and accordingly drew near. They listened with respectful attention and evidently with deep interest until he closed, when one of their number, a man about fifty years of age, who had evidently seen much backwoods service, stood leaning on his rifle, regarding the young speaker with a fixed and most sagacious look. He was apparently the Nimrod of the company, for he exhibited every characteristic of a mighty hunter,—buckskin breeches and hunting shirt, coon-skin cap, black, bushy beard, and a visage which, had it been in juxtaposition with his leathern bullet-pouch, might have been taken for part and parcel of the same. At his belt hung the knife and hatchet, and the huge indispensable powder-horn across a breast bare and brown as the bleak hills he often traversed, yet which concealed as brave and noble a heart as ever beat beneath a fairer covering. He beckoned with his hand to Mr. Clay to approach him, who immediately complied. 'Young man,' said he, ' you want to go to the legislature, I see?' ' Why, yes,' replied Mr. Clay, ' yes, I should like to go, since my friends have seen proper to put me up as a candidate before the people ; I do not wish to be defeated.'—'Are you a good shot?' —'The best in the county.'—'Then you shall go ; but you must give us a specimen of your skill ; we must see you shoot.'—'I never shoot any rifle but my own, and that is at home.'—' No matter, here is old Bess, she never fails in the hands of a marksman ; she has often sent death through a squirrel's head at one hundred yards, and daylight through many a redskin twice that distance ; if you can shoot any gun you can shoot old Bess.' 'Well, put up your mark, put up your mark,' replied Mr. Clay. The target was placed at a distance of about eighty yards, when, with all the steadiness of an old, experienced marksman, he drew old Bess to his shoulder and fired. The bullet pierced the

target near the centre. 'Oh, a chance shot! a chance shot!'
exclaimed several of his political opponents. 'A chance
shot! He might shoot all day and not hit the mark again;
let him try it over, let him try it over.' 'No, beat that, beat
that, and then I will,' retorted Mr. Clay. But as no one
seemed disposed to make the attempt, it was considered
that he had given satisfactory proof of being the best shot
in the county; and this unimportant incident gained him
the vote, which was composed principally of that class of
persons, as well as the support of the same throughout the
county."

Another instance similar to the above has been related of
Mr. Clay. While a candidate he met an old hunter who
had previously been one of his warm supporters, but who
now opposed him on account of his action on the Compensation Bill. "Have you a good rifle, my friend?"
asked Mr. Clay.—"Yes."—"Does it ever flash?"—"Once
only."—"What did you do with it, throw it away?"—"No,
I picked the flint, tried again, and brought down the game."—
"Have I ever flashed but on the Compensation Bill?"—"No."
—"Will you throw me away?" "No! no!" quickly replied
the hunter, nearly overwhelmed by his enthusiastic feelings;
"*I will pick the flint and try you again!*" Ever after he
was the unwavering supporter and friend of Mr. Clay.

While Mr. Clay was dining at Lord Castlereagh's in London, with several other distinguished Americans, the British
Commissioners, and some of the British ministers, directly
after the battle of Waterloo, and while the country was filled
with rejoicings for the victory, it was suggested at table
that, as it was not known where Napoleon was, he might
possibly flee to America for an asylum. "Will he not give
you some trouble if he goes there?" said Lord Liverpool
to Mr. Clay. "Not the least, my lord," said Mr. Clay. "We
shall be very glad to see him, will entertain him with all due
rites of hospitality, and soon make him a good democrat."

Mr. Clay's opponents often ascertained, to their cost, that
he could be witty, sarcastic, ironical, and satirical, but he
usually resorted to these weapons for purposes of defending

himself against unjust attacks, and was not often, himself, the aggressor.

Soon after his entrance into the United States Senate he made his first speech on internal improvements. His speech did not suit an elderly member who had more presumption than sagacity. As he was much Mr. Clay's senior, he attempted to prove him guilty of being a young man, and, with ludicrously affected airs of superior wisdom, attacked him with that intent, advising him to modesty corresponding with his years. Mr. Clay, in his reply, quoted the following lines :

> " Thus have I seen a magpie in the street,
> A chattering bird we often meet,
> With head awry and cunning eye,
> Peep knowingly into a marrow-bone."

It is said that the application of the manners of the magpie to those of the reverend Senator was so just that it was immediately perceived by the Senate, and excited much and hearty laughter. The supercilious critic after this encounter gave Mr. Clay no further trouble.

A public dinner was given to Mr. Clay after his return from Ghent, by his friends at Lexington, when " the negotiators of Ghent " were toasted, in whose behalf Mr. Clay made a pertinent speech. But when the last toast was read—" Our guest, Henry Clay: we welcome his return to that country whose rights and interests he has so ably maintained, at home and abroad,"—his feelings were deeply affected, and he made the following brief but witty reply with great difficulty :

" My friends, I must again thank you for your kind and affectionate attention. My reception has been more like that of a brother than a common friend or acquaintance, and I am utterly incapable of finding words to express my gratitude. My situation is like that of a Swedish gentleman at a dinner given in England by the Society of Friends of Foreigners in Distress. A toast having been given, complimentary to his country, it was expected, as

is usual on such occasions, that he would rise and address
the company. The gentleman, not understanding the English language, rose under great embarrassment, and said:
'Sir, I wish you to consider me a *foreigner in distress.*' I
wish you, gentlemen, to consider me *a friend in distress.*"

A certain member of Congress noted for his long, dry
speeches, on one occasion, in Committee of the Whole, having bored the members more than usual, said to Mr. Clay,
who sat near him, in a low voice, while pausing for a fresh
start: "You speak for the present generation, I speak for
posterity." "Yes," replied Mr. Clay, "and you seem resolved to continue speaking till your audience arrives."

It is well known that Mr. Clay was accused by General
Jackson and his friends of unnecessarily defending himself
against the charge of bargain in the election of Mr. Adams,
and that he attempted to create a sympathy for himself by
his repeated appeals to the public. Of course the accusation
was not well founded, for it was unreasonable that he should
have started a subject of that character under the circumstances. Mr. Clay, in a speech at Cincinnati, in 1828, said:
"My traducers have attributed to me great facility in making
a *bargain.* Whether I possess it, or not, there is *one* bargain which, for their accommodation, I am willing to enter
into with them. If they will prevail upon their chief to acknowledge that he has been in error, and has done me injustice, and if they will cease to traduce and abuse me, I will
no longer present myself before public assemblies, or in
public prints, in my own defence. That is a bargain, however, which I have no expectation of being able to conclude;
for men who are in a long-established line of business will
not voluntarily quit their accustomed trade and acknowledge
themselves *bankrupts to honour, decency, and truth.*"

In support of a pension bill before the House of Representatives, Mr. Lincoln, of Maine, broke out into a rhapso-
dical apostrophe—indicative certainly of good feeling—and
said: "Soldiers of the Revolution! live for ever!" Mr.
Clay, not less zealous in so good a cause, could not, however, resist the temptation to say: "I hope my worthy

friend will consent to a compromise of 'forever' to nine
hundred and ninety-nine years."

Replying to Mr. Calhoun's notions of free trade, March
22, 1832, in the Senate, Mr. Clay said : "Yet still he [Mr. Cal-
houn] clings to his free-trade doctrine, though it has proved
so ruinous to his own State, and to Southern interests, as
well as to Northern ; to that free trade which has depressed
the price of cotton to a point below what it has ever brought
since the close of the last war.   In spite of all the teachings
of experience, as well in his own, as in all other nations, still
he deafens us with the cry of '*free trade !*'   Really the case
of the honourable gentleman is without any parallel that I
know or ever heard of, unless it be that which we find in the
immortal work of Le Sage.   Gil Blas was engaged in medical practice with the far-famed Dr. Sangrado, and after
having gone as far as his conscience and his feelings could
at all endure, he came at last to the Doctor and said to him :
'Sir, your system won't do.   I have been bleeding and administering warm water with unflinching resolution, and the
consequence is—and I must tell you frankly—all our patients
—nobles, gentlemen, bourgeois, men, women, and children—
all, all are dying !   I propose to change the system.'   'What!'
said the astonished Sangrado, 'change our system? change
our system ?   Why, sir, do you not know that I have written a BOOK, and that I must preserve my CONSISTENCY?
Yes ; and sooner than change my system, or write another
book to prove it false, let nobles, gentlemen, bourgeois, men,
women, and children, and all, go to —— I will not say
where.'   The honourable Senator seems to act on the self-
same plan.   Instead of recommending hot water and bleeding, he recommends *free trade ;* and though he sees, from
year to year, that his prescriptions are killing all his patients,
he spurns the idea of changing his system, because he must
preserve his CONSISTENCY !"

Mr. Clay died on the 29th of June, 1852.   Tributes of respect from all classes of men were offered to his memory.
Henry Clay was, by universal acknowledgment, not only one
of the greatest men in this country, but of the age in which

he lived, and, happily, his moral were not inferior to his mental endowments.

It is usual to find persons who are highly distinguished in particular walks—in the forum, the senate, and the cabinet, but a character pre-eminent in them all constitutes a prodigy of human greatness. Yet such a character was Mr. Clay. The versatility of his powers was as remarkable as their strength. As a statesman his resources were inexhaustible, and his powers transcendent. His ability and eloquence at the bar were at once the delight and astonishment of his countrymen.

Attainments so extensive, multifarious, and lofty, with endowments so brilliant, have but rarely fallen to the portion of man.

Mr. Clay was singularly free from the irregularities and vices which sometimes follow in the train of greatness. The welfare of his country was the idol of his affections. He was orderly, temperate, and methodical. Before acting, he bestowed on his subject all the attention that would have been given it by a man of ordinary ability. He studied it with patience till he thoroughly understood it. The reader will come to the conclusion from this description of him, that his greatness was achieved, and not "thrust upon him." Such was Clay, the profound statesman, the eloquent orator, and the man of probity, tried and spotless. Mr. Clay was six feet and one inch high, and rather slender; his arms were long, but his hands small. In standing, talking, or walking, he was always remarkably erect. His head was exceedingly well-shaped. His mouth was very large. His eyes were expressive, and were blue in colour. His nose was prominent, and his visage spare. His forehead was high and sloped backward. His hair, before it was frosted by age, was light. His person was well-formed and commanding.

Mr. Clay's manners were charming. He was remarkably self-possessed, and always at ease in society. He was noted for his affability, his dignity, general courtesy, and quick discernment of character. He captivated the plainest people, as well as the most cultivated. He had the power of accommodating his manners to the dispositions and characters of all persons with whom he came in contact.

The voice of Mr. Clay was one of great compass, power, and melody. In the modulation of his voice, for oratorical purposes, Mr. Clay was instructed .by nature, rather than art. His voice was naturally sweet and clear, and it is said that spectators in the galleries of the Senate-chamber have often heard his voice in private conversation at his desk below, while another Senator was making a speech. This sufficiently illustrates the penetrating character of its most common colloquial notes.

The following sketch of Mr. Clay was drawn some years before his death :

" There is a tall, light-haired, blue-eyed individual, sixty years old or more, who occupies a seat in the Senate at the Capitol. He has not what would be called a handsome face, but one of the liveliest, or, if we may so speak, one of the most *looking* faces that ever fronted a head. It is because he has a *looking* organisation. You catch not him asleep or moping. He seems to see everybody that comes in, or goes out, and besides, to have an eye on, and an ear for, whatever honourable Senator may occupy the field of debate. If his own marked political game is on foot, he is then *Nimrod*, a mighty hunter. He can see just what fissure of inconsistency, nook of sophism, or covert of rhetoric is made a hiding-place. At the right moment, he aims a rifle pretty sure to hit, if his powder is good ; and his friends say that he uses the best. Grand fun it is to stand by and see this keen sportsman crack off, and especially to hear him wind ' the mellow, mellow horn,' which his mother gave him a long while ago. To leave our hunting-ground metaphor for the plain beaten way, this individual is the veteran statesman from Kentucky. Now, just come and look at his head, or seek his portrait, at least. You will see how his *Perceptives* put themselves forth in front, just as if they were reaching after their objects, as it were, for a long pull and a strong pull, to fetch them into keeping. Then, in speech, with what ease, grace, order, and effect, he can fling forth his gatherings. His mind has been developed by the exciting circumstances of active life, rather than by the speculations of 'quiet books.' Henry Clay is therefore a *practical man.* He is pre-eminently *perceptive.* He knows the whom, the what, the where, the when, the which first, and the how many, as well perhaps as any public man living. A very long political life has put him to the test. We do not aver that he never made mistakes, or that he is politically and positively right; *we intimate, moreover, nothing to the contrary.* We would simply convey that, of all the great statesmen of our country, he particularly illustrates the faculties just had under review!"

The following remarks of Mr. Underwood, his colleague, delivered in the Senate of the United States, are worthy of insertion here :

" The character of Henry Clay was formed and developed by the influence of our free institutions. His physical and mental organisation eminently qualified him to become a great and impressive orator. His person was tall, slender, and commanding. His temperament ardent, fearless, and full of hope. His countenance clear, expressive, and variable—indicating the emotion which predominated at the moment with exact similitude. His voice, cultivated and modulated in harmony with the sentiment he desired to express, fell upon the ear like the melody of enrapturing music. His eye beaming with intelligence, and flashing with coruscations of genius. His gestures and attitudes graceful and natural. These personal advantages won the prepossessions of an audience, even before his intellectual powers began to move his hearers ; and when his strong commonsense, his profound reasoning, his clear conception of his subject in all its bearings, and his striking and beautiful illustrations, united with such personal qualities, were brought to the discussion of any question, his audience was enraptured, convinced, and led by the orator as if enchanted by the lyre of Orpheus.

" No man was ever blessed by his Creator with faculties of
28

·a higher order of excellence than those given to Mr. Clay. In
the quickness of his perceptions, and the rapidity with which
his conclusions were formed, he had few equals, and no superior. He detected in a moment everything out of place or
deficient in his room, upon his farm, in his own, or the dress
of others. He was a skilful judge of the forward qualities
of his domestic animals, which he delighted to raise on his
farm. I could give you instances of the quickness and the
minuteness of his keen faculty of observation, which never
overlooked anything. A want of neatness and order was
offensive to him. He was particular and neat in his hand-
writing, and his apparel. A slovenly blot, or negligence of
any sort, met his condemnation ; while he was so organised
that he attended to and arranged little things to please and
gratify his natural love for neatness, order, and beauty, his
great intellectual faculties grasped all the subjects of juris-·
prudence and politics with a facility amounting almost to in-
·tuition. As a lawyer he stood at the head of his profession.
As a statesman, his stand at the head of the Republican
Whig Party for nearly half a century establishes his title to
pre-eminence among his illustrious associates.

   " Mr. Clay throughout his public career, was influenced by
the loftiest patriotism. Confident in the truth of his convictions and the purity of his purposes, he was ardent, some- ·
times impetuous, in the pursuit of objects which he
believed essential to the public welfare. His sympathies
embraced all. The African slave, the Creole of Spanish
America, the children of renovated classic Greece—all families of men, without respect to colour or clime, found in his
expanded bosom and comprehensive intellect a friend of
their elevation and amelioration.

   " Bold and determined as Mr. Clay was in all his actions,
he was, nevertheless, conciliating. He did not obstinately
adhere to things impracticable. If he could not accomplish the
best, he contented himself with the nighest approach to it.
He has been the great compromiser of those political agita-
tions and opposing opinions which have, in the belief of thousands, at different times, endangered the perpetuity of our

Federal Government and Union. He was no less remarkable for his admirable social qualities than for his intellectual abilities. As a companion he was the delight of his friends, and no man ever had better or truer. They have loved him from the beginning and loved him to the last. His hospitable mansion at Ashland was always open to their reception. No guest ever thence departed without feeling happier for his visit."

The following remarks by Mr. Colton, upon the attributes of Mr. Clay's oratory cannot fail to interest, deeply, a student of eloquence : " But the attributes of Mr. Clay's eloquence extend to a wider range than that of voice. His person, tall, erect, commanding ; his countenance, as well as his voice, capable of expressing every feeling and passion of the human soul, pleasure or pain, satisfaction or discontent, hope or fear, desire or aversion, complacency or contempt, love or hatred, joy or grief, ecstacy or anguish, valour or cowardice, kindness or cruelty, pity or revenge, resolution or despair ; his large mouth, and swollen upper lip, working quietly, or in agony, as occasions require ; his eye resting in calmness, or beaming with lively emotion, or sparkling with strong feeling, or flashing with high passion like the thunderbolts of heaven in the darkness of the storm ; his arms, now hanging easy by his side, now outstretched, now uplifted, now waving with grace, or striking with the vehemence of passion ; his finger pointing where his piercing thoughts direct ; the easy, or quiet, or violent movements of his whole frame ; the bending of his body forward, or sidewise, or backward ; the downward or upward look ; the composed or suffused or impassioned countenance ; the watchful, shifting glances, taking in the field of vision, and making each one feel that he is seen and individually addressed ; the theme ; himself ; his audiences ; his fame ; his position on the subject in debate or under discussion ; his relation to the assembly or the body before him ; the respect and esteem in which he is held by them ; his dignity, courtesy, deference ; his disinterestedness, his philanthropy, his patriotism ;—*all* these, and many others that might be named, are among the attributes of Mr. Clay's eloquence,

and appertain to that accumulation and concentration of influences which have given his popular harangues, his forensic
efforts, his various public addresses, and his parliamentary
speeches so much power over the minds, the hearts, and
the actions of his countrymen.

"Purity of diction cannot be separated from the attributes
of Mr. Clay's eloquence. It is not less true that language,
properly selected and composed, is eloquent, than that sentiment and passion are; and the eloquence of passion depends on that of diction. Passion may even be spoiled by
its dress, and lose all its force. Purity of diction is to
thought, sentiment, and passion, as the well-made toilet of a
lady is to her charms. It is a transparent medium, through
which the observer looks into the soul, and beholds all its
movements. When the diction is pure, all occasions of criticism, as to dress are absent, and what is in the mind and
heart of the speaker passes directly into the mind and heart
of the listener. The effect of pure diction is the same on
the clown as on the scholar. The former cannot criticise, if
he would; the latter rejects his prerogative; and both are
lost in satisfaction, if both are interested in the subject, and
otherwise equally attracted. But if the language were not
pure, both would not feel it, though possibly but one could
point out the defect or blemish. Nature, in the rudest state,
however, is often endowed with the highest attributes of
criticism. A much admired painting of a peasant girl feeding the pigs had sustained the severest scrutiny of connois-
seurs, with triumph; but, when a negro slave, used to that
business, looked at the picture, and exclaimed, 'Who ever
saw pigs feeding, without one foot in the trough?'—the
painting was thenceforth good for nothing! The best test
of Mr. Clay's language, both in colloquial and rhetorical applications, is, that it is suited to all classes of persons.

"Faith in the validity and sincerity of Mr. Clay's own convictions, arising not less from faith in his general character,
than from the artless and feeling manner of his utterance,
carries with it an irresistible influence. All who hear him
are fully persuaded, from what they know of him, and by

his manner, that he himself believes what he says. Their sur-render of opinion and feeling, therefore, or their acquies-cence, is measured only by their will, or their interest, or their confidence in his judgment, or by a combination of such influences. No small part of the eloquence of Mr. Clay lies in this faith, which is a moral band between him and those whom he addresses, dissolving in a common crucible the feelings of the two parties."

Choate.—Rufus Choate, one of the greatest orators and statesmen this country has produced, was born in Essex County, Massachusetts, on the 1st of October, 1799.

He was noted while at school for his close application to study and for his extraordinary powers of memory. He graduated at Dartmouth College in 1819. He began the study of law at Cambridge, and afterward entered the office of the celebrated William Wirt, at Washington, D. C. He was elected to the Senate of his native state in 1830. He was chosen as a representative in Congress in 1832. He was elected a United States Senator from Massachusetts in 1842, and resigned in 1845, and was succeeded by Daniel Webster.

Mr. Choate was one of the most gifted forensic orators that ever lived. He began his legal career at Danvers and Salem, Massachusetts.

His intellect, naturally powerful, he developed by exact and laborious study. His powers of discrimination and abstraction were marvellous. He was endowed by nature with a sparkling wit, a lively fancy, and an enthusiasm which was overwhelming. While speaking, Mr. Choate narrowly and keenly watched the faces of his auditors, and if he noted the slightest look of dissatisfaction, he changed his course, and, with the great tact for which he was distinguished, he would modify, or change the obnoxious statement until he would meet the approbation of his most stubborn listeners. His voice was indescribably sweet and musical, and no orator was ever listened to with greater delight.

One of his biographers says of him : " I have no words to

describe the effort of this remarkable man. The fluency, rapidity, and beauty of his language, his earnest manner, his excited action, and his whole being, conflicting with the most intense emotion ; he was all nerve ; each sense, each faculty was absorbed in the great duty of the day ; and sometimes it seemed that tears alone could relieve the uncontrollable agitation which thrilled through his frame, and quivered on his lips, and trembled in his voice; the strong nerve of a man alone enabled him to command his struggling feelings. His memory supplied quotations, learned and to the point ; his imagination called each poetic fancy quick to his aid ; and his voice of music attuned itself to all the varied tones of his discourse, awakening in every breast the sentiments and impressions of his own. He is the Proteus of eloquence."

Much time is wasted by studying subjects which are interesting, but practically useless. Mr. Choate was ever on his guard against subjects of this character, and it is said that early in life he refused to follow a friend into the labyrinths of German mysticism, or to study the doctrines of Swedenborg. Mr. Choate was earnestly desirous of mastering the law as a science, and of understanding the art of oratory.

One of the perils which attend men of great ability is the danger of their becoming victims of a delusive self-confidence. They are sometimes led by the whispers of vanity to depend upon their natural talents, and to neglect those studies, which they must pursue if they ever attain eminence. Mr. Choate, however, properly regarded genius as the mere capacity to acquire knowledge and to use it, consequently he was untiring in his efforts to cultivate his mental faculties to the fullest extent to which they were susceptible of being cultivated. When a young man he often read law until two o'clock in the morning.

Later in life, however, Mr. Choate became less exclusive in his legal studies, and sought a broader and more generous culture than the law could give.

In his preparation of cases Mr. Choate was extremely industrious. Although one of the most profound lawyers that ever lived, Mr. Choate did not neglect the study of the law governing each case which was entrusted to his management. Often the labour of preparation was comparatively light because of his familiarity with the general principles of the law. Chief Justice Parsons, himself an eminent jurist, said, in speaking of Mr. Choate's legal knowledge: " I have, indeed, no hesitation in saying that he was one of the most learned lawyers I have ever met with. And his learning was excellent in its kind and quality."

Mr. Choate's method of examining witnesses was undoubtedly the most successful which he could have adopted. He rarely, either in his examinations in chief, or in his cross-examinations, spoke harshly to a witness, but when severity was necessary no one could be more severe.

Mr. Choate once said to a friend, " Never browbeat a witness on the cross-examination ; it only makes him more obstinate and hostile. When I began to practise law, I used to think it very fine to be severe, and even savage, towards my opponent's witnesses ; but I soon found it would not do, and I reformed my method altogether. Violence does no good : the gentle method is the best. It is the old story of the sun and the wind."

The notes taken by Mr. Choate in court were always ample and complete. To a student who was going to take the depositions of some witnesses he said : "Take down every adjective, adverb, and interjection the witnesses utter."

Although his briefs were sometimes lengthy, he did not always confine himself to them while addressing juries. In the argument of questions of law to the court, he followed his notes closely, as a general rule.

Professor Brown says : " In determining the theory of his case, he was never satisfied until he had met every supposition that could be brought against it. But he had no love for a theory because it was his own, however great the labour it had cost him, but was perfectly ready to throw it aside for another, when that appeared better. This change of front he sometimes made in the midst of the trial, under the

eye of the court, and in the face of a watchful and eager
antagonist. He was never more self-possessed, nor seemed
to have his entire faculties more fully at command, nor to
exercise a more consummate judgment, than when in the
very heat of a strongly contested case, where a mistake
would have been fatal. In the preparation of a case, he left
nothing to chance; and his juniors sometimes found themselves urged to a fidelity and constancy of labour to which
they had not been accustomed."

In 1853 a vigorous effort was made in the Massachusetts
Convention to change the tenure of the judicial office to a
term of years, from a tenure of good behaviour. Mr. Choate
was opposed to this change, and the speech which he made
on that occasion was exceedingly eloquent and able. In
the course of his speech he drew an admirable portrait of
a good judge: " In the first place, he should be profoundly
learned in all the learning of the law, and he must know
how to use that learning. Will any one stand up here
to deny this ? . . . Will any one disgrace himself by
doubting the necessity of deep and continued studies, and
various and thorough attainments to the bench ? He is to
know not merely the law which you make, and the Legislature makes, not constitutional and statute law alone, but that
other ampler, that boundless jurisprudence, the common law,
which the successive generations of the State have silently
built up ; that old code of freedom which we brought with us
in the *Mayflower* and *Arabella*, but which, in the progress of
centuries, we have ameliorated and enriched, and adapted
wisely to the necessities of a busy, prosperous, and wealthy
community—that he must know.

" And where to find it ? In volumes which you must
count by hundreds, by thousands ; filling libraries ; exacting
long labours—the labours of a lifetime, abstracted from business, from politics, but assisted by taking part in an active
judicial administration ; such labours as produced the wisdom
and won the fame of Parsons, and Marshall, and Kent, and
Story, and Holt, and Mansfield. If your system of
appointment and tenure does not present a motive, a help

for such labours and such learning, if it discourages, if it disparages them, in so far it is a failure.

" In the next place, he must be a man not merely upright ; not merely honest and well intentioned—this of course,— but a man who will not respect persons in judgment. And does not every one here agree to this also? Dismissing for a moment all theories about the mode of appointing him, or the time for which he shall hold office, sure I am that, as far as human virtue, assisted by the best contrivance of human wisdom, can attain to it, he shall not respect persons in judgment. He shall know nothing about the parties, everything about the case. He shall do everything for justice, nothing for himself, nothing for his friend, nothing for his patrons, nothing for his sovereign.

" If, on one side, is the Executive power and the Legislature and the people—the sources of his honours, the givers of his daily bread—and on the other, an individual, nameless and odious, his eye is to see neither great nor small, attending only to the trepidations of the balance. If a law is passed by a unanimous Legislature, clamoured for by the general voice of the public, and a cause is before him on it, in which the whole community is on one side and an individual nameless or odious on the other, and he believes it to be against the Constitution, he must so declare it, or there is no judge. If Athens came there to demand that the cup of hemlock be put to the lips of the wisest of men, *and he believes that he has not corrupted the youth, nor omitted to worship the gods of the city, nor introduced new divinities of his* own, he must deliver him, although the thunder light on the unterrified brow.

" And, finally, he must possess the perfect confidence of the community, that he bear not the sword in vain. To be honest, to be no respecter of persons, is not yet enough. He must be believed such. I should be glad so far to indulge an old-fashioned and cherished professional sentiment as to say that I would have something venerable and illustrious attach to his character and function, in the judgment and feelings of the Commonwealth!

"But if this should be thought a little above or behind the time, I do not fear that I subject myself to the ridicule of any one when I claim that he be a man toward whom the love and trust and affectionate admiration of the people should flow, not a man perching for a winter and summer in our court-houses and then gone forever ; but one to whose benevolent face, and bland and dignified manners, and firm administration of the whole learning of the law, we become accustomed ; whom our eyes anxiously, not in vain, explore when we enter the temple of justice ; toward whom our attachment and trust grow ever with the growth of his own reputation. I would have him one who might look back from the venerable last years of Mansfield or Marshall and recall such testimonies as these to the great and good judge :

" ' The young men saw me and hid themselves, and the aged arose and stood up.

" ' The princes refrained from talking, and laid their hand upon their mouth.

" ' When the ear heard me then it blessed me, and when the eye saw me it gave witness to me.

" ' Because I delivered the poor that cried, and the fatherless, and him that had none to help him.

" ' The blessing of him that was ready to perish came upon me, and I caused the widow's heart to sing for joy.

" ' I put on righteousness and it clothed me. My judgment was as a robe and a diadem. I was eyes to the blind, and feet was I to the lame.

" ' I was a father to the poor, and the cause which I knew not I searched out.

" ' And I brake the jaws of the wicked, and I plucked the spoil out of his teeth.'

" Give to the community such a judge, and I care little who makes the rest of the Constitution, or what party administers it. It will be a free government I know. Let us repose secure under the shade of a learned, impartial, and trusted magistracy, and we need no more."

A cashier of one of the South Boston banks, was tried for embezzlement. Mr. Choate appeared for the defence.

He contended that the cashier was compelled to do what he had done by his superior officers, the directors; that *they* had swindled the public; that *they* were the responsible parties, and should suffer the punishment. He was proceeding to flay the directors, when one of them rose in court, and in great anger began to denounce Choate who, hardly allowing himself to be interrupted, said mildly: " I beg the director to be seated, as he wishes to be treated with moderation in a court of justice." And then instantly breaking out into a scream, and with the greatest impetuosity, he exclaimed: " I tell you, gentlemen of the jury, my client was as helpless in the hands of these directors as an infant surrounded by *ten thousand Bengal tigers!*"

The author who relates this incident says, in commenting upon it: " No one, however, smiled; every one looked grave, and full of sympathy for the unfortunate infant thus encircled, and ready to bewail the inevitable catastrophe."

A story is told of Mr. Choate, for the truth of which, however, the writer will not vouch. A stranger called to see him, and said that he had called to consult him about a very important matter. His cause of grievance was that at a hotel he had had a dispute with one of the waiters, who finally told him to go to h—l. " Now," he continued, with an air of great importance, " I ask you, Mr. Choate, as one learned in the law, and as my legal adviser, what course, under these very aggravating circumstances, is it best for me, in your judgment, to pursue?" Mr. Choate requested him to state again, in order of time, everything that occurred, and to be careful not to omit anything, and, when this had been done, remained for a few moments as if lost in deep thought. At last, with the utmost gravity, he spoke: " I have been running over in my mind all the statutes of the United States, all the statutes of the Commonwealth of Massachusetts, and all the decisions of all the judges thereon, and I am satisfied there is nothing in them that will require you to go to the place you have mentioned; *and don't you go.*" Mr. Choate's client doubtless followed this sound advice.

Mr. Choate always spoke with great earnestness. The style of forensic oratory in his day was somewhat different from the style at present, although he would now be heard with just as much pleasure as he was in his own time, if he were alive. It is said that at times while speaking every portion of his frame quivered with emotion, his eyes flashed fire, his gestures were vehement and energetic, and his voice would rise to a scream."

A writer, Mr. Parker, happily says, that Mr. Choate did not think that truth lies in *still* waters. " He appeared rather to be of opinion that it was a goblet of gold cast into a furious and foaming whirlpool,—as in Schiller's ballad,—into which he who would rescue it must plunge, and contend for it with the raging waters; and so, like the daring youth in the story, he would leap into the boiling, hissing, frightful vortex, pluck from its dark womb the golden prize, bear it with upraised hand through surging billows and assailing enemies back to the welcome shore, and place it in the hands of the virgin goddess, Justice, to give to its rightful owner."

The writer is inclined to believe that some of the accounts of Mr. Choate's extravagance in the use of violent and declamatory gestures, as well as his screaming at the top of his voice, have been exaggerated. Mr. Choate, notwithstanding his genius, was a man of excellent judgment and of exceedingly good taste. It is quite certain that the voice of ex-Governor William Allen, which is said to have been of "forty-bull power," greatly displeased him. It is said that he was once invited to address the people of the United States from the steps of the Capitol in Ohio. His voice almost stunned the Senators of the United States who heard him. He and Mr. Choate were members of that Senate at the same time, and on one occasion the latter remarked humorously to a friend that Allen repeatedly violated that clause of the Constitution of the United States which forbade the infliction of "cruel and unusual punishments."

Mr. Choate was unequalled in tact by any of his contemporaries. No forensic orator was ever better acquainted with the means of investing the most common theme with interest, and no one could attract and hold the attention of the jury as long as he could. Speaking of the origin of an assault, he said : " It was a mere accidental push ; such a mere jostle, Mr. Foreman, as you might give another in coming out of a Union Meeting at Faneuil Hall " (he knew the foreman was a Webster Whig) ; " or a Friday-evening prayer meeting " (looking at another and very religious juror) ; " or a Jenny Lind concert " (looking now at still another juror, who was a musical man).

In the trial of a patent case the opposing counsel said to him : " There 's nothing original in your patent ; your client did not come at it *naturally*." Choate replied, with a half-mirthful, half-scornful look : " What does my brother mean by *naturally ?* Naturally ! We don't do anything *naturally.* Why, *naturally* a man would walk down Washington Street with his pantaloons off ! "

He said of one of his female clients : " She is a sinner,— no, not a sinner, for she is our client ; but she is a very disagreeable saint."

That Mr. Choate sometimes indulged in exaggeration the following passage in his speech before a committee of the Legislature of Massachusetts on a question of boundary between that State and Rhode Island shows. He said :

" I would as soon think of bounding a sovereign state on the north by a dandelion, on the west by a blue-jay, on the south by a swarm of bees in swarming time, and on the east by three hundred foxes with fire-brands tied to their tails, as of relying upon the loose and indefinite bounds of commissioners a century ago."

Mr. Choate was not quite six feet in height. His breast was full and deep ; legs rather slender ; head remarkably well shaped, and covered with a fine suit of black, curly hair ; forehead high, broad, and almost perpendicular. His face was handsome ; mouth and nose large, lips thin and long, and eyes large, black, and lustrous.

In manners he was always gentlemanly and courteous. He was always particularly respectful to the aged, and he

treated young people, invariably, with the greatest kindness.

His vocabulary was practically unlimited. His voice was
sonorous, musical, and capable of expressing every shade of
feeling.

Mr. Choate was fond of the study of the Bible—especially
of the New Testament, and on one occasion Daniel Webster,
while looking through his library, said: "Thirteen editions
of the Greek Testament, and not one copy of the Constitution of your country." He translated many of the Greek
and Latin classics into English. He was extremely fond of
books, and an extract from his remarks on the consolations
of literature may prove of interest to the reader:

"I come to add the final reason why the working man—
by whom I mean the whole *brotherhood of industry*—should
set on mental culture and that knowledge which is wisdom,
a value so high—only not supreme—subordinate alone to
the exercises and hopes of religion itself; and that is, that
therein he shall so surely find rest from labour; succour under its burdens; forgetfulness of its cares; composure in its
annoyances.

"It is not always that the busy day is followed by the
peaceful night. It is not always that fatigue wins sleep.
Often some vexation outside of the toil that has exhausted
the frame: some loss in a bargain; some loss by an in-
solvency; some unforeseen rise or fall in prices; some triumph
of a mean or fraudulent competitor; 'the law's delay, the
proud man's contumely, the insolence of office, or some of the
spurns that patient merit from the unworthy takes '—some
self-reproach, perhaps, follow you within the door; chill the
fireside; sow the pillow with thorns; and the dark care is
lost in the last waking thought, and haunts the vivid
dream.

"Happy, then, is he who has laid up in youth, and has held
fast in all fortune, a genuine and passionate love of reading.
True balm of hurt minds; of surer and more healthful
charm than 'poppy or mandragora, or all the drowsy syrups
of the world '—by that single taste, by that single capacity,

he may bound, in a moment, into the still regions of delightful studies, and be at rest.

" He recalls the annoyance that pursues him ; reflects that he has done all that might become a man to avoid or bear it ; he indulges in one good long, human sigh, picks up a volume where the mark kept his place, and in about the same time that it takes the Mohammedan, in the *Spectator*, to put his head in the bucket of water and raise it out, he finds himself exploring the arrow-marked ruins of Nineveh with Layard ; or worshipping at the spring-head of the stupendous Missouri with Clarke and Lewis; or watching with Columbus for the sublime moment of the rising of the curtain from before the great mystery of the sea ; or looking reverentially on while Socrates—the discourse on immortality ended—refuses the offer of escape, and takes in his hand the poison, to die in obedience to the unrighteous sentence of the law; or, perhaps, it is in the contemplation of some vast spectacle or phenomenon of Nature that he has found his quick peace—the renewed exploration of one of her great laws—or some glimpse opened by the pencil of St. Pierre, or Humboldt, or Chateaubriand, or Wilson, of the ' blessedness and glory of her own deep, calm, and mighty existence.'

" Let the case of a busy lawyer testify to the priceless value of the love of reading. He comes home, his temples throbbing, his nerves shattered, from a trial of a week; surprised and alarmed by the charge of the judge, and pale with anxiety about the verdict of the next morning, not at all satisfied with what he has done himself, though he does not yet see how he could have improved it ; recalling with dread and self-disparagement, if not with envy, the brilliant effort of his antagonist, and tormenting himself with the vain wish that he could have replied to it—and altogether a very miserable subject, and in as unfavourable condition to accept comfort from wife and children as poor Christian in the first three pages of the *Pilgrim's Progress.*

" With a superhuman effort he opens his book, and in a twinkling of an eye he is looking into the full ' orb of Homeric or Miltonic song'; or he stands in the crowd breath- · less, yet swayed as forests or the sea by winds, hearing and to judge the Pleadings for the Crown ; or the philosophy which soothed Cicero or Boëthius in their afflictions, in exile, in prison, and the contemplation of death, breathes over his petty cares like the sweet south; or Pope or Horace laugh him into good humour, or he walks with Æneas and the Sybil in the mild light of the world of the laurelled dead, and the court-house is as completely forgotten as the dream of a pre-Adamite life. Well may he prize that endeared charm, so effectual and safe, without which the brain had long ago been chilled by paralysis, or set on fire by insanity ! "

Mr. Choate's originality was never questioned. He copied no one, in language or style of argumentation. He was always natural and unaffected, and was beyond question one of the most powerful advocates that ever addressed a jury. At the time of his death he was at the head of the American bar. He discharged his duty to the letter in every relation of life, public and private. No good man was his enemy, and for the respect of the vicious he was not solicitous.

Mr. Choate was extremely courteous and kind to his juniors, and he was sincerely mourned by them at his death. His fidelity to the interests of clients knew no bounds. His life was a useful one, and so perfect a character should be looked upon as an example by the younger members of the legal profession worthy of their closest imitation. The more carefully they read the history of his life and his utterances in public the greater will be their reverence for him.

He died at Halifax, on the 13th of July, 1859.

THE END.

INDEX.

449

CPSIA information can be obtained
at www.ICGtesting.com
Printed in the USA
BVOW06*0814240717
490098BV00004B/9/P